Inscriptions

Inscriptions

Between phenomenology and structuralism

Hugh J. Silverman

ROUTLEDGE & KEGAN PAUL

New York and London

*First published in 1987 by
Routledge & Kegan Paul Inc.
in association with Methuen Inc.
29 West 35th Street, New York, NY 10001*

*Published in the UK by
Routledge & Kegan Paul Ltd
11 New Fetter Lane, London EC4P 4EE*

---

*Phototypeset in 10 on 12pt Times
by Input Typesetting Ltd, London
and printed in Great Britain
by T. J. Press (Padstow) Ltd,
Padstow, Cornwall*

This collection copyright © Routledge & Kegan Paul 1987

Library of Congress Cataloging in Publication Data

Silverman, Hugh J.

Inscriptions: between phenomenology and structuralism.

*Bibliography: p.
Includes index.
1. Philosophy, Modern—20th century.
2. Phenomenology. 3. Structuralism. I. Title.
B804.S565   1987   142'.7   86–31521*

British Library CIP Data also available

ISBN 0–7100–9831–6

For Claire and Christopher

CONTENTS

Preface: inscribing the place between   ix

Acknowledgments   xiii

Introduction: continental philosophy in America   1

I   Phenomenology   11
    1 The self in Husserl's *Crisis*   13
    2 Dasein and existential ambiguity   29
    3 The identity of difference   44
    4 Thinking and being: the essential relation   52
    5 Merleau-Ponty's human ambiguity   63

II And Structuralism   93
    6 Merleau-Ponty on language and communication   95
    7 Merleau-Ponty and Heidegger: interpreting Hegel   108
    8 Re-reading Merleau-Ponty   123
    9 Merleau-Ponty and the interrogation of language   152
    10 Sartre's words on the self   172

III Versus Structuralism   195
    11 Sartre and the structuralists   197
    12 Sartre/Piaget: biographical situations, cognitive
       structures and human development   219
    13 Sartre/Barthes: writing differences   236
    14 Sartre/Foucault: dialectic and episteme   254

Contents

15 Sartre versus structuralism

IV The Difference Between (and Beyond)   265
   16 The limits of logocentrism
   17 Self-decentering: Derrida incorporated   279
   18 Foucault and the anthropological sleep   281
   19 From utopia/dystopia to heterotopia: 294
      an interpretive topology   316
   20 For a hermeneutic semiology of the self

                           326
Notes   338

Bibliography   346

Index   375

                           383

PREFACE:
INSCRIBING THE PLACE
BETWEEN

The place between phenomenology and structuralism does not occupy any space. It only marks the place between two methodologically parallel yet historically converging paths. At the limit of one, signs of the other are already plotted. At the frontier of the other, the former is incorporated and advanced. Yet structuralism does not take over where phenomenology ends. Nor does phenomenology succeed where structuralism fails. Often presented as antipodean ways of thinking, phenomenology and structuralism indicate two very different orientations in recent continental thought. Often compared for their respective virtues, they each represent dominant methodologies for the human sciences, social and cultural criticism, and the study of literature. They each build upon a separate theoretical base which allows for and even promotes a philosophical practice or practices in their own right. Their respective proponents differ widely—even to the extent of sometimes denying association with the general movement and type of thinking itself. The gaps between Husserl and Sartre, Heidegger and Merleau-Ponty are significant, and yet they fall under the broad head entitled phenomenology. With structuralism, the case is even more radical. Although de Saussure, Lévi-Strauss, Lacan and Barthes would all admit to some connection with structuralism, the positions of Foucault and Derrida are more divergent. Indeed Foucault, in the name of an archaeology of knowledge, and Derrida, in the language of grammatology and deconstruction, depart explicitly from the structuralist and phenomenological camps—though they each draw heavily upon both in terms of what might be described as a post-phenomenology post-structuralism. In certain respects, Foucault and Derrida mark out the place signified by the intersection of phenomenology and structuralism albeit not reducible to either.

The deaths of Jean-Paul Sartre and Roland Barthes in the spring of 1980 circumscribe the end of an era. From 1938, with the successful publication of *Nausea*, and then with the celebrated *Being and Nothingness* in 1943, Sartre reigned supreme as the dominant figure in French existential phenomenology just as Martin Heidegger prevailed in Germany from the publication of *Being and Time* in 1927 until his death in 1976. Had Merleau-Ponty lived past 1961, and enjoyed the same longevity as Sartre and Heidegger, he too might have extended the Husserlian shadow beyond its self-ascribed limits. With the possible exceptions of Dufrenne, Ricoeur and Gadamer, the grand European tradition of phenomenology in its transcendental and existential varieties has now come to an end. This is not to say that a new generation of younger phenomenologists are not marking out original paths in phenomenological research. Indeed, they are particularly pronounced in disciplines outside philosophy such as sociology, psychology, communication theory and literary studies. However, even in philosophy, hermeneutics as a direct outgrowth of phenomenology still has a bright future.

The case of Barthes is different. While Sartre had lost any significant voice in French intellectual life more than twelve years prior to his death, Barthes was still looked to for new directions in semiological—he would recall in his Ecole Pratique des Hautes Etudes seminar that it was Jakobson who opted for the term "semiotic"—and structuralist studies. Barthes was ten years younger than Sartre. With the exception of Lévi-Strauss, who was sketching out directions for structuralist studies in anthropology in the late 1940s, Barthes's essays, beginning with *Writing Degree Zero* in the early 1950s, began to map out its implications for literary and cultural criticism in the ensuing three decades. Lacan, whose psychoanalytic work was known to some, including Merleau-Ponty, in the early post-war period, translated Heidegger's "Logos" essay and entered the fray in the mid-1950s. The most pronounced years for the development of structuralism came in the mid-1960s—just before the May–June revolts in 1968. Thus Barthes's *Elements of Semiology* (1964) and his *Critical Essays* (also 1964) cleared the terrain for Lacan's *Ecrits*, Foucault's *The Order of Things*, and Benveniste's *Problems in General Linguistics*, all published in 1966, and for Derrida's *Speech and Phenomena, Of Grammatology* and *Writing and Difference*, all appearing in 1967. Even Godard's *La Chinoise* (1967) was an index of the ferment.

Lévi-Strauss filled the late 1950s and early 1960s with theoretical essays and treatises establishing the links between linguistics and anthropology, between structuralism and the human sciences. Without *Tristes Tropiques* (1955), *Structural Anthropology I* (1958), *Totemism* (1962) and *The Savage Mind* (1962), structuralism would not have had a voice. His four-volume *Mythologiques* (1964–72) is a magnificent demonstration and symphonic elaboration of his prior theoretical commitments, particularly with respect to his study of kinship relations.

Structuralism in the 1970s has been largely an extension and reformulation of positions taken before May 1968. Roland Barthes's own *S/Z* (1970), a detailed rewriting of a Balzac short story, sets the pattern for the type of restatement that he himself offers in *The Pleasure of the Text* (1973), *Roland Barthes* (1975), *The Lover's Discourse* (1977) and *Camera Lucida* (1980). Although Lévi-Strauss continues into the 1980s, the figures who occupy the dominant places have been Lacan (whose dissolution of the Freudian school and whose death in 1983 fragmented the psychoanalytic explosion), Foucault (whose concerns with the history of sexuality and confession opened new ways of thinking the will to say the truth), and Jacques Derrida. The places now claimed by Deleuze, Lyotard, Kristeva, and perhaps Lacoue-Labarthe, Nancy and Descombes also inscribe the *topos*—the language and place—of difference.

Developments and extensions of phenomenology and structuralism have not been entirely independent of each other. On the phenomenological side, Merleau-Ponty was doubtless the most adventurous. His early reading of de Saussure (in 1946–8) set a pattern for his subsequent interrogations of language. His friendships with Lévi-Strauss and Lacan led him to follow structuralist research rather closely. The position announced in "Philosophy and non-philosophy since Hegel," which he was formulating at the time of his death, clearly indicates the possibility of operating in the place between phenomenology and structuralism.

Preface: inscribing the place between

Similarly Derrida—whose earliest work is devoted to a reading of Husserl, as in his *Introduction to the Origin of Geometry* (1962) and *Speech and Phenomena* (1967) and whose subsequent writings take up not only Hegel, Nietzsche and Heidegger, but also de Saussure, Lévi-Strauss, Lacan and Foucault—enters and delimits the spaces of difference between phenomenology and structuralism. While Merleau-Ponty stands at the opening of the place between, Derrida formulates its closure.

The essays in this volume set the parameters for the frame of reference announced by Merleau-Ponty and signed by Derrida. They trace a pattern for phenomenology from the later Husserl through Heidegger to Merleau-Ponty and for structuralism from de Saussure through Lévi-Strauss to Lacan. They re-inscribe the language and place of difference as a post-phenomenology and post-structuralism—as a provisional hermeneutic semiology of the self-language-world complex.

ACKNOWLEDGMENTS

This book has been a long time in the making. The essays incorporated here have, in many cases, already been disseminated in a variety of contexts. Nevertheless they have been revised for the purpose of inclusion in this volume—which was their purpose all along. I am grateful to the following editors and their journals for publishing these pieces in the first instance and for permitting their reinscription back into this book: John Sallis, editor of *Research in Phenomenology*, Wolfe Mays, editor of the *Journal of the British Society for Phenomenology*, Robert Lechner, editor of *Philosophy Today*, David Rasmussen, editor of *Philosophy and Social Criticism*, Amedeo Giorgi, editor of the *Journal of Phenomenological Psychology*, Paul Piccone, editor of *Telos*, Norris Clarke, editor of *International Philosophical Quarterly*, and Tony O'Connor, editor of the former Irish journal *Seminar*. Also three of these essays have appeared in collected volumes of essays, and to their editors I express my thanks as well: Frederick Elliston, editor of *Heidegger's Existential Analytic* (Mouton), David Wood, editor of *Heidegger and Language* (Parousia Press), and Hugh J. Silverman and Frederick Elliston, editors of *Jean-Paul Sartre: Contemporary Approaches to his Philosophy* (Duquesne and Harvester). The essay in *Heidegger and Language* was also republished in *Man and World* and in *Phenomenology and the Human Sciences* (both Martinus Nijhoff), edited by J.N. Mohanty. A portion of the introductory remarks have been translated into Dutch by A. Peperzak and published in *Wijsgerig perspectief op maatschappij en wetenschap* (1984–5).

Acknowledgments

My debts of incorporation for this volume are numerous. At last, it is time to express my profound gratitude to my teachers Norman Melchert, Philip Rhinelander, John Goheen, Dagfinn Føllesdal, Alphonse Juilland, Kurt Müller-Vollmer, Lucio Ruotolo, Mikel Dufrenne, Roland Barthes, Paul Ricoeur and Michel Foucault. Although I never met them personally, Maurice Merleau-Ponty, Jean-Paul Sartre and Martin Heidegger have certainly marked my thinking and writing. And to Jacques Derrida, whose path has crossed my own many times since that small three-day seminar at the Ecole Normale in the spring of 1972, I owe what cannot be owed: my scars from the texts of his philosophical practice.

Many friends and colleagues have followed me on this itinerary—some of them as the Society for Phenomenology and Existential Philosophy has grown to middle age, others as the Stony Brook Philosophy Department has achieved a position of prominence on the American philosophical scene. After Stanford, Stony Brook has been my intellectual home—most of this book grows out of that context: the debates and disagreements, the projects and expectations, the joys and achievements that have taken place here. In particular, Don Ihde, David Allison, Ed Casey, Dick Howard, Patrick Heelan, Donn Welton and Mary Rawlinson have been my worthy counterparts on this journey. Over the years, my graduate students not only at Stony Brook but also at Duquesne, New York University, and the Collegium Phaenomenologicum in Perugia (Italy), as well as my undergraduates at the University of Warwick, have been my most persistent and devoted interlocutors. I am indebted to so many of them, but in particular I should like to thank Jeff Gaines, who worked with me on the final stages of the manuscript, Leonard Lawlor, who prepared the Index with efficiency and elegance, and J. Barry, whose support and encouragement is more than material. I have learned as much from James Bernauer, Richard Hart, Fred Evans, Stephen Watson, Dorothea Olkowski, Leonard Lawlor and Gary Aylesworth as they may have learned from me.

Portions of this book have been presented as invited papers or lectures at a wide variety of universities and colleges, including Northwestern, Purdue, Chicago, Dayton, Akron, Dickinson, Duquesne, Warwick, Essex, Oxford, Leeds, Sussex, Manchester, Manchester Polytechnic, Huddersfield Polytechnic, Trinity

Acknowledgments

College Dublin, Cork, Groningen, Delft, Brussels, Uppsala, Nice, and at the Merleau-Ponty Circle, the Society for Phenomenology and Existential Philosophy, the American Philosophical Association, Eastern Division, the Warwick Workshop in Continental Philosophy, the Collegium Phaenomenologicum, the International Society for the Comparative Study of Civilizations, and the Society for the Study of the History of Philosophy. I am grateful to those colleagues and participants whose reflections and reactions have led me to reformulate my views and positions.

Support for this project has been provided by a Stony Brook Graduate School Grant-in-Aid (1978–9), SUNY Faculty Research Summer Fellowships (in the summers of 1977, 1978 and 1981), and an American Council of Learned Societies Fellowship under a grant from the National Endowment for the Humanities, along with a sabbatical year from the State University of New York at Stony Brook in 1981–2. Furthermore the Stony Brook Philosophy Department has now made xeroxing available to aid in the material needs of this sort of research. I am glad to acknowledge all of these sources of funding which have helped me significantly in the advancement of this work.

The idea for this book was first hatched during a conversation with David Godwin, then of Routledge & Kegan Paul, during an American Psychological Association meeting in Toronto, Canada. After a number of discussions with him in the United States and then in the London office, the volume began to take shape. Later Stratford Caldecott took on the project and has been a strong and supportive editor in this and another project. Elizabeth Francis has lent a friendly ear and a critical eye to the enterprise—both of which have been greatly appreciated. Robert Bernasconi read the manuscript early on. With John Sallis, Tony O'Connor, Christina Howells, Jacques Taminiaux, Mikel Dufrenne, Dominique Janicaud and Michel Haar, I have found friendship and generous collegiality over the years. But these acknowledgments would not be complete without my expression of deepest thanks to David Wood who has been my persistent interlocutor, intellectual companion, running partner, soul-saver and friend throughout it all. Michel and Françoise Autrand have not only housed me in Meudon at various stages in the writing of this volume, but they have also provided the moral support that one often needs. It would be unfair not to mention L. Theresa Watkins, who was

Acknowledgments

present during the early stages of this book and who bore the
brunt of my laboring. And as this project has come to a close,
Patricia Athay has been my interlocuter at many of those crucial
times when not only intellectual challenge but also warmth and
understanding are called for. She has read just about all of it and
has now urged me to complete it. The book is dedicated to Claire
and Christopher, my children, who have remained with me
through it all.

INTRODUCTION: CONTINENTAL PHILOSOPHY IN AMERICA

I

Continental philosophy is one of the dominant faces of philosophy in America.[1] What I am calling continental philosophy is that orientation which tends to draw its inspiration, contacts, and style of formulation from the various traditions prevalent in Europe. While analytic philosophy—comprising the inheritors of logical positivism, ordinary language philosophy, and linguistic analysis—draws primarily upon models established in Britain and arising out of eighteenth century empiricism, continental philosophy appeals to the modes of articulation operative in Western Europe since Descartes and the rationalists. More commonly, continental philosophy in America is understood to mean those types of thinking which are consistent with work on the continent from the appearance of Husserlian phenomenology at the beginning of the twentieth century. Although Kant, Hegel, Marx, and Nietzsche are considered dominant figures within the tradition, continental philosophy as it is practiced in America tends to construe its active phases as beginning with Husserl.

There would be no point in designating a German, French, Italian, Dutch, or Belgian philosopher as a continental philosopher. Continental philosophy has come to describe quite precisely what we do here in America. Europeans are often surprised to find that American continental philosophy has taken directions and conducted research in ways which diverge quite significantly from what is current in their own context. The commonality of a theoretical language with overlapping reference terms and texts makes it easier for communication to take place—sometimes more so than with other American philosophers of an alternative orientation. Nevertheless just as American analytic philosophy is often not the same as its British counterpart, continental philosophy tends to stand on its own apart from its European proponents.[2]

Continental philosophy in America has many aspects. Until recently, the commonly acknowledged source was Husserlian transcendental phenomenology. The language of noetic-noematic structures, the theory of consciousness with its objective meaning contents imbedded within pure subjectivity, and the appeal to descriptions of experience was considered essential to serious work in the continental style of philosophizing. Although this assumption has been predominant for almost half a century, the Heideggerian existential analytic has often played a contrapuntal role. In a few instances, continental philosophers have by-passed Husserl and drawn their primary inspiration from Heidegger—even to the extent that the Husserlian language is as unfamiliar as Russell's theory of descriptions. Unlike Husserlians, Heideggerians tend to speak of fundamental ontology, temporality, and authentic modes of existence. American phenomenologists tend to be either more Husserlian or more Heideggerian. The contribution of one or the other tends to be a *sine qua non* for communicative discourse among continental philosophers in this country.

The incorporation of Hegelian and Marxian thinking along with a heavy dose of Kierkegaardian existentialism (in the case of Sartre) or Bergsonian vitalism and Gestalt psychology (in the case of Merleau-Ponty) provides two other dominant places of reference for American philosophical research. Still broadly phenomenological, but distinctively existential in orientation, the writings of Sartre and Merleau-Ponty (largely out of favor in Europe) have prompted a considerable range of original investigations in America. Those who draw upon the work of Sartre or Merleau-Ponty ought to know the relevant Husserlian and Heideggerian texts—though this does not always occur. And some simply find the psychological, social or political orientations of Sartre and/or Merleau-Ponty more congenial than their German antecedents.

Less dominant but not inconsequential for the broad spectrum of philosophers in America are those who appeal to the "existential" versions offered by thinkers as divergent as Kierkegaard, Nietzsche, Jaspers, Marcel, Mounier, Buber, and Ortega y Gasset. These existential strains made it possible for psychologists, sociologists, political theorists, theologians and literary critics to take philosophy seriously. Hence many of those who found existential approaches conducive to their own thinking took what they learned from philosophy and developed it in their respective fields. All along, they would continue to draw upon their European sources and more significantly upon their American philosophy teachers for guidance. At the same time, philosophers who found or find the existential and phenomenological ways of thinking plausible tend to expand their own research into these related disciplines. Sometimes the effect of this sort of spreading out is a broader range of thinking, occasionally less exact because of its scope, usually more meaningful to those who look to philosophy for an understanding of human experience and interaction.

Hermeneutics, taking its lead from Heidegger but also from Schleiermacher and Dilthey, has become a distinctive branch of continental philosophy. Its spokesmen Paul Ricoeur and Hans-Georg Gadamer have spent much of their time in recent years teaching and lecturing in America. Their adherents, students, and commentators are numerous. Proponents of the art or science of interpretation have spread into many other fields, but philosophers continue to work out its fundamental tenets, its methodological considerations, and its implications in relation to specific issues such as metaphor, religious thought, text theory, the history of philosophy, and the philosophy of language. The hermeneutic strain in continental philosophy is still very much alive, well, and growing in American thought.[3]

While transcendental, existential, and hermeneutic phenomenology have been the most identifiable aspects of continental philosophy in America over the past several decades, new forms have taken shape and come to stand beside the others. Although Husserlian, Heideggerian, Sartrian, and Merleau-Pontean approaches remain the principal corner stones, additions have been made. The semiology of Saussure and the critical theory of Adorno have marked a broad spectrum of research in the past fifteen years or so. From Saussurian semiology have come the structuralisms of Lévi-Strauss in anthropology, Lacan in psychoanalysis, Barthes in literary criticism, and Althusser in political theory. Unlike existentialism, where its philosophy has crept into other fields, structuralism has entered into philosophical research from related disciplines. Questions of methodology, the status of the subject or self, the implications of a synchronic conception of history—just to cite some examples—have become important issues for continental philosophers. The number of Americans who write in a semiotic style has not spread widely, though many of the concerns of structuralism were already indicated by Merleau-Ponty.[4] Enthusiasm for structuralism in America is on the rise even though it is now fading in Europe.[5]

The status of critical theory is a somewhat unusual one. Although the interest of Marx and Hegel is perennial and anyone seriously engaged in continental philosophy cannot ignore them, the cultural, social, and political theories of Adorno, Horkheimer, Benjamin, Marcuse, and, separately, Lukács and Goldmann have spawned a considerable range of adherents in America since the late 1960s. In recent years, their work is less that of political activism and more that of detailed critical investigation focusing on specific theoretical topics.[6] The renown of Habermas has given new impetus to corresponding research in America.[7] While some of the studies are done in sociology, political science, literature, and art departments, philosophers do account for many of those working actively in critical theory.

The final aspect of the continental face that I should like to consider is post-structuralism. Perhaps more than any of the other aspects, post-structuralism is establishing itself at the vanguard of continental thought. Post-structuralism is also implicitly post-phenomenology. Its major proponents are Jacques Derrida, Michel Foucault, Jean-François Lyotard, Gilles Deleuze, and Julia Kristeva. Although Derrida and Foucault are more commonly appealed to for their deconstruction and archaeology of knowledge respectively, their thought has been insinuating itself into a wide variety of philosophical studies in the past few years.[8] Their writings serve as reference texts for many individual studies articulated in corresponding modes and styles. Since they involve a radical critique of phenomenology and structuralism, in very different ways, to fully appreciate their contribution the whole twentieth century continental tradition has to be taken into account.

II

If the aspects of the continental face of philosophy in America includes phenomenology, existential philosophy, hermeneutics, structuralism, critical theory, and post-structuralism, what are its basic characteristics? Although their subject matter is shared with analytic and other philosophies (similar topics, issues, and areas of concern) what does distinguish them are (1) their style of philosophizing, (2) their reference texts, (3) their common language, (4) their relevant traditions, and (5) the significance of their enterprise. Continental philosophy is not one style but many, though there are some common features. Continental philosophers look for connections among a variety of disparate human concerns. They try to establish an interpretation or reading of their meaning or signification. Methodology tends to be taken seriously and explicitly. Implicit methodologies or ideological bases are suspect. The status of the self, inquirer, or investigator— how introduced, where situated, and in what manner incorporated into the field of relevant elements—is of paramount importance. Similarly the nature of that which is under investigation is regarded as intricately bound up with the investigator whether as subject, structure, or ideological construct. In practically all cases, the relations or systems of elements within the whole cannot be ignored or left aside without dire effects. If not synthesis, then the particular manifestations of the dispersion need to be assessed and brought out in the inquiry. Continental styles tend to eschew formalisms and reductionisms unless they can be shown to be structures imbedded within the world, the experience of the world, or the human productions and artifacts that give meaning to the world as it is lived and known.

The reference texts tend to be quite determinate and distinctively different from those of analytic philosophies. Although analytic philosophers may take an interest in and even write about some of the same reference texts, the styles and manners of approach are easily distinguished. Reference texts include the writings of Husserl, Heidegger, Sartre, Merleau-Ponty, Ricoeur, Gadamer, Adorno, Habermas, Foucault, and Derrida—to cite some of the more dominant ones. Unlike analytic philosophers, continental philosophers tend to cite these reference texts more commonly than they mention each other. This is not because they are not significant, but because the style is less argumentative and disputative. Continental philosophers are more concerned with extending the understanding of an issue as it has been initiated in the methodology or concerns of its reference texts. Continental philosophers are not usually taken up with problems that require analysis, dissection, and argument. Their interest is more with the description of a phenomenon, topic, structure, or cultural production through elucidation, elaboration, and demonstration of difference from related domains.

That this interest is undertaken with respect to specific reference texts tends to create a common language or set of common languages. If the specific reference texts are not cited, usually the mode of thinking, terminology, or methods of approach are invoked. They are often simply assumed and employed. If each study were obliged to defend the style, language, and approach, there would be no time or place to advance research in the area. Just as those who use a symbolic logic for arguing a point or claim without defending the symbols themselves, continental philosophers tend to proceed with the tools at hand.

Although the traditions appeared to overlap significantly with those of other philosophies—Plato, Aristotle, Descartes, and Kant are not the property of continental philosophers by any means— the common base can be more confusing than helpful. Interpretations of the history of philosophy are on occasion accepted or rejected because the account arises out of a different basic style of philosophizing. What counts, what matters, what is meaningful in the interpretation or reading will differ from style to style and hence the assessment of potential worth is made at the preliminary pre-interpretational level. The same holds for studies of different reference texts. The analytic reading of Heidegger, the hermeneutic account of Wittgenstein, and the deconstructionist assessment of Austin will (or may) be irrelevant for those who operate with these writings as reference texts. And certainly new research, new interpretations, new findings in any one style of philosophizing will depend upon its already established foundations. Even what Thomas Kuhn calls extraordinary science (call it here: extraordinary philosophy) will depend upon, respond to, arise out of a determinate philosophical style, with specific reference texts, a common language, and a particular tradition.

6

III

The task of this volume is to offer a persistent reading of the continental tradition. Its style is markedly continental. Although seeded and grown on American soil, its commitment to a philosophical orientation that depends upon and arises out of a tradition of European texts is paramount. The reference texts are the very texts that are offered for detailed readings: Husserl, Heidegger, Merleau-Ponty, Sartre, Piaget, Barthes, Foucault, and Derrida. This volume is highly self-conscious. It is engaged in a rereading of the very texts that constitute its tradition and system of reference considerations. Its task is to inscribe itself in the context of its own tradition, to re-inscribe the tradition itself so that it can articulate its own place and position. The position announced at the end of this volume goes under the name of a *hermeneutic semiology*. This name is provisional and yet it demonstrates the dual response to seemingly opposed and incompatible philosophical commitments. Phenomenology—as elaborated by Husserl, Heidegger, Sartre, and Merleau-Ponty—offers a full-scale attempt to understand the self-world relation. To the extent that language is inserted within this self-world relation, it is almost as an afterthought. The fundamental relation is epistemological: how the world can be experienced, known, understood—intentionality, consciousness, interpretation, and perception are the principal modes according to which the self-world relation is elaborated. That language comes to be inserted within the activity of these differing modes is both significant and important. Structuralism—as inaugurated by de Saussure and as carried on by Lévi-Strauss, Piaget, Lacan, and Barthes—begins with language. Whatever can be said of a self or world would depend upon the construction of the sign (signifier-signified relation). To the extent that the signified invokes a world, it does so only through the concept that assigns itself to a word. The conjuncture of these two separate enterprises, one: phenomenological and hermeneutic, the other: structuralist and semiological, opens up the space of difference between. I have called it a "hermeneutic semiology."

The present study however is inscribed in the place between phenomenology and structuralism. This space of difference is the place which Merleau-Ponty and the later Heidegger on the one

7

hand, and the later Barthes and Foucault on the other, entertain as the place where their own philosophizing can occur. This place—and the language of place is significant—is where a hermeneutic semiology opens onto a deconstruction, a reading of texts in terms of their differential, marginal, indecidable features. Language as written in the self-world relation but as reformulating that relation in terms of its own signifying practices offers a system of differences which constitute the place between phenomenology and structuralism. But the place between is not just a between—slash theory as it might be called. The place between is also beyond either phenomenology and structuralism. The place between must be at least a post-phenomenology and a post-structuralism. But the beyond is not a Hegelian *Aufhebung*. The beyond is inscribed entirely within the frameworks of a continental tradition and set of reference texts which it can go beyond only by operating within its contexts. The place of difference is where philosophy can find its place at the margins of its own traditions.

Inscriptions: Between Phenomenology and Structuralism is not a philosophical treatise. Yet it is a coherent and thoroughgoing inquiry into the contemporary status of continental philosophy and an offer of a position of its own within the continental tradition. *Inscriptions* is written in essay form. It is an interwoven set of investigations into the differences between phenomenology and structuralism—sometimes they are treated independently, sometimes they are brought into conjuncture with each other. By first building on the phenomenological tradition it becomes evident that the self-world relation also requires a consideration of the place of language in that relation. Taking Sartre as paradigmatic of the various strains in the phenomenological tradition, his phenomenological views are juxtaposed with those of different structuralist alternatives on the themes of language, structure, the unconscious, psychological development, literature, and history. Since Merleau-Ponty took it upon himself to incorporate features of structuralism into his phenomenology, his differing positions on the role of language lead into the juxtapositional studies of Sartre and the structuralists. The third section of the book explores the implications (and fate) of the theory of the self in a post-phenomenological, post-structuralist context. The accounts offered by the later Heidegger, Ricoeur, Foucault, and Derrida are crucial here. In effect, then, this book moves toward the inscription of the place between phenomenology and structuralism as a series of inscriptions, essays at opening the space of difference for a theory of incorporated self-decentering, an interpretive topology, or a hermeneutic semiology, in short, for a theory of textuality.

PART I

PHENOMENOLOGY

1

THE SELF IN HUSSERL'S
CRISIS

. . . no one actually arrives in his [ordinary] self-knowledge
(*Selbsterkenntnis*) at his true and actual self (*wahres und
wirkliches Selbst*), the being which is his own as ego-subject
(*Ichsubjekt*) and as the subject of all his world-knowledge
and mundane accomplishment (*weltlichen Leistungen*), . . . all
this shows itself only through the reduction, and that pure
psychology is nothing other than the infinitely toilsome way
of genuine and pure self-knowledge; but the latter also
includes knowledge of human beings (*Menschenerkenntnis*),
as knowledge of their true being and life as egos or as souls;
and then [it includes also the knowledge of] the true being of
the world, which in principle no positive science, no matter
how successful, can ever attain. (E. Husserl, *Crisis*, p. 261)

I DESCARTES'S MISTAKE

Gilbert Ryle is renowned for having proposed that Descartes
made a mistake—a category-mistake. His point was that Descartes
took the ego to be a substance of some sort and therefore fell
into the trap of naming and giving meaning to this ghost in a
machine. Husserl's critique of Descartes is of another type.
Instead of trying to show that Descartes was wrong in formulating
a notion of the ego as a thinking entity, Husserl thought that
Descartes did not go far enough. Instead of rejecting claims to
private access, Husserl claimed that Descartes was on the verge

of a great discovery: a means of access to the true and actual self (*wahres und wirkliches Selbst*).

According to Husserl, Descartes was on the right track. His methodology was sound in that he took a sceptical attitude. He doubted all forms of knowledge, hence performing the pyrrhonist *epoché*. This suspension of judgment brought Descartes back to the *ego cogito*, from which he could then reconstruct a knowledge of self and world. Descartes's mistake, however, was that he did not dwell upon the intricate characteristics of the *ego cogito:* he mistook the soul as identical and only identical with the *ego* of the *ego cogito*. Since Latin is an inflectional language and *cogito* is already "I think" (the *ego* is necessary simply for emphasis), Descartes may have found it unnecessary to focus upon the *ego* in the *cogito* of *cogito ergo sum*. Thus in his discussion of the passions of the soul (*l'âme*), he did not detect that there might be a distinction within the notion of the *ego* such that it might not be entirely equivalent in all respects to the soul. Descartes did not distinguish between (1) the psychic ego (*das seelische Ich*)— note that *die Seele* translates *l'âme*, which in turn is what we call "the soul"—and (2) the transcendental ego. For Husserl, this distinction is crucial and fundamental to a full and clear understanding of the self.

Descartes also misses a second distinction which Husserl finds to be critical: the relationship between the *ego qua cogito* (the "I think") and the actual cogitations or thoughts of the ego (the *cogitationes*). According to Husserl, wrapped up in Descartes's notion of the *cogito* is not only the *ego*, but also the acts of the *ego*, its directedness toward objects in the world (transcendent objects). This directedness, following Brentano, is called intentionality: having something consciously, the appearance of something. The *cogitatio*, as the giving of meanings to the ego, is what Husserl referred to in *Ideas* (*Ideem I*) as *noesis* (the act of thinking, related to the Greek equivalent of *cogito*, i.e. *noéo*). The ego thinks, but Descartes did not recognize that the ego-aspect and the thinking-aspect might require separate elucidation.

The third element, the *cogitatum*, was clearly an issue for Descartes (cf. Husserl, *Crisis*, sec. 50). How could he have made his systematic doubting of the world without recognizing that that which is thought is separate from the "I think", the *res cogitans* (i.e. *ego* plus *cogitationes*). In order for Descartes to doubt the

14

tower in the distance, the chair before him, his hand, his whole body, he was forced into formulating a notion of "that which is thought" (*cogitatum*). These *cogitata* are referred to by Husserl as "manners of givenness," "manners of appearing," "meanings," "intentional objects," for Husserl, they are not actually the objects in the world (the transcendent objects), but rather the way in which they appear to the thinking ego. At the time of *Ideas I* Husserl called these *cogitata noemata:* the meanings given in intentional acts.

Descartes's mistake, then, was to have equated the ego with the soul and subsequently to have included thinking along with the ego that thinks. Simply to indicate that Descartes erred, however, is only the first step. What is crucial for an understanding of Husserl's view of the self is to see how these distinctions become important in his phenomenology, to see the full implications of the ego—cogito—cogitatum structure.

II DIFFERENCE AND IDENTITY: SOUL AND EGO

The ego—cogito—cogitatum structure is already a transcendental structure. It is not possible to understand this threefold distinction without having performed the phenomenological reduction, just as Descartes could not have discovered the *cogito* without his method of doubt, his *epoché*. For Husserl, however, the ego that doubts is not entirely the same ego as the one which acts, sees, knows, and understands in the natural, naive attitude.

This latter ego is the ego which Descartes called the soul. It is the psychic ego, the empirical ego (an expression which Husserl avoids in the *Crisis*), the ego of psychological immanence. This is the self of everyday life and experience. It is the self of the natural scientist who performs his various investigations; the self which loves, which desires, which hopes; the self which decides that a clear, pure, and transcendental understanding is necessary for a full knowledge of itself.

Once this natural self takes up the sceptical, phenomenological attitude, it begins to distrust the individual validities (*Geltungen*) that are provided by a natural self. It begins to doubt that universal apodictic knowledge can be acquired by such a self. At this point, the empirical ego performs a reduction on the world and on it(s)self. The phenomenological reduction (both the transcendental and eidetic reductions) is not an act of destruction; its bracketing procedure does not eliminate that which is seen from the natural attitude. Rather it leaves the natural world aside temporarily in order to study it more clearly. On the other hand, the phenomenological reduction is not an ability which some people may have, but which is not available to others (e.g. mental telepathy). We all can perform the phenomenological reduction by learning to examine the essence of what is under consideration (eidetic reduction) and by bringing the existence of assumptions and presuppositions of what is under consideration into full view so that they will not be confused with the essential meaning (*epoché*, or transcendental reduction). In the *Crisis*, Husserl says relatively little about the procedure of the phenomenological reduction. Yet we must note that, by this procedure, the natural self is transformed into a transcendental self. The psychic ego is transformed into an absolute ego; psychological immanence becomes egological immanence; psychic, inner, or self-perception take the form of egological self-perception.

What is the nature of this transformation from the natural self to the transcendental self? The claim to transformation is a suggestion that the self takes on a *new* form. In this sense the soul is different from the pure ego; the natural self is different from the transcendental self. The change of form, however, is like a masquerade in which all of a sudden everyone removes his or her mask. We see everyone as he or she truly looks and is. Each person is, in fact, the same person whether wearing a mask or not. However, with the mask on, others may be deceived. The task of phenomenology is to minimize deception, to see things as they really are. In this sense, the empirical, natural self is quite the same self as the transcendental self, except that the transcendental self is the appearing of the empirical self as it really is.

A critical difficulty arises when one seeks to reveal one's own transcendental self. The ego in the natural attitude is the starting point in everyday perception, everyday investigations. Similarly, in the transcendental field, the realm of transcendental subjectivity, the pure ego is the starting point of phenomenological investigations. As such, the pure self is an ego-pole. It is directed toward something. Husserl sometimes calls it an ego-subject. The ego-subject is directed toward an objective something (*cogitatum*)

16

through ego-acts (*cogitationes*). These three elements are the components of transcendental subjectivity. I—intend—the meaning of something. The something, for example, a book, as it sits there on the table is part of subjectivity only as a meaning given intentionally by a pure ego. This ego-pole is like a point. The distance between two points is a line. One of those points is part of the line only in the sense that it is an end-point. Similarly, the ego-pole is part of subjectivity only as the source of direct-edness. In the transcendental realm the other point is the object-pole, that is, the *cogitatum*. However, for one pure ego, there can be many *cogitata*.[1] The pure ego, Husserl says, is an ego-pole along with whatever is peculiar to its identity. The ego's identity is not available to the different *cogitata* (*noemata*) given in different *cogitationes* (*noeses*) by the transcendental ego. Although we must recognize that the soul or natural ego is different from the tran-scendental ego in that the natural ego is phenomenologically uncritical, the two egos are the same: their field is identical and their directedness is identical. The transcendental ego, however, is the empirical ego phenomenologically refined to a point that the self *qua* empirical ego can be examined fully (in its essential form and without hidden presuppositions).

We are not to conclude that Husserl is proposing a theory of a schizophrenic self (a divided self). Rather the transcendental ego is psychologically identical with the empirical ego. Consideration of the ego as a psychological (or psychic) fact is to speak of the empirical ego. To refer to the ego as a phenomenological fact is to describe the transcendental ego. Questions of schizophrenia necessarily deal with the psychic ego. Now it may be possible to examine phenomenologically the psychic aspects of the empirical ego, but this would be to take the empirical ego as the specific theme of phenomenological reflection. In such a case, the tran-scendental ego, as in all intentional acts, undertakes the investi-gation. It investigates itself (constitutes itself) in that the self is not other—it is not the self of another. This empirical ego (soul) is the transcendental ego's own self. No psychological distance is possible.

The transcendental ego must be the self conducting (through *noeses*) a study of itself. The true and actual self becomes evident only when such an investigation takes place. The conscious life of the empirical ego serves as the necessary conditions for the consciousness in which the transcendental ego participates. However, a totally different consciousness cannot be derived from the conscious life and activity of a mundane empirical ego. Phenomenological consciousness must be developed out of a natural consciousness—it cannot arise from spontaneous generation or the like. The focus of the self is in its consciousness. Hence the phenomenological self can be correlated through its consciousness with the natural self.

In refuting psychologism and introspectionism, Husserl wants to avoid viewing the inquiring self as occupying the same ontological and epistemological status as the examined self. He would also argue that the phenomenological self can be correlated with the natural one. I (transcendental ego) can study myself (empirical ego) under the special phenomenological attitude. That there is a correlation and some identity of the selves is critical for the study to be a self-study (i.e. self-knowledge and not knowledge of another). If this were not the case, Husserl would be asserting a pure idealism in which no experiential relationship between the two "selves" would be possible.

Phenomenology must be a study of what appears there—the thing itself, in this case, the self. The reduction permits empirical egos to be treated as "phenomena," but *my* empirical ego appears to me transcendentally as a phenomenon in the form of a transcendental ego. Thus the transcendental ego is both what I find when reflecting upon the empirical ego and that which is the condition for transcendental acts.

Although the soul and the transcendental ego are identical, in that they are the same self, they are nevertheless different. The soul is the psychological-human ego "made worldly in the spatio-temporal world," while the transcendental ego carries with it "its ego-life, and its accomplishment" (Husserl, *Crisis*, sec. 58). This ego-life and its accomplishment include various transcendental aspects, such as horizon, thetic component, meaning, internal time-consciousness, etc. The self simply does not recognize these aspects under a natural, everyday perspective:

> . . . in my naive self-consciousness as a human being knowing himself to be living in the world, for whom the world is the totality of what for him is valid as existing, I am blind to the immense transcendental dimension of problems. This

dimension is in a hidden [realm of] anonymity. (*Crisis*, sec. 58)

Since it is possible, however, for this "I" to examine itself from a transcendental perspective, a new view of its natural life becomes available. This "I can" (*Ich kann*)—emphasized by Merleau-Ponty[2]—is what philosophers, e.g. Quine, have questioned. In what sense is it possible for me to take on a transcendental attitude in which I become—and re-orient myself into—a phenomenological point of view? Quine's problem of the indeterminacy of translation (cf. *Word and Object*) is significant in that he questions the very existence of a transcendental self. Sartre also responds to the issue by claiming that the transcendental ego is, in fact, transcendent—that the self must be pure consciousness, totally free, and not anything.[3] Otherwise, it will be a reified something, objectified, and in-itself. Michel Foucault has also entered the fray by proclaiming the disappearance and absence of the transcendental ego or subject as a concept that no longer has a place in a contemporary *epistemé*.[4] My task here however is to elucidate what Husserl construed to be the nature of the self, which necessarily entails a discussion of the transcendental ego.

III THE ENDURING SELF

A particular feature of the self, according to Husserl, is that it endures. Hume's doubt arose at this juncture: how can I be certain that the various impressions that I have of myself amount to more than a bundle of impressions? No unified view of the self seemed possible. Hence the whole problem of personal identity (cf. *A Treatise of Human Nature*, Bk I, Part IV, vi). Husserl however did not locate the self in the acts of the ego and its contents. As we have seen, Husserl finds the self in the ego: both empirical and transcendental. This difference is crucial for the question of personal identity. If the self is the ego-subject, then the problem of the multiplicity of impressions does not become focal. The ego, according to Husserl, carries through all of its acts, but it does not ever become the contents (the *noemata*) of its acts; it always remains behind each of its acts. We cannot say, however, that it exists independently of its acts, for that would deny the principle, reiterated in the *Crisis*, that all consciousness must be consciousness of something. Hume could not affirm any connection between his different impressions. If, however, the self is the ego and if that ego endures, then the self must endure. If the self endures, then the acts of the self must be interrelated. Personal identity hinges upon this connection between the acts (or impressions) of the self.

Husserl does assert that the ego endures (similar in character, but not in structure, to his contemporary Bergson's notion of *la durée*):

> Let us here point out only what is most important, the most general aspect of the ego-form, namely, the peculiar temporalization by which it becomes an enduring ego (*einem dauernden*), constituting itself in its time-modalities: the same ego, now actually present, is in a sense, in every past that belongs to it, another—i.e. as that which was and thus is not now—and yet, in the continuity of its time it is one and the same, which is and was and has its future before it. The ego which is present now, thus temporalized, has contact with its past ego, even though the latter is precisely no longer present: it can have a dialogue with it and criticize it, as it can others. (*Crisis*, sec. 50)

The ego, *qua* transcendental ego, endures in that it is present. Its continuity is that it remains present. It abides (cf. *Cartesian Meditations*, sec. 32). This is the continuity of internal time-consciousness. However, although present, the self is related to the past. Some pasts actually belong to this particular present. Husserl has carefully elucidated the nature of these pasts in his *Phenomenology of Internal Time-Consciousness* where he distinguishes the past of primary memory, or "retention," and the past of secondary memory, or "remembrance." Both forms of the past are specifically related to a "now," which is the "now" of the transcendental ego, of the self. Included in the horizon of the intentional act, which is "now," are both retentions, the immediate fading away of a present experience, and remembrances, the recollections that require new intentional acts (presentifications) to render them present. There are also "protentions," that is, expectations about the future experience of that which is under phenomenological investigation.[5]

The continuity of the past and the future which belongs specifically to this particular ego characterize its continuity. Husserl places a clear emphasis upon the ego as present. The self must always be present in one fashion or another. Thus the self, given through phenomenological intuition, is apodictic. However, adequate evidence of the self is available in that only the ego's "living present" can be experienced with "strict adequacy" (cf. *Cartesian Meditations*, sec. 9). This is to say that past and future of the ego, except as given within the horizon of possibilities, cannot render adequate evidence.[6] Only intuitions which are lived in the present can be strictly adequate. The apodicticity of the correlation between a present "I" and a past "I" is what affirms the continuity of the self:

> . . . through the transcendental exposition of recollection, . . .
> to what is recollected, what is past (which has the ontic
> meaning of a present having passed) there belongs also a past
> "I" of that present, whereas the actual original "I" is that
> of immediate presence; to this presence, recollection belongs
> as a present experience, in addition to what appears as the
> present sphere of facts. Thus the immediate "I" performs an
> accomplishment through which it constitutes a variational
> mode of itself as existing (in the mode of having passed).
> (*Crisis*, sec. 54b)

The past "I" is correlated with the present "I" by the fact that I experience the past "I" as an "I" that I recollect in the present. A subsequent present "I" is already recollecting the past "I" in a slightly different fashion and so on continuously throughout the life of the ego. This continuity is the temporalization of the enduring self.

IV PHYSICAL BODY AND LIVING BODY

Since the self is localized in the ego—in the transcendental ego when in its purest form—one might question the relevance of the body in this discussion. In fact, Husserl himself did not consider the body to be of major importance until the last few years of his life. In the *Crisis* (1934–37), the body becomes an issue worthy of Husserl's attention. It may also be significant to note that

The self in Husserl's Crisis

Merleau-Ponty, known for his discussion of the body, studied the *Crisis* at the Husserl Archives in Louvain. Merleau-Ponty however would surely incorporate the body within his concept of the self. Husserl on the other hand remains more strictly within the Cartesian tradition. We cannot forget that Husserl's 1929 Sorbonne lectures were published as *Meditations cartesiennes* in the 1931 French translation. And Descartes always distrusted the certainty of the body and sense-experience.

Although the body is not contained in the self for Husserl, the self must express itself in terms of the body. This point was not clear in Husserl's earlier work. In the *Crisis* the body is discussed in two ways: as physical body [*Körper*] and as living body [*Leib*]. These English equivalents for *Leib* and *Körper* are offered by David Carr in his translation of the *Crisis*. Carr notes further that "*Körper* means a body in the geometric or physical sense; *Leib* refers to the body of a person or animal" (*Crisis*, p.50). When first introduced, Husserl is talking about Galileo who fell victim to the substitution of the "mathematically substructed world of idealities for the only real world" (*Crisis*, sec. 9h). Husserl then states:

. . . everyday induction grew into induction according to scientific method, but that changes nothing of the essential meaning of the pregiven world as the horizon of all meaningful induction. It is this world that we find to be the world of all known realities. To it, the world of actually experiencing intuition, belongs the form of space-time together with all the bodily [*körperlich*] shapes incorporated in it; it is in this world that we ourselves live, in accord with our bodily [*leiblich*], personal way of being. But here we find nothing of geometrical idealities, no geometrical space or mathematical time with all their shapes. (*Crisis*, sec. 9h)

We live in the world which bears within it bodily [*körperlich*] shapes. We live in this world "in accord with our bodily [*leiblich*], personal way of being." This "we" is the self. Bodily [*körperlich*] shapes include not only stones, tables, and books, but also our physical bodies. The physical body of the self is the same body in accord with which the self has its personal way of being. The physical body and the living body are identical. But the self experiences them from different perspectives.

22

The physical body [*Körper*] corresponds with the self as psychic ego (soul). This is the psycho-physical relation which is presumed by the behaviorist whose experimentation focuses on the physical "behaviour" of the body. The psychosomatic relation is that which occurs between soul and body. Freudian psychoanalysis proposes to study this second relation, where there is some suggestion that the body is viewed principally as the living body [*Leib*]. Yet the trinity of id-ego-superego, with the self expressing itself normally as ego, would probably remain for Husserl the psychological ego. The psychosomatic relation then is the psychological or empirical ego and the living body. The third relation and the one which Husserl would subscribe to as meriting the fullest investigation is between the transcendental ego and the living body.[7] This we may call the phenomenological-human relation.

These three types of relations are based on a coincidence of what Husserl would call the self and the body. Just as the empirical ego and the transcendental ego are both identical and yet different, so too the physical body and the living body are identical and different. *Körper* and *Leib* correspond in that they occupy the same location here in the literal sense of locus, place, and space. The living body cannot be anywhere else except where the physical body is located. The living body would not correspond to a stone, for example, but only to the physical body where the living occurs. Yet to emphasize the irreducibility of the one to the other, Husserl says, "purely in terms of perception, physical body and living body are essentially different; living body, that is, [understood] as the only one which is actually given [to me as such] in perception: my own living body" (*Crisis*, sec. 28). Only in the phenomenological-human relation is the living body given to the self *qua* transcendental ego. Here the living body is not simply an object of an intentional act (i.e. transcendent object), nor is it an intentional object (*cogitatum* or *noema*). Of course, the phenomenologist may take the body as a theme, in which case it would be first an object of an intentional act (a transcendent object) and then a *noema*. But when conducting a phenomeno-logical investigation of something other than the body, the body is given to the self in perception as that which the self lives through. It is the status of "being an ego through the living body" [*die leiblich Ichlichkeit*]. The self experiences the body in terms of sensibility, kinesthesis, and motility. Seeing, hearing, moving, and doing are all kinesthetic functions of the living body. The appearances of objects for the self are all bound up with these kinesthetic functions.

What Husserl emphasized in *Ideas* as hyletic data, the material aspects of phenomenologically appearing objects, are surely another way of indicating the role of the living body in transcendental subjectivity. Furthermore, the question of whether hyletic data belong entirely within the transcendental field or whether they also partake of the object under scrutiny may be due to the pervasiveness of the living body in phenomenological experience. Since the living body is also connected immediately with the physical body such that they are spatially the same, the reason why hyletic data straddle the transcendent and the transcendental may become clearer. While hyletic data are a component of the transcendental field along with *noema*, *noesis*, and transcendental ego, the living body is not a specifically transcendental component, although it can be experienced fully (apodictically) only when the self is in the phenomenological attitude. The psychosomatic relation is not full in that phenomenological intuition is not available to the psychoanalytic self. In the psychophysical relation, neither the actual transcendental self nor the living body are brought into play. Yet the corresponding presence of the psychophysical relation along with the phenomenological-human relation links the realm of pure subjectivity with the object of an intentional act (a transcendent object). The psychophysical relation is only bracketed out, suspended from consideration within pure subjectivity; it is not eliminated from the world. We may wish to characterize the continuing connection between the physical body of the psychophysical relation and the living body of the phenomenological-human relation simply as hyletic data, except for one proviso. The hyletic data (the material aspects of the object under consideration) do in some ways extend to that object. However, the link must pass through the living body and correspondingly through the physical body as well.

The physical body is a body among other bodies. It is the body of a particular self, but not specifically of *my* self. Now, *my* self may be one of those particular selves, but it is the body of *my* self only as living body. The self does not live through its physical body *qua* physical body. It only lives through its physical body *qua* living body. The physical body can be contiguous with a transcendent object. Physical body P can be sitting in a chair C, where P and C are contiguous. But true self S is touching C in that S is living through living body L (if and only if P is the same body as L). Touching is what S does. Contiguity is how P and C are related. But P cannot touch C; only S can touch C through L. Yet in order for S to touch C, P must be contiguous with C. P is like C in that it is a physical entity. L, however, has no characteristics in common with C. C is in the world; L is in the life-world. The bearing that S has with these two types of world is the theme of what follows.

V LIFE-WORLD AND SELF-KNOWLEDGE

The self *qua* transcendental ego is related specifically to a living body. This living body occurs in the life-world. The self *qua* empirical ego is related specifically to a physical body. This physical body occurs in the world of objective science. Again the life-world and the world of objective science are different modes of understanding the same world since there is only one real world.

One physical body can be compared to another with respect to distance, size, color, shape, etc. A physical body may be compared to another entity within the world of objective science in a similar fashion and according to the same qualities. The living body does not compare with a physical entity in these same terms. The living body has no size, color, shape, distance from physical bodies and entities, yet the living body can be experienced as having such properties. When the self experiences its living body as having these properties it experiences the immediate connection between the living body and the physical body. The self lives with objects and other persons through the living body and in terms of the physical body with its various properties. These properties can be compared and measured. When however they are formulated into a mathematical world of idealities, the self of such a theoretical act conceives of itself in purely empirical terms. A distance is set up between these idealities and what Husserl calls the plenum [*die Füllen*]. The plenum is the world as it really is with its specifically sensible qualities (cf. *Crisis*, sec. 9c). This establishment of a distance seems to be what the objective or natural scientist does.

The issue at hand for Husserl is to return to this plenum and in its purified and purest form is the life-world.

The life-world is the context for the living body as experienced by the true self (the transcendental ego). The life-world corresponds to the plenum world. The objective sciences create their world of idealities from this plenum world. The phenomenological self also begins to survey the plenum world as it really is from within the very same plenum world. Such surveying however can occur only by living in the plenum world and by seeing it as a life-world, as a context for human and cultural life.

A full examination of the true self, living through its body in the life-world, is the task of the phenomenological human sciences. This task will also be the mode of self-understanding, in that once the self understands the context in which it lives and its manner of living through the body intentionally along with the appearing of elements from the life-world in the realm of transcendental subjectivity, the self will reveal itself more clearly. That which is for the self will be juxtaposed with that which is in the self. The self cannot study only what is in itself; the self must also study that which is for itself. Only in this way can the self distinguish the two and affirm its own identity. All that is for the transcendental ego is other than itself (the transcendental ego). All that is in the transcendental ego is what is identical with it. The discovery of this identity is the identity of the true self and the manner in which it can recognize, understand, and know itself.

The self does not generally recognize itself as the true self:

> . . . I am a transcendental ego, but I am not conscious of this; being in a particular attitude, the natural attitude, I am completely given over to the object-poles, completely bound by interests and tasks which are exclusively directed toward them. (*Crisis*, sec. 58)

The daily demands and concerns of the plenum world as the self sees them draws its attention away from its transcendental life— the values and interest of pure knowledge. Yet as philosopher,

> . . . it is I who practice the *epoché*, I who interrogate, as phenomenon, the world which is now valid for me according to its being and being-such, with all its human beings, of whom I am so fully conscious; it is I who stand above all

26

natural existence that has meaning for me, who am the ego-pole of this transcendental life, in which, at first, the world has meaning for me purely as world; it is I who, taken in full concreteness, encompass all that. (*Crisis*, sec. 54b)

In encompassing all that—the acts, functions, possibilities, position, etc. of the transcendental ego—the self is brought into self-consciousness by recognizing its acts, functions, possibilities, position, etc. To understand that this knowledge must always pass through the living body of the physical body to the life-world of the plenum world is perhaps the purest form of self-realization.

VI THE INTERHUMAN PRESENT

A discussion of Husserl's conception of the self, particularly in the *Crisis*, would not even approach completeness if the inter-human aspect were omitted. Suffering under the charge of solipsism in his earlier work, Husserl devoted the fifth and last of his Cartesian Meditations to an exposition of the intersubjective aspect of the transcendental ego. There he proposed that by a special procedure of reducing to the sphere of ownness (*Eigenheitssphäre*) the self could discover what is unique to the transcendental ego. But then by separating out what is peculiarly mine, a realm similar to Kant's transcendental unity of apperception could be obtained; that is, a realm which is common to the selfhood of all persons. The notions of "empathy" and "pairing" complete the procedure. Empathy is a recognition of the commonality of nature and interests of the self and pairing is the unification of that commonality of nature and interests to form an intersubjective self. Thus to speak of the self is to also speak of the self of others. Since the self must always adjust to the necessary presence of others, any phenomenological theory of the self will also be a social theory.

By the time that Husserl wrote the *Crisis*, several years after *Cartesian Meditations*, his references to transcendental intersubjectivity were interwoven throughout his discussion of self, body, and world. Within the realm of the true self, derived through the eidetic and transcendental reductions, we find: "we-subjectivity" (*Crisis*, sec. 28), "communalization of ego-subjects" (*Crisis*, sec.

48), "cosubjects of experience" (*Crisis*, sec. 47), "I-the-man among other men" (*Crisis*, sec. 54b), and "the horizon of transcendental others as cosubjects within the transcendental subjectivity which constitutes the world" (*Crisis*, sec. 54b).

Not only do we recognize that the present of the self is an interhuman present through the community of physical bodies in the plenum world, but also we find by way of Husserlian phenomenology that the life-world is an interhuman world. We find that in living through the body, we are given particular existence as separate from other bodies. But we know that these other bodies in the life-world are lived through just as ours is, because the communalization of the self at the transcendental level renders our understanding of other phenomenological-human relations as paired with our own. The self sees itself as social. Only as a psychophysical relation can the physical body be taken to exist without the living body that corresponds to it. As a psychosomatic relation, where a psychic ego experiences a living body, what remains lacking is the very "we-subjectivity" of the transcendental self. The phenomenological-human relation, however, is precisely a human present that necessarily implies and includes humans (other persons who populate the real world which we know phenomenologically through our living bodies to be the life-world). We our*selves* are human.

2

DASEIN AND EXISTENTIAL AMBIGUITY

The tri-partite structure of *Dasein-Verstehen-Zeitlichkeit* in Heidegger's account of human experience can be given a name. The name which I propose is "existential ambiguity." The structure has its founding in *Being and Time* and its elaboration as a fundamental ontology provides a sketch of how we as human beings exist within the world. The totality formed by *Dasein* (Being-there), *Verstehen* (Understanding), and *Zeitlichkeit* (Temporality) combines three mutually dependent axes of experience. The rationale for speaking of that totality as "existential ambiguity" is the principal concern of this essay.

In my interpretation of Heidegger's account as an expression of existential ambiguity, I will demonstrate eight major points.

(i) Dasein is the ontological status of existential ambiguity.

(ii) Existential ambiguity is the only situation in which more than one meaning (*Sinn*) occurs in the same self-interpretive act.

(iii) The meanings which occur in one act are inexhaustible, indeterminate, and in flux (i.e., never static or fixed).

(iv) Understanding brings existential ambiguity to disclosedness.

(v) Interpretation is the articulation of the meanings of existential ambiguity.

(vi) When Dasein is *mis*-interpreted as meaningless, absurdity rather than ambiguity is its fundamental mode of disclosure.

(vii) Temporality reveals, through interpretation, the relational structure (datability) of the meanings present in existential ambiguity.

(viii) The measures of world-time (clock time) cannot account for the meanings of existential ambiguity; an appropriate description of the many meanings which are in flux both characterizes and occurs within human temporality.

I EXISTENTIAL AMBIGUITY

Existential ambiguity unites three distinct perspectives: the ontological, the epistemological, and the temporal. "Meanings" play a central role in each case, since they form the node of interrelationship for the three perspectives. Ontologically, these meanings are multiple and inexhaustible. No set of particular meanings, however determinate or fixed they may be, can exhaust the ontological reality of man. A human being is a unified whole which is greater than the sum of its component meanings. Epistemologically, this totality of meanings is interpreted experientially as indeterminate. However, any particular meaning or set of meanings is available for determination and specification. Each specified and determined meaning is selected from the indeterminate whole. Its isolation from the totality does not deny the totality itself. Temporally, meanings are never fixed nor static while they partake of the experiential totality. They are always changing, evolving within the context of human life and action. This flux is different from their inexhaustibility and indeterminateness in that it characterizes them from a temporal perspective.

To determine a meaning, it must be posited or distinguished as primary. Due to the inexhaustibility and flux of meanings in existential ambiguity, such positing involves a choice. If I determine only one meaning, then ambiguity as such is no longer in question. Our task, however, is to describe existential ambiguity prior to the specification and isolation of individual meanings. Therefore, we must discover the two or more meanings (the multiplicity of meanings) that are unified in experience and which change through time. To describe *human* existence, more than one meaning must be present at the same time.

Existential ambiguity, as I have presented it, is different from what Heidegger calls *Zweideutigkeit*. For Heidegger, ambiguity *qua Zweideutigkeit* is a condition of the everydayness of the "There" along with the categories of curiosity and idle talk.

> When, in our everyday Being-with-one-another, we encounter the sort of thing which is accessible to everyone, and about which everyone can say anything, it soon becomes impossible to decide what is disclosed in a genuine understanding, and what is not.[1]

In referring to this condition as "ambiguity," Heidegger treats that which is open to a variety of interpretations and assessments as usual and exhibitive of its everydayness. The inability to arrive at a "genuine understanding" prohibits disclosedness (which Heidegger associates with the presentation of truth). Such disclosedness is inadequate and incomplete. Taking knowledge from ambiguous disclosures can lead only to confusion and false belief. Ambiguity, then, is inauthentic. It does not help to bring an understanding of something into the world, of our Being-with-one-another, or of Dasein's Being towards itself. *Zweideutigkeit*, for Heidegger, involves our inability to distinguish one meaning from another, one truth from another. Therefore, it is to be left behind in the move toward more authentic modes of existence, such as care. In the authentic condition, we can understand a disclosure as a truth—the deceptions of ambiguity do not hinder us. Ambiguity, then, is like the morality of the herd for Nietzsche or like the world of appearances for Plato. In each case, only illusion and opinion are possible.

In existential ambiguity, however, we are not led astray from the full disclosure of Being. Existential ambiguity is the description of how we are in the authentic mode. That which Heidegger sees as leading to our fallen condition and which confronts us deceptively from an epistemological point of view is only one of many types of meaning. Heidegger's *Zweideutigkeit* is fixedly and determinately there for us in its inauthenticity. Existential ambiguity, on the contrary, is the description of human being as it is able to understand whatever is disclosed. The experience of what is disclosed occurs in a temporal flux. Existential ambiguity is a fundamental ontological description of Being in its relation to particular entities. It is not an incidental experience to be overcome.

With this caveat, an interpretation of Heidegger's formulation of what I have called existential ambiguity is now possible. In order to do so, we must clarify the nature of meanings. Methodologically, Husserl has provided the groundwork for assisting us in our purpose.[2] By studying *noemata* after the phenomenological reduction (transcendental and eidetic reductions) has been performed, we can concern ourselves with meanings (*Sinne*). Such procedures, according to Husserl, will allow us to exclude preconceptions, i.e., to suspend judgment concerning the existence of objects (the transcendental reduction or *epoché*) and to exclude accidental features of objects (the eidetic reduction). Furthermore, they will allow us to perform the special, phenomenological reflection on noematic *Sinne* (meanings as they appear for consciousness).

Husserlian phenomenology seeks to concentrate conceptual thought on *noemata* as meanings given in noetic acts.[3] An examination of *noemata* would show that they are bordered by horizons. The inner horizon characterizes my expectations (protentions) and primary memory (retentions) of a particular object, while the outer horizon describes the whole world as possibility for my intentional consciousness.[4] Furthermore, the noema has a thetic component, which involves a positing of Being. This positing is temporal and is implied in beliefs and other acts.

For an understanding of existential ambiguity, we must ask: what, in phenomenological terms, is the content of the *noema* of various modes of Being? Husserl does not concern himself in any primary way with this question. Heidegger, however, makes it the focal point of his work. *Being and Time* is the study of the *Sinn* [meaning] of *Sein* [Being]. And "in the meaning of Being, those entities which have the character of Dasein are what is primarily interrogated" (*SZ*, p. 41; *BT*, p. 65). In moving specifically to the phenomenology of Being, Heidegger establishes the foundation for a theory of existential ambiguity. The tripartite structure of *Dasein-Verstehen-Zeitlichkeit* brings together the three perspectives of existential ambiguity while also providing an interpretation of the human meaning of Being. In this case, *Dasein*, as I shall show, delineates the meaning-level; *Verstehen*, its understanding or givenness; and *Zeitlichkeit*, is continued, active, horizonal character.

II DASEIN: THE MEANING(S) OF BEING-THERE

Dasein is an entity (*ein Seiende*):[5]

> Looking at something, understanding and conceiving it,
> choosing access to it—all these ways of behaving are
> constitutive of our inquiry, and therefore are modes of Being
> of a particular entity, of *the* entity, which we, the inquirers
> are ourselves. Thus to work out the question of Being
> adequately, we must make an entity—the inquirer—
> transparent in his own Being. The very asking of this question
> is an entity's mode of *Being;* and as such it gets its essential
> character from what is inquired about—namely, Being. This
> entity which each of us is himself and which includes Being's
> possibility of inquiring, we shall denote by the term "Dasein."
> (*SZ*, pp. 7; *BT*, pp. 26–7)

Dasein could be translated as Being-there. I am that entity who
is there. I perform the inquiry and my being there allows me to
inquire. I, as an entity (Dasein), am my possibilities. In Husserlian
terms, each of my possibilities is a component of a noematic
horizon. When constituted, these non-thetic components are not
fixed (i.e., maintained in the same form and position) from one
act to another, even though the noematic *Sinne* (meanings given
in acts) are filled. Each successive intentional act reveals a
meaning which is comprised of different possibilities. The filling
of a *noema* implies that I have constituted an object without a
subsequent explosion of the *noema*, that is, without rejecting the
meaning that was previously given protentionally. In the case of
an explosion of a *noema*, one would expect the possibilities to
change. But possibilities also change when the *noemata* are filled.
Ambiguity occurs when there is more than one noematic *Sinn* for
an act where all the *noemata* are filled. Technically, for Husserl,
this situation should not arise. A noetic (meaning-giving) act
should reveal only one noematic *Sinn* (meaning-given) with its
corresponding possibilities. For Heidegger, when speaking of
human being, the object of a self-reflective noetic act is Dasein,
but Dasein is also the subject—the entity doing the inquiring.
Hence, if Dasein were to constitute itself as both "subject" and
"object,"[6] then both meanings would be given and filled in a
single act. The possibilities of a "subject" and those of an "object"

would be combined in the same experience. More than one noematic *Sinn* would be entailed by a reflective act. The self-constitution need not be consciously turned upon itself. Human experience per se brings together the meaning(s) of subjectivity and the meaning(s) of objectivity at the same time in the same experiential act. In fact, the experience of Dasein may be the only case in which more than one filled noematic *Sinn* is possible in a particular intentional act.

Existential ambiguity occurs when many meanings are experienced together, where the whole formed by those meanings is experientially irreducible, where the context does not allow any one of the meanings to be determined as primary or de facto separate from the others, and where the meanings themselves are never fixed or static. If we consider the filling of more than one *noema* in several acts, where each act has only one noematic *Sinn*, then we would have nothing other than the regular temporal perception or constitution of a physical object (although in an art object, there is the possibility of a special kind of constitution).[7] If there is only one act with several noematic *Sinne*, then ambiguity is present, for many meanings are experienced at the same time, none of which are determinate. To be determinate is for one noematic *Sinn* to be explicitly distinct from all others. The multiplicity of human meanings is given as a whole at the same time, in the same act. To determine a meaning would dissolve the totality and spread it out into separate acts. It now remains for us to show in what way Heidegger claims that Dasein constitutes itself as both "subject" and "object" in a given act, for in that way a multiplicity of noematic *Sinne* are given at once.

Dasein is existing:

> Dasein always understands itself in terms of its existence—in terms of a possibility of itself: to be itself or not itself. Dasein has either chosen these possibilities itself, or got itself into them, or grown up in them already. Only the particular Dasein decides its existence, whether it does so by taking hold or by neglecting. The question of existence never gets straightened out except through existing itself. (*SZ*, p. 12; *BT*, p. 33)

Being-there is as Being there can be and might be. Dasein passes judgment on its own existence. Therefore, Dasein has its existence as its own. Dasein can fall into inauthenticity or it can maintain its authentic Being. Whichever, Dasein must recognize itself as existing. It should also be noted that Heidegger places emphasis on Dasein as a particular, for it is only as an individual that Dasein must choose. What is to be understood here is that Dasein is both subject and object since, among its various activities, it chooses itself.

"The 'essence' of Dasein lies in its existence" (*SZ*, p. 42; *BT*, p.67). This often cited remark is helpful in phenomenological terms since "existence" will be the essence remaining after the eidetic reduction, even though it is existence, according to the Husserlian transcendental reduction, about which we suspend our judgment. Yet when examining Dasein, existence is precisely what comes under scrutiny—what is to be reflected upon noematically.

"Dasein has in each case mineness (*Jemeinigkeit*); thus one must always use a personal pronoun when one addresses it: 'I am,' 'you are' " (*SZ*, p. 42; *BT*, p. 68). Since Dasein is addressed, it is an object. Dasein is that to which one speaks. But at the same time it is a subject: "Because Dasein is . . . essentially its own possibility, it *can*, in its very Being, 'choose' itself" and win itself; it can lose itself and never win itself; or only "seem" to do so (*SZ*, p. 42; *BT*, p. 68). Dasein is both active and passive, constituting and constituted. But most importantly, it is not now one and now the other, rather it is experienced as both at the same time.

"Being-in is the formal existential expression for the Being of Dasein, which has Being-in-the-world as its essential state" (*SZ*, p.54; *BT*, p. 78). Although Dasein exists and is mine, although it is both subject and object and therefore existentially ambiguous, it must be described as having the basic state of Being-in-the-world. Without Being-in-the-world, Dasein would not be spatial. Without spatiality, Dasein would only be constituted as an intellectual creation. Existential spatiality is Dasein's thereness, its thereness as in-the-world—Being-there-in-the-world.

"Being-in-the-world" is a unitary phenomenon:

> The compound expression "Being-in-the-world" indicates in
> the very way we have coined it, that it stands for a unitary
> phenomenon. This primary datum must be seen as a whole.
> But while Being-in-the-world cannot be broken up into

35

contents which may be pieced together, this does not prevent it from having several constitutive items in its structure. (*SZ*, p. 53; *BT*, p. 78)

The word "constitutive" describes components which make up the whole, but which cannot be reduced to its parts.[8] When Dasein is constituted phenomenologically, Being-in-the-world as existence presents itself for noematic-reflection. Being-in-the-world is a whole, but it also has constitutive items in its structure. In the case of the physical object, such constitutive items would be aspects (*Abschattungen*) of a noematic *Sinn*, but in the case of Being-in-the-world, they are each noematic *Sinne* with horizons, thetic components, hyletic data, etc. Dasein is multi-noematic and Being-in-the-world is multi-noematic. Without this special multi-noematic character, the possibilities of Dasein would be the same as the possibilities of a physical object. Furthermore, the multi-noematic quality renders the possibilities of Being-in-the-world particularly meaning-laden and meaning-ful.

III *VERSTEHEN*: INTERPRETATION AND UNDERSTANDING

Dasein is its own disclosedness:

If we inquire about Being-in as our theme, we cannot indeed consent to nullify the primordial character of this phenomenon by deriving it from others—that is to say, by an inappropriate analysis, in the sense of a dissolving or breaking up. But the fact that something primordial is underivable does not rule out the possibility that a multiplicity of characteristics of Being may be constitutive for it. (*SZ*, p. 131; *BT*, p. 170)

We approach Dasein as Being-in-the-world, we do not propose to analyze it by breaking it up into its component parts[9]—thereby regarding each act as having one and only one noematic *Sinn*. Rather, we consider it as a unitary phenomenon. In Heidegger's statement, Dasein must be interpreted in a special way. If it is improperly interpreted, Dasein will not reveal itself in its wholeness. Thus,

even though Being-in-the-world is something of which one
has prephenomenological experience and acquaintance
[*erfahren und gekannt*], it becomes *invisible* if one interprets
it in a way which is ontologically inappropriate. (*SZ*, p. 59;
BT, p. 86)

Interpretation will be the constitution of Dasein as visible, as
disclosedness. "The existential proposition, 'Dasein is its
disclosedness,' means at the same time that the Being which is an
issue for this entity in its very Being is to be its 'there' " (*SZ*, p.
133; *BT*, p. 171). Thereness is the possibility of being visible, of
being disclosed. Entities have the possibility of departing from
their concealed condition—even though they are, in fact, "there."
Interpretation requires an effective description of thereness.
Interpretation of Being-in-the-world requires a full presentation
of Being-there as disclosed.

Dasein is a state-of-mind. "Existentially, a state-of-mind implies
a disclosive submission to the world, out of which we can
encounter something that matters to us" (*SZ*, pp. 137–138; *BT*,
p. 177). When I am in a good mood, my Dasein appears to me as
full of meaning, which is Dasein's authentic condition. Existential
ambiguity at such moments is at its most creative level, for here
the many meanings, which are inexhaustible and indeterminate,
appear in their most seminal, most clear, and most complete form.
At such moments, Dasein's possibilities are experienced in their
plenitude, because Dasein's disclosedness is effectively brought
forward in interpretation.

Dasein is engaged in understanding and understanding is the
Being of potentiality-for-Being:

Possibility, as an *existentiale*, does not signify a free-floating
potentiality-for-Being in the sense of the "liberty of
indifference" [*libertas indifferentiae*]. In every case Dasein, as
essentially having a state-of-mind, has already got itself into
definite possibilities. As the potentiality-for-Being which it *is*,
it has let such possibilities pass by; it is constantly waiving
the possibilities of its Being, or else it seizes upon them and
makes mistakes. But this means that Dasein is Being-possible
which has been delivered over to itself—*thrown possibility*
through and through. Dasein is the possibility of Being-free
for its ownmost potentiality-for-Being. Its Being-possible is

37

transparent to itself in different possible ways and degrees.
(*SZ*, p. 144; *BT*, p. 183)

Understanding is the disclosedness (self-transparency) of Being in
terms of meanings. The disclosure of meanings includes the
making visible of horizons, where possibilities come into view.
Such possibilities can be described as a sense of what I might be
if I were to choose myself in that way. Understanding is my
awareness of what I am and what I might be. Surely, there will
be instances of my not becoming what possibilities appear to
reveal. However, freedom to become my possibilities characterizes the Being of my understanding. Execution of my possibilities
is my potentiality-for-Being. Understanding is the disclosure of
my possibilities. Therefore, my understanding is the Being of my
potentiality-for-Being.

Interpretation is the development of the understanding:

As understanding, Dasein projects its Being upon
possibilities. This Being-towards-possibilities which
understands is itself a potentiality-for-Being, and it is so
because of the way these possibilities, as disclosed, exert
their counterthrust upon Dasein. The projecting of the
understanding has its own possibility—that of developing
itself. This development of the understanding we call
"interpretation." In it the understanding appropriates
understandingly that which is understood by it. In
interpretation, understanding does not become something
different. It becomes itself. Such interpretation is grounded
in that understanding; the latter does not arise from the
former. (*SZ*, p. 148; *BT*, p. 188)

Just as understanding comes to grips with the horizon of *noemata*,
understanding is a horizon itself for itself. Just as understanding
is the Being of potentiality-for-Being, it is also potentiality-for-
Being for itself. This potentiality-for-Being for itself is interpretation. Interpretation is the development of the mode whereby
existential ambiguity is understood. Existential ambiguity includes
the possibilities, potentialities, and actualities for Being in terms
of meanings. Understanding can understand meanings too. Therefore, interpretation *qua* development of the understanding is the
bringing of existential ambiguity to disclosedness. Dasein is

disclosedness. We now have only to investigate the Heideggerian description of meaning.

"Meaning is that wherein the intelligibility (*Verständlichkeit*) of something maintains itself. That which can be articulated in a disclosure by which we understand, we call 'meaning' " (*SZ*, p. 151; *BT*, p. 193). Articulation is the mode of interpretation (hermeneutics).[10] When something is disclosed to me such that my understanding can grasp it and I can articulate it, then it is a meaning. Once given, a meaning can maintain itself, for articulation is maintaining. Maintained meanings bring out their condition as experienced and as understood.

Meaning is the formal-existential framework of disclosedness:

> In so far as understanding and interpretation make up the
> existential state of Being of the "there," "meaning" must be
> conceived as the formal-existential framework of the
> disclosedness which belongs to understanding. Meaning is
> an *existentiale* of Dasein, not a property attaching to entities,
> lying "behind" them, or floating somewhere as an
> "intermediate domain." Dasein only "has" meaning, so far
> as the disclosedness of Being-in-the-world can be "filled in"
> by the entities discoverable in that disclosedness. Hence only
> Dasein can be meaningful [*sinnvoll*] or meaningless [*sinnlos*].
> (*SZ*, p. 151; *BT*, p. 193)

Meaning is the form which understanding and interpretation provide. In Husserlian terms, it would be the noematic *Sinn;* disclosedness would be the transcendent object which is constituted by the understanding. But as an existential structure meaning is something which only Dasein *has*. Everything else must *be* a meaning *for* Dasein. Everything else is by virtue of Being-in-the-world. Dasein has meaning(s) since it is both subject and object. Dasein is meaningful when existential ambiguity is completely understood. Dasein is meaningless when it does not disclose itself fully or when its intelligibility does not maintain itself. Indeed, Dasein could not be interpreted if it were without meaning or absurd. Dasein is existentially ambiguous when it can be interpreted. Thus Dasein is *not* existentially ambiguous only when it is without meaning. "Only that which is without meaning [*das Unsinnige*] can be absurd [*widersinnig*]" (*SZ*, p. 152; *BT*, p. 193). This absence of meaning is not one of Dasein's authentic possibilities—though it could fall into such a state inauthentically. Its meaningful self-understanding would not be denied thereby.

IV *ZEITLICHKEIT*: TEMPORALITY AND THE EXPERIENCED FLUX OF MEANINGS

Temporality is the meaning of the Being of Dasein:

> Time must be brought to light, and genuinely conceived, as the horizon for the understanding of Being, and for any way of interpreting it. In order for us to discern this, time needs to be explicated primordially as the horizon of the understanding of Being, and in terms of temporality as the Being of Dasein, which understands Being. (*SZ*, p. 17; *BT*, p. 39)

What is the meaning of having many meanings which are never static? If I constitute Dasein, I constitute many meanings which are never fixed and unmodifiable at a future moment. When I constitute myself or something, I perform an act. The performance of such an act cannot be conducted outside of time. In fact, whenever I am conscious of Dasein or of something else, I am conscious of the "now" phase of the *noema*. I can be conscious of Dasein only through understanding, for understanding is the Being of potentiality-for-Being. Potentiality-for-Being is the delineation of my possibilities. The Being of the delineation of my possibilities is my horizon. Understanding addresses itself toward horizons in order that the possible meanings might be interpreted. Each addressing itself is an addressing of time. Human time, specifically, reveals Dasein as existentially ambiguous.

All of Dasein's behavior is to be interpreted in terms of its Being—that is, in terms of temporality:

> In the "then," concern expresses itself as awaiting; in the "on that former occasion," as retaining; in the "now," as making present. In the "then"—but most unexpressed—lies the "now-not-yet;" that is to say, this is spoken in a making-present which is either awaitingly retentive or awaitingly forgetful. In the "on that former occasion" lurks the "now-no-longer." With this, retaining expresses itself as a making-present which

awaits. The "then" and the "on that former occasion" are
understood with regard to a "now;" that is to say, making
present has a peculiar importance. Of course, it always
temporalizes itself in a unity with awaiting and retaining, even
if these may take the modified form of a forgetting which
does not await anything; in the mode of such forgetting,
temporality ensnares itself in the present, which in making
present, says pre-eminently "Now! Now!" That which concern
awaits as what is closest to it, gets addressed in the "forth-
with;" what has been made proximally available or has been
lost is addressed in the "just-now." The horizon for the
retaining which expresses itself in the "on that former
occasion" is the "earlier;" the horizon for the "then" is the
"later on" ("that which is to come"); the horizon for the
"now" is the "today." (*SZ*, pp. 406–7; *BT*, pp. 458–9)

This long description expresses what Heidegger takes to be
Dasein's behavior. It relates the way Dasein presents itself. And
clearly it presents itself in terms of temporality. Each moment is
described in a relational structure, which Heidegger calls
"datability." Datability is a characterization of horizons. If I
perceive Dasein as "now," I am at the same time perceiving it as
a whole relational structure. In the horizon of a "now" *noema*—
if the noematic *Sinne* characterize Dasein—all of its temporal
possibilities are constituted.

Because temporality is ecstatico-horizontally constitutive for
the clearedness of the "there," temporality is always
primordially interpretable in the "there" and is accordingly
familiar to us. (*SZ*, p. 408; *BT*, p. 460)

Temporality is responsible for the clarity of existential ambiguity.
The many meanings of thereness can be interpreted by Dasein as
Being-there. The temporal presentation of this thereness reveals
Dasein's possibilities as the Being of potentiality-for-Being (which
is understanding). Dasein's horizons are revealed temporally, and
for this reason, temporality is familiar to us. In fact, without
temporality, Dasein would not recognize itself, for its meanings
could not be given. As Husserl demonstrates in *The Phenomenology of Internal Time-Consciousness*, meanings may be atemporal, but they must be given temporally. Existential ambiguity

41

must be temporal, for the fact that many meanings, which are neither static nor fixed, are given in one temporal act is what distinguishes them from other noematic *Sinne*. Without temporality, the many meanings would be atomically mingled with all other meanings. I would then be unable to distinguish myself from a chair. Furthermore, it would be impossible for such meanings to be interpreted, for articulation is laden with temporality.

The temporality of Dasein is within-time-ness:

> Along with the temporality of Dasein as thrown, abandoned to the "world," and giving itself time, something like a "clock" is also discovered—that is, something ready-to-hand which in its regular recurrence has become accessible in one's making present awaitingly. (*SZ*, p. 413; *BT*, p. 466)

Dasein's temporality finds itself in relation to "world-time." World-time is characterized by chronological measurement—the time of a clock. Thus when Dasein constitutes itself as having many meanings, it also constitutes itself in relation to measured time. In this way, Dasein experiences itself as within-the-world. The Being of temporality as Being interpreted within-the-world is the Being of existential ambiguity. Ambiguity understands itself as measurable by world-time, but as distinct from it. Thus ambiguity can be characterized by world-time from what Husserl calls the natural or naive attitude. Temporality, not world-time, describes existential ambiguity phenomenologically. The temporality of existential ambiguity shows Dasein in relation to world-time and within-time (within-world-time), but not exhausted by world-time. Its meanings are disclosed for understanding, not for clocks.

In reuniting our various considerations, we find that the structure of *Dasein-Verstehen-Zeitlichkeit* fills out the fundamental features of existential ambiguity. Dasein shows itself as a multiplicity of meanings (noematic *Sinne*) brought about by the co-givenness of subjectivity in objectivity and objectivity in subjectivity. This co-givenness creates a constitutive complexity in which whatever entities Dasein might be, they also involve the interpretive activity that seeks to understand them. But in the case of Dasein's self-understanding, the fullness of meanings is disclosed when Dasein constitutes itself. In constituting itself, the meanings now articulated become reformulated in terms of the horizontal possibilities of Being-in-the-world and Being-within-time. Temporality accounts for the dynamic character of the experience of meanings. This movement and reformulation of a totality of meanings in the mode of self-interpretation is named existential ambiguity.

3

THE IDENTITY OF DIFFERENCE

In Martin Heidegger's *Being and Time*, the self is situated in the place occupied by what he calls *Dasein*. However, this place is also where the traditional concept of "man" would be located. An assessment of Heidegger's position since *Being and Time* (1927) demands a clear understanding of how the two concepts of "self" and "man" have been formulated in Western thought. On that basis, it will be possible to demonstrate the respect in which the later Heidegger is consistent with his earlier position.

I

In dealing with the problem of human nature, two basic formulations recur: one is in terms of "man;" the other is in the language of "the self". Associated with "man," I would suggest that one can find alternate descriptions that consider questions of "the person," "personal identity," "the individual," "relations between the body and soul," and so on. The question of the "self" can be related to discussions treating the "ego," "mind," "consciousness," etc. The former, that is "man," is generally presented by distinguishing various parts of the soul and their relationship to the body (for example, Plato indicates the rational, spirited, and appetitive and shows how such a soul is imprisoned in the body). Aristotle and St. Thomas present man as a functional relation between form and matter compared to seeing and the eye which sees. Lucretius, La Mettrie, and Skinner seem to be content with a view of man that is reduced to a series of sensations or stimulus-response reactions. Hume's discussion of personal identity differs from this view only in that impressions are related to ideas, but his conclusion as to the identity of man can at best be described in terms of a bundle of impressions with little hope for unity. Strawson restates the issue by considering the relation between that to which states of consciousness and that to which certain corporeal characteristics are ascribed. His conclusion is that a "causal relation" relates a person's body to each of his various kinds of perceptual experience. The last type of discussion about man which I will consider here is the one that presents man in terms of his place in the nature of things. Augustine's conception of man's sinfulness is necessarily related to the perfect state before the fall of Adam and to the need for faith in God. Pico della Mirandola revises this earlier Platonism and finds man at the center of the universe. (Protagoras's idea that man is the measure of all things, seen in the light of the Renaissance, leads directly to the dignity of man.) Pico establishes the dignity of man in his capacity to raise himself up to the level of angels or to descend among the lower forms of being. Where Hobbes focused on the fact that man's life is solitary, poor, nasty, brutish, and short, Rousseau sought perfection and goodness in the noble savage whose origin is outside society. But it was Darwin who rediscovered man's place in nature. Man's evolution from monkeys is not only temporal like Augustine's and Rousseau's models, but it is also classificatory like that of Protagoras and Pico. Perhaps Scheler's contribution is that he has returned the biological model to a cosmological one in which man has importance as well as place in the world.

Now the other type of concern with human nature is in terms of the self. When Heraclitus says: "I have searched myself" (ἐδιζησάμην ἐμεωυτόν), when Socrates appeals to his daemon in the *Apology* or when he says in the *Phaedo* that he himself (i.e., his soul) will no longer be there after death, when Epictetus appeals to that which is within our power (meaning specifically, "opinion, aim, desire, and aversion"), when Boethius seeks consolation from the projection of his twofold personality in Lady Fortune and then Lady Philosophy, when Montaigne proposes to portray himself and Pascal rejects Montaigne's claims by saying, "It is not in Montaigne, but in myself, that I find what I see in him," when these formulations of the search for the self are put forward, we become aware of a different kind of discussion from that of the first type. The first type, the problem of "man," is concerned with the whole individual in all his order manifestations and aspects.[1] "Man" encompasses whatever proposition, whatever description that might deal with "you" and "him" or "her." The "self," however, is focused. The "self" is concentrated in the core of the person, or in the nucleus of "man." The self is that which one might call what is truly "me," what is not, and cannot be, someone else. This difference becomes particularly apparent when the self is construed as the "ego" or "I." The major theories in this area include: the Cartesian cogito, the Kantian transcendental unity of apperception, the Hegelian consciousness, the Freudian threefold unity of id, ego, and superego, the Husserlian transcendental ego, the Jamesian pure ego and the Sartrian for-itself.

Rather than giving further examples of these two types: that is, (1) man and (2) the self, I should now like to focus on a particular aspect of Heidegger's thought and indicate how he has integrated these two ways of discussing human nature into a structure that allows for the possibility of unifying the two types into a single description. In other words, Heidegger is able to talk about both man and the self in terms of a conceptual scheme that does not require that they be distinct. My thesis here is that Heidegger's concern with what I will call the identity of difference is precisely the locus of these two types of description. Where traditionally a distinction has been necessitated by the nature of the description, in Heidegger's work, the identity of difference is both man and the self.

II

In English, we do not hear or write the difference between difference (*Differenz*) and difference (*Unterschied*). *Differenz* suggests a difference in the accidental features of the particular or in number, but not in the kind of entity.

For example, *Differenz* is the difference between four people and five people in an elevator, where all are nevertheless people. *Unterschied* implies a radical separation in kind—a distinction, as it is sometimes translated. (This would be the difference between two people and two lions in an elevator.) From now on, I will refer to *Unterschied* as difference$_2$ and *Differenz* as difference$_1$. The difference$_2$ (*Unterschied*) between difference$_1$ (*Differenz*) and difference$_2$ (*Unterschied*) cannot even be *seen* in English. We both hear and see it as "difference." That is, we both hear and see (read) the "difference" as identity.

The problem that poses itself in a reading of Heidegger is that in attempting to re-evaluate human nature, we always return to the same: the man *per se*, or the person. I will focus my discussion on "man," but it will soon be clear that there is also no other place for the "self." For our understanding of man, we do not experience the difference$_2$ of difference$_1$, since it appears as identity. We do not experience difference, but only identity and we discover our self in the search for an ample description of man. In fact, when a difference does appear, this difference must be mediated so that we might understand the identity.

Heidegger claims that there is a difference between *Sein* and *Seiende*. *Sein* is usually translated as Being (usually with a capital "b"). *Seiende* has a number of equivalents in English. Essentially, it means "that-which-is." Ralph Manheim in his translation of *Einführung in die Metaphysik* (*An Introduction to Metaphysics*) has rendered it as "essent" (a neologism which, as Manheim states, "is based on the fiction that *essens, essentis*, is the present participle of *sum*."[2] The currently accepted French translation of *Seiende* is *étant*.[3] Thus there is a difference$_1$ between Being and that-which-is, between Being and essent. This difference is what Heidegger has called "*die ontologische Differenz*."[4] This "ontological difference" is to be distinguished from "*das Unterschied von Sein und Seiendem*" (the difference$_2$ between Being and essent). That is, *die ontologische Differenz* (the ontological difference) characterizes the Being of that-which-is. This ontological difference is perhaps analogous to what Merleau-Ponty (after Bergson) has called the lived (*le vécu*).[5] It may, therefore, be accurate to refer to this ontological difference as a lived difference which is to be distinguished from an analytic one. Thus the ontological difference is not the difference$_2$ that we remark when we read Heidegger (the difference$_2$ between *Differenz* and *Unterschied*), but rather the difference that installs itself in human life. The ontological difference is the true ontological status of man. The difference$_2$ between Being and essent (*das Unterschied von Sein und Seiendem*) is the difference that we make for purposes

47

of clarity. When speaking of the nature of man the difference$_2$ between Being and that-which-is (the essent) is the ontological difference.

In a seminar held in 1968 on Hegel's *Differenzschrift*, Heidegger warned of a danger in the ontological difference. The report of this seminar was published in France in a limited edition by a number of eminent French Heidegger scholars. In his summary for the September 5 session, Michel Podgorny writes (and I translate): "The danger is that, in the horizon of metaphysics, the difference might lead one to represent Being as an essent."[6] What he is saying here is that one must not begin to consider Being as a thing-which-is. Being cannot be reified. This is also partially why the ontological difference is not entirely a "between"—between Being and the essent. For the ontological difference to be a "between," Being would have to be localized and simply become another essent. But it is the nature of Being to continually escape becoming an essent. Being continually differentiates itself (difference$_2$) from the essent. Being has no location since it is always at the horizon. For Heidegger, the peculiar nature of man is that he is an essent who is distinguished by always having Being at the horizon. This distinguishing is what I have called difference$_2$, that is, man is different from other essents, other entities. Man is always differentiating himself from other essents. At the same time, it is difference$_1$ in that man is the essent which is related to Being, and he is related to Being by differentiating himself from the essent which he is.

In the 1968 seminar, Heidegger noted that the ontological difference can be understood in two ways:

(1) the expression: "the ontological difference" is constructed like the proposition: "the tree is green;" ontological is therefore the adjective of the substantive difference. From this first point of view, it is the difference itself between Being and essent which is "ontological" as one might say of the leaf that it is green.

(2) the difference itself between Being and essent carries and renders ontology possible as a fundamental discipline of metaphysics.[7]

Heidegger is thus suggesting, by the comparison of two ways to understand the ontological difference, that the first might render

Being an essent, in that the difference would be an essent. This would carefully localize Being as metaphorically the wall (Being) against which the ladder (the ontological difference) is leaning while stationed on the ground (essent). It would make the difference into a thing with an attribute: that it is ontological. The second interpretation suggests that there would not even be any ontology, any human being, if there were no difference between Being and essent. That is, ontology would not be possible if Being and essent were identical. The first interpretation describes the ontological difference as difference₂ (*Unterschied*) while the second interpretation is an affirmation of difference₁ (*Differenz*). Both interpretations are interpretations of the ontological difference. Both interpretations allow for a description of man.

We must now try to discover precisely man's relation to the ontological difference so that we can consider the relation of man to the self. In order to do so, I suggest that we consider the following passage from Heidegger's book on Nietzsche:

> Ontology is founded on the differentiation (*Unterscheidung*) between Being and essent. The "differentiation" is more appropriately called by the name *Differenz*, since it announces that essent and Being are in a sense brought into distinction one from the other: separated and yet still related to one another. All this comes from themselves and is not due to an "act" of differentiation (*Unterscheidung*). The difference (*Unterscheidung*) as difference (*Differenz*) means that a divergence (*Austrag*) exists between Being and essent.[8]

We have become aware of the ontological difference as separation or distinction, that is, difference₂ (*Unterschied*). Now we learn that this difference *qua* separation is in fact an active separating (*Unterscheidung*). Yet it is not effected by an act, which someone, some ego, might perform. The separation is not total. We recall that the ontological difference installs itself at the horizon of the essent. This helps us to understand that "essent and Being are still related to one another."

We must now ask the question: what is this relation of the essent to Being? The answer is: man. Man is the relation of the essent to Being in terms of an act of separating or differentiating, which is not initiated from a focal point, from a nucleus, from a center. Hence if there is a self, it is intimately involved in the active separating; it is not that which initiates the active separating.

In his work on Nietzsche (1961), Heidegger states: "We situate ourselves in the differentiation (*Unterscheidung*) between essent and Being. This difference supports the relation to Being and it supports the relation to the essent" (p. 207). "Man as such situates himself in the relation to Being" (p. 206) And "that which we announce under the indeterminate title of the 'relation of man to the essent' is in its essence the relation of man to Being" (p. 206). Thus we find Heidegger stating that "one takes one and the other, the relation to the essent and the relation to Being, as the 'same' thing" (p. 205). Since man is both relations, the two relations are, in a sense, the same. As we say sometimes in English, it is the same difference. Man is the same difference, that is both the relation to Being and the relation to essent.

In this same study of Nietzsche, Heidegger metaphorically calls this relation "a little passage" (*Steg*): "The differentiation between Being and essent is the little passage which everywhere, in every form of behavior and in every attitude, leads us from the essent to Being and from Being to the essent" (p. 246). Again, man is this little passage. No matter which way one goes, from essent to Being or from Being to essent, the little passage remains the same. Man is this going in both directions at once. One might call this going in both directions at once an ambiguity, but an ambiguity that establishes the existence of man and not an ambiguity to be eliminated. We realize however that this little passage is only an image and that in fact the relation is not between two points, not between a start and a finish, not between an ego and an object in the world, but is ontologically elaborated as difference. There is no need to go out to Being any more than it needs to come back again. Being is always differentiated ontologically from an essent and it always depends upon an essent in order to be.

The differentiation, as we have seen, is an active differentiating. The active differentiating delineates the ontological difference and the ontological difference can be described in terms of a difference (*Unterschied*)—difference$_2$. But, in fact, difference$_1$ and difference$_2$ are identity in that *qua* difference, they are the relation that Heidegger has called "man." We cannot, of course, be content with simply calling this relation, this identity of difference, man. We have sought the locus of the self and have found that it cannot lie behind acts, it cannot be the center of active differentiating any more than it is the initiator of the active differentiating itself. If the self cannot be the center, the nucleus of the active differentiating, it must describe some aspect of the individual. And if man is this active differentiating, this relation between essent and Being, this identity of difference, the self must also be this very same relation. Thus the dichotomy between the two types of human nature announced at the beginning of this essay turn out to be the same in Heidegger's language.

The implication of such a view is that Heidegger has refused the distinction (between man and self) which was established by Descartes and consummated by Husserl and James in their focus upon the ego as the true self. Their position had been to allow doubt to be placed upon the fullness of the person as an integrated relation of body and soul, of personal identity, and of the dignity of man in the universe. Heidegger's conception returns the locus of the self to the same place, the same relation, in which he finds man. If man and the self are different, it is an identity of difference.

4

THINKING AND BEING: THE ESSENTIAL RELATION

To be and to think can be construed as separate domains of experience—one, ontological; the other, epistemological. For Heidegger, however, the two are intimately bound up with each other. Indeed, the relationship is both active and essential to human life. What I propose to develop here is precisely their manner of relatedness.

I THINKING AND BEING AS BELONGING-TOGETHER

In his lecture on "Moira" and again in *Identität und Differenz*, Heidegger cites a fragment from Parmenides: "Thinking and Being are the same thing."[1] In *Identität und Differenz*, he comments: "Thinking and Being are two different things, apprehended here as 'the same.' "[2] Furthermore, "thinking and Being have their place in the same and hold each other out of this same."[3] And finally, "We have established the meaning of the identity of thinking and Being within the interval (*Inzwischen*) by defining it as the belonging-togetherness (*Zusammengehörigkeit*) of the one and the other."[4] Thinking and Being are then the same but in a very special sense. Their sameness is not pure identity of equivalence. What is named here by the belonging-togetherness of Being and thinking is not that the two can be considered interchangeably. Both are out of the same, that is, they are both founded in that which is (the essent).[5] This founding, however, is based in the fact that thinking and Being are both differentiated

52

from that which is. We should therefore attend more carefully to
"the possibility of apprehending the '*Zusammen*' (together) out
of the '*gehören*' (belonging) instead of representing for ourselves
the 'belonging' out of the 'together' " (*ID*, p. 16). This is to say
that if Being and thinking are principally *together*, we cannot
distinguish their relationship. However, if we realize that Being
and thinking are principally *belonging*, then we can examine
precisely the fashion in which they *belong* to one another—belong
to one another together. Being and thinking do belong. They
belong together as the essence of man.

Heidegger claims that "thinking is present because of the duality
(*Zweifalt*), which is never spoken. The approaching (*An-wesen*)
of thinking is on the way toward the duality of Being and essent"
(*VA, III*, p. 38). The duality is the "locus" of the ontological
difference (*Differenz*) between Being and essent.[6] It is also the
"locus" of thinking. The sameness of thinking and Being take
place within this *Differenz*. Where Being is differentiated ontologically, thinking is differentiated epistemologically. Here Being
is a "being-before" while thinking is a "letting-be-before."[7] But
both occur within the *Zweifalt* of Being and essent.

That the belonging-togetherness of Being and thinking is a
togetherness and yet also a difference is not easily understood. In
their belonging, they are the same because they are together. Yet
in the context where they belong they are difference (*Differenz*).
Thus we read in *Was Heisst Denken?*: "How can thinking and
Being ever be identical? They are precisely what is different (*das
Verschiedene*): presence of what is present and taking-to-heart."[8]
Presence of what is present and taking-to-heart cannot be the
same. But they can be the same difference (*Differenz*) as indicated
epistemologically (*der Unterschied*) and as experienced ontologically. They both belong together in the ontological difference
between Being and that which is. In that difference, Being is the
presence of that which is present (*Anwesen des Anwesenden*) and
thinking is the taking-to-heart (*In-die-Acht-nehmen*). Furthermore, the presence of that which is present is precisely what must
be thought. The presence of that which is present must be taken-
to-heart. Taking-to-heart is the living of the difference. This is
why Heidegger cites a line from Hölderlin's "Socrates and Alcibi-
ades" in his lecture "What Does 'Thinking' Mean?": "He who
has thought most profoundly loves that which is most alive."[9]

Thinking profoundly is fully grasping the presence of what is
present. And fully grasping what is present is fully grasping "that
which is most alive." Fully grasping is taking-to-heart. Therefore,
taking-to-heart is grasping that which is most alive, which is the
presence of that which is present. Or, in other words, thinking is
grasping Being as that which is most alive. This is all to say
that the difference to which Being and thinking belong is a lived
difference. It is lived as the presence of what is present and as
the taking-to-heart of that presence.

> We do not think Being as it is except if we think it in the
> difference (*Differenz*) which distinguishes it from the essent
> and if we think Being in the difference which distinguishes it
> from Being. In this way, the difference becomes
> appropriately visible to us. (*ID*, p. 53)

Becoming visible here means coming alive, even being alive (in
much the same sense as Merleau-Ponty conceived of visibility).[10]
Thus we think Being in the difference. By thinking Being in the
difference, we take it to heart. Taking-to-heart is fully grasping
what is alive in the difference, i.e., the presence of what is present,
the Being of what is. This is what we see when we understand
how Being and thinking belong together.

To think "living being" is a task: "Of all that which is, living
being is probably the most difficult for us to think, for if it is, in
a certain sense, our closest parent, it is at the same time separated
by an abyss of our ek-sisting existence."[11] If we specify that "living
being" is the nature of man, this will help us to understand the
belonging-togetherness of Being and thinking. What is most
difficult to think is precisely the essence of man. Man is the living
being that is so close to us and at the same time separated by an
abyss of our "ek-sisting existence." Man is the Being-there (*Dasein*) that is also expressed by the ontological difference. Man is
this "ek-sisting existence" that is there. To think this existence,
to take-it-to-heart, is not easy. Yet this is precisely what man must
do in order to be, for Being and thinking belong together. The
abyss that separates them is the ontological difference that brings
them together. It is the multiplicity of human meanings rendered
whole *qua* ambiguity because what is taken-to-heart is the whole
and not just each individual meaning, each individual point of
difference between Being and that which is. This is why Heidegger

has noted that "the search for thinking Being without that which is becomes a necessity."[12] To accomplish this would be to truly accomplish a full grasp of the essence of man. To think the being present without that which is present would be to pass through the difference of being present and that which is present, for to take being present to heart is to manifest the fullness of Being without reducing it to a single meaning. To fully think Being or being present is to fully think the ambiguity of man in its wholeness. To think Being as that which is would be to reduce it to a single meaning. To think Being in its Being as differentiated from that which is is to take the essence of man to heart.

To think Being, as differentiated from that which is (the essent), is nevertheless to think Being out of that which is. What is really being thought is the difference, since, if what is thought were a thing (and not a difference), then one would be thinking an essent and not thinking Being. Thus "to think Being on its own asks us to turn away from Being, inasmuch as Being, as in all metaphysics, is fathomed and displayed only out of the essent and for the essent as its foundation" (*ZS*, p. 24). Thinking out of the essent is to found Being in the essent. It is the expressing of the difference by founding Being in that which is, by thinking Being in its difference from the essent.

In the "*Es gibt Sein*" of the Being-there of Being, thinking is the giving of *Dasein*, of man. "We think the destinying which *gives* Being as a donation" (*ZS*, p. 34). When Being is given as donation, man appears. The giving is the rendering present of that which is present. Since man is the presence of that which is present, that which is present in man is given by thinking. Thus thinking is not only the taking-to-heart of that which is, but it is also the giving as donation of that which is. This *Zweifalt* is again expressed through the ontological difference. In the giving, we discover a letting-lie-before-us as well as a taking-to-heart. This giving is both an arriving of that which is and an appeal to Being out of that which is. Thinking is the rendering of the in-between (*Zwischen*). Because of this duality, which we can now call ambiguity, "that which is when correctly thought, stands up to correct thinking."[13] That which is present through thinking presents itself as present. Thinking is both giving Being to that which is present and taking-to-heart that which is present. This double-pronged activity goes in both directions at the same time. And when it is

55

a question of man, the going-in-both-directions-at-the-same-time is living the Being of what is as a whole.

The going-in-both-directions-at-the-same-time can be named by the reciprocal genitive: "This genitive says that Being as such (*das Seyn*) shows itself at the same time as that which is to be thought and that which needs thought to answer it."[14] However, here the genitive is the genitive in the "thinking of Being." But when Being is thought, "the Being of that which is" is also thought. The thinking of Being is a genitive that names the belonging—togetherness (*Zusammengehörigkeit*) of Being and thinking. The thinking of Being moreover occurs within what is named by the reciprocal genitive: the ontological difference.

In *Kant und das Problem der Metaphysik*, Heidegger referred to thinking as a "preconceptual comprehension of Being." "This preconceptual comprehension of the Being of the essent in all its constancy, amplitude, and indeterminateness is given as something completely beyond question."[15] It is beyond question because it expresses itself in the ontological difference. The comprehension of Being is the fully grasping and taking-to-heart of that which is. It is also the full giving of Being. "On the basis of the comprehension of Being, man is present (*Da*) with the Being which takes place in the revelatory (*eröffnende*) irruption into the essent" (*KPM*, p. 207; English tr., p. 237). Through the comprehension of Being, man is rendered present, Being is given as there (*Dasein*), as whole. The rendering is the full grasping of all the differentiating meanings in the ontological difference. Comprehension is the encompassing of the Being of that which is. Thinking is comprehending the ontological difference. Thinking is comprehending the possible multiplicity of meanings as ambiguity. True thinking is comprehending man. This is to say that knowing as experience comprehends man.

"For all comprehension (*Vernehmen*) of that which is in its Being, Being itself is already illuminated (*gelichtet*) and happens (*ereignet*) in its truth" (*UH*, p. 54). In comprehending man, there is both illuminating and happening. What is illuminated is the Being of that which is (i.e., man). What happens is the essent in its Being. The presence of what is present is illuminated and what is present happens in its presence. This is the comprehending of Being, the relationship between Being and thinking, which belong together.

56

Heidegger refers to thinking as "working to construct the house of Being" (*UH*, p. 154). Thinking is building, building up the house of Being which surely is the being present of that which is. Thinking takes the initiative to undertake the project and at the same time thinking is commissioned to do it. Thinking does what it does and thinking happens as it happens. In *Unterwegs zur Sprache*, we hear again and again that language is the "house of Being." If thinking works at constructing the house of Being, then what it works at constructing is language. Language is then that which is constructed out of the relationship between thinking and Being. And language names the relationship. Thus we find in *Aus der Erfahrung des Denkens:* "if thinking has the courage to come to the call of Being, then that which has been distributed to us finds its language."[16] Out of the relationship between thinking and Being, language appears. As thinking constructs the house of Being, it constructs language. Referring again to a line from Hölderlin, Heidegger repeats: "We are a sign, emptied of meaning."[17] Man is a sign; but man is only a sign emptied of meaning because his meaningfulness needs to be built. This building is the project of thinking. Thinking constructs the house of Being. Out of the thinking of Being comes language. The meanings that are constructed are the meanings given life by thinking in its comprehension of the Being of that which is. These meanings are named by language, but they are the meanings of human ambiguity. They are the fullness of the ontological difference—as it expresses itself through language. Without thinking, there would be no house of Being. Without Being, thinking could not comprehend or take-to-heart or give. This is why thinking and Being belong together.

II DIE SACHE: THE QUESTION OF THINKING

To understand thinking, it will be necessary to know what is the matter in question when thinking occurs. This matter in question, this question of thinking is *die Sache*. Heidegger has even entitled a recent collection of his papers (1969): *Zur Sache des Denkens.* What is this matter of thinking that is in question?

Surely it is that which merits being thought (*das Denkwürdige*). All that thinking comprehends merits being thought. If it did not, thinking might go astray, which it cannot do since it always belongs together with Being. Since it cannot be other than belonging together with Being and since Being merits being thought, thinking cannot go astray. Being merits being thought because it must be rendered present for it to be ontologically different from that which is present. It cannot be rendered present in that way, as we have seen, without thinking. And without rendering Being present, there would be no meaningfulness, no human ambiguity, and hence no man. But that would be impossible since man is precisely that which appears for his own consideration.

> We said that man is the *animal rationale;* but does this definition exhaust the essence of man? Is the last word which can be said of Being: Being means reason? Or the essence of man, his belonging to Being, the essence of Being: does all that still continue to be, and in an even more disconcerting fashion, to be that which merits being thought (*das Denkwürdige*)? If it is as such, do we have the right to abandon it for the benefit of a frenetic research which only knows how to count, but whose successes are grandiose? Or are we bound to discover the routes by which thought can answer that which merits being thought rather than ignore it, enveloped as we are by thinking which is limited to calculating.[18]

Can that which merits being thought, i.e., the Being of that which is, be ignored? Clearly Heidegger's answer is in the negative. That which merits being thought must be thought. To ignore it is, in fact, to think it in the mode of ignorance or forgetfulness. Forgetting Being (*Seinsvergessenheit*) is another mode of thinking in its full sense. Heidegger's project however is to suggest that Being ought not to be forgotten, that by thinking the difference between Being and that which is (the essent), Being will not be forgotten. What merits being thought is the essence of man. It is precisely by thinking that the essence of man is thought, that the ontological difference between Being and the essent is given and, at the same time, taken-to-heart.

That which merits being thought—the Being of that which is—cannot be thought fully "by counting." For Heidegger, thinking is an experiential knowing and does not restrict itself to knowing only this or only that. Thus he makes the distinction between the

activities of logic and *logos*. "By a constant reference to that
which is logical, one gives the appearance of Being engaged on
the path of thinking, when in fact one denies it" (*UH*, p. 126).
The denial, however, cannot be a full rejection. The referring to
what is logical is nevertheless thinking, but it is forgetting that
one is thinking; for "counting" is taken as that which merits being
thought. Here one becomes misguided. Thus even when counting,
that which merits being thought should be thought. "Logic understands thinking as the representation of that which is in its Being,
since representation gives itself the generality of the concept. But
what reflection (that is, thinking) is there in representation that
thinks the truth of Being?" (*UH*, p. 126). Thinking the truth of
Being is what most merits being thought. And the truth of Being
is Being's disclosedness (ἀλήθεια). Being is unconcealed or
disclosed by being present. Thinking is rendering present that
which is present. However,

> thinking against "logic" does not mean breaking a lance in
> favor of the illogical, but only to return to the *logos* in one's
> reflection and to its essence as it appears in the first age of
> thought, that is, to finally prepare oneself for such a reflection
> (*Nachdenken*). (*UH*, p. 126)

One must, according to Heidegger, prepare oneself for going
towards thinking (*nachdenken*) in one's thinking. The return to
what the Greeks called *logos* is then the direction that thinking
should take. By referring to his lecture of 1951 entitled "Logos,"
we discover that, in terms of an appeal to Heraclitus, "*Logos* is
the name which designates the Being of the essent."[19] *Logos* is
the name (given through thought) of the Being of that which is,
otherwise known as the ontological difference. By thinking *logos*,
we think the ontological difference, we think the multiplicity of
human meanings by rendering them ambiguous. *Logos* is the
name for this ambiguity. *Logos* merits being thought. Thinking
logos, in *Sein und Zeit*, is the interpretation of the disclosedness
of Being. Again the disclosedness of Being, *qua* essence of man,
is what merits being thought.

"To determine that which concerns thinking, that which never
ceases to be a question, that which is the point itself of the
question,—that, in German, is the word *Sache:* the matter in
question" (*ZSD*, p. 67). "What really must be thought keeps itself

turned away from man since the beginning" (*WHD*, p. 4; Eng. tr. p. 7). and yet it is precisely what really must be thought (*die Sache*) that merits being thought. What merits being thought is that which never ceases to be in question. The ontological difference never ceases to be a question because it can never become an essent. Human ambiguity can never become that which is. It is always difference (*Differenz*)—the difference between Being and that which is. We are always questioning this difference. We are always asking it anew. This is the repetition that never repeats itself. It is always difference: "Being—a question (*eine Sache*), but nothing of that which is" (*ZS*, p. 20). Being is always escaping through its difference. The difference is therefore always the matter in question—that which merits being thought.

"By stepping back, we liberate the question (*die Sache*) of thinking, Being as difference, we permit it to present itself to us in an encounter which can remain entirely empty of objects" (*ID*, pp. 55–56). The step back is reflection (*Nachdenken*)—the step towards. By stepping back, we think towards Being as difference, we come closer to comprehending the essence of man. Heidegger understands this step back as a return to Greek thought. But it is also the stepping back of Being from that which is. It is also the ontological difference differentiating itself through thinking.

There is, however, another important element to this stepping back. At the same time that it accomplishes an approach to that which merits being thought, it collects together that which has been thought. Essential to thinking in the essence of man is memory:

> What is most thought-provoking (*das Bedenklichste*) could be something lofty, perhaps even the highest thing there is for man, provided man still is the Being who *is* insofar as he thinks, thinks in that thought appeals to him because his essential nature consists in memory (*der Gedächtnis*), the gathering of thought. (*WHD*, p. 12; Eng. tr, p. 31)

The ontological difference is continually expressing itself. Being is continually differentiated from that which is. Meanings are formed in the ambiguous totality and meanings are left along the way. However, through the gathering of thought, through memory, thinking collects the difference as it was. In this way it establishes a continuity to the rendering and taking-to-heart of thinking. In this way, thinking gathers as well as gives the ontological difference. The question of thinking, then, is the Being of that which is through memory as well as through thinking. What is food for thought is what is given to us through the gathering of thought—which itself is a task for thinking.

III THE ESSENTIAL NATURE OF MAN

Being and thinking belong together. The question of thinking is that which merits being thought. What most merits being thought is the Being of that which is. How do thinking and Being relate to man's essential nature?

Heidegger speaks of this issue in *Was Heisst Denken?*:

> No way of thought, not even the way of metaphysical thought,
> begins with man's essential nature and goes on from there
> to Being, nor in reverse from Being and then back to man.
> Rather every way of thinking *takes its way* already *within*
> the total relation of Being and man's nature, or it is not
> thinking at all. (*WHD*, p. 74; Eng. tr. p. 80)

Thinking cannot be a starting point that goes from one point to another, from Being to the essential nature of man or from the essential nature of man to Being. In the first place, we already know that neither Being nor the essential nature of man are "points" from which there can be departure or arrival. We know that Being is always differentiated from that which is. We know that the essential nature of man is that difference—but it is that difference as it is thought. Thus it would be impossible to speak of either as "points." In announcing the essential nature of man here we have just noted that it is the ontological difference "as it is thought"—this is the question of thinking. Since Being is differentiated from that which is, since the essential nature of man is that difference, since thinking belongs together with Being, and since the essential nature of man cannot be described without also describing thinking, thinking must take its way *within* the total relation of Being and man's essential nature.

This "being within" accomplishes itself in the vitality of living, named through language, and is unable to escape its relation to Being and the essential nature of man.

> Thinking accomplishes the relation of Being to the essence of man. It neither constitutes nor produces this relation for itself. Thinking only presents it to Being as that which is remitted to itself by Being. (*UH*, p. 26)

Thinking therefore is the vitality of the relation between Being and man's nature. This is the encompassing vitality that renders the totality of human meanings whole. These meanings, expressed through the ontological difference, are ambiguous because thinking comprehends them. "The relation of the truth of Being to the essence of man is conceived as comprehension. But here the comprehension is at the same time conceived out to the unconcealedness of Being."[20]

To assemble what we have discovered from our examination of the relationship between thinking and Being, we may conclude that man is the ambiguity that happens out of the belonging—togetherness of Being and thinking. Where Being is differentiated from that which is, thinking is the comprehending of that ontological difference. Thinking takes the ontological difference as precisely the question at hand. And within that difference, thinking discloses the Being which is necessary for the presence of man and the human essent which is necessary for the presence of Being.

5

MERLEAU-PONTY'S HUMAN AMBIGUITY

The work of Maurice Merleau-Ponty has been referred to as a philosophy of ambiguity. For the most part, however, "ambiguity" has served merely to label his philosophical writings, while there has seldom been a careful attempt to articulate its nature. Discussions of ambiguity in Merleau-Ponty's philosophy have usually focused on the importance of the body as cutting through the subject/object view of man, on the primacy of perception, on the centrality of temporality, etc., but very little indication has been given as to why the writers of these critiques have chosen to link the term "ambiguity" with these notions. I shall review some of the commentaries in which ambiguity is taken to be a central aspect of Merleau-Ponty's thought. Then I shall consider how Merleau-Ponty himself employed the term: *ambiguïté*. Finally, I shall inquire into the import of his work for a theory of human, or existential, ambiguity.

I THE PHILOSOPHY OF AMBIGUITY

One of the first commentators to cling to the term "ambiguity" was Ferdinand Alquié (1947), who carefully indicated that Merleau-Ponty was in search of a normative conception of the human individual.[1] He rightly saw that Merleau-Ponty's project was to challenge and overcome a dualistic view of the self. Alquié remarks that Merleau-Ponty "at the same time rejected the two correlative ideas of absolute objectivity and absolute subjectivity,

63

of the World-in-Itself and of Mind; instead of allowing them to alternate as both true, he took them both to be false" (Alquié, p. 54). To posit the truth of both objectivity and subjectivity, both being-in-itself and being-for-itself, is to assert a dualism. To deny their separate existence is the first step towards a revised description of human activity. Ambiguity then could be founded upon the rejection of a dualism and the reconstruction of the self concept as an interwoven, experiential whole: being-in-itself-for-itself.

In assuming a monism, Alquié asserts that, on the one hand, the *subject*, for Merleau-Ponty, is the body. But the body is also the fundamental *object* in the life of the human being. Human existence cannot be considered apart from the body. The body is both subject and object as one form of being. "The ambiguous existence of the body is existence itself" (Alquié, p. 55). In claiming that the body is ambiguous, that the body is the unitary manifestation of human existence, Alquié establishes the locus of ambiguity. However, to say simply that human existence is ambiguous because the body is both subject and object will not suffice. One must also indicate the ontological status of the body as a manifestation of perception, experience, and temporality. In short, ambiguity must be shown to be a phenomenon of human existence and not simply as a posited conception.

Alquié notes some of these features when he states that for Merleau-Ponty,

> class and nation are "modes of existence." And, in the natural
> world as in the social world, the immanence of
> consciousness, a notion which is very dear to idealism, and
> the transcendence in relation to consciousness, which
> sustains realism, coincide. These two worlds have "an
> immanence in principle and a transcendence in fact." As in
> existence itself, they are ambiguity. (Alquié, p. 57)

The "in here" and the "out there" form one. Immanence and transcendence, idealism and realism, the world of thoughts and the world of international conflict are not two parts of a whole, but rather an experiential unity. "There is never absolute determinism for me, nor am I ever pure consciousness: I am existence, I am time, that is *ambiguïté*" (Alquié, p. 59). Alquié wants to account for Merleau-Ponty's work in terms of a Cartesian world. To do so he must show that there is only one world of human existence, and he must do so against a background that posited two worlds in conflict. But Merleau-Ponty would hold that the self is ambiguous, irrespective of Descartes's position. Yet, like Alquié, Merleau-Ponty continually felt obligated to answer his philosophical tradition. Hence his dialogue with dualists tends to overshadow the importance of ambiguity as a phenomenon *per se*.

Alphonse de Waelhens (1949) focuses his attention on the notion of perception.[2] Having borrowed his title from Alquié, he likewise stresses the denial of dualisms in order to establish a theory of ambiguity. According to de Waelhens, the *bête noire* was Sartre. Sartre's discussion of being-in-itself and being-for-itself constituted the contemporary dualism that had to be attacked:

> We have even lost the right to get more or less out of trouble, as Descartes and Spinoza had done, by calling it a confused idea. Once the for-itself and the in-itself are radically separated, once consciousness becomes a spectator without consistency in its own right, the die is cast: such a consciousness will know or not know, but it cannot know in several ways or be related to the in-itself in an ambiguous fashion. (de Waelhens, *SC*, p. viii)

Ambiguity is grounded upon a rejection of the separation between the for-itself and the in-itself. Perception should ambiguously relate the for-itself to the in-itself in a variety of ways. Perception should itself be ambiguous, since the human self is whole. To perceive is not a disembodying activity. We cannot be spectators of the world without also implicating the body.

With de Waelhens, then, ambiguity is presented in connection with perception, but still in terms of a rejected dualism. Although we are all involved in our historical context, our positions are not always completely conditioned by our response to that context. We can answer our traditions, but philosophy is not simply a response. It is also the description of phenomena as they appear. Perception can appear as ambiguous without a polar view which asserts a complete dichotomy. As in the case of language, a metaphor such as "metaphors are pretty little maidens" is not exclusively and exhaustively bound to the context of metaphor and to the context of pretty little maidens. It can have an importance as a phenomenon by itself in its own metaphorical context. Perception can be ambiguous, whether Sartre claimed that the in-itself and the for-itself are separate or not.

John Wild (1963) has clarified the perceptual character of *ambiguïté* without an *argumentum ad traditionem*. In his Foreword to the English translation of *La Structure du comportement*, he states:

> Merleau-Ponty's account of the lived body is marked by a
> high degree of both perceptiveness and originality. This
> body, as I live it from the inside, is quite different from the
> objective body which is observed, though each perspective
> is legitimate and the two overlap at certain vital points, which
> introduces an essential ambiguity into the whole situation of
> man. He is both a being among other beings in the world,
> and at the same time an originating source of the whole
> world order in which he exists.[3]

Here ambiguity accounts for the whole situation of the self as a phenomenon in its own terms. The ambiguity is a description of the lived body. Two perspectives overlap at vital points. That is, ambiguity occurs not only because we are in the world, but also because we are an originating source of the whole world order in which we exist.

What remains unclear, however, is precisely the manner in which the overlap occurs. What are these vital points which allow us to say that the self is ambiguous? How are we ambiguous if the body is both "lived from the inside" and observed from the outside? Although Wild is clearly attempting to bring out the conditions for the presence of ambiguity, such language can also be misleading. His interpretation suggests that we are like a moving box: inside, there is a little machine or a little "man within a man" (homunculus) which guides what is seen from the outside. If there is any doubt about Merleau-Ponty's position in *Phénoménologie de la perception*, *Le Visible et l'invisible* is explicit on this point. He eschews terms such as "inside" and "outside" when describing the human self. We are visible (are seen), but we are also invisible (because we see). The visible is seen and the invisible is the seeing. However, the seeing (the invisible) is not "from the inside." To have a body is to be seeable; it is also to see. The seeing is just as much an integral aspect of the body as its visibility. Marc Richir, for example, has characterized this distinction by the metaphor of ruins.[4] The ruins are seen, and yet we know well that there is a great deal that we are not seeing. There is the visible and the invisible, but there is no outside and no inside. Both visible and invisible are present in the ruins and integral to the existence of ruins *qua* ruins: If we had been there when the ruins were not ruins, but were a magnificent medieval castle, there would be nothing invisible. However, there is no such counterfactual conditional for man. Under no circumstances could we ever have been wholly visible. The empiricist's dream is doomed to be only a dream. We must be ambiguous, and the empiricist will always be forced to reduce the invisible either to the visible or to non-existence.

While these various interpretations of Merleau-Ponty's notions of ambiguity are largely only sketches, at least they concentrate upon some helpful aspects of the problem. Henri Lefebvre, however, in an article entitled "M. Merleau-Ponty et la philosophie de l'ambiguïté" (1957), offers innumerable references to the notion of ambiguity in extremely varied and imprecise contexts. For example, we read:

> From a historical perspective, the philosophy of ambiguity is
> defined as an *eclecticism*. Moreover, every eclecticism has
> an ambiguous character, and we can imagine how profound
> Victor Cousin must have appeared to his contemporaries
> because he was eclectic, incomprehensible, and ambiguous.
> He would glide from a cartesian "rational" psychology to a
> platonic ontology and from a theory of philosophical history
> tainted with hegelianism to a kind of secularized theology.[5]

Ambiguity, then, we are to assume, is associated with the eclectic and the incomprehensible (*insaisissable*)—features which make a philosophical work appear profound. Is Lefebvre saying that Merleau-Ponty's work is eclectic and hence ambiguous because he relies upon investigations in phenomenology, Gestalt theory, organicist psychology (Goldstein), etc.? It would be a superficial account to invoke "ambiguity" simply because one makes use of theories and experiments from a number of different points of view. Merleau-Ponty's philosophy of ambiguity requires that we go beyond an eclectic self, that a person is whole and not divided up into parts or sections, that one's understanding of this wholeness should form itself in terms of that whole and not in terms of its parts. In examining the wholeness of the phenomenon of the self, a variety of theories can partake of that totality of human being in its ambiguity. However, the simple addition of a number of theories is insufficient.

Elsewhere, Lefebvre approximates more closely the sense of "ambiguity" as discussed by the other commentators already mentioned. He states:

> The central nervous system is the place where a "total image of the organism" is formed, an image of the whole which directs the distribution of motor influxes. An "image" (a mode of ambiguous existence, half-physiological, half-psychological) can be total only when the whole organism is involved. (Lefebvre, p. 49)

An image or mode of existence is ambiguous because it is both mental and physical, internal and external (Lefebvre, p. 47), yet neither separately. Again, it is the resolution of a dualism. However, Lefebvre's description of ambiguity as an intermediary between subject and object has disastrous implications, for an intermediary posits that what it mediates still exists, that the troika of object, intermediary, and subject is present. In Merleau-Ponty's ambiguity, the "intermediary" is ambiguity, because ambiguity is all there is. The organism is the "intermediary" with nothing to mediate between.

After largely inadequate or generally superficial commentaries, finally Xavier Tilliette's *Merleau-Ponty: ou la mésure de l'homme* (1970) offers a brief but substantive attempt to understand the nature of ambiguity in Merleau-Ponty's work. He cites two passages from *Phénoménologie de la perception*:

> The same reason for my presence here and now and for my presence elsewhere and always accounts for my being absent from here and now and absent from all places and all times. This ambiguity is not an imperfection of consciousness or existence, it is the definition of them.[6]

And further:

> I know myself only from my inherence in time and in the world, that is, in *ambiguïté*. (*PdP*, p. 397; *PoP*, p. 345)

These two passages are central, and Tilliette attempts to clarify them:

The ambiguity or equivocation, reverberating at all levels, translates better than other words (e.g., duality, duplicity, polarity), because of the halo of unclarity (*indistinction*) which surrounds it, the fleeting character of existential consciousness and the "knot of relationships" which constitute it: self—body—world, motricity—objectivity, meaning—signified, perception—reflection, etc. It harbors the dialectical ferment, the acidity of negativity, which lends to the descriptive method its secret power. The interpreter, whom we are accompanying, takes it largely as a driving bolt.[7]

Tilliette emphasizes the importance of choosing ambiguity over other terms. As a phenomenon, *ambiguïté* is perfectly clear. Perhaps "indistinctness" (rather than "unclarity") is a more accurate translation of Tilliette's term "*indistinction*." A dualism or polarity, for example, indicates a precise distinction between two elements. *Ambiguïté* has no distinctions, only aspects or structures. Such aspects or structures in existence are indistinct, inseparable, and irreducible from one another. Presumably Tilliette means the temporal aspect of existential consciousness when he refers to its "fleeting character." Without temporality, consciousness would be static, for temporality is a necessary condition for the ongoing existence of the human self. Finally *ambiguïté* is what Tilliette calls the "knot of relationships." The knot includes its aspects—relationships—but it does not distinguish them. With *ambiguïté*, the knot is the inherence of the relationships and that which is related. However except for the fact that Merleau-Ponty discusses the issues mentioned by Tilliette, i.e. self—body—world, motricity—objectivity, meaning—signified, perception—reflection, it is not at all clear why, whether, or how these specific relationships interrelate to form the "knot" in question.

Tilliette goes on to tell us that *ambiguïté*, used as a noun, does not conform very well to the project that Merleau-Ponty set before himself. It is better considered as the adjectival "ambiguous" with "intentionality" as the substantive. Hence, after praising the term *ambiguïté*, our author wants to take the emphasis off *ambiguïté* and put it on the Husserlian notion of intentionality. The task is to focus on ambiguous intentionality as a characteristic of human existence. Intentionality has a body but this body is ambiguous. Since corporeal intentionality is ambiguous intentionality, there is no longer any distinction between self (*moi*) and world. Ambiguous intentionality is that relationship, which, by its very existence, dissolves the two elements to be related. On this score, Tilliette is helpful, but we will have to question further into the nature of this ambiguous intentionality, for, as I shall show, ambiguous intentionality is *ambiguïté*.

II MERLEAU-PONTY AND *AMBIGUÏTÉ*

Let us now inquire into the precise fashion in which Merleau-Ponty himself used the term *ambiguïté*. This will provide a basis for a full articulation of human or existential ambiguity.

In *La Structure du comportment*, Merleau-Ponty employs various senses for the term *ambiguïté*. As linguistic ambiguity, we find explicit uses of it both on a practical and on a theoretical plane.

In its practical use, that is, where ambiguity appears simply as a term implying several possible senses which occur together, we find him claiming that the notion of form is ambiguous. Indicating that behavior is a form, he goes on to show that form is neither the juxtaposition of externally associated terms, nor relations which are intrinsic to thought. Form is ambiguous because it does not require us to consider it solely in one direction or the other. Form includes both, for as Merleau-Ponty remarks: "This notion must be understood in itself, with which the philosophical significance of what precedes would remain equivocal" (*SC*, p. 138; *SB*, p. 128). Even though Merleau-Ponty's employment of ambiguity here stresses its linguistic meaning (i.e., the *term* "form" is ambiguous), there is an acute sense of the possible implications of this usage. ("Form" could be construed to take on ontological dimensions.) Furthermore, he is very careful to distinguish "ambiguity" from "equivocation," in which two elements still maintain an independent existence. With ambiguity, the distinctiveness is dissolved. With the notion of form in higher types of behavior, a positive understanding is achieved. Form assists in understanding; its ambiguity is desirable and ought not to be reduced—unlike linguistic ambiguity which must be eliminated for the sake of clarity. With the notion of ambiguous form, we understand behavior better!

From a theoretical point of view, Merleau-Ponty offers an example which clarifies the nature of ambiguity, albeit still linguistic. This is no longer an ambiguity of use (hence, practical), but rather an ambiguity of meaning (hence, theoretical). The following example demonstrates a textual ambiguity, in which the text is a musical text. However, the ambiguity under discussion is not yet existential ambiguity:

> If all musical texts were lost with the exception of one page concerning which one did not even know that it represented music, it would be noticed that the signs of the page can be distinguished by their position on the staff, by adjoining secondary signs (those which distinguish a white from a black) and by their variable groupings within certain units of space (measures); the internal analysis of the text would determine the external contours and the principal dimensions of the universe which is expressed in it. If, by chance, another universe than the universe of sound possesses the same characteristics of structure, the text remains ambiguous. But this ambiguity does not prove that the relation of signs to the signified is contingent: on the contrary it is due to the fact that two possible significations have the same structural properties in common. (*SC*, pp. 132–3; *SB*, p. 122)

The ambiguity occurs because the two or more significations have the same structural properties, that is, because the same constituents of one signification are paralleled in the other. And the signification is not simply the relation between the signifier (*signifiant*) and the signified (*signifié*), but it exists on its own, submerging the relation within it. The text, then, is ambiguous because there are similar structural qualities between the various possible expressions of the same text and between these two different texts. These structural qualities appear in the significations—not in the signifier or the signified. Yet the text (with its internal and external contours)—not the significations— is ambiguous. By analogy, the human self (like the text) is ambiguous. Similar structural qualities arise between the significations (or meanings) of one person and those of another. Both individuals have the same form of experience though the interpretive and significative context may differ. For this reason, we will claim that an existing person is ambiguous. The structural qualities in my meanings are in common with those of other persons. This is certainly not to say that if I am a person who is happy, someone else must be happy as well (he may be sad when I am happy), but the structural qualities (whereby each person can be happy or sad, or some similar state) are the same. The analogy between linguistic ambiguity and existential (i.e., human) ambiguity as articulated here by Merleau-Ponty is strikingly clear.

When discussing "the human order," he is careful to articulate the role of ambiguity, but now it appears as *ambiguïté* and no longer as a linguistic concept.

> The meaning of human work is the recognition, beyond the present milieu, of a world of things visible for each "I" under a plurality of aspects, the taking possession of an indefinite time and space; and one could easily show that the signification of speech or that of a suicide and of the revolutionary act is the same. These acts of the human dialectic all reveal the same essence: the capacity of orienting oneself in relation to the possible, to the mediate, and not in relation to a limited milieu; they all reveal what we called above, with Goldstein, the categorial attitude. Thus, the human dialectic is ambiguous: it is first manifested by the social or cultural structures, the appearance of which it brings about and in which it imprisons itself. But its use-objects and its cultural objects would not be what they are if the activity which brings about their appearance did not also have as its meaning to reject them and to surpass them. (*SC*, p. 190; *SB*, pp. 175–6)

Here the human dialectic is ambiguous. But what is the human dialectic? It is the tension of the actualization of significations in an ongoing experience. This dialectic not only reveals actualities (a limited milieu), but it also reaches out into the possible. There is a similarity of structures between individuals—the human aspect, and also the projective or creative character of that ambiguity. The dialectic which reveals a person as ambiguous does so not only on the static plane, not only in terms of the defined milieu in which specific acts occur, but also in terms of the possible and the capacity to go beyond the socio-cultural structures which imprison us. This creation of meanings occurs within structures which indicate that we are of a particular social political, economic, etc., milieu, but also that with each given meaning, there is surpassing—with each context, there is projection beyond it. The human dialectic never simply treads water, it is always advancing, projecting, creating, surpassing itself. This temporal-psychological aspect of human being (the human order) is a necessary condition, but not a sufficient condition for existential ambiguity.

Also necessary and perhaps even sufficient in Merleau-Ponty's view is perception. For Merleau-Ponty, perception is central.

> We find ourselves in the presence of a field of lived perception which is prior to number, measure, space and causality and which is nonetheless given only as a perspectival view of an objective world and an objective space. The problem of perception consists in trying to discover how the intersubjective world, the determinations of which science is gradually making precise, is grasped through this field. The antinomy of which we spoke above is based upon this ambiguous structure of perceptual experience. The thesis and antithesis express the two aspects of it: it is true to say that my perception is always a flux of individual events and that what is radically contingent in the lived perspectivism of perception accounts for the realistic appearance. But it is also true to say that my perception accedes to things themselves, for these perspectives are articulated in a way which makes access to interindividual significations possible: they "present" a world. (*SC*, pp. 235–6; *SB*, p. 219)

Particularly in *Phénoménologie de la perception*, and its prolegom-enon, *La Structure du comportment*, the self is described as this "ambiguous structure of perceptual experience." For Merleau-Ponty, perception is ambiguous because it is neither the "flux of individual events," which characterize the "subjectively" initiated acts resulting in a Cartesian *res cogitans*, nor the appearing of the things themselves, to which Husserl continually sought to return. Perception is ambiguous because it makes significations possible. Significations are the manner of relating the flux of individual events to their appearing. The ambiguity is attained *qua* ambiguity in that many of these significations occur at the same time. Signifi-cations can only arise in an inter-individual world (a world which is neither intersubjective nor interobjective). Neither individual events nor a series of objectifications make up an inter-individual world. The former would be a world of egos and the latter a world of things. *The* world is neither of these hypothetical worlds, *the* world is an inter-world, an inter-individual world, which is continually marked by significations. These significations constitute the individual through perception, which can never be either a world of egos, nor a world of things. Perception, then, is the world as it appears in terms of significations. We are those significations.

How do we gain access to significations? Consider our grasp of the phenomenal object:

> The phenomenal object is not spread out on a plane, as it were; it involves two layers: the layer of perspectival aspects and that of the thing which they represent. This ideal reference, this ambiguous mode of organization, can be described or understood, but not explained—with the help of a psycho-physiological law, for example—as if the "mental image" were another retinal image the size of which could be measured and related to certain variables. (*SC*, p. 210; *SB*, p. 219)

This "ambiguous mode of organization" is the same as the "ambiguous structure of perceptual experience" cited above. We are informed that it "can be described or understood, but not explained." Methodologically, this point is important. Why can't it be explained? What is there to explanation that is contradictory to the project of description or understanding? And why are the latter two acceptable, while explanation is not? In English we have the verbs "to explain" and "to explicate". These are both rendered in French as "*expliquer*". *Expliquer* must then cover both senses. It must cover the subsuming of a particular under a rule (as in the relationship between a mental image and a retinal one) and also a pulling apart, an unfolding (as is metaphorically suggested in the etymology of *expliquer*). In the first case, that which is to be studied is left aside in favor of the rule or general principle. In the second, the phenomenon of perception is folded up in its "natural" state, that is, the state in which it exists, the state in which it manifests itself. To explain it is to unfold it, to spread it out, and hence to present it in a way in which it does not appear. What is crucial for philosophy—a theme to which

Merleau-Ponty returned throughout *Le Visible et l'invisible*—is to reintegrate itself into experience.[8] The way for philosophy to reintegrate itself into experience is either to describe and understand or to disappear altogether. Assuming that one does not wish to submit to the latter, the role of philosophy is to describe and understand.

Both of these philosophical activities (describing and understanding) do not adversely affect the phenomena. Understanding may even be a corollary of description. Some may advocate the necessity of explanation for understanding, but Merleau-Ponty argues that understanding will never follow from explaining. Explanation leads only to misunderstanding or, in hermeneutical terms, explanation leads to misinterpretation. Description is the project of approximating what is to be understood without altering it. Description is clarification, illumination, making visible. This is not the clarification of the biologist who seeks to understand the workings of his laboratory rat by dissecting it. The dissection destroys the life of the rat. For *ambiguïté*, to be dissected is also to be destroyed, which, Merleau-Ponty would claim, is what dualists have done for centuries. His demand is: tell me how it is, but don't touch it. Added difficulties arise when the phenomenon is *ambiguïté*, for the person doing the prescribing is also manifesting *ambiguïté*. The same would hold for the person engaged in explanation or any other activity. Since to describe *ambiguïté* is also to manifest it, we cannot metaphorically say: don't touch it. In fact, we cannot stop touching it. Description is the attempt to become aware that we are touching. Explanation is the attempt to cut off our hand so that we can isolate the touching. We learn, in the "Preface" to *Phénoménologie de la perception*, that the tool of explanation is analysis, for analysis is the breaking up or dissection which purports to understand, but which only misunderstands. Description is the manner in which the philosopher must learn to understand:

> Seeking the essence of consciousness will therefore not consist
> in developing the *Wortbedeutung* of consciousness and
> escaping from existence into the universe of things said; it will
> consist in rediscovering my actual presence to myself, the
> fact of my consciousness which is in the last resort what the

word and the concept of consciousness mean. (*PdP*, p. x;
PoP, p. xv)

This rediscovery is the path toward an articulation of existential
ambiguity.

For Merleau-Ponty, this rediscovery of one's actual presence to
oneself is not a retreat into the transcendental realm of subjectivity, as in Husserl's project, Merleau-Ponty endeavors to put
himself at the heart of experience itself:

> Experience anticipates a philosophy and philosophy is merely
> an elucidated experience. But now that the phenomenal field
> has been sufficiently circumscribed, let us enter this
> ambiguous domain. (*PdP*, p. 77; *PoP*, p. 63)

After his discussion of the phenomenal field, where this passage
occurs, and which serves as his introduction to the phenomenology
of perception, philosophy only follows experience itself (which
is always primary). Philosophy—or phenomenology—attempts to
clarify experience (the "ambiguous domain") through description.
What Merleau-Ponty describes as "ambiguous" in *Phénoménologie de la perception* seems to vary. However, there is only one
human ambiguity, although it manifests itself in terms of (1) sense
experience, (2) human existence, (3) perception, (4) the body,
and (5) temporality. Since *ambiguïté* is unique, and since each of
these aspects of human life is ambiguous, they are synonymous
in Merleau-Ponty's understanding.

(1) *Sense éxperience*. The phenomenal field, as I have noted, is
the field of experience, an "ambiguous domain." On the level of
sense experience, this ambiguity manifests itself synesthetically. It
is particularly intensified under the influence of mescalin (*PdP*, p.
263; *PoP*, pp. 227–8). He gives the example of an auditory rhythm
which accounts for the running together or fusing of the cinemato-
graphic image or picture. Without sound, Merleau-Ponty notes,
the picture would manifest a markedly distinct succession of
images, but with the two senses together, the experience reveals
itself as ambiguous. In everyday life, all our senses coincide, and
for this reason, our sense experience is ambiguous. That is, our
experience is not a series of independent images, sounds, feelings,
smells, or tastes; rather it is the concurrence of them all together.
Thus ambiguity manifests itself on the level of sense experience.

(2) *Human existence*. Ambiguity is also characteristic of human existence, which is not limited to the specific senses. For example it is manifested in our sexuality:

> Sexuality, without being the object of any intended act of consciousness, can underlie and guide specified forms of my experience. Taken in this way, as an ambiguous atmosphere, sexuality is co-extensive with life. In other words, ambiguity is of the essence of human existence, and everything we live or think has always several meanings. (*PdP*, p. 197; *PoP*, p. 169)

Sexuality provides an ambiguous atmosphere because it is that through which experience occurs. Though continually present in human life, sexuality is seldom rendered explicit. Since sexuality is co-extensive with human life, sexual meanings occur along with meanings arising from a particular situation. In a person's existing, no matter what the situation may be, sexual meanings are unavoidable. Hence this ambiguous atmosphere is essential to human existence. Merleau-Ponty uses the term "*équivoque*" instead of "*ambigu*" when he concludes that "ambiguity is of the essence of human existence" (although he did speak of an "*atmosphère ambigue*"). The adjectives "*équivoque*" and "*ambigu*" are not precisely synonymous. In this case, however, it is acceptable for the English translator to have used the word "ambiguous" in both cases because, when describing human existence, Merleau-Ponty states that "everything we live or think has always several meanings." This plurisignification is crucial to the understanding of *ambiguïté*. There are always several meanings for everything we live or think, but they are really ambiguous only when considered together as a whole. In terms of sexuality, these meanings form a situational wholeness, without which they are merely equivocal, i.e., various separate meanings that characterize what we live or think.

(3) *Perception*. While sense experience is ambiguous because there is always synesthesia, while human existence is ambiguous because many meanings cohere in a whole, perception is ambiguous because there is no lived distinction between perceiving and the thing perceived.

If seeing or hearing involved extricating oneself from the

impression in order to lay siege to it in thought, that is ceasing to be in order to know, then it would be ridiculous to say that I see with my eyes or hear with my ears, for my eyes and ears are themselves entities in the world and as such are quite incapable of maintaining on the hither side of it that area of subjectivity from which it is seen or heard. Even by making them instruments of my perception I cannot ensure that my eyes and ears retain any cognitive power, for the notion of perception is ambiguous: they are instruments of bodily excitation only, and not of perception itself. There is no middle term between *in itself* and *for itself*, and since my senses, being several, are not myself, they can be only objects. I say that my eyes see, that my hand touches, that my foot is aching, but these naive expressions do not put into words my true experience. Already they provide me with an interpretation of that experience which detaches it from its original subject. Because I know that the light strikes my eyes, that contact is made by the skin, that my shoe hurts my foot, I distribute through my body perceptions which really belong to my soul, and put perception into the thing perceived. (*PdP*, p. 246; *PoP*, pp. 212–13)

Ceasing to be in order to know is, of course, experientially impossible. However, we can decide to know in order to be by performing a particular kind of reflective act. This sort of distantiation does not *in fact* separate us from lived perception, it only allows us to think that we have done so. What we say can often be misleading if understanding is what we are seeking. For me to say that my eyes see, that my hand touches, that my foot is aching are all metaphorical expressions. We can say them, but we cannot *be* them. It would be equally possible to take another metaphorical point of view and say, as Merleau-Ponty suggests, that the light strikes my eyes, that contact is made by the skin, that my shoe hurts my foot. Merleau-Ponty's phenomenology suggests that we must place description within that realm to which our metaphors point. It suggests that one does not necessarily get at experience, human existence, or perception by considering only what we say. It suggests that perception is not divided up, but that we divide it by specific cognitive acts. Description must survey and inventory perception as we experience it and as it is. The phenomenologist with his description must, above all, realize that he too perceives and that his description is hardly separate from the perception he describes. Thus Merleau-Ponty finds that perception is ambiguous: perception does not manifest itself as the meanings which come from inside, nor does it come from the outside, the thing perceived, for the perceived and the perceiving both partake of the same activity and are indistinguishable in perception itself. There is no middle term between a Sartrian in-itself and for-itself because there are no poles.[9] All that exists is the ambiguity which is perception.

In "An Unpublished Text," Merleau-Ponty sums up his whole project by distinguishing two kinds of ambiguity:

> The study of perception could only teach us a "bad ambiguity," a mixture of finitude and universality, of interiority and exteriority. But there is a "good ambiguity" in the phenomenon of expression, a spontaneity which accomplishes what appeared to be impossible when we observed only the separate elements, a spontaneity which gathers together the plurality of monads, the past and the present, nature and culture into a single whole.[10]

In *Phénoménologie de la perception*, Merleau-Ponty did not refer to this "bad ambiguity" as an ambiguity. He only discussed its occurrence in previous philosophical thought. The "good ambiguity" is what he always calls *ambiguïté*. This is the ambiguity which incorporates what is whole and describes it as such. Perception, in particular, has this characteristic. The *study* of perception could lead to a bad ambiguity, but this is simply what I have been calling a dualism—particularly one in which subject and object are treated as separate entities. Good ambiguity, which "gathers together" a plurality of meanings and considers them as one, is what Merleau-Ponty sought to articulate and defend. Existential ambiguity is a "good ambiguity."

(4) *The body*. If one were to ask about the place of perception, human existence, and experience, Merleau-Ponty's answer would have to be: the body.

> What enables us to center our existence is also what prevents us from centering it completely, and the anonymity of our body is inseparably both freedom and servitude. Thus, to sum

up, the ambiguity of being in the world is translated by that
of the body, and this is understood through that of time.
(*PdP*, p. 101; *PoP*, p. 85)

The most concrete manifestation of our ambiguity is through our
bodies. At the same time, our body binds us to the world, because
it cannot escape the world, and yet we also choose where we go
in terms of the body. That I am a person who is free is expressed
in terms of my body, but also in terms of my body, I am a person
who is enslaved by the situation in which I find myself. My body
is my being-in-the-world. My body is my ambiguity.

Merleau-Ponty offers a helpful case in which he demonstrates
this aspect of *ambiguïté*.

When I press my two hands together, it is not a matter of two
sensations felt together as one perceives two objects placed
side by side, but of an ambiguous set-up in which both hands
can alternate the roles of "touching" and being "touched".
(*PdP*, p. 109; *PoP*, p. 93)

For Merleau-Ponty, there are not two separate appearances; the
touchante and the *touchée*, any more than there are two separate
phenomena: the *visible* and the *invisible*. The touched is always
touching and the touching is always touched. They are all one
phenomenon: human ambiguity. The body is a "circuit of existence," we are ambiguous. My right hand does not touch the left
any more than the left touches the right. I am a circuit of existence
which meets itself at my hands. At the same time that I am a
person whose right hand is pressing against the left, I am also a
person whose left hand is pressing against the right. While I am
both of these persons, I am neither one nor the other, for they
are not two persons. I am ambiguously one person, who is visible
in that I can be seen, touched, etc., and invisible in that I can see,
touch, etc. In *Le Visible et l'invisible*, Merleau-Ponty describes this
ambiguity as *la chair*, or, sometimes, visibility. These terms
suggest the total fusion of the visible and the invisible. In *Phénoménologie de la perception*, this fusion and annihilation of
elements was described as the body. The body as both corporality
and visibility is a manifestation of ambiguity.

(5) *Temporality*. Merleau-Ponty remarks above that the "ambiguity of being in the world is translated by that of the body, and

this is understood through that of time." Thus we also understand ambiguity through the being of time. Merleau-Ponty adds:

> What needs to be understood is that for the same reason I am present here and now, and present elsewhere and always, and also absent from here and now, and absent from every place and from every time. This ambiguity is not some imperfection of consciousness or existence, but the definition of them. (*PdP*, p. 383; *PoP*, p. 332)

Now we can understand the ambiguity, which we have considered in its other aspects, in terms of time. When we attempt to understand ourselves in terms of time, we find that: there is time and we are temporal. Time is absent from here and now and absent from every place and every moment only when we examine it. By examining it we observe from our transcendental telescope and find that time is there, and not here and now. But when we realize that we cannot escape time, when we realize that time is always with us, we find that it is always present in every place we go and at any time we consider it. It is only absent from all places and all times when we think that we can objectify human existence. With Merleau-Ponty's help, we become aware that we are this ambiguity. I am the person who tries to consider myself apart from time, and I am the person who can never be outside of time. There are not two times, as Bergson suggested; there is only one. This time is ambiguous, since the ambiguity of my meanings can never escape their temporality. I am that ambiguity.

This point returns us to the question of self-knowledge invoked by the Delphic oracle centuries ago: if I am ambiguous, how do I know myself. Here the circle completes itself. "I know myself only in so far as I am inherent in time and in the world, that is, I know myself only in my ambiguity" (*PdP*, p. 397; *PoP*, p. 345). Any self-knowledge must necessarily come in terms of the very ambiguity which I am. Since sense experience, human existence, perception, the body and temporality are all ambiguous, since they are all manifestations of ambiguity, an understanding of these aspects of ambiguity will lead one to an understanding of oneself. But again this understanding or self-knowledge will not itself be separate from the experience of being ambiguous. I am the same person who knows through experience that he is ambiguous and who appears to himself as ambiguous. We are always in that

81

situation. Hence our contact with ourselves will always be within the sphere of ambiguity. Our knowledge of ambiguity will be in terms of our ambiguity. In fact, our knowledge of ambiguity will be our ambiguity.

III MERLEAU-PONTY AND EXISTENTIAL AMBIGUITY

We have examined Merleau-Ponty's work as it is understood by others and as he has spoken of ambiguity. Let us now look at the implications of his work for the understanding of existential ambiguity.

(1) *Ontology*. In the "Preface" to *Phénoménologie de la perception*, which sets forth his understanding of the Husserlian project, Merleau-Ponty states that "because we are in the world, we are *condemned to meaning*, and we cannot do or say anything without its acquiring a name in history" (*PdP*, pp. xiv-xv; *PoP*, p. xix). Just as Sartre proclaimed that we are condemned to freedom, Merleau-Ponty informs us that we are condemned to meaning. We are not condemned to meaning because we are determined in any substantial way, but rather because in any consideration of the human self, some meaning arises, that is, we can be described in a certain way and as the potential subject matter for the historian. Yet we could be condemned to meaning without historians to record it. We are not all Charles de Gaulle; our meanings are not all surveyed and examined by someone in terms of the diverse moments in our lives. And yet in another sense, we are all chronicled. We are in the world; we are in the world with others; and these others help to account for our meaning. Whether these other people write down our meanings is immaterial to the existence and thriving of our meanings. Other people confirm our meanings, for our meanings are inter-individual, in the sense that they are actualized in a world with others. Hence, they are supported in their existence by the presence of other people.

The meaning (*sens*) of a person is not only confirmed by others, it is also confirmed by oneself. We experience the meanings which constitute our being. Remaining on the ontological plane, we must try to understand what Merleau-Ponty takes to be the nature of these meanings. In de Saussure's terminology, we might say that

we must understand these meanings (*significations*) synchronically. Then we will be able to examine the systems and syntagms
in which they are experienced, and finally the diachronic actions
of actualizing these meanings.[11]

This synchronic aspect implies that meanings are understood at
a given time. Indeed, this is the only sense in which we are able
to articulate the meaning that a person is. Each enumeration of
a person's meanings is a determination, a reduction, a distinction
of one meaning or of one set of meanings from another. The only
set of meanings or structure of meanings that is whole is the one
which is given at one time and characterized by the descriptive
terms: self or human nature or person or individual, etc. To be a
person is to be significant, to be full of meaning (*sens*). Merleau-
Ponty does not tend to speak of man as an experienced totality
of many meanings which all cohere without ontological distinction
between them, but it is clear that, for Merleau-Ponty, phenomenology is a philosophy of meaning. The meaning that a person is
in a given perception is what the historian would record. It is also
that which the phenomenologist would describe. This meaning is
a person's signification. Signification (*signification*) is a descriptive
phenomenon, while meaning (*sens*) is ontological. In a phenomenology of human nature, the two must necessarily coincide, that
is, they must be identical. A person's signification is his meaning
and his meaning is his signification. The phenomenologist seeks
to describe the manner in which a person is or exists, and that
which he describes is precisely the being of the person. At the
same time that a person has significations, he is also meaningful,
i.e., significant. Merleau-Ponty would prefer to call a person
meaningful rather than full of significations. To say that the self
is meaningful translates into French as *plein de sens*, which does
not characterize the ambiguity of the meanings as well as our
English expression: meaningful. The English: "meaningful," in
fact, characterizes quite precisely the experienced coherence of a
multiplicity of meanings to form existential ambiguity, viewed
ontologically. For Merleau-Ponty, a person's significations are the
conditions of being meaningful. To be described by many significations, on different levels, at the same time, is the constant state
of the self: a signifying and meaningful being (*homo significans*).

What is it for Merleau-Ponty to speak of the self as meaningful
(or significant)? Let us first examine this concept in terms of his

"unfinished symphony:" *Le Visible et l'invisible*. Here he distinguishes between the visible: that which can be seen and the invisible: that which does the seeing (*le voyant*). But the split (*l'écart*) between seeing and being seen, between perceiving and being perceived (to return to the language of *Phénoménologie de la perception*), is not an abyss, as Sartre has suggested. This real and lived aspect of human life is *la visibilité* (visibility). *La visibilité* is the *chiasme* of the visible (seen) and the invisible (seeing). It is *ambiguïté* itself.

> One should not even say, as we did a moment ago, that the body is made up of two leaves, of which the one, that of the "sensible," is bound up with the rest of the world. There are not in it two leaves or two layers; fundamentally it is neither thing seen only nor seer only, it is visibility sometimes wandering and sometimes reassembled. And as such it is not in the world, it does not detain its view of the world as within a private garden: it sees the world itself, the world of everybody, and without having to leave "itself" because it is wholly—because its hands, its eyes, are nothing else than— this reference of a visible, a tangible-standard to all those whose resemblance it bears and whose evidence it gathers, by a magic that is the vision, the touch themselves.[12]

Visibility is the entity which constitutes seeing and seen, person seeing and thing seen; it is *ambiguïté* because it does not distinguish between seeing and seen, seer and seen; it is the person as a whole who subsumes the separation. As an existing human being, the person is *ambiguïté* or, in this case, what Merleau-Ponty calls visibility. But visibility is also significance. A person's significance is his coherence of seer and seen, seeing and seen, toucher and touched, etc. Significance does not distinguish the elements. It only presents itself as meaning.

In *Phénoménologie de la perception*, Merleau-Ponty called this visibility a person's "circuit of existence." The circuit of existence passes through the body, as does visibility. It comprehends seeing and seen. The body is seen (*vu*) by others as by oneself, but it is also filled with seeing or seer (*le voyant*). It is a circuit, because it is always closed. There is no way for the seer to escape being also seeable. And for a person to be seen is also to include the fact that he sees. For the individual, this is a continuous circuit of existence, which is always lived, and which constitutes his being. Since a person is entirely meaningful, the whole circuit of existence is significant. This is to say that one's circuit of existence can be described in terms of significations, experienced as meaningful, and hence significant. By describing a person's significations (those having to do with seeing and those manifested as seen), we describe that person's circuit of existence *qua* significant visibility.

We noted in our discussion of the philosophy of ambiguity that Merleau-Ponty has been interpreted as setting this phenomenon off against a dualist background. From this point of view, he is responding to the dualist, and his position is one which attempts to put the phenomenon of man back together again. Hence, visibility, circuit of existence, significance, and *ambiguïté* are descriptive responses to the dualist who speaks of mind and body, soul and body, for-itself and in-itself. Merleau-Ponty's *ambiguïté*, therefore, continues to bear a trace of dualism. His *ambiguïté* is the resolution of mind and body, soul and body, for-itself and in-itself, mental and physical, transcendental and empirical. The resolution comes in terms of the seer and seen, the touching and the touched, work and the consciousness of work, etc. Existential ambiguity, however, need not be a situation of meaningfulness where the meanings are only binary. Some meanings may form structures, such as those that are constituted as roles, emotions, intersubjectivity, communicability, sociality, etc. Any meaning which constitutes who a person is will participate in existential ambiguity as significance. It need not and does not restrict itself to traditional philosophical dilemmas.

(2) *Epistemology*. If we consider significance to be a horizontal (ontological) phenomenon, that is, an essential characteristic of being, then we might consider the "intentional arc" to be a vertical (epistemological) phenomenon, in that it activates and gives presence to significance. For Merleau-Ponty, the "intentional arc" is what constitutes the self as meaningful. It gives life to significance, in that it is essential to the lived aspect (*le vécu*) of significance. The "intentional arc" is the experience of the meaningfulness of an individual, i.e., *his* "intentional arc," *his* experience. The "intentional arc" personalizes as it actualizes significations as meaningful and significant.

The "intentional arc" renders significance cognitive. Significance becomes not only *my* significance, not only *my* experienced significance, but also *my known* significance. This is a special and general kind of knowing as distinct from reflective knowledge, as Merleau-Ponty makes quite clear in his critique of reflection, i.e., Descartes. Reflective knowledge makes a phenomenon of the world into a thought-object. It replaces the "world" with "being-thought." Instead of taking the world and human life as that which is to be approached, reflective thought tries to make the world and human life conform to that which is thought. The phenomenon then becomes the object of thought (Descartes's towers and his doubting), and not human being, not the self (which is presumably what reflective thought proposes to be discussing). The "intentional arc" passes through the body. It therefore includes all sense experience. It characterizes human existence and has its expression in the world of men and women. It is delimited by a circuit of existence and, therefore, does not go outside of what is felt or experienced by an individual person. In the often discussed example of the phantom limb, the amputee still feels the presence of his hand, even though it is absent. In bodily terms, his circuit of existence goes only so far as his lived body. But the presence of the absent hand is also part of this circuit of existence. Clearly it is not bodily presence. But it is a cognitive presence. It is experienced as there. Of course, when the amputee goes to pick something up with the missing hand, its absence is clear. But it is cognitively clear. The "intentional arc" grasps it as absent.

We find a similar situation with what has been called our knowledge of the external world. The ash tray is a part of the circuit of existence when it is experienced as "there." It can also partake of the circuit when it is experienced as "not there," that is, when there is openness onto the presence of its absence, when an object or a space does not manifest itself as anticipated. For example, if one is walking down a dark alley, there may be the expected presence of "no one there" and the hope that this absence continues to be present. The circuit of existence, therefore, includes and encompasses only that which is present. There is no question of doubting or of being certain of such objects, unless doubt itself is present, or unless the absence of certainty is immanent: the world of experience activated by the "intentional arc."

This intentional arc is projective:

86

The life of consciousness—cognitive life, the life of desire or perceptual life—is subtended by an "intentional arc" which projects round about us our past, our future, our human setting, our physical, ideological and moral situation, or rather which results in our being situated in all these respects. It is this intentional arc which brings about the unity of the senses, of intelligence, of sensibility and motility. (*PdP*, p. 158; *PoP*, p. 136)

The intentional arc reaches out into the future and back into the past of one's experience. It manifests itself from a particular standpoint; it projects from here and now; and it is the life of consciousness here and now. As a cognitive life (*une vie connaiss- ante*), it is epistemological. It accounts for the unity of all the senses and of all intelligibility. This situation, by which Sartre describes our context, is experienced: at once temporal, physical, ideological, moral, and political. This life of consciousness includes all forms and types of knowing.

The example of a person walking around in the dark further characterizes the intentional arc. As I have noted, the intentional arc is projective; it reaches into past and future; and it extends out into the inter-individual world, from which it cannot escape. In the dark, there are still the past experiences of walking around in the dark, and there are those expectations that might arise as this person gropes about. But unlike walking about in the daytime, the person cannot see what is around him: what he touches has only the form of that which is immediately touched, what he smells is perhaps more acute than usual and yet it is more mysterious, unqualified, etc. He does not have very much "play" (*Spielraum*) between the aspects of his intentional arc which include the limits of his body and that which projects into or permeates the world. In darkness this "play" is very slight. The "lived distance" between seer and the seen is at a minimum. The person, therefore, cognitively experiences himself as isolated and alone. The "lived distance" or "play" allows him, in daylight, to feel at ease, flexible, and free, because he has more of a lag with which to play. He can distance himself. In darkness, distancing is more difficult.

Similarly, in dreaming, a person's distance from himself is prac- tically eliminated. He has to wake up to reassure himself that the snakes biting his feet are not really there. In the dream itself, there is no lag, no lived freedom, no play. The intentional arc is foreshortened; it does not project out into the everyday inter-individual world. It activates only the world of the dream. We might even say that his circuit of existence is short-circuited. It does not manifest its everyday characteristic of having a lived distance between the immediate body and the whole phenomenal field. Here the body and its world of dream is the phenomenal field. All expectations in the future of possibilities are in terms of the dream. The past is the past of the dream. Only the possibility of awakening differentiates the lived dream and the phenomenal field. This possibility, when actualized, becomes the reactivation of the person's lived distance, his ability to extend his intentional arc.

The motion of extending the intentional arc in everyday experi-ence is a return to the metaphor of verticality. As I have indicated, the intentional arc activates and provides the lived aspect to sign-ificance. This type of intentionality has its tradition in Brentano and Husserl, but also an affinity with the Hegelian dialectic. It surpasses (*aufhebt*) subjectivity and objectivity into the intentional arc itself. The intentional arc does not distinguish between visible and invisible, between ego and object, between mind, body, and world. Our subject-predicate sentence structures would convince us that it is performative. Yet there is no agent and no patient being acted upon. All there is, for Merleau-Ponty, is the signific-ance that arises as the intentional arc occurs. The arc neither moves forward nor backward, it simply spans. But its cognitive expanse reveals its describable significations, its experienced meanings, and its ontological significance.

(3) *Psychology*. Psychology here is taken in a particular sense, emphasizing the temporal dimension of human ambiguity. Its concern is with the self's changeability through time when acting and being acted upon. This acting involves creating meanings, the creation of the significance which one becomes. But this part of creation is not subject-initiated, nor object-stimulated. It occurs within the projective activity of the intentional arc. Acting in this sense is not an "I" doing something. It is rather the doing as it occurs and as it forms an entity or totality of meanings. This formation of the totality of meanings is the continued living of the person. Ambiguity is not fully existential ambiguity (as opposed to

simply an intuited essence) unless it is interpreted as manifesting the flux of human experience. Human experience, understood epistemologically, cannot be viewed without concern for the aspect of change, the creation of new meanings, which is the ongoing aliveness and existing of the individual. Therefore, one must describe this psychological aspect of human being in order to offer an elucidation of the wholeness of the phenomenon of the human self.

"Man," Merleau-Ponty indicates, "taken as a concrete being is not a psyche joined to an organism, but the movement to and fro of existence which at one time allows itself to take corporeal form and at others moves towards personal acts" (*PdP*, p. 104; *PoP*, p. 88). We are not simply the epistemological tension in which meanings are actualized, but also the "to and fro of existence" which manifests itself as body expressing itself in terms of personal acts. These personal acts are the creation of meanings, the continual actualization of new meanings. The body is the expression of and participation in personal events. *Qua* expression and *qua* participation, the body is the phenomenal field of significance. This field is not static; it is always manifesting itself in new ways, in terms of new meanings. Its totalization is never the same. In response to the traditional Cartesian dualism, Merleau-Ponty argues:

> The union of soul and body is not an amalgamation between
> two mutually external terms, subject and object, brought
> about by arbitrary decree. It is enacted at every instant in the
> movement of existence. (*PdP*, p. 105; *PoP*, p. 89)

This enactment is the creation of meanings: human action given as thematically temporal.

Temporality is the movement of human existence. For Merleau-Ponty, this description of the human condition characterizes an "inner necessity" that a person be temporal. Temporality is not a compulsion, nor a desire, but rather a fundamental structure of human being. Merleau-Ponty has said that it "is not by reason of some vagary of the human make-up" that the self is temporal. A person continues living by his very actability and creatability. If we did not act, we could not create new meanings. If we could not create new meanings, we could no longer exist as a human being. To exist is to be temporal. Hence, temporality becomes a

Schopenhauerian will to life, a Darwinian survival of the fittest, and a Platonic eros. It defines life; it constitutes life; it conditions life; and it accounts for life. Temporality is the actualization of the projective aspect of epistemology. Without it, which is an impossible counterfactual, a person would not exist and could not live. Temporality is the oxygen of existential ambiguity.

Personal acts are expressed temporally. Time "arises from *my* relation to things." (*PdP*, p. 471; *PoP*, p. 412) Time is not something that I perceive as a relation, similar to the perception of the relation between two objects on a table. I can never escape it. It is always with me, because it it essential to my being human. Temporality is the continual revealing of my encounter with things as I cognitively encompass my significance. I am related to the apple on the table, in that I am a person who sees an apple on the table. But this meaning never occurs in isolation, as I must express it here. It occurs as a relation, but a relation that is always changing. When I am a person who is eating an apple that was on the table, this too is a relation. But the relation continues to express itself in connection with other meanings.

Human temporal movement is not a succession of individual meanings like the succession of frames on a film. It is projection toward what will be and what might be; it is the expectation of the manifestation of possibility. Merleau-Ponty calls it "prospection." But prospection is not just the Husserlian protention: the expected possibility that I will be a person who will enjoy that apple. Prospection is defined by Merleau-Ponty as "anticipatory retrospection." That is, the creation of new meanings is anticipated, expected, but they are anticipated and expected, in short, created, in terms of past experience. And retrospection is "prospection in reverse." Retrospection is the remembered possibility of being a person who saw an apple on the table and who then began eating it. Time then is a continuum, but it is a continuum which never halts, never stops to look forward (protention) nor to look backward (retention and memory); it simply keeps on passing, keeps on creating new meanings in terms of the significance that one is.

"I am myself time, a time which 'abides' and does not 'flow' or 'change' " (*PdP*, pp. 481–2; *PoP*, p. 421). The self is time, because time is always present. It continues to live with us and it never changes because it is always present to our intentional arc. The

90

presence of significance or meanings is the presence of time. In terms of our experience, time is always there. Yet time is also that very aspect in which new meanings are created and are added to those that we are. Time is the actualization of our totality of meanings. Always actual, it is also projective. Time continually pushes forward and backward, but never goes beyond us. It is one's action itself.

By taking temporality as the focal point of the manifestation of the psychologically creative aspect of human nature, Merleau-Ponty de-emphasizes the actual creation of meanings and the manner in which they are created. Yet this focus also helps us to recognize the continually dynamic but always present enactment of being, that is, the psychological manifestation of human ambiguity. It allows us to rediscover the wholeness of the existing human being and the impossibility of separation because of the irreducibility of ontological presence. Action is projective, but present. Action—and all action is temporal—renders the human self cognitively significant and inextricably ambiguous.

PART II

AND
STRUCTURALISM

6

MERLEAU-PONTY ON LANGUAGE AND COMMUNICATION

In 1947–8, Maurice Merleau-Ponty taught a course at the Université de Lyon entitled "Language and Communication." The
course was concerned with three basic issues: (a) the critique of
scientism—particularly in psychology, linguistics, sociology, and
history, (b) the relationship between language and thought, and
(c) the role of the speaking subject in communication. Although
the content of this course has not been published, student lecture
notes are available.[1] In this essay, I review the material covered
in "Language and Communication" and compare it with issues
raised in *Consciousness and the Acquisition of Language* (the
published lectures for the 1949–50 Université de Paris lectures).
The juxtaposition of these two courses, which took place at a time
when Merleau-Ponty was developing and expanding his interrogation of language, serves as a framework for the relationship with
subsequent formulations in phenomenological and structuralist
theories of language.

(a) In Merleau-Ponty's critique of scientism, he tried to elucidate the differences between philosophy, psychology, and science;
but he did not study them as three separate realms. His aim was
not to widen the rift between philosophy and scientific psychology,
rather he hoped to indicate how they might be reconciled.

Physiological psychology (G. Fechner[2] in particular) studies
stimulus-response relationships. It circumvents the very issue with
which psychology ought to be concerned: describing the particular
laws that interpose themselves between the stimuli and the
responses. Fechner's quantitative evaluation of sensations and

excitations suggests an upsetting of the balance of our organism; however, as Merleau-Ponty indicated in the *Structure of Behavior*, these processes are more appropriately understood not as the loss of an equilibrium, but as its reorganization.

An alternative to Fechner's conception of psychology is Koehler's attempt to study the structure of the ape's universe.[3] Merleau-Ponty explicitly calls Koehler's psychological method "phenomenological:" a method which does not seek a false objectivity by purging itself of all anthropological terminology. All interpretation necessarily includes a human aspect. Hence it is not improper to interpret the ape's behavior in terms of "invention," "good fortune," etc. Merleau-Ponty makes this same point in *Consciousness and the Acquisition of Language* when demonstrating the advantages of the phenomenological method over the reflexive and inductive methods.[4] Furthermore, just as he also points out the distinctions between the human, vital, and physical orders in the *Structure of Behavior*, in "Language and Communication" he stresses the importance of achieving access to the internal laws of the organism itself. Such a procedure will necessarily confront us with a study of language, for language is one of the most essential structures of the human organism.

Scientism was also evident in certain domains of linguistics. Experimental phonetics finds the causes of speech in the phonatory organs. Language is turned into a thing. But just as physiological psychology was confronted with the theories of Koehler, scientistic linguistics encountered Ferdinand de Saussure. In support of his thesis that there are alternatives to scientistic linguistics, Merleau-Ponty cites von Wartburg's *Problèmes et méthodes de la linguistique*.[5] Von Wartburg's publications on the evolution and structure of the French language[6] are extensive and they exemplify how one might study a language with some of the distinctions that Ferdinand de Saussure offered at the beginning of the century.[7] One distinction which is mentioned in the 1947–8 Lyon course is the opposition between the diachronic and the synchronic. The diachronic aspect of linguistics is the historical development of languages (e.g., from Latin to Old French to Modern French). The synchronic aspect is an atemporal structure (or sometimes a time-slice) where each particular fact must be viewed in relation to an individual language (e.g., contemporary French). However, as Roman Jakobson indicated in his 1972

Collège de France lectures, Saussure did not intend these two notions to be distinctions in the sense of irreconcilable opposites. In characteristic fashion, Merleau-Ponty moves toward a reconciling tension or dialectic between the two—in this case in terms of "lived language." Diachrony is the perspective whereby a unified element or elements in a language are traced through time, while synchrony is the approach which interrelates a number of disparate and multiple contemporaneous elements. According to Merleau-Ponty, we must consider what language is for a speaking subject. A "lived language" (*langage vécu*) like French both has its historical origins in Latin and is the language spoken by contemporaneous individuals. De Saussure characterized "speech" (*la parole*) as that language which is spoken by individuals; and he considered "language" (*la langue*) as not only that which comes from the past but also that which tends towards the future. To know a language, Merleau-Ponty claims, one must know both its past and its present orientation. In this way, we overcome the exclusive postulates of positivism.

In this context, Merleau-Ponty appeals to another linguist whom he does not mention in *Consciousness and the Acquisition of Language*. A. Meillet[8] surpassed the positivist ideal by regarding language as a totality rather than a table of juxtapositions. In Latin, for example, pronouns change their meaning as block, as a system, and not one after another. Similarly, as the reader of *Consciousness and the Acquisition of Language* knows, Gustave Guillaume considers Greek conjugation, for example, as an architechtonic of time. A sublinguistic scheme extends beneath a given language and informs us about the temporal architechtonic in that language. In the Lyon course, Merleau-Ponty claims that to speak of a linguistic scheme, one must reach the deep facts of language and abandon positivism. It is insufficient to simply add up facts without any formulation of their relationship to thought. The goal of linguistics, Merleau-Ponty states, is to rediscover one or several sub-linguistic schemes. Furthermore, when compared to Noam Chomsky's structural linguistics, Guillaume's deep facts of language, which form a sublinguistic scheme, occupy a position similar to the notion of deep structure as opposed to surface structure in the study of syntax.[9]

Merleau-Ponty's task is to show the inadequacies of behaviorism, positivism and empiricism. However, he does not want to reject their findings altogether—he wants to understand them as incorporated within lived experience as a whole. He claims that in psychology, one cannot be docile before facts; one must interpret them (with all the fullness that interpretation as an activity can reveal); and in order to understand facts, one must try to link them to one another. In linguistics, one cannot allow language to become a pure object, for at the same time that it has certain schemes or structures, it is also in a process of temporal evolution. Both of these aspects are actualized in the speaking subject.

While in the 1949–50 Paris course Merleau-Ponty reserves his comments of a general sociological nature (as philosophical implications of the problem of language) for the concluding pages of his investigation, in the 1947–8 Lyon lectures, examples from sociology and history are introduced rather early in the presentation. There is a reason for this. In the earlier course, he is trying to show how scientism pervades certain areas of human activity; in the later series, he wants to show how men make their history just as they make their language. In *Consciousness and the Acquisition of Language*, he assumes that scientism has been surpassed. Two years earlier, it was necessary for him to point this out.

Just as scientism invades psychology (taking physiological data as necessary and sufficient for an ontology) and linguistics (taking language as a pure object), sociologists have attempted to create a science of nature where social facts are interpreted as things. The sociologists in question ignore both meaning and thought. Durkheim,[10] for example, develops concepts of the religious and the sacred; he understands these concepts as correlates of the social; but he does not examine the social itself. He only notes the coincidence of the sacred and the social. Mauss,[11] on the other hand, would not reduce the sacred to the social. According to Merleau-Ponty, he would reintegrate the two domains into a totality. There is not just one "social force," but rather a whole system of signification that allows for relations between individuals: between barbarian and citizen, slave and free man.

The same kind of assessment can be made of history. Bossuet[12] in the seventeenth century thought of himself as an absolute observer (just as the King of France was an absolute ruler). He understood history as unfolding itself before him. But historians recognized that they themselves were historical. This meant that they had to allow for a dialectic between the objective and the subjective. In order to demonstrate the implications of such a dialectic, Merleau-Ponty asks the following question: did Rabelais believe in God? The problem of belief or disbelief was a post-eighteenth century issue. To understand Rabelais, Merleau-Ponty suggests, one must reconstruct the "mental equipment" [*l'outillage mental*] of his period. By discovering the fantasms and attitudes of the period, we can enter into a subjective-objective dialogue with the past. We must, in fact, recognize that this dialectical relationship is "indissolvable," that we are bound to our link with former epochs. Hence, Merleau-Ponty notes the the *cogito* is a synthesis of the personal and universal—a kind of paradox which did not exist at the physical level. The position of Rabelais with respect to God is a personal matter, but one situated within a universal setting. In order to provide an account of that relationship, we must enter into a similar dialectical relationship in which the question itself is meaningful. Its meaning however is situated within our experience of Rabelais's world. By going beyond scientism in physiological psychology, in linguistics, in sociology, and in history, we come to understand our own relation to them. The physiologist cannot separate himself from his organism; the psychologist is vitally linked to behavior; the sociologist is immersed in society; the historian understands history; and the linguist speaks a language. They are all dialectics in dialectical relation with one another, because they form the human context, which Merleau-Ponty (elsewhere) called "the phenomenal field."[13] We cannot put the knowing subject in the object that he seeks to know. The linguist is in a reciprocal relation with the language he studies. In this way, Merleau-Ponty announces a metaphysics that brings us out of objectivity. It shows us that human subjectivity is irreducible. If we are made by our society, we, at the same time, make it. Merleau-Ponty says that the scientific world is "flat;" by their juxtaposition, all elements are rendered equal. What scientists often do not realize is that the same studies which make claims to objectivity place subjectivity in relief. As Merleau-Ponty describes it, I must rediscover the intentions of others. Thus in sociology, for example, the intention to be retrieved is the intention of another person as he lives through and contributes to the elements of his society. I am constantly confronted by the problem of communication with others—not as a theoretical propositon, but as a reality that I cannot escape. In our world, we are placed directly in the face of other subjects—yet it remains difficult to grasp them as subjects. As Merleau-Ponty puts it, this is the paradox: the object can be found only by manifesting itself out of our subjectivity. This same subjectivity makes us enter into human structures. It forces us to realize our particularities. Our particularities as structures of experience in turn permit us to communicate with other periods and other mentalities. Merleau-Ponty further claims that in the respect in which this paradox is ultimate, it is "*the* metaphysical consciousness." Metaphysics shows that this condition of subjectivity producing structures is not an illusion and that man has always known it. However, a "vulgar realism" has allowed him to ignore the possibility of understanding it.[14]

(b) The second major concern of this 1947–8 course was the relationship between language and thought. Merleau-Ponty claims that the psychologist, like the linguist, is a speaking subject. We are not situated in language like a stone in a magnetic field, for even when I reflect on language, it is still language which allows me to clarify my thoughts. In fact, it would be impossible for there to be a link between the subject and language as two different substances. And yet this is precisely what the objective study of language proposes. The objective study of language does not try to deal with the language of the speaking subject. It gives up immanence. The notion of sympathy with other people drops out. Sign and signification become fixed, since they become the object of investigation.

The objective study of language, as in behaviorism, defines language as verbal reactions and conditioned reflexes. According to this view there are two kinds of reflexes: innate reflexes and conditioned reflexes. Innate reflexes are previous outlines of behavior which the anatomy of the phonatory organs determine from birth. Conditioned reflexes have a modicum of flexibility by contrast with innate ones. Pavlov,[15] for example, defines language as the sum of simple reactions. These reactions are assessed in terms of localizations in which there is a certain stimulus evoking a corresponding response. The question of consciousness does not arise. Signification is fixed by a word and a few images traced in the brain. Verbal behavior is defined as a one-to-one relation: word to localization in the brain.

In questions of aphasia (in cases of the subject's inability to find words to express his idea), some difficulties with the objective approach arise. How can aphasics find words in certain practical situations, while they can not find these same words in other situations? The notion of a localization breaks down when one considers the case of cerebral lesions. Linguistic facts and cerebral facts cannot be held in an absolute correspondance. One might show the fact of localization in the brain; but the brain is only a means of access to language. From Merleau-Ponty's perspective, all attempts to replace lived language by a study of localizations are not science. They are postulates. We must not confuse the requirements of the mind and the postulates of a mechanism. Thus Gelb and Goldstein[16] have shown that a subject who is no longer able to recognize colors does not have a loss of significations. He is only unable to group significations. He has lost the possibility of categorial judgment. Merleau-Ponty has more to say about this categorial function in *Consciousness and the Acquisition of Language*.[17] Here, however, he distinguishes two manners of speaking: (1) an automatic manner of speaking: this is the one cited by Pavlov, where a man can live in spite of certain weaknesses; (2) the true manner of speaking: this is the establishment of original relations between the self and things and between the self and others.

Merleau-Ponty cites Kurt Lewin[18] as having examined the relations between a word and the image that comes to mind. According to Lewin's theory, the same grammatical category can be found in the mind as in the word. Images are an act of consciousness. Alain[19] however criticized this view on the grounds that one can look into an image but in fact not see anything. To give body to our belief, we borrow from reality: e.g., this shadowy contour of a bush becomes a bandit lurking in the dark. We use the sensible to incarnate our own convicitions. This is the orientation which Sartre developed in *The Psychology of Imagination*.[20] One cannot actually observe an image—to do so the image would have to have a place in the body. We find that the image of Peter who is absent is not like a photograph of him. It is more like an intermediary between me and him. For Sartre, there is no association of images, since in reality there is only one consciousness. Merleau-Ponty claims that the image is the sedimentation of a total life which gives that life its meaning. This is also important for the place of thought in language. Language is not a sonorous phenomenon; it is not purely physiological. There is only an intentionality of language. The adherence of meaning to the word shows that I rejoin myself in speaking. Language is a manner of speaking. There is a signification of the word that is to be distinguished from the pure concept of the word. Outside the thematic dictionary signification, the word is surrounded by a halo of meaning.[21] The presence of this halo of meaning points to a new connection between language and thought.

Language, Merleau-Ponty says, is a manifestation of thought. Language can be studied in two ways: (1) it can be studied according to the relations between phenomena (which is the task of psychology); (2) it can be studied according to the foundations which render these phenomena possible (which is the task of philosophy). From the psychological perspective, the intention of language must be grasped in each case of its expression. But the psychologist starts with the very presuppositions which it is the task of the philosopher to critique. The philosophy of language must go beyond the pure phenomenon of language.

However, the psychologist as well must go beyond the realism of the common sense view of language, which understands language as the sum of signs and images. Merleau-Ponty indicated to his students that psychology is concerned with a certain sector of being, while philosophy is concerned with being in general. Nevertheless, a conscientious psychology will very quickly go beyond itself toward philosophical thinking. The moment that one introduces the conscious subject, it is clear that the conscious subject is coextensive with its own existence, with human nature. As soon as we see that the conscious subject is coextensive with nature, psychology and philosophy can no longer be distinguished. Of course, the psychologist will not admit this. He will maintain his initial ontology. Psychology alone avoids piercing the ceiling of the phenomena. However, Merleau-Ponty notes that psychology can also be reflexive, just as Husserl asserted the existence of noematic reflection. If one follows the developments of objective knowledge, one will see that there is an interior to the phenomenon. And this path is how we arrive at philosophy. I might add that in his own career Merleau-Ponty wove in and out of psychology, an oscillation which he reiterated later in terms of a dialectic between philosophy and non-philosophy.[22]

Linguistics also provided Merleau-Ponty with a means of access to philosophy. In this Lyon course, he was explicitly concerned with the fundamental relationship between language and thought. In *Consciousness and the Acquisition of Language* he was more interested in the actual "genetic" aspects (as Piaget would call them) of this relationship. Yet as Chomsky and students of Chomsky are well aware, the language-thought relation is also basic to language acquisition.

The problem of linguistics is parallel to that of history. Since the nineteenth century, we have been aware that humanity cannot be considered as a simple juxtaposition of consciousnesses. The communal life of consciousnesses constitutes a human milieu which is exterior to the individual consciousness. With historical objects, there appears a level of being between physical being (e.g., a stone) and the being of individual consciousnesses. This historical level is a mixed one. The historical milieu depends on man while at the same time it is conditioned by physical factors. History is mind poured out into cultural objects. It is not the mind of the *cogito*. This indicates that, for Merleau-Ponty, there is mind outside of self-consciousness. This has its implications in linguistics as well. Since linguistics recognizes a logic in language, it might be tempted to say that language is logic, just as history, which recognizes physical factors in itself, might be tempted to claim that history is the physical factors which contribute to it. In linguistics, we have to understand the nexus: language-mind. In fact, language carries the mind well, but it is not the cause of thought. We must unite and articulate the objective mind and the subjective mind. This means that we must not regard language as a purely historical phenomenon, as Valéry does in his essay on Leonardo da Vinci.[23] Saussure warned us against purely diachronic studies. The *cogito* is formulated; its words say something. If we return to the tacit *cogito* that concerned Merleau-Ponty at the end of the *Phenomenology of Perception*. we discover the *cogito* which gives being to my consciousness, we rediscover an inseparable thought of a certain historical and linguistic thickness. Everything that I now say is conditioned by my linguistic learning. The presence of my thought is a presence through the already accomplished, the already seen (*déjà vu*).

(c) This point brings us back to Saussure. Language exists only in speaking subjects. It appears at a certain moment, but it is in the process of becoming. Language changes. It is like a symphony.

There is language (*langue*) and speech (*parole*). There is the musical score and there is the particular orchestra that is playing the symphony. Language is the totality of permanent principles. Speech is the totality of what people say, the initiatives of all those who speak the language in question. There is an interdependence between language and speech, which can be studied synchronically—at a particular time or period. But again one must be wary of studying language as a reality-in-itself. Because there is a multiplicity of speaking subjects, language must envelop each one. Language is a means which is offered to each subject—so that both will understand.

In the Paris course, Merleau-Ponty considers this problem of communication principally in terms of children. In the Lyon course, he discusses language only in general terms. Language is carried by inter-subjectivity. To speak does not mean that one makes use of a sum of discrete words; rather it is to have a system of non-separable signs. It is a totality of signs, a currency which comes out of our relations with others. The problem is to know how and why a system of signs without a distinct individuality is linked to a system of significations without a distinct individuality. Between the two systems, the relationship may be intrinsic, with common structures. The relationship between concept and word, however, is arbitrary. Saussure distinguishes the signification of a word from its linguistic value. Language is not a simple nomenclature. Language is a creation of linguistic values. We learn our thought through our language. Since to understand someone is not to place concepts behind words, there is a grouping of concepts in us. We must adhere narrowly to signs. We take up and silently reaccomplish the intentions of the person who speaks.

This is the link with Husserl's fifth cartesian meditation, where the problem of intersubjectivity is explored and which Merleau-Ponty interprets as the problem of communication with others. As Merleau-Ponty notes, the certainty that I have of my self comes from what I think. To represent to myself that there is another consciousness that can think, that can annul my own results, is to affirm that there is, in being, something other than what I would know to recognize. Similarly, others annihilate me; I am only a phenomenon for others. On the plane of thought, there cannot be a solution, for other people's thoughts kill my own. The behavior of others allows a coupling. The sexual instinct is a capacity for an act which the subject must reintegrate according to an innate knowledge. Similarly, my speech couples itself to the language of others. I grasp a behavior as comprehensible. The paradox is that, at the moment that I believe I can communicate with others, I do it with a language which is only a manner of expression, for there are many languages, and even if I speak a foreign language, I retain my maternal language. We are not subjected to any language. In all cases, our universality has no meaning unless it realizes itself in a particularity. The universality is not given to us. This is the manner in which Merleau-Ponty comes to grips with the problem which he sets out to consider in the Lyon course: the problem of language and its role in communication.[24]

Merleau-Ponty's subsequently published writings on language include: the section on "Linguistics" in "Phenomenology and the Sciences of Man" (1951), which is contained in *The Primacy of Perception;* "On the Phenomenology of Language" (1952) and "Indirect Language and the Voices of Silence" (1952) both of which are reprinted in *Signs;* "The Sensible World and the World of Expression" (1953), "Studies in the Literary Use of Language" (1953) and "The Problem of Speech" (1954), all three of which are summarized in *Themes from the Lectures;* and the posthumous *Prose of the World*, which was probably written between 1950 and 1952. In many of these texts, particularly *The Prose of the World*, we find an analogue to the scientism which Merleau-Ponty criticizes in "Language and Communication." This analogue is the idea of an algorithm, a universal or pure language, which Merleau-Ponty rejects as untenable. The problems with such an algorithm are paramount. Above all, the result is that:

> the word possesses no virtue of its own; there is no power hidden in it. It is a pure sign standing for a pure signification. The person speaking codes his thought. He replaces his thought with a visible or sonorous pattern which is nothing but sounds in the air or ink spots on the paper. Thought understands itself and is self-sufficent. Thought signifies outside itself through a message because it attaches the same signification to the same sign, whether by habit, by human conventions, or by divine institutions. In any case, we never find among other people's words any that we have not put

there ourselves. Communication is an appearance; it never brings us anything truly new. How could communication possibly carry us beyond our own powers of reflection, since the signs communication employs could never tell us anything unless we already grasped the signification?[25]

It should be clear from these remarks, written about three or four years after the Lyon course, that Merleau-Ponty maintained his concern with the enterprise that seeks to separate language from thought. The end-result is the production of another dualism in which thought and language, subjectivity and objectivity, self and signs are divorced from one another. In order to demonstrate that this dualism is an impossible condition, Merleau-Ponty describes the unavailability of multiple significations when a pure sign stands for a pure signification and the limited powers of communication when it has to turn back upon itself without the possibility of new meaning.

For Merleau-Ponty, language is imbued with thought and thought is already a language. The speaking subject is the active, dialectical uniting of thought and language in a communicative situation. Communication arises out of a condition in which it is evident that the embodied, speaking subject is speaking with others. The speaking subject is already a communicative *Mitsein*. Thought, novel thinking, unperceived perspectives are brought into language in the speaking of it. This sort of communicative practice is announced by Saussure in terms of *parole* as to enactment of a *langue*.[26] Where Roland Barthes, in his early work, stressed the textuality of an enacted *langue* in terms of a *langage* (or discourse), his more recent writing introduces the notion of pleasure which can only be achieved by the speaking of "desire" through the text.[27] The respect in which, according to Barthes, this "pleasure" achieves "*jouissance*" is, in many respects, a return to the experiential knowledge production to which Merleau-Ponty continually appealed in his descriptions of communication as the appearance of thought in the subject's speech. Although Merleau-Ponty had described speech and expression in terms of gesture and bodily articulation in *Phenomenology of Perception* (1945), signs that Saussurian semiology had begun to take effect on Merleau-Ponty's thinking are already evident in the 1947–8 course on "Language and Communication." Furthermore, this was one of the clearest formulations of the developing intersection between phenomenology and structuralism—a link which is still open to further exploration.[28]

7

MERLEAU-PONTY AND HEIDEGGER: INTERPRETING HEGEL

In the last year of his life, Merleau-Ponty gave his lectures on "Philosophy and Non-Philosophy since Hegel" at the Collège de France. These reflections offer interpretations of Hegel and Marx.[1] The first part of the study focuses on the celebrated "Introduction" to Hegel's *Phenomenology of Mind*. Curiously, however, Merleau-Ponty did not turn directly to the Hegelian text itself. Rather he worked out of Heidegger's essay "Hegel's Concept of Experience" which is collected in *Holzwege* but published for English-speaking readers as a separate volume.[2] Heidegger divides Hegel's "Introduction" into sixteen numbered paragraphs and comments upon each one in turn.[3] According to Heidegger, the 1807 title of the *Phenomenology of Mind*, i.e., "Science of the *Experience* of Consciousness," represents "experience" as the fundamental concern of the phenomenological enterprise. Indeed, the discussion of Hegel's "Introduction" develops an understanding of that very notion of "experience." Since Merleau-Ponty comments upon Hegel through Heidegger's text, it is not at all surprising that the concept of experience is also central to Merleau-Ponty's interpretation of Hegel. The confrontation of these two philosophers with Hegel is also their confrontation with each other and this encounter will be the subject of this essay.

INTRODUCTION

Merleau-Ponty provides little direct commentary on Heidegger's interpretations of Hegel. Much of the dialogue is internal to Merleau-Ponty's own presentation of the Hegelian position. The absence of direct reference to Heidegger is not unusual. In fact, Merleau-Ponty rarely discusses the work of his German post-Husserlian counterpart. One of the few exceptions to this silence occurs in Merleau-Ponty's course outline for 1959 ("Philosophy as Interrogation"). He notes that through an inquiry into Being, Heidegger seeks

> to integrate truth with our capacity for error, to relate the incontestable presence of the world to its inexhaustible richness and consequent absence which it recuperates, to consider the evidence of Being in the light of an interrogation which is the only mode of expressing this eternal elusion.[4]

The passage is significant in that it embodies precisely the interchange and dialogical structure which is present throughout the two-pronged response to Hegel. By distinguishing the specific understanding which Heidegger holds toward Hegel and by contrasting that response with the Merleau-Pontean position, the interrogation which Merleau-Ponty announces with respect to Heidegger can be re-directed back to Hegel and forward to contemporary thought. Hence without examining the particular statements that Merleau-Ponty has made about Heidegger or attempting to surmise how Heidegger would respond to Merleau-Ponty's incarnate philosophy and his move to visibility, our attention will be turned away from a direct confrontation. The Hegelian problematic will therefore serve as an instrument for the introduction of triangularity, as a model against which the two versions of modern phenomenology can show their differences, and as a point of inversion from the nineteenth century to the twentieth.

In order to give form to our own interrogation, it will be necessary to establish a triple tripartite set of relations. All nine terms are concerns introduced by Heidegger in his reading of Hegel's text. Yet it is precisely this text which Merleau-Ponty also reads in the move from philosophy to non-philosophy, or, as he says in the 1959 course, from "philosophy as a rigorous science" to philosophy as pure interrogation. Indeed, Merleau-Ponty cites this path as the same path "that led Heidegger from the negativist and anthropological themes to which the public reduced his early writings, to a conception of Being which he no longer calls philosophy—but which, as it has been well remarked (J. Beaufret), is certainly not extra-philosophical" (*TL*, p. 105). In a fashion similar to Heidegger's itinerary from philosophy to Being, Merleau-Ponty establishes the sojourn from philosophy to visibility, from philosophy to experience, and from philosophy to non-philosophy.[5] Just as he says of Heidegger, the result is "certainly not extra-philosophical" any more than it was for Hegel, who announced the end of philosophy before them.[6]

This retracing of steps affirms, in the first instance, the triad of (1) presence, (2) appearance, and (3) presentation; in the second case, (4) representation, (5) natural consciousness, and (6) real consciousness; and in the third account, (7) truth, (8) experience, and (9) phenomenology. The movement from presence to phenomenology follows the form of philosophy becoming experience (Merleau-Ponty) and establishes itself in the ontological difference between Being and beings (Heidegger). By detailing each of these triads, first from a Heideggerian perspective and second from a Merleau-Pontean point of view, the identity of their difference will become evident. Each element of the triple structure is thematized in Heidegger's essay "Hegel's Concept of Experience," and reformulated by Merleau-Ponty in his own terms and in his own response to Hegel.

I THE FIRST TRIAD

(1) *Presence*. For Heidegger, the presence of that which is present establishes a difference.[7] This ontological difference, already announced above, is not only the difference between Being and beings, but also the presence in that which is present (*das Anwesen in seinem Anwesende*). The difference cannot be marked, it can only be re-marked in that which is present. The presence of the present brings Being to what is there. The "there" simply takes the forms, shapes, and sizes that it has. As a difference that is established on the horizon of what is there, this difference (presence of the present) illustrates the philosophical understanding of what is present by clarifying what needs to be

known. As object of knowledge, that which is present is available for scrutiny. But its availability for scrutiny is affirmed by its presence (*Anwesen*).

A philosophical hermeneutic seeks to reveal existence as presence in its self-appearance. The enterprise, however, reveals only that which is present (*Anwesende*) and not necessarily its presence (*Anwesen*). Philosophy, for Heidegger, examines the ontic (that which is present). Yet it continually finds itself falling into the ontic, rather than affirming its presence as the ontological character of what is there.

For Merleau-Ponty, philosophy must become the texture of existence. Just as Heidegger in *The Introduction to Metaphysics* associates the mistranslation of φύσις with the Latin *natura*, Merleau-Ponty in *The Structure of Behavior* takes the "physical order" as the first of three differentiated levels of human existence (with the vital and human orders each, in turn, fulfilling the conditions of nature). By reiterating this concept of nature *qua natura naturans* in *Phenomenology of Perception* and *qua* "concept of nature" in the Collège de France courses for 1957 and 1958, he demonstrates the "presignificatory" character of "brute being"— what Bergson viewed as "a primordial lost undividedness" and what Husserl found in "the sphere of 'pure things' " (*blosse Sachen*) (*TL*, p.78), (*TL*, p.79). In each of these cases, nature is present, but undifferentiated by human understanding. Nature is that to which philosophical thought must always return and that which it must become.

(2) *Appearance*. Heidegger calls for the appearance of knowledge—thereby seeking to realize the presence of that which is present. In order for that which is present to appear, it must have a place. The place is the ontological space of the differencing of Being from beings, of presence from that which is present. In other words, an investigation of absolute knowledge requires a standard of measurement. Appearance is that standard. Knowledge of what is present can only be established through the appearance of that which is present. Its appearance, then, is the marker according to which its Being can be announced. Knowledge can be ascertained by the appearance of something. Although the appearance cannot be regarded as static and fixed, it does require a point of emanation. In coming about (appearing),

111

appearance realizes knowledge. Indeed, appearance depends upon performance for the realization of knowledge.

According to Merleau-Ponty, the appearance of knowledge also depends upon an investigation. However, philosophical inquiry itself makes knowledge appear. As knowledge becomes evident, philosophy is mobilized at the level of appearing. In terms of *The Visible and the Invisible*, which he was developing at the same time as "Philosophy and Non-Philosophy Since Hegel," appearance depends upon the intertwining of the visible and the invisible into pure visibility. The standard of measurement is pre-objective being itself. Appearance, for Merleau-Ponty, is philosophizing and not the standard of measurement. Philosophizing must return to pre-objective ("brute") being. Philosophy becomes non-philosophy, i.e. the fulfillment of *praxis*, and the absolute. when the appearance of knowledge brings the absolute to presence.

(3) *Presentation.* According to Heidegger's interpretation, presentation aims at the appearance of knowledge. In order to achieve the presence of that which is present, knowledge must appear. Presentation is the performance according to which knowledge will appear. Presentation is the active function which brings about the appearance of that which is present in terms of its presence. The knowledge which appears according to presentation is phenomenal knowledge. Such knowledge depends entirely upon appearance taken as the standard of measurement. By checking phenomenal knowledge against appearance, that which is present becomes evident only when it is presented as an appearance. Phenomenal knowledge, as its etymology suggests, is the manifestation of beings (entities, essents, etc.) as they are brought to the fore within a particular context.

Merleau-Ponty indicates that the presentation, which is the way knowledge appears, cannot bring about the appearance as if it were an external force or condition. He would affirm Heidegger's position that "with the characterization of the science which presents phenomenal knowledge in its appearance, we suddenly become involved ourselves in the presentation" (*HCE*, p. 92). Our involvement, however, is not a conscious choice, a decision that we can or cannot make. Rather the very appearance of knowledge in the presentation is our embodied and expressive engagement with that which is present.

Merleau-Ponty would agree with Heidegger that "we are

involved already, since what the presentation presents is 'for us' "
(*HCE*, p. 92). Yet, this "for us" is not to be regarded as a passive
involvement. Merleau-Ponty's fundamental conception of our role
in the presentation prescribes our active engagement in the
appearing of knowledge. No detachment is possible. The presentation is not *to* us. We effect it by presenting the appearance
of the absolute, by our intentional projections throughout the
phenomenal field of appearing knowledge. The presentation of
that knowledge can occur only by our inhabiting it.[8]

In this first triad, the result of the movement is phenomenal
knowledge. For Heidegger, phenomenal knowledge is the presentation of that which is present as an appearance which announces
its presence. The appearance differs (itself) from that which is
present, while the presentation affirms its identity with the presence of that which is present. For Merleau-Ponty, the result is a
phenomenal field of expression and visibility, but the result is the
same as the beginning: what appears has already been presented
and what has been presented is already knowledge of that which
is present. At this point, what we now know is only what appears
to us (Heidegger) and through us (Merleau-Ponty).

II THE SECOND TRIAD

(4) *Representation.* A mental representation (*Vorstellen*), in
Heidegger's understanding, is the basis of self-certainty. The
object appears to the subject as a representation of itself to itself.
Representing here means making the absolute available to itself
as presence. This being present (*parousia*) is a self-presentation.
In the first triad, presentation was the presentation of that which
is present according to its appearance. No conditions were shown
as to how the presentation takes place. In representation ("giving
again" and "placing in front"), we now find that bringing to
presence comes in terms of a self-presentation. The object (which
is present) is brought to appearance by the object itself: the object
presents itself for itself and to the subject. As a re-presentation,
the object's presence to itself is self-certain. It needs no external
standard of measurement apart from its appearance, through
which it is given again to itself.

As the self-presentation of that which is present, representation is natural representation. In representing itself to itself, the performance is self-motivated. Phenomenal knowledge, of which representation is a type, presents itself as true knowledge. In the mental appearance of the object, the knowledge that results is true because the truth (*a-letheia:* bringing out of concealedness) is in the belonging-together (*Zusammengehörigkeit*) of (1) that which is represented, (2) that which represents, and (3) the act of representing. As to the full understanding of truth, we must wait for the third triad, but as to the triple unity of representation, it occurs when appearance emerges from concealedness to unconcealedness, from that which is present to presence—by an additional performance of a presentation.

Representing something in natural knowledge, that is, the knowledge of everyday awareness, maintains its own identity as mineness (*Jemeinigkeit*). *Qua* representation, opinion arises as belonging to someone. Such opinion takes three forms: (1) an unmediated focusing on something, (2) trusting acceptance of what is given, and (3) what is received, held and accepted as our own. In each case, what is mine is that which is represented as present, indisputably and convincingly. The presentation of phenomenal knowledge as opinion is accepted (by a subject) as the presence of what is present.

The two forms of representation, (1) self-representation as a mental appearance to the self or subject, and (2) natural representation as possessed, are both modes of rendering something cognitively present. Merleau-Ponty's approach would avoid self-representedness as a type of self-reflection. Philosophical knowledge does not come from either the mental or natural representation of an appearance to oneself. Rather philosophical knowledge is based on the move to participate in the absolute as it reveals its phenomenal character. This move is not the vision of a mystic such as Bonaventure, nor is it the pantheism of a Wordsworth. Rather the move to participate in the absolute is the intentional arching of the subject and the object, the future and the past. This arching is a lived activity which permits neither the object to represent itself to itself by itself nor the subject to make the object represent itself to the subject by incorporating it into the subject's own sphere. For Merleau-Ponty, the incorporation must be in the representation itself. Philosophical knowledge must be the representing of what is present to the subject as an intermingling of the subject with the object and the object with the subject. Philosophical thought must enter into the self-presentation of phenomenal knowledge such that the repeated presence of the world in its various manifestations becomes the place of philosophical representation. Thus philosophy takes on the character of representation as it enters into the texture of the world's appearances, problems, and proposed solutions.

(5) *Natural consciousness.* Of the two ways in which Heidegger considers consciousness, the first, drawing upon the Husserlian conception of the natural attitude, indicates that Hegelian sense-certainty overlooks the Being of beings, the presence of that which is present. In this first instance, natural consciousness—as a type of representation—finds only beings, only that which is present. All presentations are simply tied to that which is present. The appearance which is the standard of measurement for the presentation, has no place in the context of the ontological difference (between Being and beings). Natural consciousness finds only beings, entities, essents. Beings appear in their everyday, existing form. Known in their ontic, rather than their ontological, character, beings do not participate in subjective experience as such. They are presented to a consciousness that treats them as objectivities, entities to be known, but not to be interpreted fully. The natural attitude in Husserl is restated in Heidegger as a consciousness incapable of articulating the Being of beings—the lived ontological difference by which presence can appear.

Merleau-Ponty does not accept the distinction between a natural and a phenomenological consciousness, which is implied in Heidegger's consideration of this first instance of natural consciousness. From the early *Structure of Behavior*, Merleau-Ponty shows (as we have noted in terms of "presence") that the physical order is integrated with the vital and human orders, such that nature is already consciousness of nature, life is already consciousness of life, and work is already consciousness of work. Although he would agree with Heidegger that consciousness of nature (or natural consciousness) is by itself inadequate, he would also wish to point out that it cannot exist by itself in the first place. The appearance of each level of consciousness is also its self-comprehension (*Selbst-verständlichkeit*). Merleau-Ponty would deny the necessity of the distancing process: the separation of Being from beings, presence from what is present. For

Heidegger, the understanding of what appears comes only with the establishment of a difference, given in the genitive form: the Being of beings. For Merleau-Ponty, nature must be lived through—the process is one of integration. In the later philosophy, nature is united with *la chaire* (the flesh). Hence, philosophy must not separate itself from lived experience. Instead it must participate even in everyday experience *qua* non-philosophy. In that respect, even if natural consciousness is concerned only with beings, entities, essents, it is nevertheless consciousness and it has a vocation.

The second instance of Heideggerian natural consciousness moves toward the appropriation of its own abode. With *das Ereignis*—being as appropriation or advent—consciousness seeks to fulfill its own horizons. For natural consciousness to appropriate its own abode, it must become fully present to itself. Such self-representation in effect goes beyond natural consciousness toward the realization of the absolute. The absolute is achieved when natural consciousness surpasses itself.

Here again, although Heidegger indicates that natural consciousness is not entirely enclosed upon itself, it does nevertheless require an act of self-overcoming in order to establish its place in the ontological difference, that is, to announce the presence of Being. For Merleau-Ponty, however, philosophizing moves into the embodied arena of practical life. The absolute is not beyond nature, it *is* nature appearing as a lived presence through the intentional experience of the individual. In suggesting a return to nature, Merleau-Ponty is closer to Nietzsche than to Hegel—who would propose a surpassing. The Nietzschean return is the affirmation of what was as what will be. Merleau-Ponty finds that return within the interwoven flux of the presence of an incarnate consciousness of nature *qua* natural consciousness, i.e., *qua* presentation of the absolute in phenomenal knowledge.

(6) *Real consciousness*. Real consciousness, in Heidegger's assessment of Hegel, is different from natural consciousness. The natural is not the real, any more than natural consciousness is real consciousness. The natural stems from nature, while the real is what truly is. Nature is the ground according to which the real is understood. Real consciousness reveals what truly is, i.e., nature as a phenomenon. The representations of nature are re-interpreted according to real consciousness. The representations of

116

natural consciousness simply return nature to itself, beings to beings, ontic to ontic. Real consciousness, however, opens up the possibility of the real, of Being, and of ontological conditions in general. Yet real consciousness is natural knowledge, a real phenomenom of nature. Like Husserl's phenomenological atti- tude, real consciousness cannot place itself in a realm that is different from that of the natural attitude.[9] Rather it is a new way of seeing, a more firmly grounded mode of interpreting what is. For Heidegger, natural consciousness is not-yet-true, since its truth is real consciousness. Real consciousness is then natural consciousness becoming its truth. In other words, real conscious- ness includes both the measure of truth (the real) and that which is measured (nature). As we have already seen, the standard of measurement is the appearance itself. The real as measure is opposed to nature as measured. The movement of one to the other is established according to the appearance of that which is present in nature. By examining itself (*qua* measure), conscious- ness shows itself to natural representation (*qua* measured). By its self-representation, consciousness combines both theoretical and practical understanding—real knowledge is established in relation to nature, the relation in which the ontological difference is realized.

What is important here is that Heidegger points out the conditions for philosophy to develop in the context of the real, although always defining it from the natural. Merleau-Ponty, however, insists upon the presence of the real in the natural. Nature is informed by what truly is such that its realization is nature appearing as presence of the absolute through body, speech, and political action. Interrogation is not a new mode of knowing that sets itself apart from nature and the absolute. Interrogation goes directly to nature and the absolute in order to bring out the visibility that is already there. Interrogation must therefore negate itself as a separate philosophy, as a theoretical model that distinguishes itself from what is and what is present. Its difference occurs by becoming what is and what is present. Its negation is its affirmation. Its nature is its reality among the things of the world.

In this second triad, we have noted the self-representational character of the first triad (presence, appearance, and presen- tation). By representation, presentations are made available for a natural consciousness. Yet a natural consciousness can only treat what is present; it cannot account for the presence of the ontological difference. For Heidegger, the introduction of real consciousness succeeds where natural consciousness fails. For Merleau-Ponty, however, such a distinction is both artificial and mis-directed. The directionality must return real consciousness toward nature rather than away from it.

III THE THIRD TRIAD

(7) *Truth.* In order to represent the consciousness of nature to real consciousness, Heidegger claims that truth must appear. The necessity of the appearance of truth has already been noted, but without the possibility of indicating its realization. Only here, in the third triad, is there an understanding of the representational forms of presentation. In order to have an understanding of that which is present (nature), truth must appear. But truth reveals itself only for real consciousness. Truth arises out of the measure (the real) of nature (the measured). Indeed, truth is the fulfillment of the conditions of measurement in that the standard of measurement is appearance as understood by real consciousness. Truth is bringing that which is hidden in nature out of concealment (*Verborgenheit*). Truth as a *a-letheia* (away from the forgotten—the river Lethe as the veil over appearance) demonstrates the overcoming of forgetfulness (*Seinsvergessenheit*). The Being of beings, the presence of that which is present, are brought to the fore in a representational act. Natural consciousness is brought to real consciousness. That which is present is shown to be differed by Being such that its presence is known in its truth. Truth appears in the Being of beings, for truth is the self-realization of the ontological difference.

Merleau-Ponty would reserve the presence of truth for the lived phenomenon. The appearance is also the knowing. Truth cannot wait for real consciousness to bring about an understanding of the presence of that which is present. For Merleau-Ponty, truth has its origins in visibility. According to the pre-1959 working notes, what circulates as *The Visible and the Invisible* could have been entitled "The Origin of Truth" or "Genealogy of the True." Indeed, from the early 1950s Merleau-Ponty had been working on a theory of truth or at least a study of its origins and development. Truth is grounded in pre-objective Being. Its appearance is visibility itself. But truth in this sense is the fulfillment and realization of nature. Nature's visibility is called corporeality in the earlier view, and established as "inter-mondial" in the later position. Truth need not appear to a real consciousness in order to bring about this visibility *qua* natural interworld. The sources and manifestations of truth are in the chiasm of the visible and the invisible, which corresponds to the Heideggerian ontological difference and which carries the name of visibility, but which is already present in beings and in that which is present.

For Merleau-Ponty, knowing the truth is not formalized. Consciousness is achieved in the act, as he showed with Bukharin making his choice in favor of the party and against his own objective factual condition. Here philosophical knowledge becomes true in its own self-denial. By refusing autonomy for itself, philosophy announces the truth of the world. By becoming non-philosophy, philosophical knowledge takes on the style and prose of the world.

(8) *Experience*. In Heidegger's understanding of Hegel, the appearance of truth is both experience and experienced. Experience gathers itself together by attending to the immediate present—not to the future, nor to the past. The presence of the present when represented by natural consciousness to real consciousness as truth is experienced within the temporal present (*Gegenwart*). In other words, experience becomes the absoluteness of the absolute by bringing to presence that which is present. In this *Ereignis*—presenting that which is present to presence or appropriating the absolute—experience brings truth to light.

For Heidegger, experience remains inaccessible to natural consciousness. Experience is both real and the principal activity of real consciousness. It cannot be known as an object, as an element of nature —nor can it be known as pure Idea. Experience is the beingness that arises out of the Being of beings. Hence, experience is the truth of the ontological difference.

In response to Heidegger's understanding of Hegel's "Introduction" to *The Phenomenology of Mind*, Merleau-Ponty emphasizes the importance of experience as *praxis*. *Praxis*, for Merleau-Ponty, *is* the absolute; and the absolute is nature, visibility, the phenomenal field. Hence, as in the case of presentation, representation, and consciousness, experience does not separate itself off from that which is present. Experience is not "in-between" (*dia*) Being and beings, but rather "throughout" it. The task of the philosopher who seeks to interrogate the world is to experience what appears in order to participate in the absolute. Where Merleau-Ponty wishes to interrogate the world, Heidegger questions Being. Just as the *Seinsfrage* crosses out the inscription of Being,[10] philosophy denies itself as experience apart from the world. What is different is that, for Merleau-Ponty, philosophy moves toward and becomes the experience of the world, while for Heidegger philosophy questions the Being of beings. In other words, instead of questioning Being, Merleau-Ponty interrogates the world. In Merleau-Ponty's view, experience is the delineation of the ambiguous truth of life itself.

(9) *Phenomenology*. Since phenomenology is the study of appearances, we are returned to the question of the first triad: appearance taken as the standard of measurement. In fact, we can carry out the necessary examination only because experience is the standard. Experience, as we have seen, is the truth brought about by a real consciousness of nature. Experience, however, also depends upon a presentation of the appearance of that which is present. Seen from this third perspective, the presentation is phenomenological, but its performance does not simply present that which is. It reveals the truth of that which is in its ontological status. Indeed, phenomenology is the truth of experience.

Phenomenology, in Heidegger's understanding, is the project which seeks to know the absolute as absolute. The absolute is known through real consciousness as it represents itself in a presentation of what is generally available to natural consciousness. The real consciousness of the absolute establishes the truth of what appears. Phenomenology gathers together the truth of what appears in order to understand it. Thus although Heidegger speaks of the "end of philosophy" (in his interpretation of Hegel and Nietzsche), he does not reject philosophizing himself. Phenomenology *qua* philosophy is that which both brings knowledge of the world and explores the world of knowledge. Phenomenology can affirm that experience is the true experience of presence.

In "Philosophy and Non-Philosophy Since Hegel," as in *The Visible and the Invisible*, Merleau-Ponty reorients the specifically phenomenological character of his enterprise. We find claims to the appearance of the absolute and visibility, but we learn that the absolute is also the phenomenon. In *Phenomenology of Perception*, the absolute would have been the phenomenal field with its circuits of existence, its intentional arcs, and its corporeal expressivity. In his final writings, the absolute is the realization of a perceptual faith which goes by the name of pre-objective Being and which we know only by living through it. Knowledge of what appears is the experience of what appears. As consciousness unravels its truth, it does so at the level of experience. Experience, for Merleau-Ponty, is phenomenology become *praxis*. Living, expressing, and acting are philosophy at work, philosophy negating itself as separate philosophy.

This philosophy bears no resemblance to that of the tradition. We find no Platonic ideas, no Aristotelean observation, no Cartesian sceptical rationality, no Kantian critique. . . . What appears is philosophy that has denied its theoretical stance in order to be its greatest achievement. This dialectical phenomenology is a non-philosophy—thought become the texture of an inter-human world of experience—the world of Dante, Shakespeare, and Beethoven, but also of the "common" man.

In this third triad, truth, for Heidegger, is shown to be the full appearance of beings as presented in the relation to Being. The experience of truth is the understanding which phenomenology can bring to the study of the presence of that which is present. Merleau-Ponty's position, however, is that one need not come so far in order to recover the things themselves. Phenomenology is a return to pre-objective Being by a perceptual faith which cannot allow for a forgetting of the Being. On the contrary, phenomenology is authentic only when it negates itself and becomes the experience of the world. Its truth is in the style of the world as it makes itself visible and as we enter into its visibility. This double articulation is the intertwining of visible and invisible, Being and non-being, philosophy and non-philosophy.

CONCLUSION

In our tripartite triadic structure, philosophy (questioning) follows the Heideggerian path of Hegel interpretation. Along the way we have shown (a) the inadequacy of appearance as a standard of measurement in relation to that which is measured, i.e., the ontic realm, (b) the reorientation of such presentations as representations, which natural consciousness makes available for real consciousness, and (c) the fullest understanding of that which is present as placed representationally within the ontological difference and as realized at the site of that difference. The name of this latter understanding is phenomenology. By contrast, in Merleau-Ponty's interrogation of the Hegelian dialectic, (a) the appearance of the absolute is its own standard of measurement, (b) the representation of real consciousness is visibility within nature and is distinguishable from real consciousness, and (c) philosophical self-negation becomes experience as the texture of the world. The name of this latter self-negation is non-philosophy.

The purpose of our study has been to juxtapose two readings of Hegel so that we could read the readings and so that their identical tasks could be established as the place of their difference from each other. Merleau-Ponty's continued struggle against a tradition that allows for the separation between nature and reality, objectivity and subjectivity, appearance and truth is evident in his response to Heidegger's position. Even in his later writings, Heidegger is also struggling to show that to fall into the ontic, inauthentic, realm of beings forces us to forget the ontological difference which brings the truth of our experience and demonstrates the vocation of phenomenology. The Heideggerian fall, however, is at the same time a call to stand up again in the opening (*Lichtung*), to experience what a natural consciousness does not understand. The Merleau-Pontean leap into the texture of the world, with its corporeality, and its visibility is hardly a fall. It is an achievement: the success of Western philosophy which negates itself in order to live, to understand, and to act. The truth of the ontological difference is the experience of visibility.

8

RE-READING
MERLEAU-PONTY

In *Philosophy and Non-Philosophy since Hegel* (1960–1),[1] Merleau-Ponty reassesses the European philosophical tradition which highlights the names of Hegel, Marx, Nietzsche, Kierkegaard, Husserl, Heidegger, and Sartre. His problematic is the status of philosophy in relation to its non-philosophical sources and goals. I shall propose that *Philosophy and Non-Philosophy since Hegel*, Merleau-Ponty's last course, elaborates a thematic which is both critical to his earlier philosophical activity and transitional to the increasingly significant "structuralist" perspectives—even to their current "post-structuralist" phases. The central role that Merleau-Ponty's thought plays is decentered into its actual expression just as much as his positions demand particularized formulations in order to be understood. Thus Merleau-Ponty's influence cannot be revealed only through explicit references to his name and writings. Rather what concerns us is the conceptual dissemination: his collaboration and "quarrels" with Sartre, his characterization of behaviorism, freudianism, and gestalt psychology, his response to the 1937 Stalin purge trials, his existentialized conception of Husserlian phenomenology, and his rethinking of philosophy in its history. These elements of a philosopher in the making—*se faisant* as he said of Bergson—are reconstituted in the light of Saussurian linguistics (which Merleau-Ponty taught at the Ecole Normale Supérieure in 1948–9), Lévi-Strauss's structural anthropology (the subject of an essay entitled "From Mauss to Claude Lévi-Strauss" which was first published in 1959), Lacan's neofreudianism (referred to in *Consciousness and the Acquisition of Language* of 1949–50), Althusser's break with the young Marx (signalled in the *Adventures of the Dialectic* of 1955 and especially *Philosophy and Non-Philosophy since Hegel*), and the revived return to an archeological Hegel in the forms Foucault offers (developed out of Hyppolite's commentaries and essays). As for the post-Merleau-Ponteans (Derrida, Lyotard, and Deleuze), invoking philosophy as becoming non-philosophy by inscribing itself in our own lives is echoed throughout grammatological traces, libidinal economies, and rhyzomal dispersions. This Merleau-Pontean context, as transformed into a multiplicity of texts, continues to announce its presence as ambiguous radicalism (and radical ambiguity) within considerations of language, anthropology, psychoanalysis, political theory, and history. By entering these various disciplines, by passing through their domains of expertise, by thinking their content, and by bringing understanding out of them, philosophy can reach its fullest achievement as non-philosophy. Non-philosophy is philosophy rendered experiential. What must be shown is how philosophy *qua* conceptualization can become absolute in the various realms of our practical life.

I PHILOSOPHY BECOMING EXPERIENCE

Merleau-Ponty's sudden death in 1961 has been described, on various occasions, as the termination of a thought in the act of becoming. To substantiate the point, we were first presented with *The Visible and the Invisible* (1964), that monument to the survival of ontology in an age when the whole domain was about to be relegated to an archive somewhere. Then for those of us who did not hear him at the Collège de France, summaries of his courses from 1952 to 1960 were published as *Themes from the Lectures* (1968). Finally, *The Prose of the World* appeared in 1969 with a philosophy of language, developed in the early 1950s, but announced previously only in essays now found in *Signs* (1960) and in some early courses, such as *Consciousness and the Acquisition of Language* (1949–50).[2]

Could we have expected that there was more to come? The answer is given in the form of a response to those who might have also wondered what Merleau-Ponty would have entered in the

Collège de France Bulletin at the end of 1961—*Themes from the Lectures* ends with 1960. The content of the answer is now given in terms of working lecture notes entitled *Philosophy and Non-Philosophy since Hegel*,[3] published by Claude Lefort. Merleau-Ponty's work in the year of his death establishes not only themes and concerns that occupied him many years earlier, but also new directions of thought. In both cases, however, the pervading interest was for philosophy to accomplish what he took to be its ultimate task: becoming experience.

Of the two posthumous books *The Visible and the Invisible* and *The Prose of the World*, the latter was written earlier, specifically in the year or so prior to *In Praise of Philosophy*,[4] his inaugural Collège de France lecture delivered in January 1953. In one sense, then, *The Prose of the World* cannot be regarded as chronologically representative of Merleau-Ponty's final philosophical position. In another sense, the formulations of the early 1950s are also expressions of a position taken a decade later. The problematic of *In Praise of Philosophy* is concerned with the dialectic of history and philosophy (Hegel and Marx; Marx and Hegel) resolving itself into an ambiguity of philosophy and absolute being. From the Hegel who identifies philosophy and history "by making philosophy the understanding of historical experience, and history the becoming of philosophy" (*Praise*, p.48) to the young Marx who said that "one 'destroys' philosophy as a detached mode of knowing, only to 'realize' it in actual history" (*Praise*, p.51), we find the basis for the recovery of meaning that takes possession of itself, through philosophy, in the "fecund moments" of experience (*Praise*, p.58). We are told that the philosopher takes a distance (the Heideggerian interpretation of the Husserlian *epoché* as "stepping back") in order to see a meaning; it "comes to itself only by ceasing to coincide with what is expressed" (*Praise*, p.58). But if philosophy remains at a distance, this *pensée de survol* (overview thinking) cannot fulfill the philosopher's vocation. Philosophy cannot maintain itself outside history and common experience. Hence "in order to experience more fully the ties of truth which bind him to the world and history, the philosopher finds neither the depth of himself nor absolute knowledge but a renewed image of himself placed within it among others" (*Praise*, p.63). This earlier formulation of philosophy becoming non-philosophy is itself parallel in structure to the incarnate phenomenology of *Phenomenology of Perception* (1945). There the non-philosophical experience of spatiality, motility, and even freedom are an elaboration of a lived, pre-objective philosophy.

In *The Prose of the World*, Merleau-Ponty sought to relate Hegel's claim that the Roman state was the prose of the world to the view that "the category of Prose [goes] beyond the confines of literature to give it a sociological meaning."[5] Here the theme of transition from philosophy to non-philosophy is given expression through various types of language, from the most formal, as in the algorithm, to the most indirect, as in painting and gesture. Meaning enters into the presence of the world through language and the various forms of prose. As he had indicated in the "Preface" to *Phenomenology of Perception*, "we are condemned to meaning."[6] In *The Prose of the World*, not only is meaning expressed through prose, but prose is extended throughout the inter-world (*l'entre-monde*). Philosophical meaning then becomes the lived expressive world, a *Lebenswelt*, which does not fulfill the conditions of Husserl's transcendental reduction requiring that existence be placed in suspension. In this sense, philosophy can become what Merleau-Ponty (in 1961) characterizes as non-philosophy.

The seeds of this non-philosophy were already germinating in *The Prose of the World*. Just as he often opposes a "bad ambiguity" to a "good ambiguity,"[7] Merleau-Ponty considers (and rejects) the possibility of a non-philosophy that will be the complete annihilation and denial of philosophy. He writes: ". . . no philosophy of history has ever carried over all the reality of the present into the future or *destroyed* the self to make room for the future. Such a neurotic approach to the future would really be non-philosophy, the deliberate refusal to know *that in which one believes*."[8] Hegel certainly does not introduce history as a brute necessity which obliterates judgment and suppresses the self; on the contrary, history is their true fulfillment. Like Heidegger, Merleau-Ponty espouses a philosophy of presence. Just as Heidegger's Presence (*Anwesenheit*) has, as its ontic correlates, the present (*Gegenwart*) of presence (*Präsenz*), similarly Merleau-Ponty cannot envision philosophy finding a home solely in the future. Such a utopian outlook would deny philosophy its lived aspect. For philosophy to become non-philosophy, non-philosophy must be on-going experience, and such experience cannot be in the future.[9] The movement of intention and expression must appear now in order to fulfill the philosophical, i.e., phenomenological, enterprise. Since philosophies have dealt either with "mediating transcendences" or with "how the self makes itself world or culture which in turn must be animated by the self" (*PW*, p.84), true history must be lived and expressed in the present. Thus of the two types of non-philosophy, the one, which translates as a future in which the self is destroyed, is unacceptable. The other, described in 1961, is to be investigated within a signifying perceptual field and within a language of experience which *means* but does not *propose*.

Unlike *The Prose of the World*, Merleau-Ponty did not put aside (or abandon) *The Visible and the Invisible*.[10] Clearly it occupied his attention even in the final year of his life since the last entry of the "Working Notes" is dated March 1961 (less than two months before he died).[11] The book was to be entitled *The Origin of Truth*, for the return to origins (the *arché* and *genesis* of knowledge) would uncover the source of truth. The notes begin with the truth of being and the being of truth, which are the ontological conditions for "our state of non-philosophy" (*VI*, p.165). But what, in effect, can non-philosophy be? Merleau-Ponty proposes a dialectic between two alternative solutions (dialectics): "either the 'bad dialectic' that identifies the opposites, which is *non-philosophy*, or the 'embalmed' dialectic, which is no longer dialectical. End of philosophy or rebirth?" (*VI*, p.165). Either the dialectic selects discrete entities (facts) and hence cannot escape disparate multiplicity or it becomes solidified and devoid of movement. The very dialectic between the two alternatives: the end of philosophy (which Heidegger has proposed)[12] and the renaissance of philosophy (which philosophers tend to wish for) is inherent in the problematic itself. Is non-philosophy then a termination of and conclusion to philosophy or is it the basis for a revival? Only the former was suggested in *The Prose of the World*. In the 1959 note, a dichotomy is indicated: non-philosophy could establish either complete positivity or complete negativity. And philosophy itself might serve as the bridge between those two forms of non-philosophy.

The only other explicit reference to non-philosophy in the "Working Notes" reiterates its duality: "philosophy is not immediately non-philosophy—it rejects the positivism in non-philosophy, a militant non-philosophy—which would reduce history to the visible, would deprive it precisely of its depth under the pretext of adhering to it better: irrationlism, *Lebensphilosophie*, fascism and communism, which do indeed have philosophical meaning, but hidden from themselves" (*VI*, p.266). Philosophy looks within itself in order to fulfill itself, in order to become lived experience. As philosophy becomes non-philosophy, its self-givenness may appear in a harmonious functional form in which non-philosophy—living—is precisely what was sought by philosophy. The risk, however, is that non-philosophy may be the destruction (without possibility of renewal) of philosophy. If history is reduced to the visible, or the produced, the vital dialectic of visible and invisible cannot be realized. Since history is in production (in the making), its invisibility is as present as the specifically visible. The heart of philosophy is its *chiasm* (or intertwining) of taking and being taken, seeing and being seen, touching and being touched, perceiving and being perceived, enveloping and being enveloped. Within this mutual coincidence (*Ineinander*) (*VI*, p.268), this "identity difference of difference" (*VI*, p.264), this "interrogative ensemble" (*VI*, p.187), "the becoming-man of nature" (*VI*, p.185), leaves no space for a metaphor to occur in between (*VI*, p.221).[13]

Though some may wish to argue that the position is a new direction in Merleau-Ponty's thought—and it is true that the language has changed from the formulations of the early 1940s—the basic structure of the position is the same. What is now non-philosophy as the fulfillment of philosophy was then an "intentional arc" (*PoP*, p.136) and a circuit of existence delineating a phenomenal field, experienced as already there. Or even earlier in *The Structure of Behavior* (1942). Merleau-Ponty indicated the necessity of recognizing the originality of the dialectical pair "perceived situation-work" as much as the irreducibility of "vital situation-instinctive reaction" to the pair "stimulus-reflex."[14] Each subordinated dialectic is fulfilled as it is surpassed in another pair. Nature, life, and mind are the successive moments in a series of visible-invisible relationships. They are also the expression of philosophy becoming non-philosophy in a meaningful fashion.

The dialectic of philosophy and non-philosophy is another form of the ambiguous life which permeates Merleau-Ponty's various perspectives. In each case, the rethinking of this ambiguous domain has been central to his formulation of the dialectic. This was particularly the case in *Humanism and Terror:* "The dialectic of the subjective and the objective is not a simple contradiction which leaves the terms it plays on disjointed; it is rather a testimony to our rootedness in the truth."[15] As he was to develop in *The Visible and the Invisible*, the subjective-objective dialectic is the locus of meaning, visibility, ambiguity, truth. The revealing of truth (as in Heidegger's *Unverborgenheit*) is the bi-directionality of philosophy coming out of individual knowledge and entering into the common domain. In connection with Bukharin and the ambiguity of history, bi-directionality is expressed as the opposition between the Commissar and the Yogi: "the true nature of tragedy appears once *the same man* has understood both that he cannot disavow the objective pattern of his actions, that he is what he is for others in the context of history, and yet that the motive of his actions constitutes a man's worth as he himself experiences it. In this case we no longer have a series of alternations between the inward and the external, subjectivity and objectivity, or judgment and its means, but a dialectical relation, that is to say, a contradiction founded in truth, in which the same man tries to realize himself on the two levels" (*HT*, pp.62–3). For the same person to express both philosophy and non-philosophy is not a simple task. Yet it is the banner under which Merleau-Ponty operates both in 1947 and in 1961.

To indicate, in another area, this repetition of the same, we find the concluding passage to the essay on "Trotsky's Rationalism" delineating the Scylla and Charybdis of philosophy's move to non-philosophy. On the one hand, we find a utopianism, on the other, a dogmatic philosophy of history: "Marxism does not offer us a utopia, a future known ahead of time, nor any philosophy of history. However, it deciphers events, discovers in them a common meaning and thereby grasps a leading thread which, without dispensing us from fresh analysis at every stage, allows us to orient ourselves toward events" (*HT*, p.98). This final self-orientation toward events—similar to the "tending toward expression" by which Merleau-Ponty characterizes the child's imitative behavior—is the ultimate realization of philosophy. Philosophy cannot satisfy itself with analysis, nor even with description. For Merleau-Ponty, it must initiate a movement in the direction of actual lived experience (*Erlebnisse*). This can be accomplished through Marxist *praxis* only if one carefully interprets social phenomena. The traditional Heraclitean metaphor of life as a flowing river is here transformed into a *curriculum vitae*— a course of life—which the philosopher thinks and writes about in order for it to enter into the texture of the world. Each person must, however, enact his own course of understanding—as Merleau-Ponty did from *Humanism and Terror* to *The Prose of the World* to *The Visible and the Invisible*.

The initial phases of the basic themes, later developed in *Philosophy and Non-Philosophy Since Hegel*, were begun at the time of *The Adventures of the Dialectic* (1955).[16] or, more precisely, in 1956, when Merleau-Ponty offered his Thursday course on "Dialectical Philosophy."[17] Although a continuation of the recently published book, the lectures also explored new ground. After moving from the "fecundity of contradiction" and "the labor of the negative" in Hegel to the "subjective reflection" of Kierkegaard and Heidegger, Merleau-Ponty then turned to a "circular dialectic" in which "the *experience* of thought" undergoes a journey to learn "what was already there, 'in itself,' before reflection." This itinerary, which takes him through Hegel, Feuerbach, Marx, Kierkegaard, Heidegger, and Sartre establishes an uneasy equilibrium between the negative and the positive, the one and the many, the subjective and the objective, the null and the total. These different dialectics might be said to return eternally— as Nietzsche claims of life in general—to the same: philosophy and non-philosophy.

Each equilibrium reintroduces the question of the status of non-philosophy in its relation to philosophy. In order to clarify the question, Merleau-Ponty takes up the role of nature. His studies on nature are not to return to a physicalism. Nor is this nature precisely the *physis* of the ancients—though it is accompanied by a *logos* that seeks to know it. In Aristotle's *logos* of *physis*, the structure of the natural world is known by living in it and observing one's surroundings. However, for Merleau-Ponty, what counts is not the distance between *logos* and *physis*, but the immediacy of the former in the latter.

The interrogation of nature is philosophy's move toward nature. In contrast to classical metaphysics which establishes the distance between philosophy and nature, Merleau-Ponty's metaphysics is an ontology *of* nature, i.e., a natural ontology. In "The Possibility of Philosophy" (1959), philosophy interrogates its foundations. When it becomes evident that nature is foundational, the question arises as to whether philosophy occupies a place apart from nature? With Hegel the answer is negative—"something comes to an end" (*TL*, p.100), and philosophy is denied a special status. In the process, a philosophical void is created by the denial. The filling that Marx, Kierkegaard, and Nietzsche offer is itself a destruction of philosophy. The end of philosophy begins where philosophy becomes nature.

With the naturalization of philosophy, "we enter an age of non-philosophy. But perhaps such a destruction of philosophy constitutes its very realization. Perhaps it preserves the essence of philosophy, and it may be, as Husserl wrote, that philosophy is reborn from its ashes" (*TL*, p.100). The problem is not whether philosophy is such a phoenix, but rather how it is reborn from its ashes. The preoccupations, obscurities, equivocations, and interpretations of these post-Hegelian thinkers do not solve the problem any more than the numerous commentaries on their writings. What is philosophical in non-philosophy is not a series of recommendations for our own time. Thought can no longer provide guidelines, evaluations for present and future action. Whatever we discover in Marx, Kierkegaard, and Nietzsche, it is not a picture of how they understood their era. On the contrary, we find in them the very condition of our own time: "They live on in us rather than our having a clear perspective on them and we involve them in our own problems rather than solving theirs with ours" (*TL*, p.101).

Their philosophy of non-philosophy is to become our non-philo-sophical philosophy. The history of non-philosophy is a continual restatement of a negated metaphysics. At each moment that a philosopher refuses to accept the standard metaphysical assertions in favor of a renewed understanding of life, then non-philosophy is at work. Non-philosophy is not anti-philosophy, for the former is philosophy put to work, while the latter runs counter to the enterprise of understanding itself. By interrogating the meaning and possibility of non-philosophy, philosophy is reborn in nature and in experience. Philosophy inserts itself into everyday life such that the interrogation is a realization of our own activity. Along the path of its history, Heidegger, following Husserl, moves to interrogation—not of the *Lebenswelt* as such, but rather of the ontological conditions of existence. Merleau-Ponty's identification of Heidegger as embarking on the path of non-philosophy signals a certain change in orientation. Throughout Merleau-Ponty's work, we find explicit reference to Husserl, while the insertion of Heidegger into his corpus only a year prior to *Philosophy and Non-Philosophy since Hegel* suggests that he has made the very ontological turn which determines the direction of *The Visible and the Invisible*.

Following Heidegger, some, such as Sartre, spoke of man as negated being and the being which negates. Merleau-Ponty is aware that the early translations (by Henri Corbin) of *Dasein* as *la realité humaine* (human reality) led directly to the substitution of humanism for metaphysics. The end of philosophy was understood as the end of metaphysics. However humanism, in the sense of a philosophy of the human, would triumph. For Merleau-Ponty that was a misinterpretation. Certainly humans are implicated in the experience of the world—but they need not be glorified. Heidegger sought "through *Dasein*, to bet at Being, to analyze certain human attitudes only because man *is* the interrogation of Being" (*TL*, pp.109–10, translation revised). Human being enters into the interrogation and is interrogated along with Being. But it does not appear as an isolated entity. Humans participate in "pre-objective Being" just as much as any other essent or being. For philosophy to enter into such participation through understanding is for philosophy to become non-philosophy. By expressing and describing our living through pre-objective Being, i.e., nature, philosophy can return to what is fundamental, and hence to what is not philosophical.

If the fundamental is not philosophical, which is Merleau-Ponty's position in his 1959 course, a clarification of what is fundamental comes in the next year. *Eye and Mind*, his last publication, explores vision. Understood in terms of "visibility" in his working manuscript, vision is nature at work. Philosophy surrenders to vision as is exemplified in the activity of a painter such as Cézanne who interprets how we see by making us see.[18] Unlike thought with its Cartesian supports through construction and transformation, vision goes to the things of the world in order to uncover their sense. This necessarily corporeal vision delineates the zone of Merleau-Ponty's post-Hegelian philosophy.

Space is

> reckoned starting from me as the zero point or degree zero
> of spatiality. I do not see it according to its exterior envelope,
> I live in it from the inside; I am immersed in it. After all, the
> world is all around me, not in front of me. Light is viewed
> once more as action at a distance. It is no longer reduced to
> the action of contact or, in other words, conceived as it
> might be by those who do not see in it. Vision reassumes its
> fundamental power of showing forth more than itself.[19]

Vision enters into spatiality and participates in more than it
reveals. The task of philosophy is to take thought to the spatiality
of vision. Once there, philosophy must divest itself of its pretensions. Philosophy learns that the study of painting can teach us
how to understand the world as non-philosophy. "The painter's
vision is not a view upon the *outside*, a merely 'physical-optical'
relation with the world. The world no longer stands before him
through representation; rather it is the painter to whom the things
of the world give birth by a sort of concentration or coming-to-
itself of the visible" (*EM*, p.181). The painter reveals nature as
the emergent meaning of the visible. As Being arises, the painter
enters into the painting. On this basis, he can return to himself
in order to complete his vision, his understanding. "Vision alone
makes us learn that beings that are different, 'exterior,' foreign
to one another, are yet absolutely *together*, are 'simultaneity' "
(*EM*, p.187). The unity of beings is the unity that philosophy
seeks to know, but which it can know only by experiencing them
in their spatiality and visibility.

   Merleau-Ponty finds an unmediated expression of Being in
literature which is similar to the "meaning of the visible" in
painting, for they both activate an "intentional arc." From among
his writings in 1961, Merleau-Ponty left five notes on the novelist
Claude Simon.[20] The three principal themes of these notes, (1)
vision, (2) *Vorhaben*, and (3) the felt, are reformulations of the
same experience. One asserts: "To see is to allow us to avoid
thinking a thing, *since we see it*" (*Entre Fiens*, p.42). Cartesianism
requires that whatever is thought be included in the *cogito*. The
cogito cannot itself allow us to enter the world of things in order
to see them. We must in fact suspend our thoughtful judgement
in order to perceive what is there. Vision is itself a grasping of

what is already there (*vorhaben*). To speak of the *Vorhabe* as pre-objective experience is to include what is imaginary as well as perceptual. In both cases, the task of the novelist is to describe what is felt. Without the work (*le travail*) of the novelist, "feeling, living, and sensorial experience are not worth anything. Work does not involve simply the conversion of the lived into words, but rather *making what is felt speak*" (*Entre Fiens*, p.45). The philosopher is also engaged in making what is felt speak—but not in sensorial language. The philosopher must return to experience in order to develop the language of experience. But that language is an elaboration of whatever achieves meaning in our daily lives.

II PHILOSOPHY AND NON-PHILOSOPHY

Merleau-Ponty's 1960–1 course explores the relationship between philosophy and non-philosophy in two distinct parts. In the first portion, after some introductory remarks concerning the appearance of the absolute, he identifies the absolute with the phenomenon, establishes the relationship between knowledge and experience, proposes a phenomenological dialectic, develops the place of self-consciousness, and indicates Hegel's failure to link philosophy and non-philosophy. The second part focuses on stages in Marx, immediate philosophy, Marx's critique of Hegel, the possibilities of praxis, Marx as philosopher, and the relationships between thought, man, and nature. Although Merleau-Ponty is moving toward a unified thematic, the cryptic form of the work makes this difficult to perceive readily. The directions that he had developed prior to 1961 all point to the possibility of philosophy becoming non-philosophy. First Hegel, then Marx, serve as the means of articulating this movement.

In exploring Hegel's "Introduction" to the *Phenomenology of Mind*, the absolute appears in such a way that the phenomenon is the whole truth. Since the phenomenon must appear, its manner of appearance encompasses all that is, i.e., the absolute. This means that philosophy cannot present itself in any way other than as non-philosophy. Philosophy must be engaged in questioning. Heidegger's understanding of the question of Being and Sartre's discovery of the origin of negation in the interrogative attitude establish characteristic modes of philosophical questioning. In

Nietzsche's claim that the Greeks knew how to live, the stress on appearance as life manifesting itself places them at the level of the phenomenon, at the level of non-philosophy. Philosophy, through its questioning, interprets and thereby transfigures what is lived.

In order to interpret experience, philosophy sets itself apart from experience. When Nietzsche proposes the absolute of appearance, he sets the stage for Heidegger to claim that the absolute is "a-philosophy" and for the Sartre of *Critique de la raison dialectique* to assert that Marxist *praxis* offers the best example of an unsurpassed philosophy. Accordingly philosophy for Heidegger and Sartre becomes non-philosophy, experience, life.

Philosophy has no access to the absolute through understanding (*Erkennen*). Understanding, which seeks to know the absolute, requires some instrument or medium by which it can approach the absolute *qua* appearance. In mediating between the philosopher and the absolute, understanding serves as an indicator of appearance. However, it reveals only an empty space or a pure directionality. Because of this mediating function, understanding cannot succeed in bringing out the appearance in its absolute form. As a substitute for understanding *qua* mediating function, we would have to become understanding itself. This could be accomplished in history if life were to make itself into a type of knowledge and knowledge were to make itself into life. In that way, the relationship between the absolute and our acquaintance with it would be realized in our own experience.

To accomplish this task, a recognition of the identity of the phenomenon with the absolute is required. Philosophy is not understanding because philosophy demands that understanding perform a mediating function. If understanding mediates, then acquaintance-knowledge (Bertrand Russell's formula for *Erkennen*) of the absolute will differ from the appearance of the absolute. For the absolute to be true, it must be known in its truth and it must appear in its truth. Furthermore, understanding must be the manner of revealing the truth of the absolute. Thus revealing the phenomenon is presence of the absolute.

In the appearance of the absolute, natural consciousness seeks to be the real accomplishment of knowledge. However, since there is also a *natural* unconscious, which Merleau-Ponty attributes to

Marx as well as to Freud, knowledge cannot grasp the totality of the phenomenon. The structure of consciousness is such that the phenomenon is not fully revealed. Because the phenomenon is both in relation to itself and in relation to the external world, a chiasm is formed. By this chiasm, consciousness interweaves the phenomenon within its natural context. "Nature," which was the theme for Merleau-Ponty's lectures in 1957–9, provides an environment whereby consciousness can be its own concept, but not its own self-realization. Consciousness must also become nature in order for it to realize itself in addition to manifesting its identity.

Such a consciousness is engaged in negation. What is negated is not the for-itself, as in Sartre. According to Sartre, the for-itself negates itself so as to give itself a being which it is not and to project beyond that being. But its projects define itself as another in-itself. The operations of consciousness force the in-itself into transcendent objectification. For Merleau-Ponty, consciousness negates in order to affirm its own movement to a new form of being and expression. In this way, the intertwining of the relation to self with the relation to the external world is a dynamic orientation toward an unfulfilled self-realization and not a denial of true identity as in Sartre. Its *telos* is to be unified with itself and nature. But since that unification is not possible, consciousness must be unhappy. As long as it remains unhappy, divided within itself, and alienated, it cannot become the absolute unification that it seeks.

What appears out of this impossibility for consciousness to achieve unification is the intentionality of consciousness. Intentionality is itself experience (*Erfahrung*)—but it is a restless experience. It is never content in that it continues to delineate the chiasm (the intertwining). As long as the chiasm exists, a polarity will be found within natural consciousness. The measure of experience, then, will be the identification of what is measured and that by which it is measured. This binary opposition between *mésurant* and *mésuré* parallels that of the *signifiant* and *signifié* in a semiological formulation. Since the standard of measurement cannot be what is measured, the measurement *qua* experience or knowledge cannot be the appearance of the absolute. The absolute must remain unachieved.

To measure consciousness is to make it a mediated intuition.

But if it were a mediated intuition, how could consciousness learn anything? On the one hand, consciousness is the standard of measurement and the external world is measured in order to establish what consciousness knows. In the first case, consciousness is philosophical, in the second, consciousness is natural. Since, however, these two types of consciousness can exchange their roles, they can each be subject or object for the other. They are the same for each other—even though together they cannot be absolute, for measurement is the denial of the absolute.

For the attainment of the absolute, knowledge must be experience. But in order for this to be true, knowledge must undergo a transformation. Knowledge, that is knowledge of the object, is insufficient. After the dichotomy between subject and object, and between the standard of measurement and what is measured, what remains is "a pure act of vision." Though Merleau-Ponty finds this formulation in Hegel, it is repeated in his own work: the surpassing of these dichotomies is visibility, or, to put it otherwise, ambiguity. Both visibility and ambiguity are restatements of intentionality, the dual process which unifies the opposition within it. The bi-directionality of standard of measurement to what is measured and vice versa establishes the relation as pure unmediated experience.

The exchange between standard of measurement and what is measured is dialectical. The dialectic arises out of the tension between the relation to self and the relation to a transcendent object. This dual relation characterizes the function of consciousness, which accomplishes its tasks through experience. Such experience is ambiguous (*zweideutig*) in that its many meanings are unified in a synthetic activity.

If we examine the role of ambiguity in this connection, we find that it is at once phenomenological and dialectical. It is phenomenological in that consciousness comprehends itself in a moment. That moment is the full revelation of the phenomenon as neither object nor subject but as "the co-givenness of both" (*für dasselbe*). Consciousness stands out as meaning: the signification of the relation as the appearing of appearances. Since nothing can enter phenomenology from the outside, it is unmediated. As a description of experience, phenomenology brings out the various dimensions and aspects of that experience as it takes place.

Ambiguity is also dialectical in that it moves in two directions, integrating whatever enters its path and surpassing itself by preserving its own integrity. As dialectic, ambiguity is the operation of knowledge (*Wissen*) upon the object and the object delimiting the extent of knowledge. The dialectical relation is surpassed in experience itself. What remains is the ambiguous totality that is no longer differentiated. In its totality, the dialectic forms the absolute. Merleau-Ponty illustrates this notion of the absolute by mentioning the historical conditions underlying the purge trials of 1937, which he had discussed at length in *Humanism and Terror*. Here experience has brought out the ambiguous alternatives and resolved them into the nakedness of events, i.e., the absolute of appearance.[21]

A consciousness that is truly self-conscious, Merleau-Ponty claims, is empty. The case in point is Hegel's assumption that his own self-consciousness (which would be analogous to the bourgeois state) is identical with consciousness in general (which would be similar to the state). But the bourgeois state cannot fulfill itself (become fully aware of itself) if it assumes that it is the state. The state must be conscious (i.e., appear in consciousness). Since consciousness permeates what appears through experience, it must permeate the state. The state cannot be limited to its determination of itself as the bourgeois state would do. Therefore, the bourgeois state is not fully self-conscious.

Because experience operates within a total situation, *praxis* must *be* the absolute (full consciousness in self-consciousness). To become itself, consciousness must tear itself away from itself so that it may participate in the absolute. Although consciousness "designates" absolute knowledge, it can only become that absolute by entering into it experientially, by practicing it in action.

Though Hegel sets up the move to the absolute through consciousness, he does not link philosophy and non-philosophy. Both the relation to the self and the relation to the external world are preserved. Consciousness remains ambiguous without the necessary experiential unification. The absolute here is absolute negation or absolute affirmation. It cannot be both at the same time. Yet for philosophy to become non-philosophy, experience of the world as an appearance, it cannot maintain the disjunction between affirmation and negation. That disjunction signals the continuance of philosophy and the refusal of non-philosophy. For the possibility of non-philosophy, pure *praxis* must take place. Here neither affirmative nor negative judgement can play a part—only experience in its fullness is necessary. Since Hegel is still involved in negation and positive surpassing, one must look beyond him for the requisite move to the absolute.

The early Marx is Hegelian in orientation, attempting to reform philosophy by dissociating himself from Feuerbach. Merleau-Ponty refers to this point in Marx's development as the "philo-sophical" or "pre-Marxist" period and argues that it is followed by a break with philosophy as a form of alienation.[22] Two problems characterize this change. First, in the early period, views which are reminiscent of Feuerbach are mixed with those which are non-Feuerbachian. For example, we find the claim that the destruction of philosophy must be its realization and its realization must destroy philosophy. The latter formulation cannot be simply a return to speculative philosophy. It must mean that philosophy is itself transformed—a position which Feuerbach did not take. Thus inherent in the early Marx are signs of a move to non-philosophy.

The second problem concerns the role of a Hegelian dialectic in the case where socialism is to be scientific. If philosophy has become socialism in its rigorous and non-utopian form, has Hegel's method also been excluded? If so, can the move to non-philosophy maintain its signification and importance, or is philos-ophy reified and excluded (as a positivism), rather than reinte-grated in another form? Merleau-Ponty would wish to support the dialectical reintegration. Thus to those who charge Marx with not having written a *Logic*, the answer that *Capital* is its substitute can indeed provide a basis for understanding Marx's later project. In the orientation toward appearance by means of essence, we find a reconstruction of experience. The structure of that movement is fully Hegelian. Hence the scientific socialism proposed through *Capital* is actually philosophy following out the movements of experience. The later Marx is therefore both the refusal and the reintegration of his earlier philosophy.

Merleau-Ponty attempts to understand this reunification by asking whether it is a question of logic (*Sache der Logik*) or a logic of the thing in question (*Logik der Sache*). If it is a question of logic, then it has little importance for the material conditions at work in society. If, however, it is a logic of the thing in question, where what is in question is historical materialism, then the project

139

for philosophy is to become that logic which brings out the very thing in question. In reformulating the lived ambiguity, what is to be surpassed here is the distinction between idea and thing. In history, the difference becomes the identity of the thing in question with its intrinsic logic.

Such an identity of the thing in question with its logic goes by the name of immediate philosophy. Here philosophy is unavailable for mediation. When Hegel understands and conceptualizes experience, the absolute is self-presentational, self-enclosed, and self-defining. It is mediated only by its affirmation of itself as absolute. With this affirmation, the absolute gives itself as true. The movement of truth brings consciousness. Consciousness renders the truth of the absolute evident for itself. But since this movement is pure conceptualization for Hegel, Marx's mandate is to return to immediate philosophy. With Marx, experience no longer becomes philosophy, conceptualization, and self-presentation. Now philosophy becomes experience, pure movement, and immediate philosophy.

At the same time that the Marx of *Capital* believes he has abandoned philosophy by presenting the realities of inter-human economic relations, in effect he has rediscovered philosophy in its experiential form. The negation of philosophy is its revival as non-philosophy. Realizing non-philosophy is the fulfillment of philosophy becoming world and the recognition that it is no longer necessary for the world to become philosophy. What was self-consciousness is now *praxis*, for *praxis* is philosophy in its immediacy. Where Narcissus required the river in order to see himself, self-consciousness is mediated by its conceptualization of itself. In *praxis*, Narcissus no longer looks at himself in order to know himself. Now he goes for a swim. . . . Conception becomes action within concrete conditions.

Such a reversal involves an implicit critique of Hegel. However, Marx also engages in an explicit critique. His writings in 1843 and 1844 revise Hegel in favor of embodied man and non-philosophy. The movement toward the realization of incarnate reality and the movement from philosophy to non-philosophy represent an identical directionality. Where the Hegelian philosophy was a philosophy of the concept and thought, the Marxian formulation is the presumed denial of philosophy *per se* and the introduction of *praxis* as the inheritor of absolute knowledge. The absolute

140

therefore becomes bodily experience, that is, openness to material need, exchange, and alienation. Since *praxis* is both "the head and heart of the Revolution," Marx views philosophy as a hindrance to the realization of the Revolution. However, if philosophy becomes non-philosophy, then *praxis* can operate freely within the historical reality that founds it.

The move from philosophy to non-philosophy is not a pure denial of philosophy as such. Rather it is a reunion of philosophy with non-philosophy, in which a philosophy of the concept will no longer dominate over a philosophy of experience. Philosophy is not therefore annihilated. On the contrary, it achieves life through negation. The negation of philosophy *qua* non-philosophy is both the failure and the realization of philosophy. When the specific relation between philosophy and world has been overturned (*verkehrt*), the world and its problems prevail.

The Marxian critique of Hegel rejects the non-engagement that is characteristic of the Hegelian State. An action which evolves according to the highest principles is an intellectual's *praxis*. Such *praxis* is anti-philosophical (not non-philosophical) and hence it is another form of philosophy. What it requires above all is a realization of its possibilities in the proletariat, not in the conceptual realm. Merleau-Ponty speaks of this realization as the positive possibility of the German emancipation in the proletariat. What he means is that the full freedom of the proletariat in Germany, as envisioned by Marx, is also the fulfillment of philosophy as a meaningful enterprise. With the proletariat as "universal spirit" (*Weltgeist*) comes negativity (reaction against the bourgeoisie) and a dialectical union of philosophy and the proletariat. The proletariat negates its oppressor; philosophy negates its conceptual orientation.

The superstructure needed to carry out the movement of negativity is not a philosophy of consciousness, but a philosophy of incarnate human being. Thus we find mirrored in the Marxian critique of Hegel, the Merleau-Pontean response to Husserl.[23] Just as Hegel integrates phenomenology into knowledge as soon as he sees that he is part of that knowledge (what appears is known for the self), Marx returns to his early essays in order for them to become true in *Capital* and in its self-surpassing, i.e., the denial of capitalist production.

In *Capital*, Marx has moved from reality (the actual capitalist conditions of production) to appearance (the proletariat which comes into view as an oppressed class). The task of *Capital* is to give a basis to proletarian philosophy as a movement of things. It also brings about a consciousness of separation between the *de facto* proletariat and the philosophico-historical function which conditions it.

For Marx *qua* philosopher the task is to provide critique, which Merleau-Ponty sees as taking four forms: (1) the critique of philosophical exhaustiveness, i.e., philosophy cannot cover existence in its entirety; (2) a critique of the pretensions of self-consciousness, i.e., by knowing oneself one does not know all of one's historical and material conditions; (3) a critique of the negation of negation, i.e., the success of the proletariat will be an affirmation and not another negation; and (4) the critique of objectivity, i.e., objectivity is an alienation of subjectivity in the object.

The Marxist philosopher recognizes that his true *Dasein* is in nature. Nature is the locus in which the man's existence is realized as ambiguous. This ambiguity is not the "bad" ambiguity of contradiction and duality in subjectivity and objectivity. This ambiguity indicates a multiplicity of meanings unified through experience in concrete situations. When object-being is alienated, consciousness has ground for action. However when consciousness is experienced as pure object-being, it loses its range of possibilities. Self-affirmation is dependent upon the recognition of one's alienated state. Alienation arises when the self responds to the will of the other, which denies the selfness of the first. This type of negativity, which Hegel called the desire of the other as it occurs in the master-slave relation, is nevertheless the ground for the possibility of self-affirmation in a concrete socio-historical context.

In Hegel, nature and man are extracted from thought (*Denken*). Hence, thinking and pure knowledge are primary. However, if reversed, if nature or man were predicated upon consciousness, the problem would still not be rectified. What is needed is a single being in which negativity can operate. This singularity, repeated in Sartre's "singular universal,"[24] has the character of ambiguity without the divisive aspects of duality and multiplicity. Marx would understand such a being to be concrete reality informed by history with signification.

Nature is transformed in the movement of history by "sensuous-practical man," that is, by a meaning-laden human *praxis* which takes on a carnal, "material" shape. While history is produced by man, it also produced him. Merleau-Ponty quotes Jean Hyppolite as claiming that "human nature will resolve itself after the resolution of historical conflict." Once we recognize that man's self-estrangement and self-consciousness are not reserved for the mind, we see that they are realized only in surpassing (*aufheben*) history. As a self-surpassing and a self-conserving process, man's true being is revealed within nature's movements. The advances and retreats of non-philosophy occur within history and nature in such a way that philosophy surrenders its autonomy in order to live as flash in the world.

Where philosophy for Hegel was the absolute appearing in experience, that experience remained a phenomenon in thought. The presence of philosophy at work provides a place for Hegelian thinking. Non-philosophy for Hegel can, at most, be another type of negation within thought. With Marx, however, the reversal, by which philosophy becomes historical experience, *praxis*, and the concrete, is a revitalization of philosophy. This revitalization does not occur as philosophy, but rather as non-philosophy, the historical conditions of embodied human beings confronted with the realities of exchange and alienation. However, by rendering these conditions evident, philosophy is revived like a phoenix through and out of non-philosophy.

III THE DISSEMINATION OF CENTRALITY

The reconstruction of phenomenology that accompanies Merleau-Ponty's work is based in an understanding of Husserl, Heidegger, and Sartre. We cannot trace the full development of this reconstruction here, though its outlines can be sketched. The presence of a transcendental ego in Husserl as the condition, and source, of all intentional acts give the self and hence all philosophical reflection a well-defined central point of emanation.[25] Heidegger replaces the focus on the transcendental ego with an emphasis on the movement between Being and beings. Interpretation and the ontological difference alter the point of attention from the starting-point to the intentional relation of in-betweenness, where neither subjectivity nor objectivity prevail.[26] The Sartrian appeal to the transcendence of the ego[27] is a response to both the pure subjectivity claim and the intermediary postulate. For Sartre, what might have been called a *center* in the tradition is now regarded phenomenologically as "nothingness."[28] If a self can be identified as such, one must look to each transcendent ego that is taken as the object of a reflective act. Such selves, however, are outside consciousness and, therefore, false versions of the self. It would be bad faith to deny them. Only the unreflected or pre-reflective *cogito* might serve as a place for the truth of the self. Yet a non-place, non-entity cannot be regarded as a center. The philosophizing self finds its identity in its projects and possibilities and in the transcendent forms of its self-expression. The latter remain, in effect, a third alternative to the Husserlian and Heideggerian conceptions of self.

Merleau-Ponty moves to combine all three alternatives. His reconstruction of the immediate tradition—as well as that of Nietzsche, Marx, and Hegel, whom he discusses explicitly in *Philosophy and Non-Philosophy since Hegel*—is the basis for his own articulation of the self as ambiguous.[29] Here the self is regarded as the unifying source, the intentional activity, and the worldly transcendent form of the person. Philosophy becomes experience and hence a type of non-philosophy because it is the enactment of signification in operation delineating the incarnate importance of the individual in an intermundane context. Significations are gathered together as the expressive manifestations of consciousness in the self's relations with others.

This reconstruction is the basis for *praxis* and action. The philosophizing self cannot be isolated, cannot simply be interpretive understanding, and cannot be only a series of reflected beings-in-themselves. The philosophizing self must bring the consciousness of its own activity to action itself and that action must be philosophy in the style and form of non-philosophy.

Although Merleau-Ponty's elaboration of philosophy becoming experience can be regarded as a useful unification of what is present in his immediate tradition, what, on the other hand, is the place of his writings in the expressions of thought that have followed in the wake of his death? We may regard the post-Merleau-Pontean formulation of the movement toward "non-philosophy" as the "decentering of philosophy."

While Merleau-Ponty argues for a multiplicity of significations delineating our human experience, structuralists insist upon signs and structures. That two of Merleau-Ponty's books announce these same notions is not irrelevant. The first work, *The Structure of Behavior* (1942), refers to structures as the basis for a system of human behavior. *Signs* (1960), on the other hand, presents the signs of contemporary life at the linguistic, sociological, literary, and political level.

What is both peculiar and important in the discussion of structures and signs is expressed by the two thinkers most fundamental for post-Merleau-Pontean perspectives: Ferdinand de Saussure and Claude Lévi-Strauss. Even though the former made his principal contribution (*The Course in General Linguistics*[30]) in the first decade of this century and the latter published his principal study (*Elementary Structures of Kinship*[31]) in 1947, their renown predominates largely in the 1960s.

For de Saussure, a sign is the combination of a signifier (word) and a signified (concept). Signification is the act or process of relating signifier to signified in relation to a value system of other signs. Such a system of signs would be *langue*. When spoken or activated at a particular moment, *parole* is given expression. In combination, the speaking (*parole*) of a particular language (*langue*) gives rise to a system of use-signs, i.e., a *langage*. A *langage* is the manifestation of significatory signs within a system. Such a unity of multiplicity does not, however, establish a center. Any philosophical formulation that is in this way semiological will find itself proliferated throughout the system.

Similarly in structural anthropology, structures are formed by a combination of elements that are repeatable in different times and/or places. That which operates their production, whether in myth, kinship, or ritual, will not be a fixed, locatable subjectivity. Rather, the savage mind, as Lévi-Strauss later calls it, will reproduce itself throughout cultural products.

These two approaches within the human sciences cannot be regarded as philosophical expression. In fact, some emphasize that structuralism is a methodology and not a philosophy. If it were to be a philosophy, it could be termed "ideology" or theory. As long as it remains a *praxis* of semiological and structural operations, its status as a decentered philosophy (what Merleau-Ponty calls "non-philosophy") can be maintained.

In the work of de Saussure, Lévi-Strauss and their followers, we find a field of inquiry in common with Merleau-Ponty's interrogations. Sartre's essay on Merleau-Ponty in the special issue of *Les Temps Modernes* (1961) points to this decentered space: "He buried himself in the night of non-knowledge, in search of what he then called 'the fundamental'."[32] Sartre selects a passage from "De Mauss à Lévi-Strauss" in *Signs* to make his point. He writes: "What is of interest to the philosopher (in anthropology) is precisely that it takes man as he is, in his effective situation in life and knowledge. The philosopher interested in anthropology is not one who wants to explain or construct the world, but he who aims at inserting us more deeply into being" (S:M-P, p.211). In Merleau-Ponty's move to non-philosophy, he finds philosophy appearing in various forms of life, such as those examined by structural anthropology.

The interest in entering deeply into being is not limited to linguistics and anthropology. It also arises notably in literary criticism (Barthes), psychoanalysis (Lacan), political theory (Althusser), and the history of ideas (Foucault).

Roland Barthes distributes philosophical subjectivity throughout the surfaces of literary expression. His championing of Robbe-Grillet and other *nouveau romanciers* illustrates his orientation toward the representation of geometrical relations circumscribing the production of human acts and relations without identifying a localized human subjectivity. *The Voyeur* announces a murder.[33] We follow the expressed elements of a series of relations—an island, cigarette butts, the nape of a woman's neck, etc. Nowhere, however, do we find the establishment of a subjective perspective. Knowledge is dispersed throughout the elements of material, geometrical, geographical, interhuman relations. Events are recounted as an inventory of real consciousness distributed throughout Nature.

Barthes's own criticism also moves away from the interpretational mode. A textual reading is not an individual's personal statement of themes and images. Reading a text involves the elaboration of its semiological components: binary oppositions, myth, and structure. Writing begins and transpires at "degree zero."[34] The authorial mode remains absent. Signification is dispersed throughout the system of signs in the language (*langage*) of the novel, play, fashion, women's autobiography and photography.[35] Criticism is thus articulated at the level of non-philosophy.

Sartre, in his essay on Merleau-Ponty, comments:

> Savage and opaque, it is the work which retains being within its recesses. This unreason is the undertaking which will subsist in the community as its future *raison d'être*. And above all, it is language, that "fundamental," for the Word is only Being in the heart of man thrown out to exhaust itself within *meaning*. In short, it is man, burst forth in a single spurt, transcending his presence in being, to reach towards his presence in the other, transcending the past to reach towards the future, transcending each thing and his selfness to reach towards the sign. For this reason, Merleau, towards the end of his life, was inclined to give an ever more important place to the unconscious. He must have agreed with Lacan's formula: "The unconscious is structured like a language."(S:M-P, p. 211)

Merleau-Ponty's language of silence may well be a form of the unconscious. For Lacan, however, the Freudian unconscious is not entirely silent—it is revealed as a chain of signifiers. Freudian "condensation" and "displacement" are forms of metaphor and metonymy. The language of the self is once again dispersed throughout produced forms.

Since the psychoanalyst is limited to what the patient says, the analyst must attend to the letter and word in speech. The unconscious expresses itself in many ways. The signifying chain is dispersed such that meaning *insists* in the chain of the signifier but none of its elements *consists* in the meaning of which it is capable at a particular moment.[36] The self does not dispense meanings conscious or unconscious. Rather it maintains an "ex-centricity" that has no nucleus, only symptoms of other realms of self-expression.

Similarly in political theory, philosophy enters into the lives of human individuals in their concrete situations. Theory does not stand apart from practice. Althusser's term "theoretical practice" will show that philosophy can live, but not as separate, "high altitude" thinking. Philosophy must enter the fray. The practice of theory must itself be non-philosophy, i.e., philosophy that has become experience and action.

> Theoretical practice falls within the general definition of
> practice. It works on a raw material (representations,
> concepts, facts) which it is given by other practices, whether
> "empirical," "technical," or "ideological." In its most
> general form theoretical practice does not only include
> *scientific* theoretical practice, but also pre-scientific
> theoretical practice, that is, "ideological" theoretical
> practice. . . . [37]

Non-philosophy is not the refusal to think, to write, to uncover
the bases of social elements of knowledge. Yet it cannot at the
same time ignore concrete human concerns in their "empirical,"
"technical," and "ideological" forms. Theoretical practice is both
the practice of theory and the theory of practice. Is this position
not in effect what Sartre attributes to his fellow editor of *Les
Temps Modernes?* "Merleau's commentaries on politics are only
a political experience in the process of becoming, by itself and in
every sense of the word, the *subject* of mediation. If writings are
acts, we can say that he acted in order to appropriate his action
and to find himself in depth" (S:M-P, p. 209). The self that he
sought was not a transcendental self—nor, for that matter, a
transcendent ego. His writings were a theoretical practice which
also created self-expression.

The fourth area in which Merleau-Ponty's legacy achieves
relevance is in the history of ideas, or what Foucault calls the
history of systems of thought.[38] Uncovering the *epistemé* of a
particular set of structures, forming a system on a synchronic
plane, is once again not the building of systems of ideas. Rather
it reveals the presence of the absolute within human experience.
"Resemblance" for the Renaissance, "representation" for the
classical age, and "man" for the modern *epistemé* are forms of
the dispersal of knowledge. Yet they are also evidence of the
underlying unity of knowledge, that is, knowledge experienced as
structure.

We do not live at a particular time in relation to the discrete
development of some particular idea, concept, or scheme. We live
in an inter-contextualized set of contemporaneous domains of
knowledge production. Biology, linguistics, and economics,
although separate realms of investigation, all carry on their work
at the same time. They also affect one another because of the

types of knowledge that are produced due to interrelated conditions. The task of philosophy is not to simply explain what is, it must enter into knowledge of life, language, and labor. If it remains aloof, it will fail, if it participates in the experience of the world it will negate itself. But this latter path, though the hardest of the two, is nevertheless the vocation of philosophy. In this respect, philosophy becomes archeology: neither semiology nor hermeneutics but rather the explicitation of sign systems and the interpretation of the knowledge frameworks that they form in context.

Merleau-Ponty's unspoken presence also permeates post-structuralist activity. Dominant directions, particularly in France, continue in Merleau-Pontean fashion. We cannot even claim that the non-philosopher has been forgotten—like negative theology, his presence appears everywhere but is identified nowhere.

The blossoming of Jacques Derrida in 1967 announced grammatology as the study of writing (*écriture*).[39] Writing is situated in the exteriorization of speech. Meaning and signification do not arise out of an act, but rather throughout the appearance of writing. Writing corresponds to the visibility that Merleau-Ponty appealed to in the speaking spoken and the spoken speech which appears in a painting, in an event, or in the expression of thought. The closing (*clôture*) of the epoch in which metaphysics prevails is the insertion of speech and voice within verbal language (*langage*). The *grammé* repeats a later Heideggerian presence of that which is present (a visibility of the visible). By claiming that the distinction between *différence* and *différance* is available only in writing[40] (in spoken language the "a" is not heard), Derrida points to the "traces" or "marks" of linguistic experience.

These "traces" are an index of decentered subjectivity. The self *is* only in the *logos of grammata*, just as with Merleau-Ponty the speaking subject appears as absolute only in experience—an experience arising contemporaneously with the presence of the phenomenon. As philosophy becomes this experience, its form, as we have seen, is that of non-philosophy. For Derrida, with the absence of a reference to the subject, signification operates within the free play of differentiation between signifier and signified.[41] Meaning is disseminated[42] throughout writing—specifically, the presence of writing—the voice of silence and the silence of voice.

For Lyotard, once author of a *Que Sais-je?* volume on phenomenology,[43] the translation of intentionality into libidinal desire plays a Merleau-Pontean refrain. With Lyotard, figural expression is sent out in various directions at the level of discourse. Desire meets the painting or the text at a moment perpendicular to its formalization.[44] The field in which discourse is present indicates the place of human desire, the place in which the libidinal is at work. This unification of Freudian singularity and Marxist collectivity at the point of intersection in art is philosophy-become-text.[45] The textual presence of the unconscious, however, is also theoretical work (*travail*) announcing itself as work (*oeuvre*) of art.

Similarly all magisterial discourse has as its goal the assertion of mastery over an audience.[46] In seeking to gain the confidence of his students, the sophist entered into the art of persuasion. Persuasion became the expression of the master's desire over the language of the student. The student in speaking for himself would in fact be dispensing the desire of the other—the student's language could only be a repetition, extension, and multiplication of a discourse that belongs to his teacher and is therefore not his own. Merleau-Ponty had already noted that with non-philosophy an autonomous subjectivity does not speak. What he found in Hegel and Marx was the corporeal expression of philosophy no longer identifying itself as such. The study of magisterial discourse is the presence of the very same language. The discourse that seeks to negate that of the master takes the place of the master as in the Freudian desire for paternal replacement. Non-philosophy becomes the child and parent of philosophy.

Difference, repetition, dissemination—these are the indices of Merleau-Ponty's legacy. His unspoken presence permeates these formulations of current thought. Their presence in Deleuze's writing once again signals that the empire of signs is at work delineating the contemporary *epistemé*. Just as Deleuze sees Proust embroiled in the intricate construction of a spider's web, one would be hard put to find the place of an individual subjectivity at the center of French thought. The spider continues to weave—Marcel, the character, becomes, in the end, at the point of recovering lost time, the author of the narrative that sought the fulfillment of its temporal teleology. When the ends meet, one cannot say that a point is established. Rather, like the rhizome, growth extends outward forming a network. The end point is as undiscoverable as the starting place. Yet the web, the network, the text are non-philosophy philosophizing.

Deleuze's books on Spinoza, Kant, Nietzsche and Bergson are evident of a passing-through-philosophy.[47] Yet the return which interrogates Sacher Masoch, Proust, Lewis Carroll, Freud-Marx, and Kafka[48] is the refusal to present philosophy in a hierarchical, genealogical, linear fashion. The Merleau-Pontean flesh of the world is, in Deleuze, the transmission of the absolute at the level of textual experience.

The texture of the world becoming an interpretation of human activity and consciousness becoming carnal presence could not avoid articulation in the writing of those who developed along with Merleau-Ponty. We can only mention Ricoeur's hermeneutic, Dufrenne's aesthetic, Lévinas' metaphysic, and, of course, Sartre's dialectic, which extend the tradition that would have continued to speak.

Merleau-Ponty's philosophy is not non-philosophy in the sense of a lost philosophy. Its presence is prolonged despite his absence. The absence of a living subjectivity is not the absence of a lived philosophical adventure.

9

MERLEAU-PONTY AND THE INTERROGATION OF LANGUAGE

To interrogate language is to raise the question of its place and meaning within the frame of human experience. Maurice Merleau-Ponty never ceased to interrogate language; but in asking about language, he reformulated its character into four generally synchronic knowledge frameworks. Within what he called the primacy of perception, he wove a texture of problematics, including nature, thing, body, world, time, freedom, dialectic, art, history, and vision. Each problematic implicates and incorporates the others. Language is inscribed within the texture of problematics as the disclosure of their relationships but also according to the knowledge frame in which they operate.

Merleau-Ponty returned to the question of language again and again—from its initial formulation in *Phenomenology of Perception* (1945) to the version offered in his posthumous and unfinished *The Visible and the Invisible* (1964). Within each framework, he would retrace to a certain degree the terrain he had already traversed and each time he would reformulate his understanding of language. In each reiteration, the shape of language as a problematic itself had changed. Yet there are no radical epistemological breaks along his itinerary and there is no continuity of thought either. As he articulated his understanding of language, it underwent significant transformations in the almost two decades during which it played a role in his thinking and writing.

The framing of the four formulations includes (1) the language of the body (1945), (2) the philosophy and psychology of communication (1946–52), (3) indirect language (1952–57), and

(4) the language of visibility (1958–61). Because these frameworks incorporate texts resulting from formal lectures and uncompleted manuscripts as well as deliberate publications, a certain overlap in the dates of appearance mark the organization of texts.[1]

I shall offer a three-fold reading of the four formulations. The first and most extensive reading establishes Merleau-Ponty's appropriation of language according to the four different frameworks or formulations. The second reading offers an interrogation of language based upon its appropriation within Merleau-Ponty's own enterprise. The third reading takes the interrogation of the appropriative and appropriated language to its limits, to the place at which it no longer operates simply as a lived language of significations. This last reading moves to where its own paradoxes of expression locate a style which is not in any particular place but which ajoins, corners, and signs the inscription and interpretation of particular languages—of literature, of corporeity, of history, of sociality, etc.

For each of the four formulations, a distinctive, diacritical, and oppositive relation characterizes the appropriateness of language. The elaboration of the oppositional structure is already the interrogation of language. The elaboration does not simply announce the appropriateness of language, for it places itself in the between, at the locale in which language is questioned, where language is neither a philosophical construct nor a practical tool, where language becomes a system of significations with a style of its own. For language to have a style of its own is to take language too far, to take it to excess. For language to rely exclusively on a network of significations is to underestimate language. The limits of language occur at the juncture, at the intersection, at the cornering (*accointance*) where the ambiguity of significations[2] meets the expression of a style. This placement of language at the limits of significations on the one side and the achievement of style on the other constitutes the parameters which Merleau-Ponty announces but cannot fulfill.[3]

I THE LANGUAGE OF THE BODY

In *The Structure of Behavior* (1942), Merleau-Ponty found little place for language. The critique of early behaviorism, the building of the human order onto the vital and physical orders, and even the relations between body and soul circumvented the question of language. As far as the structures of behavior were concerned language seemed inappropriate. Because the concept of structure was identified with the notions of form and *Gestalt*, structure in the sense of de Saussure's structural linguistics did not enter into Merleau-Ponty's considerations until soon after the publication of *Phenomenology of Perception* (1945). Indeed, Merleau-Ponty's 1946 course at the Ecole Normale Supérieure was devoted to Saussure. In the following year he published his essay "The Metaphysical in Man," where he not only mentions de Saussure but also ascribes to him the view that the speaking subject lives in his language.

Between *The Structure of Behavior* (1942) and "The Metaphysical in Man" (1947), the appropriateness of language was intimately bound up with Merleau-Ponty's account of the body, particularly as the region of expression and speech. The body is transfigured by expression and speech. The dichotomy between subject and object is no longer in question, for the body appropriates meaning (*sens*) for itself in the act of speech. The speaking subject carries speech through its bodily gestures prohibiting a disincarnated consciousness. Consciousness is already corporeal and speech is already the incorporation of meaningful thought. In speaking, in gesticulating, in articulating, in signaling, the body is the locus of meaning production. Thus the body of the word, which is incorporated into speech, is the material instrument of verbal expression.

In this first formulation signalled by *Phenomenology of Perception*, Merleau-Ponty distinguishes two kinds of speech: *parole parlante* and *parole parlée*.[4] The opposition is critical; for between "speaking speech" and "spoken speech," speech appropriates its meaning. All thought is speech in a certain respect. Thought attains a body, it becomes a language when it is spoken through speech by a speaking subject. In other words, between the speaking and the spoken is a language. The language in question here is nothing other than the language of speech (*parole*). But speech is already body—the experiential use of phonatory organs, the singing of music, the reciting of words, the expression of ideas, the articulation of objects, etc. Speech announces itself as the body in action—what it produces is a "spoken speech" (*parole parlée*)—its producing is "speaking speech" (*parole parlante*). The production of spoken speech by speaking speech is the constitution of language—the assembly of meanings in order to create signification, a signifying intention which is necessarily already corporeal.

Speech of the sort I have been considering remains within the domain of verbal language; this speech produces words, sounds, and utterances. However another dimension of this phenomenal field in which language is proper to the body, in which the body is appropriate to language, is gesture. Gesture is the paradigmatic case of bodily expression. Yet Merleau-Ponty does not begin with gesture; he does not make other forms of language derivative of the gestural. In both speech and gesture, the body becomes thought, the body inscribes meaning in a texture of experience by which it speaks—not in words but in movement and in a tendency toward expression. Signalling to a friend to "come here" in Italian, shrugging one's shoulders in French, frowning in British English, and indicating quotation marks in American are all forms of gesture. They all tend toward expression. They all demonstrate the movement of thought through the living body. Such gestures are tied to specific cultural contexts and therefore partake of what seems arbitrary and conventional as in a verbal language. Even though some may claim that gestures or emotional imitations are natural signs (as Merleau-Ponty suggests) nevertheless they operate within a nature/culture opposition where natural signs are conventionalized and conventional signs are naturalized. What is eminently important here is that whether one is offering an elaborate philosophical discourse, asking the price of a beer, saying "no" with one's hands, fingers, shoulders, and head, or laughing out of joy, the body is the medium of expression. All expression is both bodily and the *topos* of meaning production. As Merleau-Ponty puts it, "the human body is defined in terms of its property of appropriating in an indefinite series of discontinuous acts, signifying kernels which surpass and transfigure its natural powers."[5] In going beyond its natural limitations, the body adopts a tendency toward cultural expression, toward a language (*un langage qui devient une langue*). This movement of the body proper (*le corps propre*), of one's own body, is itself already the appropriation of language, making language one's own in order to speak, in order to express oneself.

But without other people (*autrui*), there would be no need

to express oneself. The appropriation of language is already a movement of reciprocity, a tendency toward communication. Speaking is already a gesture which carries with it a meaning just as gesture carries its own meaning.[6] This orientation toward communication occurs in the attempt to grasp and transmit meaning, to fulfill the reciprocity between my gestures and those of others. It is "as if the other's intention inhabited my own body and as if my intentions inhabited his."[7] This contextualization of gesture, and speech which is already gesture, indicates, elaborates, and inscribes a texture for the appropriation of language.

II THE PHILOSOPHY AND PSYCHOLOGY OF COMMUNICATION

Although Merleau-Ponty introduced the question of communication in *Phenomenology of Perception*, he thematized it in the years following the war, in the years which saw the formation of *Les Temps Modernes*, in the years when he was teaching first at Lyon and also at the Ecole Normale Supérieure de Paris and then as a professor of psychology at the Sorbonne. In the span of about five years (from 1945 to 1950), Merleau-Ponty discovered structural linguistics, incorporated it into his phenomenological perspectives and addressed himself even more intensively to the problem of language and particularly that of communication. As he had already demonstrated in his principal doctoral thesis (*Phenomenology of Perception*), the appropriation of language incorporates communication. By extending his critique of Gestalt psychology, behaviorism, and psychoanalysis within the shadow of both Husserl and Saussure, he entered upon a consideration of the philosophical and psychological aspects of communication.

In his 1945–6 Lyon course, he began a systematic study of theories of language in Western philosophy from Heraclitus, Socrates, and Plato to Descartes, Berkeley, and Locke, and on to Humboldt and Cassirer.[8]

In the 1947–8 lectures on language and communication,[9] he develops his critique of scientisms in psychology, sociology, history, and linguistics in order to establish the relationship between language and thought and to articulate the role of the speaking subject in communication. The evidence of both schemes or structures and the temporal evolution of language indicates Merleau-Ponty's adoption of the synchronic and diachronic elements of structural linguistics. Both of these aspects are actualized in the speaking subject. At no time can this appropriation of language by the speaking subject allow language itself to become an object—even for the linguist, who must speak in order to carry on his enterprise. For Merleau-Ponty, the intentionality of language places thought within language such that "I rejoin myself in speaking."[10] The words that I speak are "surrounded by a halo of meaning." The philosophy of language must go beyond the pure phenomenon of language in order to appropriate it and in order for its appropriateness to take place.

In his first formulation concerning language, Merleau-Ponty did not recognize the symphonic character of language. It is corporeal, but it also has temporally changing structures. This synchronics and diachronics of language offers a framework for the experience of speaking subjects. In order to translate the experience of speaking subjects into an experience of communication, Merleau-Ponty turned to Husserl's fifth cartesian meditation. Unfortunately this threw him back again into a problem of my nihilation of others as they nihilate me in that the other's subjectivity becomes an objectivity for me and vice versa. In order to go beyond this theory of mutual objectification, which recurs in the early Sartre, Merleau-Ponty appeals to the notion of intersubjectivity as the coupling of my speech with the speech of others; hence producing communication. The difficulty which Merleau-Ponty faced was that in order to obtain a communicative appropriation of intersubjective language, he could not remain within the transcendental model which Husserl offered. De Saussure's structural considerations helped to establish the conditions for both temporality and communicability, but they could not be fully reconciled with the Husserlian perspective. He had already shown in his brief discussion which covers a few pages of "The Metaphysical in Man" that Gestalt psychology establishes a "communication between and a mixture of the subjective and the objective."[11] But Gestalt psychology is inadequate in this respect. It only sets up the possibility of the conjunction of Husserlian phenomenology and Saussurian structuralism. The linking of these two orientations seemed to be a natural outgrowth of Gestalt psychology's concerns with both intentions and structures. But as Merleau-Ponty gradually discovered, he could only incorporate the models by transforming them into an existential and developmental context. Intentionality could no longer remain transcendental and structure could no longer imply "form," "whole," "figure against a ground." The appropriation of communication would have to remain a "desire" until he could free himself fully from both the problematics of "intersubjectivity" and "holism" without at the same time falling into the formal models of structuralism. Thus he wrote in 1947:

> That general spirit which we all constitute by living our life in common, that intention already deposited in the given system of language, pre-conscious because the speaking subject espouses it before he becomes aware of it and elevates it to the level of knowledge, and yet which only subsists on the condition of being taken up or assumed by speaking subjects and lives in their *desire for communication*—this, in this field of linguistics, is indeed the equivalent of the psychologist's form, equally alien to the objective existence of a natural process as to the mental existence of an idea.[12]

The formulation of communication as a "desire" could be attributed to a variety of interests which both informed and plagued Merleau-Ponty's early work. The "desire for communication" cannot be realized because of the aporias of the Husserlian theory of transcendental subjectivity, because of the search for comprehension in forms which Kohler, Koffka, Gelb and Goldstein proposed, because of the unrealizable libido ever present in Freudian psycho-analysis, and because of the Sartrian theory of mutual objectification which Merleau-Ponty could never quite overcome.

Yet in his courses for the Institut de Psychologie at the Sorbonne in 1949–52, he sought avenues whereby the theory of communication could become appropriated into the experience of language. In *Consciousness and the Acquisition of Language*, he stressed the developmental account of language in order to uncover the manner in which a child learns to speak and communicate. This important approach which has been followed through by cognitive psychologists but which has been left largely untouched by phenomenologists, stresses linguistic diachrony—not in terms of the history of languages, but in terms of an individual person's acquisition of a language and his communication with others. Merleau-Ponty traces the child's path from babbling to the appropriation of linguistic structures including the acquisition of phonemes and the imitation of others. He was particularly interested in how children more than seven years old communicate with each other and was dismayed with Piaget's conclusion that "there is no true communication between children."[13] Piaget's limited conception of "comprehension" forces him to draw conclusions which prohibit a full description of communicative relations among children. By examining the pathology of language, he could demonstrate how in cases of verbal hallucination and aphasia, there is indeed a shrinkage of the child's appropriation of language and the possibility of communication.

Although the language which Merleau-Ponty explores in this second formulation is limited more specifically to verbal language, the language of the very young child certainly incorporates gestures which are not yet those of the speaking subject. But even if it is possible for the child to appropriate language, that is, to make it his or her own, it is more difficult for the child or even the adult to appropriate communication. Thus Merleau-Ponty turns from psychological and pathological theories to the philosophical implications of linguistic theory. Saussure's views occupy an even greater place in *Consciousness and the Acquisition of Language* than in earlier writings. The diacritical aspects of language indicate differences: conceptual differences on the side of the signified, phonic differences on the side of the signifier. And the sign itself which is composed of the signifier/signified opposition is an arbitrary relation—a relation which is itself conventional. Because the arbitrary nature of the sign results in a differential linguistic system, "each linguistic phenomenon is a differentiation of a movement of communication."[14] While "value" can be exchanged for an infinite number of objects, "signification" remains an essential part of a particular communication experience. On the basis of signification, the communicative experience spans, intertwines, and appropriates the conventional system of differences. In the articulation of signs, he writes, "each speaking subject finds himself reintegrated into the collectivity of speaking subjects. The *global will* to communicate with the *alter ego* founds the positive [aspect] of the linguistic phenomenon. But this linguistic phenomenon, considered instant by instant, is never anything but negative, diacritical. The currency for a global possibility of communicating makes up the very essence of the speaking subject."[15] Communication is appropriated only by a will, as a possibility, as the speaking subject reintegrates himself into the collectivity of speaking subjects—that is, as the speaking subject inscribes himself in the system of differences which constitutes a language.

In the year following his course on *Consciousness and the Acquisition of Language*, Merleau-Ponty began a two year course on "Phenomenology and the Sciences of Man." The English version of the text is only partial but it does include the section in which Merleau-Ponty took up the role of linguistics in Husserl's philosophy. In returning to Husserl, Merleau-Ponty is again faced with the problem of rescuing the experience of language, of liberating the speaking subject, of achieving communication among speaking subjects by avoiding the trap of an objective study of language. The phenomenologist is concerned with what the speaking subject really is, with an elaboration and adoption of language as it is spoken. "The speaking subject is turned toward the future. Language for him is above all a means of expression and of communicating to others his intentions, which are also turned toward the future."[16] This access to a speaking subject in the later Husserl is no longer a concern with a transcendental subject but with a speaking subject in a definite linguistic situation. As Merleau-Ponty puts it, "to know what language is, it is necessary first of all to speak. It no longer suffices to reflect on the languages lying before us in historical documents of the past. It is necessary to take them over, to live with them, to speak them. It is only by making contact with this speaking subject that I can get a sense of what other languages are and can move around in them."[17] In this respect Merleau-Ponty viewed Husserl as approximating the task which Saussure had set before himself: to return to the speaking subject in its linguistic context—which for Husserl is a fullness and for Saussure a system of differences. Whether it accounts for the appropriation of identity as in Husserl or the appropriation of difference as in Saussure, the appropriation itself, the making of a communicative situation in which language is lived as one's own is the formulation of Merleau-Ponty's enterprise in this second version.

The final account of this version was made clear in one of

Merleau-Ponty's last courses before moving on to the Collège de France in 1952. In *L'Expérience d'autrui* (1951–2), he distinguishes clearly between a language (*une langue*) and language (*le langage*). The language which concerns him is not a language (*une langue*) such as French, German, or English, but "*le langage* as a phenomenon of communication."[18] An interpreter employs language (*le langage*) in order to communicate a movement of thought. But, in fact, this communicative language is already the inscription of a system of significations, a system of differences which passes from language to what is meant: the sign is already structuration and structuration is already a system of significations which constitutes the communicative situation.

III INDIRECT LANGUAGE

By building a link between Husserl and Saussure, Merleau-Ponty opens up the field not only of the desire and possibility to communicate, but also the appropriation of a language which is not direct, not fully explicitated, but which speaks and which is communication itself. This is the indirect language which Merleau-Ponty examines in "Indirect Language and the Voices of Silence" (published in *Les Temps Modernes*, June and July 1952).

Retracing the steps he had left in the form of lecture notes, Merleau-Ponty reiterates the child's efforts at communication even on the level of babbling. He reiterates the importance of the Saussurian theory of the sign and he moves toward the meaning which arises at the edge of the sign, at the outskirts of the system of linguistic differences. Brunelleschi builds the cupola to the Florentine cathedral in conformity with its site. He does not accomplish his task by making references to explicit architectural signs. Rather he envelops them with an appropriative action, a speech of sorts in which Brunelleschi the architect announces the full meaning of the context. It is as if he could communicate with the site in order to fulfill its meaning:

> A language sometimes remains a long time pregnant with transformations which are to come; and the enumeration of the means of expression in a language does not have any meaning, since those which fall into disuse continue to lead

a diminished life in the language and since the place of those which are to replace them is sometimes already marked out—even if only in the form of a gap, a need, or a tendency.[19]

Further on Merleau-Ponty adds: "The meaning occurs at the intersection, in the interval between words." Thus when the meaning does arise, it fills in the gaps which were already marked out, already prepared for expression. In other words, language itself is indirect, allusive—silence. Indirect language prepares the way for speaking, writing, painting, etc. In this third formulation of the appropriation of language, language denies the presence of pure meaning, language opens up a field of differences in which significations that appear as guide posts begin to take shape. To appropriate indirect language is to bring about meaning in the intervals between significations (based on signs) which begin to appear in expression. Language for Merleau-Ponty is not only the movement toward communication but also the fulfilling of expression through the appropriation of differences in the verbal chain and through the identification of significations which we grasp in terms of a broad movement toward expression. In this third formulation, Merleau-Ponty builds upon bodily gesture and the desire to communicate, the tendency toward expression through an indirect language. The appropriation by the writer or painter of the indirect language is like the child's orientation toward speech, toward the acquisition of a conversation (and hence an intersubjective language). Yet it also carries with it an originating intention, a genesis of language out of silence, a "tacit language"—the field of speech before it is spoken.

Malraux's concerns with the development of perspective in painting, when incorporated into the lessons Merleau-Ponty has reaped from Husserl, Saussure, and the Gestaltists, establishes the domain out of which bodily expression can become communication through art. When the voices of silence speak, they speak through paintings such as those of Cézanne, Klee, and Van Gogh, through the writings of Stendhal, Valéry, and Proust—. An operant and latent meaning becomes manageable for the artist. It establishes a field of expression that, once appropriated by the artist, begins to generate meaning out of which its significations can be appropriated by others.

In this third formulation, in the years from 1951 to 1954, Merleau-Ponty draws upon his earlier study of Cézanne's experience and gives it a context as the indirect language through which meaning and hence signification can arise. As he puts it, "when one goes from the order of events to the order of expression, one does not change the world; the same circumstances which were previously submitted to now become a signifying system."[20] "The human use of the body is already primordial expression,"[21] which means that when Renoir paints his *Bathers*, his understanding of the body takes on expression in his painting. It is not simply the representation of bodies, but also the meaning of bodily expression which begins to speak through the painting as a signifying system—a framework of significations which the art historian can articulate but which the spectator appropriates in his or her own experience. In this way, culture adopts significations through the incorporation of human meaning. The process of expression gives rise to arts of expression. The artist destroys ordinary vision by realizing it just as the writer defeats the constraints of ordinary language by realizing it.[22] Or in another version, "language speaks and the voices of painting are the voices of silence."[23] The appropriation of a language which can say: "These beautious things have not been to me as is a landscape to a blind man's eye" as Wordsworth does, or the appropriation of the corporeal visible as Renoir does in *The Bathers* are the speaking of a language and the voices of silence as they enter the expressive texture of what Husserl called "intersubjectivity." Both Wordsworth and Renoir conventionalize, culturalize, and bring the indirect language into a corporeal language of communication.

In the posthumous *Prose of the World* (written primarily between 1950 and 1952), Merleau-Ponty develops even further this experience of expression. The intention to communicate (the problematic of Merleau-Ponty's second formulation) is now oriented toward the transformation of meanings into a system of expression. The painter for example paints as much by the lines he traces, the blank spaces on the canvas, and the brush strokes he does not make as much as the specific shapes he fills in. This indirect visual expression has its analogue in the truly expressive speech of the poet and prose writer. In embarking upon *The Prose of the World*, Merleau-Ponty set out to respond to Sartre's *What is Literature?* (1947) as Roland Barthes did in his *Writing Degree*

Zero (1952). He hoped to provide an account of literary experience in which communication is a central feature, but which is not simply grounded in the communication of freedom by the prose writer. The writer's task is, as he elaborates in the chapter on "Indirect Language":

> to choose, assemble, wield, and torment these instruments in such a way that they induce the same sentiment of life that dwells in the writer at every moment, deployed henceforth in an imaginary world and in the transparent body of language.[24]

Merleau-Ponty is far more concerned with "the sentiment of life that dwells in the writer" than with the priority of prose over poetry and the specific audience of writers. Indeed he is closer to the Heideggerian problematic which becomes more and more significant in his writings. Just as Heidegger seeks to think the writer's language as the opening up of a speaking of language which situates itself in the ontological difference, similarly Merleau-Ponty emphasizes the writer's dwelling in a significant texture of differences which cuts horizontally across the writer's contact with the world through his speech. That Merleau-Ponty associates the experience of the writer with that of the painter necessarily undercuts the dichotomy which Sartre establishes between the poet who is like Tintoretto painting a yellow sky as opposed to the prose writer like Malraux who is engaged in a definite situation and whose goal is the freedom of all mankind. Here again Merleau-Ponty approaches a Heideggerian meditation which brings together the experience of Van Gogh's peasant shoes with a Greek temple and Hölderlin's poetry. Thus when Merleau-Ponty writes that "all of classical painting rests on the idea of a communication between the painter and his public through the evidence of things,"[25] he is announcing and appropriating a language—an indirect language—which allows for the communication of painter and public through the embodied experience of things in the world.

Again and again within this third formulation Merleau-Ponty distinguishes the algorithm of a pure language from the literary and other types of indirect language. He rejects the ideal of a "successful" language which can stand disembodied from experience. Even the orientation toward the achievement of a universal language is continually situated within an experiential expression. The algorithm, for Merleau-Ponty, is "a revolt against language in its existing state and a refusal to depend upon the confusion of everyday language."[26] The search for pure signification is the attempt to overcome the gaps, intervals, and differences in the experience of language. In the algorithm, communication is only an appearance and never actually brings anything new. Despite its project of escape from the indirections of language and its attempt to appropriate language within a fully circumscribed and completely opaque system of knowledge, it, in fact, appropriates only a very small, limited, and direct aspect of experience. Algorithm expression remains simply secondary; it can be *exact* because it can accomplish precisely what it sets before itself as its task. It does not require appropriation because it is already proper to itself and only to itself.

In offering itself to literary language, the algorithm can avoid the problems inherent in passing from the sensible world to the world of expression, for the algorithm is pure, limited, and direct expression. It has no need of painting itself with the sensible— which, for Merleau-Ponty, is already involved in the enterprise of the creators of a universal language. By contrast, literature is in advance of the philosophy of language. Literature already incorporates and highlights the miracle of the mystical union of sound and meaning, signifier and signified. In his 1953 Collège de France lecture on "The Literary Use of Language" Merleau-Ponty builds upon what he described as the "mystery of language" in the *Prose of the World*. The mystery of language—"indirect language" is a more fortunate formulation for what Saussure characterized as an arbitrary relation between signifier and signified—indicates the difference or gap which is distributed throughout expression and highlighted particularly in literature. Freud's notion of the "over-determination of speech"—which Lacan has identified with metaphor—is another form of the expressive appropriation of language through which meaning fills the differences and sets up a system of significances. Literary speech expresses the world, so too does the overdetermined language of the patient reporting a dream. "Perhaps all men, as well as the man of letters, can only be present to the world and others through language; and perhaps in everyone language is the basic function which constructs a life

165

and its work and transforms even the problems of our existence
into life's motives."[27]

IV THE LANGUAGE OF VISIBILITY

The fourth formulation of Merleau-Ponty's considerations on
language emerges in the last two years of his life (between 1959
and 1960)—depending upon when he actually began writing *The
Visible and the Invisible*. These considerations also include his last
published work *Eye and Mind* and several brief remarks in his
last course *Philosophy and Non-philosophy since Hegel*.

The problem which inserts itself into any examination of these
texts, and particularly that of *The Visible and the Invisible*, is one
of interpreting an enterprise which opens onto an ontology of
difference, but which itself tends toward novel expression. In
short, how can the language of visibility appropriate itself to its
own enterprise. Without a doubt, Merleau-Ponty continues to
build upon his prior appropriations: gestures and incarnate speech
realize the orientation toward communication and the rounding
out of indirect language. But a new question is raised in the last
years: how can the interrogation of Cartesian reflection, Hegelian
and Sartrian dialectic, Husserlian and Bergsonian intuition open
up onto the chiasm, an intertwining which is both the difference
and identity of the visible and the invisible, the seen and the seer,
the touched and the touching?

The chiasm is a vertical, ontological relation. In one working
note, Merleau-Ponty associates it with the "ontological
difference"[28]—which is so commonly associated with Heidegger.
The ontological difference, the chiasm of visible and invisible, the
intertwining of seeing and seen, touching and touched establishes
an invisibility which is filled only by perceptual faith, which
achieves meaning only in the appropriation of a language of visibility. It would seem however that this type of visibility could be
articulated without stressing the place of language. It would seem
that the reciprocity of visible and invisible might not necessarily
appropriate language. It would seem that the difference enacted
in the intertwining need not enter into speech. But when we
remember that *la chaire* (flesh) establishes visibility, which fills
out the body and its surroundings, it becomes evident that once

again language speaks in the ontological difference, in the chiasm, in the unachieved gap between the visible and the invisible. The *écart* is opened up and appropriated in language along with the meaning which literature, music, and even the passions give it. The reversibility of the visible and invisible is also the invisibility of speech and what it signifies.[29] The signification which arises out of this vertical relation between speech and its signified is elaborated horizontally across a system of differences—the system of differences which Merleau-Ponty discovered when he appropriated the structural linguistics of de Saussure. This horizontal movement, continually opening up new horizons, cuts across the vertical *écart*, sets itself up as language and enters into an ongoing communicative movement within the intercorporeity of the interworld (*intermonde*). Thus meaning arises out of the vertical difference; a system of significations arises out of the horizontal differences; and language is appropriated in the intersection of the vertical difference and the horizontal differences.

These horizontal differences are not the object of a reflection from above (a bird's eye view of things, a *pensée de survol*), nor are they the result of a series of things which distinguish themselves from each other. The horizontal differences are proliferated at the membrane, hinge, juncture, cornering (*accointance*) of visible and invisible—they are the proliferation of speech across a whole, moving field of differences. The note which ends with "*langage et chiasm*" demonstrates Merleau-Ponty's commitment to this double crossing of difference as a fundamental orientation in which the appropriateness of language is indicated. The appropriation of language is the appropriation of flesh.

Thus the painter who adopts a fleshly understanding of the world is able to make the object he sees visible in the painting. In *Eye and Mind*, Merleau-Ponty cites Valéry as saying that the painter "takes his body with him"—and he adds "not the body as a chunk of space or a bundle of functions but that body which is an intertwining of vision and movement."[30] The painting is the silent articulation of the intertwining of "essence and existence, imaginary and real, visible and invisible—a painting mixes up all our categories in laying out its oneiric universe of carnal essences, of effective likenesses, of mute meanings."[31] In this respect, Cézanne's *Mont St Victoire* does indeed demonstrate the silent speech with its mute meanings which Merleau-Ponty described in his third formulation through the work of Malraux. What is different in this fourth formulation is that painting is a demonstration of visibility and an appropriation of a language which gives access to the structure of Being, a polymorphous Being with multiple dimensions. Language here is based on painting with its proper essence of the visible, and its doubling of the invisible. "This mute Being which speaks in painting has its analogue in the figurations of literature and philosophy—the only privilege of speaking—thought," Merleau-Ponty writes, "is to have rendered its own support manageable."[32] He suggests thereby that speech operates with a similar access to Being, a similar ontology that situates itself in the fleshly difference between the spoken and the unspoken, in the *écart* of speaking. That it is possible to appropriate the language of philosophy in a similar fashion is the topic of Merleau-Ponty's last course *Philosophy and Non-Philosophy since Hegel* (1961).[33] By identifying the difference between philosophy and non-philosophy, the appropriative dimension of philosophy is the dimension of experience in all its ambiguity.

V INTERROGATING LANGUAGE

This chapter is entitled the interrogation of language. So far the inquiry has restricted itself to the appropriation of language. Without an elaboration of what is proper to language, it cannot be interrogated effectively. Without an indication of language— as bodily gesture and speech, as communication, as the indirect expression of literature, painting, and music (by contrast to the algorithm), and lastly as an ontology of visibility and the intersection of differences—without the building of formulation upon formulation, the full interrogation of language cannot even be proposed. This means that what is proper to language (including speaking, writing, and painting), what belongs to language, and what language can call its own—once elaborated with care—enters into each formulation with an interrogative mood.

Interrogation is a dominant thematic of Merleau-Ponty's fourth formulation. He offered a course on the topic in 1959. In this course, he noted that he would concern himself with the possibility of philosophy in 1959. Interrogation situates questioning in the between, at the juncture, on the hinge. Interrogation opens up and makes what is philosophical in language (or whatever is to be interrogated) speak for itself. When interrogating philosophy itself Merleau-Ponty sought to indicate how philosophy becomes non-philosophy in the present age.[34] In this respect philosophy interrogates its own meaning and possibility—that is, it situates itself in the difference between philosophy and non-philosophy, in the system of differences which are marked by significations. Philosophy interrogates the *Ineinander* of Being in its difference from beings.

The interrogation of language situates itself as a direct repetition of the appropriation of language. The interrogation of language questions the already said of the appropriated in order to examine its meaning, its significations, and ultimately its limits. The interrogation of language asks language about its meaning and possibilities. In order to fulfill the enterprise, each of the four formulations must be reviewed one by one—each must be interrogated as a unique epistemological framework which is itself layered and stratified in order to produce an ontology of language, an ontology which establishes its own limits.

The itinerary of interrogating language in Merleau-Ponty identifies four distinct thematics: (1) ambiguity, (2) lived language, (3) the orientation toward expression, and (4) the paradoxes of expression. Each is built upon an opposition, a difference which allows for the articulation of the interrogation and the meaning of its placement.

In the first formulation, which is characterized by ambiguity (i.e., the multiplicity of meanings held in tension within the phenomenal field of the body)—the opposition between speech and expression prevails. Speech is a form of gesture which achieves meaning through its conjuncture with expression. The insertion of ambiguity between speech and expression announces the opening of a field in which verbal meanings are already experiential, in which gestural meanings are already expressive. Ambiguity is the production of a corporeal multiplicity whose interrogation announces the significance of perception in its most general characteristics.

The interrogation of the second formulation installs itself in the opposition between linguistics and the speaking subject. What is appropriate to language is this second formulation in the contribution of linguistics, particularly that of Saussure, but also

Jakobson, Goldstein, Vendreys, Guillaume and others. Structural linguistics demonstrates that language is founded on a system of differential relations which gives rise to significations. On the basis of such a system, the child acquires a language and tends toward communication, which is also the orientation of adults. The acquisition of a language, the expression of linguistic structures, and the establishment of intersubjectivity in terms of language is already accomplished by the work of the speaking subject. The speaking subject gives meaning(s) to linguistic science such that what arises out of the interrogation (in the difference) is a *lived language*. The lived language supplants and augments the thematic of ambiguity in the first formulation.

In the third formulation, the difference between the algorithm or pure language and indirect language establishes (through interrogation) the movement toward expression. Expression is not a given. It arises only out of a field of silence which is given to speaking through painting, poetry, prose, music, etc. This indirect language opposes itself to the universal, pure language which is sought after by an objective, exact science of language—by a science which reduces differences to positivities—by an enterprise which seeks to ignore the voices of silence. Nevertheless out of the opposition expression becomes possible.

The still groping, but more fully articulated form of this possibility occurs in the fourth formulation in which the tendency toward expression is replaced by the paradoxes of expression. Expression has its multiple directions, its intertwinings and crisscrossings in the differences between visible and invisible, touching and touched, in the flesh of the chiasm. There the logos of the sensible world remains meaningful and ontologically fulfilling of the expressive dimension of corporeality which is already intercorporeality and of intercorporeality which is already an interworld where expression takes place. In this respect the ambiguity of experience is a lived language which is oriented toward the achievement of the paradoxes of expression.

Significantly, and here I conclude—at least temporarily—in each of the four formulations, the place of style always stands at the edge, at the margin of the appropriation and therefore in the interrogation. Style has no definite place in the ambiguous field of bodily speech and expression—yet Merleau-Ponty announces its appearance as "Spinozist, criticist, and phenomenological."[35]

170

Style is a certain way of linking up with the natural world, a manner of speaking or even singing the world. Thus each gestural signification appropriates a style all its own. But the appearance of that style unrewinds (or deconstructs) the generality and the singularity of the expressive situation.

In the orientation toward communication, style appears in the differential structure of significations. "Style is defined neither by words nor by ideas," it possesses an oblique rather than a direct signification.[36] It announces the arrival of the "new". Thus the child imitates the style of the speaking subject and not the words themselves. Style is our "manner."[37] It is the quality of the ambiguous meanings of experience as it inscribes itself in the significative differences of language. As a text the system or horizontal differences tend toward signification. Style is the tendency toward signification in the lived language.

In the movement toward expression of indirect language, style identifies itself at the limits of language. The child adopts a "style of expression" in order to speak. Similarly style "germinates at the surface of the artist's experience"[38] where his system of equivalences begins to take on its own particular characteristics. Style is simply the speech of the voices of silence.

But finally, the allusive, elliptical style of the fourth formulation remains inimitable, inalienable and in between the inner and outer horizons of a visibility that seeks to express itself in all its multiple and paradoxical aspects. The countryside of fleshly experience, as Merleau-Ponty states in *The Visible and the Invisible*, is only a variation on speech. To speak of its "style" is to create a metaphor.[39] Style is already metaphorical of speech. Style is the paradox of expression taken to its limits. Style is the crossing out of both the ontological difference and the differential system of significations in the intertwining of the visible and the invisible. Style is visibility without either identity or difference.

10

SARTRE'S WORDS ON THE SELF

In Sartre's descriptions of the self, the function of language changes in accordance with alterations in his concept of self. The change in the relationship between the self and verbal expression is a genetic interest that can be restated synchronically by citing three moments along Sartre's way. Each stage indicates a different formulation of this relationship. What I am suggesting is that one can speak of an *episteme* at differing moments within the work of an individual rather than limiting such a consideration to a historical context, as Foucault proposes.[1] Thus Sartre's early writings (1936–44), dealing with the transcendental ego, the ontological restructuring of consciousness without an ego internal to it, presuppose that a particular linguistic determination of the self will not affect the true self in any critical fashion. Yet in *Saint Genet* (1952), as representative of the second *episteme*, the word—a dizzying word—"Thief" alters Genet's whole experience of himself and who he is. In this context, the self is formed in reaction to words. By the time of *The Words* (1964), the writer's experience of language and the linguistic analogy become the locus of self-expression. I shall examine in turn each of the three self/language binary structures.

I

The first *episteme*, that of the self without words (*sans paroles*), is most clearly formulated in *The Transcendence of the Ego* (1936)

172

and *Being and Nothingness* (1942), though the point can also be made by an examination of *Nausea* (1938) and some of the plays such as *The Flies* (1943) and *No Exit* (1944). To be *sans paroles* is to affirm the possibility of speaking about the self without the self speaking or being named. In this critique of Husserl's transcendental ego,[2] Sartre proposes a revision in the status of the ego. This revision stems from a difference of opinion as to the nature of consciousness. Husserlian phenomenology asserted that along with the noetic (meaning-giving act) and noematic (meaning-given) elements of consciousness, there is also a transcendental ego that stands behind all acts of consciousness and which serves as the source of intentionality. This transcendental standpoint operates as the subject-pole for the directedness of consciousness. Husserl distinguishes between the transcendental ego and the psychophysical, or empirical, ego, in that the latter is refined (bracketed) methodologically in order to facilitate phenomenological investigation—leaving the transcendental ego inside consciousness.[3] Within the phenomenological field,[4] only the conscious life remains. Though Husserl speaks of consciousness as a whole in terms of "subjectivity," the ego-pole is most appropriately called the self, or even the true self. The psychophysical ego corresponds to the self prior to the phenomenological reduction.

Husserl's establishment of the pure self does not depend upon the individual's recognition or experience of language. Of course, the statement of method is linguistic, but the status of consciousness is not. Similarly, Sartre's critique of the transcendental ego is not founded on linguistic conditions. Sartre claims that the ego cannot rest within the transcendental field. It must be outside consciousness, that is, temporally, it must be the ego that I just reflected upon. Whenever the ego is taken as an object of reflection, it cannot, according to Sartre, be an ego within consciousness. The ego cannot be caught red-handed in the act of reflecting upon itself.[5] It is always experienced cognitively as the self whose act is complete and which is no longer in consciousness, or as the self that is not yet, but that is projected to be.

Whatever self is reflected upon (*réfléchi*) must be an object of an intentional act. All intentional acts have objects (all consciousness is consciousness of something). When the self is reflected upon, it appears as outside consciousness, since it is an object

173

of consciousness. Consciousness therefore must be unreflected (*irréfléchi*). Meaning can arise only when consciousness is reflective. If consciousness itself is unreflected, then it must not have meaning until it is reflected. When it is reflected, the meaning is a meaning of a past self, a self that is not the self of consciousness. Since consciousness has no meaning when it is unreflected, it cannot have a content. This rejection of the Cartesian *cogito* as nonsubstantial is the basis for Sartre's conclusion that consciousness is empty.

Can we claim, however, that this empty consciousness is the true self? Clearly the projected or past (reflected) self is not the true self—even though, in Sartre's formulation, it is identical with a transcendent ego. If we do not require that the true self be the ego, and there is no reason—except for Cartesian convention—that we should, then the unreflected consciousness would be the most appropriate candidate. Precedent exists for a non-unitary conception of the ego as an alternative to the Cartesian-Husserlian view. One could die the Freudian self as a tripartite id-ego-supergo structure, the Humean self as a bundle of disparate impressions, and the Aristotelian self as a functional unity of body and soul, where each is not associated with a unitary ego. The Sartrian version is somewhat curious, by contrast, for Sartre proposes that the self is a non-self, but an active, individual non-self (unlike the Platonic world-soul or Chinese Tao). Since this self is not an ego and is without content, without a meaning to define it, there is surely no name that characterizes a particular self, no word that will serve as the predicate noun or adjective indicating who the self is. Thus, Sartre does not introduce words for the self. It has no experiential meaning; likewise, no linguistic meaning. The true self (that is, unreflected consciousness) of the first *episteme* is empty and without words. The reality of the self (Corbin's translation of Heidegger's *Dasein* was *la réalité humaine*, which Sartre employs regularly) is distinct from the words necessary to describe it. The self does not associate its experience with the names applied to it.

Non-thetic (or non-positional) consciousness is an epistemological structure. The self's attempts to posit its own ontological status as a participant in and even the center of consciousness is doomed to failure. In seeking to know who the self is, the self exhibits its own incapability: it cannot take itself as the theme of its own experience and still hope to be the self of the experience. The self-knowledge act is a self-negating act. As I attempt to know who I am, I find that I am not that which I propose to know. The thetic (noetic) act[6] should give as the meaning of its object the self that is its subject. But the bankrupt character of the traditional subject-object distinction is brought into focus here. The cognitive act that seeks to know its own subjectivity, and which must take that subjectivity as an objectivity, cannot succeed in restoring the subjectivity to a pure state. The subjectivity *qua* self must always remain other, because it has treated itself as other (that is, as what it is not). In being taken as other than what it is, the self is not the thesis of its own conscious act, for the self is not that other. The self becomes that other only when it is no longer itself. The self loses its identity and becomes an otherness when it cannot grasp itself in its own self-conscious act. Self-consciousness—consciousness (of) self—is non-thetic self-consciousness in that the self's awareness of itself is the denial of making itself other than what it is. When it becomes other, it is no longer the self. When the self refuses to be other—a self outside consciousness—it must be non-thetic.

Self-consciousness is non-self-referential. Even if language were introduced—at least a conception of language as referential (in the Fregean sense)—the self would not be characterized. Since in this sense linguistic meaning (*Sinn*) refers to some referent (*Bedeutung*), the difficulty in the case of the self is that there is a meaning (*Sinn*) but no referent (*Bedeutung*) that corresponds to the *Sinn* in question. But the self is not Pegasus, nor a unicorn. The self exists. Pegasus and unicorns do not exist, though some philosophers, such as Meinong and Russell, have claimed that they subsist. For Sartre, the self *is*, but not as referent of a cognitive or a linguistic act. That the self exists was made quite evident in *Nausea*. Roquentin experiences that which lies behind the veneer of things, that which underlies their essences. But he experiences even more strongly the existence that underlies any values or determinations that he might select for himself. To write a history of the Marquis de Rollebon might be a way of suggesting that this self is a historian, that this self can be referred to as a historian. Roquentin has a title, an essence, a name. The meaning of that essence will be his *self*—the label that he will be able to call his own. This nominalist identification is reassuring to him.

The title will comfort him. Yet when he considers whether the appellation (*historian* will in fact (-icity) be himself, he experiences nausea. He becomes aware that his self will not be identifiable with the referent *historian*. Nausea, then, is the experienced awareness that the self exists, but that it is not any particular essence. This experienced awareness of being other than essence, other than labels, is frightening to Roquentin. He is confronted with his own existence—the existence of his self, a self that has meaning but no referent. Whenever it is a referent such as *historian*, the label will be different from the self as a meaning (the meaning of the self). The nausea is what one undergoes when confronted with this unusual situation. Undergoing the nausea, as in Nietzsche's *Thus Spoke Zarathustra*, is going under (*untergehen*) in order to overcome (*übergehen*) one's self. For Dostoevsky's underground note writer, going underground and being spiteful are the analogues of experiencing nausea. In Sartre's terminology, to be nauseated is to be conscious of one's self and its existence—without linguistic reference.

What is this self that cannot be known thetically or referred to linguistically? Since it exists, its ontological mode must be its manner of being understood. *Being and Nothingness*, which occurs within this same *episteme*, is subtitled "An Essay in Phenomenological Ontology." One of the tasks here is to bring out the being of the self in order to consider it as a phenomenon. What, then, is the meaning *qua* appearance of the self? There should be "selfness," though there may not be a self that is a reflected object or a referred name. This "selfness," Sartre proposes, is nonsubstantial. It is not an object, in itself, a thing. A nonreified meaning, however, is not unusual. All phenomenological meanings (*eidoi, noemata*) are not, as such, things. Many such meanings are meanings *of* things, but this is not to suggest that they themselves *are* things. There are also meanings of poems, images, dreams, sounds, and so on. In each of these cases, that of which there is consciousness is other than the consciousness itself. We have already seen that whenever the self is other than the consciousness itself, it is not the same self that has been under investigation. If, however, the self is the same self that is conscious, it must occupy a rather unusual status. What then is the meaning of the self, the "content" of consciousness—the selfness—when the self is the very consciousness itself?

When Sartre claims that this true self is entirely for-itself (*pour-soi*), he means that it cannot be an object for itself and still be itself. So he calls the true self, this being for-itself, *nothingness*. As *nothingness* (*le néant*), the self is a meaning with no referent, an existence with no essence, a consciousness with no object that is other.

This pure unreflected subjectivity is active, always becoming (Kierkegaard's contribution). The flux of the self is its temporality. The future self (who I shall be) and the past self (who I was) are outside consciousness. Such selves cannot be identical with the self that I am. Each must necessarily be in-itself, an object for reflective consciousness, before or after my true self. When Roquentin thinks of his future visit with Anny or when he remembers his past occasions with her, he distinguishes the present self from those other selves. The self who he is can be described temporally as present. Therefore, what is present is the true self, the unreflected consciousness, the for-itself, and existence. Though present, a reflective act attempting to identify its nature will reveal only a "just-having-been," a self that is no longer the present self. Similarly, when a specific future self is projected, this self that is about to be will also distinguish itself from the present. This present is not quite a specious present, but it does clearly distinguish itself from other moments of the temporal flow. It acquires special renown in that the present is the moment of the true self. If the self is present, absence will clarify the character of that presence. Presence differentiates itself from what it is not, whether it be presence of the self or the presence of some object, a chestnut-tree root, Peter in the café, or Orestes or Electra. When the other (thing or person) is absent, then the critical question is whether that absence is present or whether it is simply absent. When Electra in *The Flies* laments the absence of Orestes, his absence prohibits her from effecting revenge and retribution upon her mother, Clytemnestra, and her lover, Aegisthus. Orestes' absence is therefore quite present to Electra. She experiences the non-presence of her brother. Again, this experience is not formulated as such in terms of words—even when he does appear, she refuses to call him Orestes until she is convinced that he is the brother who will assist her in returning justice to Argos. Even when he tells Electra his name, she does not take the name as identical with the reality. The reality of Orestes is most important to her—his name is only incidental and secondary. Thus, she will attribute the name to him only when she is convinced of the reality of his presence. This de-emphasis on the role of language in the formulation of the self is echoed in Merleau-Ponty's comment that the two lovers in the *Charterhouse of Parma* know the presence of love even before it is named.[7] The name simply confirms the knowledge—and renders it transcendent. In *The Flies*, the present absence of Orestes does not depend upon Orestes' naming himself in order for him to become a present presence. The direct experience is what counts. Electra must experience him as Orestes. The word itself will not suffice.

Sartre outlines a similar movement when he describes the experience of one's self as absent. Here, however, it is not the other who appears as absent, but rather one's very own self. The self appears as an "absent-presence:"

> Selfness represents a degree of nihilation carried further than
> the pure presence to itself of the pre-reflective cogito—in
> the sense that the possible which I am is not pure presence
> to the for-itself as reflection to reflecting, but that it is *absent-presence*.[8]

Selfness as an absent-presence is the full appearance of a meaning within consciousness, but a meaning without a referent—hence, a consciousness whose content is the presence of an absence. Consciousness cannot provide an elaboration of selfness as pure presence. The self as absent-presence indicates the emptiness of consciousness in the sense that the self's possibilities are evident though no specific definition can be made available. Once the multiplicity of possibilities has been determined as one particular formulation of the self, the self becomes pure presence. Therefore, the fundamental characteristic of selfness is its possibilities. Sartre's *No Exit* demonstrates quite vividly the absent-presence of selfness in that the three characters occupy an afterworld in which the world is still present to them. They have an openness onto what other people are still saying about them. Language identifies them but the speakers are not aware that what they say is available to the awareness of those (dead) who are under discussion (i.e., referred to). This awareness is exaggerated in that it is located in the afterlife, and hence inaccessible to the speakers on earth. Nevertheless, the absent-presence is emphasized by the dissociation between the statements about them and the consciousness that perceives their articulation. Garcin, for example, now in this hell, understands how his possibilities are limited. He no longer has the full freedom of possibilities available to the living self. Naturally, in a play, the self speaks. But Sartre does not point out that this is a speaking self. Rather, we are aware that the self's possibilities have been limited only by the situation in which the three characters find themselves. Since they cannot manifest an openness onto the future as we who are alive can, they must continue eternally in their absent-presence. When a full, living human being is in question, the totality of possibilities, which the self is qua "circuit of selfness," "is what the for-itself lacks in order to be itself." (BN, p. 102; Fr., p. 147) By passing through that which is absent, that which is lacking, the specific lack of being becomes evident. The circuit of selfness delineates the structure of the self without requiring that there be something, a content, or an in-itself, within consciousness. The circuit of selfness is the delineation of pure phenomenological meaning.

II

In 1947–8, Sartre is on the threshold of a new positivity. A new conceptual scheme begins to arise. Sartre writes *What Is Literature?* (1947) and then produces *Dirty Hands* (1948). His epistemological break with an alinguistic ontologization of cognitive experience points to a new view of the self. *What Is Literature?* provides the groundwork in that the concept of the prose writer, as one who ought to be committed to the freedom of other people, becomes the paradigm of the self expressing itself through language. Freedom, which was a well-developed notion in *Being and Nothingness*, serves as the principal feature of the self's contact with language in *What Is Literature?* In the earlier view, freedom was described as the specific character of consciousness in its field of possibilities. The very nihilating quality of consciousness-as-self is its freedom. By negating the object-like status of the in-itself, consciousness as for-itself makes its projects as free acts in a situation of possibility. In this work on the natural function and purpose of literature, Sartre proposes that freedom is intimately bound up with the activity of the writer in relation to his reader:

179

The author writes in order to address himself to the freedom of readers, and he requires it in order to make his work exist. But he does not stop there: he also requires that they return this confidence which he has given them, that they recognize his creative freedom, and that they in turn solicit it by a symmetrical and inverse appeal. Here there appears the other dialectical paradox of reading: the more we experience our freedom, the more we recognize that of the other; the more he demands of us, the more we demand of him.[9]

The notion of the self that is founded in its freedom is hereby placed in a linguistic context. The writer must necessarily write in order to be a writer, and the reader must necessarily read in order to be a reader. In both cases, writing and words serve as the medium for the expression of freedom. The dialectic between reader and writer places these particular species of self in direct relationship with words. The free self addresses or is addressed through writing. Thus, the writing functions as a means by which one self communicates with the freedom of another. What does not occur, however, is an identification of the self with the language of writing. Rather, we live within language—as Heidegger claimed, "Language is the house of Being." Language is

> our shell and our antennae; it protects us against others and informs us about them; it is a prolongation of the senses, a third eye which is going to look into our neighbor's heart. We are within language as within our body. We feel it spontaneously while going beyond it toward other ends, as we feel our hands and our feet; we perceive it when it is the other who is using it, as we perceive the limbs of others. There is the word which is lived and the word which is met. But in both cases, it is in the course of an undertaking, either of me acting on others or the other upon me. The word is a certain particular moment of action and has no meaning outside of it. (WL, pp. 14–15; Fr., p.71)

That words are bound up with action and that the self *qua* conscious being *is* only in its action indicates the central function of words in the ontology of the self. Sartre even suggests that for the "engaged" writer "words are action." (WL, p. 17; Fr., p. 73)

180

If the self *is* through its action and words are action, then, in this case the prose writer, the self can reveal its being through words. Not everyone, however, employs words as a mode of action. The committed writer and his readers are not the only possibilities. Picasso's painting of the destruction at Guernica, Merleau-Ponty's conception of gesture, and Camus's rebel are all nonverbal forms of action. In this respect, Sartre still finds validity in the priority of action over words. He would agree with Goethe's revision of the Gospel according to John, which reads: "in the beginning was the Act" (rather than the Word). Not all individuals define themselves in terms of words.

The second *episteme* enters into a living relationship between self and words, but only for selected selves, only for those involved in a committed enterprise. Presumably we are all "within language as within our body." However, only action makes the words of that language significant. Hugo, in *Dirty Hands*, knows that he talks excessively. He is called a "chatterbox." Olga tells him that he talks too much, that he talks to make sure he is alive. The words that he speaks are what confirm his life. Words even seem to define his life—he recounts in acts one through six the events leading up to his deed. But the deed achieves signification only as Hugo recounts it. Although, as Goethe says, "*Im Anfang war die Tat*," here the deed must be talked about in order for its meaning to be assessed: "Telling it, that's not hard; I know it by heart; I recited it to myself every day in prison. But what it means, that's something else again."[10] Action signifies only as it is given in words. Language (here: speech) is the mode by which action achieves phenomenological meaning (*Sinn*).

When Hugo killed Hoederer, was it an assassination or a crime of passion? Is Hugo salvageable or not? The resolution of the latter question may also depend upon history, as in Bukharin's case.[11] He is salvageable if his act was a crime of passion, if his motive was not political. Since Hoederer has been reinstated politically and his work must be carried on, his assassin cannot be salvaged (revived, brought out of the junk heap). But if the crime were committed out of jealousy, then Hugo did not kill Hoederer for political reasons. In this case, the meaning of the act as recounted to Olga is different. Like Dostoevsky's murderer Raskolnikov, whose name Hugo takes before the crime, he can be saved. Olga is his Sonya. The life after prison can be his resurrection. But the difference here is that the meaning of his deed depends upon what he says to Olga. The meaning of the act depends upon his words.

Hugo sees that the act establishes his identity and fulfills his reality, but his identity and reality attain meaning only through words. He must define himself through his deed. He is called a traitor by those who put him up to it, and an assassin by Hoederer and Jessica (his wife). But he is also accused of play-acting as both traitor and assassin. Who is he? What is the meaning of the deed when he does kill Hoederer? Was he in fact an assassin or a traitor? He has acted, but he has not chosen. Only his words two years later will define his deed and hence his being. The words will be his choice. The word that he finally chooses, "un-salvageable," is a commitment to self-destruction. Like Hoederer he will be killed and history as it is written will determine the significance of his life. His own word, "unsalvageable," the last word of the play, will finally be identified with his reality. Hugo will not be open to the charge of play-acting.

In this second *episteme*, tentative corrections are offered between verbal expression and the existing self. Hugo is a case in point. He tries out defining himself as a traitor, then experiments with assassinhood. He acts out of equivocal motives and is deemed a jealous husband by his victim and by society. Only when he calls himself "unsalvageable" does he accept a name for himself. Nevertheless, the clear dichotomy between language and reality is maintained.

In *Saint Genet*, Sartre's view is that instead of the dichotomous relationship between words and reality that is expressed in *Dirty Hands*, words are here identified with reality, play-acting and overt action are associated with appearance. This inversion of the situation in *Dirty Hands* is due to Genet's peculiar circumstances. The difference, however, expresses the same position (by negation). Just as Hugo ends with an identification of his self with a name—his condemnation—Genet begins his life with a similar identification. In both cases, the dialectic between the self and words is in operation.

Genet is orphaned. He knows nothing of his mother or father. At the age of seven, he is taken to the home of Morvan peasants, who give him everything he has. Genet owns nothing; everything is a gift. Hence, when he is caught taking a pair of scissors from the utensil drawer, it is viewed as theft. However, we are told that Genet condemns theft, since it is immoral to steal. Even so, Genet has been stealing all along without realizing it, since he does not distinguish between taking and partaking of what has been made available to him. His verbal condemnation of stealing and his action of stealing remain separate until Genet is "caught in the act."

His hand reaches into the utensil drawer and the look of the other (his foster parents) is translated into the words "You are a thief." Instead of distinguishing the words from himself, Genet takes them as a specification of who he is. He assumes that because he has been called a thief, he must *be* a thief. A spiritual death occurs. His multifaceted existence has now been given a unitary meaning: "Thief." He has been objectified and made other by his foster parents. His task remains one of determining what to do with his new-found identity (his received self).

Genet decides to be what crime made of him. He takes on the label and begins to activate the evil will that has been attributed to him. Genet is Evil, because decent folk, like his foster parents, are Good. Good folk would not steal, hence Genet is Evil because he is a thief. If Genet is Evil, an in-itself, his for-itself must express itself through a will, in Genet's case, an Evil will. He has been named an outcast by society. Now he must act as other, as when to everyone in society, as unacceptable to the community of selves.

When introducing *The Thief's Journal*, which Genet wrote in 1949, Sartre spoke of Genet as Narcissus: "Not all who would be are Narcissus. Many who lean over the water see only a vague human figure. Genet sees himself everywhere. . . ."[12] Genet is always someone other than himself for himself. Once he has identified himself with words, he cannot distinguish himself from them. His otherness has been initiated by the verbal self-definition. From then on, his selfhood will always be otherness. Hence, when Genet, like the mythical Narcissus, looks into the water, what appears is not an image of his identity—but rather his very identity. He is the thief, the beggar, the homosexual, the poet, the saint, the double, and so on. Whenever the self seeks to know itself, a word appears and the self is identified with it. The reflective consciousness must fall back into the immediate consciousness and fade out there. For the reflective consciousness was a flashlight that searched the immediate consciousness with the aim of discovering the Other there. But it failed in its task and could only produce a paltry Ego."[13] Like the attempts of a reflective consciousness to reveal the unreflected in *The Transcendence of the Ego*, the reflective consciousness here is a flashlight that cannot accomplish its task. No light is shown on the self as immediate consciousness. What appears is the "paltry Ego" that bears a name, which *is* the name: *Thief*. He finds the other, it is himself.

Rimbaud wrote: *"Je est un autre"*—I is another. In speaking of Genet, he might have added: and the other is a word. What Sartre says, however, is: I is another and the other is God. But what does it mean to be God here? By being treated as other, Genet can choose to do what he will with the identity that he has been given. Because he is other, he is alienated from himself. Just as Feurbach claims that man in his self-alienation created God (which was Feurbach's response to Hegel's thesis that God in his self-alienation created man), Sartre affirms that Genet in his self-alienation is other, is God. Because he is other, Genet is free to exercise his will in whatever fashion he may wish. In this sense he becomes pure freedom, pure will—pure evil will. Because he is pure freedom, he can be God. Since he is alienated from himself, however, he cannot be God, for God has nothing alien within him. Once otherness enters into God, it becomes demonic (according to Sartre). The otherness within Genet makes him a demon. He remains a demon because he has been called evil and because he continues to associate words with his own reality.

Normally, language is an instrument, a tool, a means to the end that is communication. Sometimes words attain a more independent status, they become miraculous, illustrating the power of language over the self. Sartre says that language is Genet's "most inward reality and the most rigorous expression of his exile." (SG, p. 276; Fr., p. 259) His reality has been defined by language. Also, language is the means by which Genet's alienation from decent folk occurred and the means by which Genet continues his exile. Society has taken care of *things;* Genet can do what he wishes with *words*. Genet is a being-toward-prison, to speak in Heideggerian terms, and no matter what he does, society has isolated him. When in prison, it does not matter whether he calls it a prison or a palace; as far as society is concerned, he has been taken care of. "What counts is the word's material presence,

184

which symbolizes the signifying content that, for Genet, is none other than the being of the thing signified." (SG, p. 280; Fr., p. 261) Genet associates the thing signified with the meaning of the word that is symbolized. The association is not, however, a correlation. Rather, it is an identification in which there is no difference. The word takes on the ontological character of the thing.

When Genet enters the bookstore with his rigged briefcase, he asks the bookseller for a rare book. The bookseller makes the normal correlation between the book requested and the words "I would like to see the book." Genet, however, proposes his own words as the thing signified. What he means is: I would like you to leave the open store. His words are the absenting of the bookseller, just as normally a rose is the red flower on the thorny bush. When the bookseller leaves, Genet places the book that really interests him in his special briefcase. The other meaning of the words "I would like to see the book" has been realized.

Similarly, when a policeman stops him (after the theft of the book) and asks him what is in his briefcase, Genet answers, "Nothing." For Genet, the reality is the word *Nothing*, the reality is not what is in the briefcase. As Genet interprets the situation, his *answer* is the thing to which the policeman's question refers. Here language is a tool in that it will dissuade his interrogator from pursuing the investigation. For Genet, what is in fact in his briefcase is an appearance, whereas for the policeman the appearance (which can be deceptive) is Genet's word. If the man does not believe Genet's negation, then Genet's word has broken down like a lawn mower that no longer works. The thing (word) will have failed to operate.

This identification of words with things is an extension of Genet's identification of words with his subjectivity. Genet's gestures are intended to derealize things. "Speech is a gesture and the word is a thing." (SG, p. 392; Fr., p. 364) By speaking, Genet gives life to the self that has become a word. Since words are things, Genet's self is a thing for himself. Yet when he speaks, he is able to go beyond his self-reification through the language and words that have been given to him. The relationship between words and speech is parallel to that between poetry and prose. This distinction, first expounded in *What Is Literature?*, is reiterated in Genet's case and again for Flaubert.

185

Genet first writes poetry "in order to be moved." Dante and Petrarch would write of Beatrice or Laura because they were moved by a *visio Dei* or a love for the woman, but Genet creates words that will stimulate his own emotion. The poetic words are written in order to activate the self: "I was twenty years old; a little girl whom I loved had died ten years before, and it was the anniversary of her death. I wrote the verses in order to be moved" (SG, p. 426; Fr., p. 396). This was Genet's first poem. By writing it he would hear himself as another. He reads his own words: they are himself but as an otherness. Because he is other for himself he can be moved emotionally by his own words, and only by writing them does the sense of loss become real.

The poetic act is a gesture. Hence it is a form of speech. The self speaks by creating words. As the words are created, the self is defined, spoken, but only in an isolated form. The poem is not an end-in-itself, rather it is a means to martyrdom. Genet martyrs himself by making the poem other. Since, however, he is already other when he writes, he must perform a double negation in order to martyr himself, that is, to place himself in a position where he has been wronged by others. When he writes "The Condemned Man," he achieves the goal. He has been called a thief by others because he possessed nothing. Now he collects the very words of his poem from other poets: Cocteau, Valéry, Mallarmé, Hugo, Baudelaire, everyone. His poem is a patchwork of phrases written by others. No one would have wanted him to be in a situation where he must steal. Hence he is pitiable. He has been wrongly persecuted and he wants to return this to society—to martyr himself before good people. Genet's poetry is not written so that we will see, since his poetry itself is theft (plagiarism). His poetry is an expression of his own experience in order to observe himself. He is the condemned man, like Villon in "The Ballad of the Hanged Man," who reflects upon his own fate. Poetry, as Sartre pointed out in *What Is Literature?*, is on the side of things, not signs. Poetry is a structure of the external world. When Genet sees himself as the condemned man, the poem serves as a mirror for his own self. In just the same way that the mirror is material, and reflects the image of the visual self, Genet's poetry is a means of placing his life before him. Sartre calls this "poetry-fatality," which has an end. It is determined and inevitable—a clear reflection of the self for itself.

186

In contrast to poetry-fatality, Sartre refers to "deliberate poetry." Deliberate poetry is founded on choice: choice of words, audience, style, and so forth. Deliberate poetry is written for a purpose. Thus Genet "puts fatality into his poems and his deliberate art into prose" (SG, p. 44; Fr., p. 412). The deliberate in prose is the presence of choice and freedom in Genet's work. Bound to himself when he writes poetry, in prose he is able to achieve his full martyrdom. He will not only be something alien for himself as he is in his poetry, but he will also be alien to other people who read his prose. Through words, he will reach beyond his personal experience to that of other people.

Writing prose is a departure from the passiveness of poetry. As a creator, Genet writes prose. Prose is factual and participates in a world of facts. But it is also "overdetermined." A multiplicity of meanings fills the prose moment. A metaphorical language appeals to the other and speaks to others with its multi-directionality. Here the artist's consciousness is not simply self-indulgent, but has a purpose, a direction, and an audience. Overdetermined prose is the medium for Genet's full self-expression.

If Genet did not write, he would be just one more thief, one more homosexual, one more person who lives in his own self-enclosed world. Yet he does write. Since *he* is in his poetry, his poetry is Evil. But when he writes prose, the poetry tampers with it—gets in the way—Evil taints the prose, which is Good. Poetry gives the prose false pretenses. The prose is a victim of the poetic activity. What is normally Good (prose) is placed on an Evil base (poetry).

Through the influence of poetry as Evil, Genet in his prose enters the homes of the Good people of society. The work of art is a substitute for crime. The work of art is a type of Apollonian dream that people experience while they are awake, as opposed to the dream of crimes occurring in their homes while they are asleep.

By writing, Genet reaches beyond the walls that have isolated him from society as a whole. Police, magistrates, and prison guards all insulate him from decent people. Society has delegated these individuals to keep selves such as Genet's away from the daily activities of society. When Genet writes, the social character of words allows them to universalize their significations. Words penetrate prison walls and social castes. When uttered, a word is as a subject speaking; but when heard, it takes the form of an object. When Genet writes, he becomes an object for himself in his poetry; and when it is deliberate *qua* prose, he martyrs himself for others. He presents himself as victim to them. But his victimization is also his betrayal. When he frightens other people, then he achieves the glory he seeks. His victory is verbal in that he restores negativity to his readers. They react against him and hence burn him at the stake. But this is what he wants.

Genet objectifies himself in the language of his autobiographical novels as we do ourselves in our dreams. He makes himself into many different characters, for example, Divine, who is living with Darling. The only way for him to believe in the real existence of Darling is to objectify himself as Divine (the queen). In that way, Genet can be with Darling and believe in him. Genet must see himself in the female role in order to create the existence of Darling. Genet is Divine, whom he has created in words. As an objectification of Genet, Divine is also an object for decent people.

Given an ego, a self, Genet wants to return it to decent people and install it within their daily experience—he wants to throw it back into their laps. Hence his use of *I* in the fictional work. The reader encounters the *I* in the novel and confuses it with his own. In referring to a subjectivity, the *I* is referred to one's own. But that *I* is of course the *I* of a thief and homosexual. In identifying his self with that of the novel, the reader is made uneasy. He is inclined to ask, "What else did I do?" (SG, p. 499; Fr., p. 461). "Genet holds the mirror up to us: we must look at it and see ourselves" (SG, p. 599; Fr., p. 550). His self penetrates into our own through the language of autobiographical fictional prose. We are forced to react because of the uneasy identification. Genet becomes a victim to us and we give him the sainthood that is his victory over us. Through words, Genet brings his self before those who read him. Because he *is* the words he creates, this particular self presents itself to other humans for their unwitting participation. Thus the universalization of the self occurs through the words that the self creates in order to communicate.

III

The third paradigm is once again a new stage of thought in the development of Sartre's philosophy. No longer is the self simply identified with words—particularly in prose writing—but now the self is articulated directly in linguistic terms. What was an aberration in Genet becomes the *modus vivendi* for the Sartrian man of the 1960s. With the appearance of *Search for a Method* (1957) as an introduction to the *Critique of Dialectical Reason* (1960) and *Words* (1963), Sartre puts forth this new position quite explicitly. A full reformulation of the relationship between the self and language is here achieved.

Only suggested in *Saint Genet*, the position that language is a social phenomenon, that words universalize, is made clear in *Search for a Method*. In emphasizing the role of social structures, Sartre points out that we are not only knowers, but we also appear as known.[14] As known, we are manifestations of the interests of a class engaged in a collective project. Class-consciousness is

> not the simple lived contradiction which objectively characterizes the class considered; it is that contradiction already surpassed by *praxis* and thereby preserved and denied all at once. But it is precisely this revealing negativity, this distance within immediate proximity, which simultaneously constitutes what existentialism calls "consciousness of the object" and "nonthetic self consciousness." (SM, p. 33n; Fr., p. 31n)

Going beyond the lived contradiction of a given class is the nature of this class consciousness. Praxis is the means by which a class goes beyond its contradictions in order to effect appropriate changes. Thus, praxis is the analogue of the non-thetic self-consciousness that was characteristic of the first *episteme*. But praxis is a social phenomenon—it is what *we* do. My praxis is paired with the praxis of others through reciprocity. We are known through the expression of our common praxis and language is one of the most central forms in which this social self is exhibited.

Sartre explains his position, particularly in footnotes to *Search for a Method*, in the light of semiological formulations. Although de Saussure thought that linguistics was merely a part of the general science of signs, Roland Barthes suggests that, on the contrary, semiology is a part of linguistics.[15] Following Barthes, to speak of the self in semiological terms is to offer a linguistic consideration. Sartre bases his own stance on the shoulders of Hegel and Kierkegaard:

> for Hegel, the Signifying (*le Signifiant*) (at any moment of history) is the movement of Mind (which will be constituted as the signifying-signified and the signified-signifying; that is, as absolute-subject), the Signified (*le Signifié*) is the living man and his objectification. For Kierkegaard, man is the signifying; he himself produces the significations, and no signification points to him from outside (Abraham does not know whether he is Abraham); man is never the signified (not even by God). (SM, pp. 9–10n; Fr., p. 18n)

That the French *signifiant* can be translated both as "signifying" and as "signifier" must permeate an understanding of Sartre's claim. For Hegel, absolute mind (*Geist*) in its movement is the signifier—that which motivates signification through signifying activity. When *Geist* achieves its fulfilment, it is the signifier-signified and signified-signifier. Sartre refers to this achievement as the absolute subject, which would be analogous to his own being-in-itself-for-itself.

The difference in translation is also worthy of consideration with respect to Kierkegaard. Man is the signifier, in this case. As an individual, he does the signifying and produces the significations. He is never the signified, because he is never an object for himself or for anyone else. But Sartre does not say "object" here. He says "signified," suggesting that a man is never linguistically specified (Genet would be an exception). Man is always linguistically specifying—he specifies what is by giving it names and labels. For Kierkegaard, the individual never specifies himself, although Sartre characterizes his nature as a signifier or as signifying.

This linguistic formulation of the self in terms of the Hegelian and Kierkegaardian views is surpassed in the Sartrian position. Sartre proposes that the Hegel-Kierkegaard conflict is resolved in that man is neither signified nor signifying (signifier). Man is *at once* both signified-signifying (signified-signifier) and signifying-signified (signifier-signified). Sartre states that this is like the Hegelian absolute subject but in a different sense (SM, pp. 165, 166n; Fr., p. 103n). In his UNESCO lecture on Kierkegaard

(1964),[16] Sartre characterized this same notion of man as "the singular universal" and as "the subject-object paradox," But in *Search for a Method*, the semiological terminology helps to clarify man's situatedness in language. Sartre's move here is to give the self the status of man, as signified-signifier and signifier-signified.[17] The self is situated squarely inside language and inside culture.

When the self is inside language, one is inside "a special field of instruments." Language is an "objectification of a class, the reflection of conflicts, latent or declared, and the particular manifestations of alienation" (SM, p. 113: Fr., p. 75). To be inside language is to be part of the social structures that characterize one's class and that represent conflicts that arise out of the presence of need in a field of scarcity. Thus, the conditions of class-consciousness through the activity of praxis in the face of practico-inert elements are worked out within language.

For this very reason, Sartre can and must, in this third *episteme*, or paradigm, discuss the self in terms of language. Where, in the first stage, the self could be discussed without reference to language and, in the second, language becomes important only for the committed writers or for one such as Genet who identifies the self with words, at this third *episteme* the self must appear within the very words that one uses. Since, in the Marxist formulation, there are only men and real relations among men, these relations also involve one's particular linguistic structures. Sartre claims that man defines himself by his project. But in *Search for a Method*, it is a collective project rather than the individual fundamental project of *Being and Nothingness*. As the self goes beyond its material conditions, it establishes significations within its social context.

> Significations come from man and from his project, but they are inscribed everywhere in things and in the order of things. Everything at every instant is always signifying and signification reveals to us men and relations among men across the structures of our society. But these significations appear to us only insofar as we ourselves are signifying. (SM. p. 156; Fr., p. 98)

Through signification we participate in the collective activity of our situation. The self signifies through its signification, through its language, from which it cannot extract itself. At most, the self can continue to signify.

The self totalizes, as Sartre points out in the *Critique of Dialectical Reason*, through a "dialectical circularity." This dialectical circularity is the first paradigm "circuit of selfness" placed in a social and linguistic context. By means of *need*, the self totalizes itself with other selves through a common praxis. Man mediates things to the same extent that things mediate man. Praxis confronts the practico-inert as much as the practico-inert, the material elements of social life, presents itself to man. The self is caught up in the dialectic and can totalize itself only in a series or group and by its act of signifying—by creating significations.

The self signifies the signified by signifying significations. Although actions signify, so too do words. *The Condemned of Altona* (1960) illustrates this point in that Franz, who has been hiding in his room for thirteen years since the Second World War, still believes that Germany is in ruins. He wants this to be true to such an extent that he says, "I'm making progress. One day the words will come by themselves, and I shall say what I want to."[18] If Franz is successful, his words will not even require a self to make them signify. They will take on the signifying by themselves. In this sense, history will follow its progressive inevitable path, as Marxists claim, and signification will be self-supporting: the self will be a signifier only when there are signifieds to actualize it.

The progressive-regressive method, however, also prescribes that one go back to the family and class conditions that make certain significations inevitable. Franz's incestuous relations with Leni close him off from events. He is unable to express his common praxis with others. Hence he can conceive of the possibility of his words signifying by themselves. As his sister-in-law says, "words don't have the same meaning up there" (CA, p. 102; Fr., p. 220). A regressive consideration will show that this is not possible: words cannot signify by themselves. Franz must leave his room and face the practico-inert or die. He selects the latter. His voice and the words on the tape recorder can only announce that he has been, that he must be responsible for and answer for what does occur among men. Like the view of Sartre's first *episteme*—for example, in *Existentialism Is a Humanism* (1946)— in choosing one chooses for all mankind, but here choice and responsibility come from a common praxis in view of common practico-inert conditions. In this third paradigm, choices must signify—perhaps they are signification itself—but in any case signifying necessarily implicates a living self (the signifier).

Franz would not deal with his family and the real responsibilities that gave him signification. Sartre takes this to heart and writes his autobiography as an attempt at a self-reflexive progressive-regressive study. He calls it *The Words*. His project: to save himself—"a whole man, composed of all men, as good as all of them and no better than any."[19] *The Words* is Sartre's attempt to show that the self must be expressed in terms of words. The self signifies particularly through the language in which it is inscribed.

Sartre writes. What he writes, like his words, is the locus of his projects. Through his books, Sartre projects himself into culture. He recognizes himself in what he writes in that writing is a product of human activity, human praxis. Because he was told by his grandfather, whom he resented, that he would make a good teacher, he decides to select the words that Blanche Picard offers for him. "The child will be a writer," she says. Sartre speaks of it as a "sign on his brow." Through this sign he will achieve signification—the progressive perspective will reveal his being. The status of his grand-parents, the early death of his father, the indenture of his mother to her parents, the absence of a requirement that he follow in his father's shoes, all form the regressive elements that contribute to a comprehension of Sartre. The self is its words—first play-acting with them, then taking them as his vocation:

> I took language for the world. To exist was to have an official title somewhere on the infinite Tables of the Word; to write was to engrave new beings upon them or and this was my most persistent illusion—to catch living things in the trap of phrases: if I combined words ingeniously, the object would get tangled up in the signs, I would have a hold on it. (W, p. 114; Fr., p. 151)

By writing words, Sartre attempted to be like Genet: to identify the words with things. But he knows that the words will signify things and that they will signify the self when it activates the words. This was Roquentin's thought when he contemplated breaking away from history writing and creating a novel. What was a possibility for Roquentin is a necessity for Sartre in his third *episteme*. As Sartre says in *The Words*, "I was Roquentin." Now he must write and create out of the significations of his social context.

Sartre's blindness in later life does not deny him the fulfilment of this third paradigm. He wrote until he could no longer write, but the end of writing is not the end of the self. There are still the very words of the speaking subject. Although he says that tape recorders are an inadequate substitute for the stylistic formation of words beneath his pen, there are those who continue Sartre's signifying activity through interviews, films and television broadcasts (with Simone de Beauvoir, Pierre Victor, Philippe Gavi, Michel Contat and others).[20]

The view that began with the conviction that the self can exist independent of words, and which turned to an interrelational notion of identity and language, concludes with the necessary role of signification in the formation of the self. With the recognition of the social nature of the self in praxis, Sartre has realized the function of language in the delineation of self-expression. Sartre's words *on* the self have become words *of* the self.

PART III

VERSUS
STRUCTURALISM

11

SARTRE AND THE STRUCTURALISTS

INTRODUCTION

During the almost forty-year period in which Sartre's thought has been inscribed in French, and more generally, world culture, structuralism has also established its own base. Structuralism, like existentialism, has specification only insofar as it can be identified with individual proponents. Indeed, although Sartre, Marcel, Heidegger, and Jaspers were all called existentialists at certain periods, they cannot be identified as holding precisely the same doctrine. Hence, although I shall take de Saussure, Lacan and Lévi-Strauss as representative of the structuralists, their individual concerns and interpretations of "structural" features differ significantly.

In selecting these three structuralists, I hope to account for both representative and diverse types of structuralist formulations. De Saussure's work in linguistics at the turn of our century, Lacan's neo-freudian psychoanalytical exploits during the past thirty years, and his contemporary Lévi-Strauss's anthropological inquiries into myth, kinship, and taboos have formed the backbone of structuralist thinking. In responding to their fundamental positions, Sartre has been able to reaffirm his own perspective and to illuminate significant aspects of the structuralist outlook.

Consistent with these interchanges, I shall focus on three specific issues that have served as the basis for controversy: the signifier-signified relation in de Saussure, the unconscious in Lacan, and the concepts of diachrony and synchrony in Lévi-

Strauss. They are related in that the Sartrian understanding of the signifier-signified combination establishes a basis for characterizing human experience. Sartre's lifelong controversy with Freudian psychoanalysis has led him to reject some hidden realm of human experience. And his affirmation of dialectical reason has placed him in opposition to those who would look beyond history in favor of invariant structures of experience. The debate between Sartre and the structuralists, then, is an exchange concerning what can properly account for human experience and its various forms of expression.

When asked by Pierre Verstraeten in a 1965 interview for the *Revue d'Esthétique* whether he distinguishes between signification (or meaning) and "that which is signified" (or simply, "the signified"), Sartre answered:

> Yes, for me the signified is the object. I define my language, which is not necessarily that of linguists: this chair is the object, therefore, it is signified (*signifié*); then, there is the signification, which is the logical totality that will be constituted by the words, the meaning or signification of a sentence. If I say: "This table is in front of the window," I refer to that which is signified (*un signifié*), i.e., the table, by the meanings forming the totality of constituted sentences, and I consider myself to be the signifier (*le signifiant*). The meaning is the noema, the correlate of the vocal elements that are uttered.[1]

Sartre here has utilized the Saussurian distinction between the signifier and the signified by transferring it to a phenomenological context. For Saussure, the signified would be the concept or notion of chair as it is signified by the word or signifier "chair." However, the English translation of *signifiant* as "signifier" eliminates the ambiguity which exists in French: *signifiant* can be both a noun or substantive ("signifier") and a present participle or process ("signifying"). Thus the *signifiant* is that which signifies, the signifier, and the signifying process—particularly in a speech act. Sartre inverts Saussure's view by making *signifiant* that which signifies, but more accurately the signifying process itself (since he rejects a substantialist view of the ego). The signified becomes the actual object, signified in the world. Sartre's signification, like Saussure's, is the act of unification whereby the signifier and the signified are brought into relation. In Sartre, signification is the meaning given in the signifying of the signified.[2] The transposition from Saussure's terminology is Sartre's way of clarifying his own notion of being in relation to structural linguistics.

As I shall show, human being (i.e., the person) is a totality of significations in Sartre's sense. Being appears in terms of signification (or meaning), which, Sartre says, is the "logical totality" constituted by the words of a sentence. Meaning is constituted being— the logical totality—which the words actualize. To consider in further detail, the meaning is not just a relationship between a word and its concept, as it is from the linguist's perspective, but rather it is an ontological phenomenon. For Sartre, the signified is a particular object which is signified. A totality of many signifieds constitutes a world of objects. That which signifies the world of objects, or particular objects as well, is not the words themselves (as Saussure would have it), but rather the particular self who does the signifying (i.e., the signifying process or *signifiant*).

When considered in terms of Sartre's philosophical work in general, this translation from one conceptual scheme to another is most informative. Sartre has already made it quite clear in *The Transcendence of the Ego*[3] (1936) that the ego is not a transcendental component in the way Husserl had proposed. The ego is not the source of intentional acts; it is not the Cartesian *ego cogito* which does the doubting. At most, the ego is a transcendent object—a "just-having-been" which can be considered reflexively only as an object. Hence from this perspective all there is for reflection is the series or totality of objects that present themselves. The ego can be an object of reflection, just like the chair, but it can never be the object of itself *as* it is reflecting. The ego is always constituted as a being-in-itself (*en-soi*) in the same sense that the chair is in-itself. In other words, the chair, *qua* signified, is given signification by the person constituting it either experientially or in terms of words. The person, then, is a signifying activity—I constitute the chair while at the same time signifying myself. But *qua* signifier, I am not a transcendental source. I am simply that being which engages in a signifying process.

What is constituted, what is actualized, is the meaning or signification which can be (but is not necessarily) referred to by words which I write or speak. This type of meaning is the human meaning which is given in experiential constitution. Linguistic meaning can be derived only from words or uttered vocal elements. To find the linguistic meaning, one must begin by a study of words and their interrelationships in sentences. Human meaning is not found, it is created. Human meaning is constituted in a signifier-signified relationship where the signifier is not the *ego* but the personal process of signifying objects in terms of words, sentences, discourse, gestures, etc. Human meaning is the uniting of the signifying and the signified in experience.

This binary character of human experience was prominent in his 1943 *magnum opus: Being and Nothingness*.[4] The signified is a being-in-itself. The chair is a being-in-itself (*en-soi*); the chestnut tree in his novel *Nausea* is a being-in-itself; the *ego* is a being-in-itself. All these forms are signified by a signifying act—a being-for-itself (*pour-soi*). But so that this being-for-itself will not be confused with transcendent objects and since it is not a transcendent object, Sartre sought to establish its nature. This being-for-itself could not possibly be any*thing*, since that would make it a being-in-itself—transcendent like the chair. Rather being-for-itself must be no*thing*.[5] Being-for-itself—the status of consciousness—is not any kind of thing and yet it is still a form of being. Its being is active and free, which, for Sartre, is to say that it never constitutes itself as an object.

What is constituted is being—existence—the I am, I exist, of any act—a Cartesian *sum* without substantialization of the self. This being, although it is not anything, is not completely without characteristics. Its most fundamental characteristic is negative: that it is never just pure consciousness. To assert the affirmative would lead to idealism—and pure idealism is unacceptable to Sartre as it was to Husserl. Consciousness is always consciousness *of* something. To be conscious of something is to be no*thing*. Yet the fact of something given is what ties or tethers being-in-itself to being-for-itself. Sartre calls this tethering "facticity." Facticity is the condition of being in a particular situation. Being in a situation is the realism in Sartre's phenomenology. Such being-in-a-situation is the status of being conscious of something in terms of the particular context in which the consciousness occurs. This is dramatized in *Nausea* where Roquentin writes:

How long would this fascination last? I *was* the root of the chestnut tree. Or rather I was entirely conscious of its existence. Still detached from it—since I had consciousness of it—and however lost in it, nothing else but it. A consciousness which was uneasy and yet one which let itself go with all its weight, brought to a state of falseness, on this inert piece of wood.[6]

This consciousness has no substance and yet it is always intricately bound up with substance. It signifies, to return to Sartre's statement of 1965; and what it signifies is substance. It signifies by establishing meanings, some of which can be characterized in terms of words. We might say that Roquentin's meanings—the aspects of his being—are established or constituted in terms of the words written in his journal.

Being, as we have seen, has an unusual status, or perhaps we should say, a very usual status, that is, one which characterizes each and every human being. For a person, being is both in-itself and for-itself. Being, then, as it is constituted, is ambiguous. Human being is both something and nothing, both signified and signifying. From an ontological perspective, this status appears as ambiguous because being is not given as unidimensional. Onto-logically, one can say, I am, I exist, but the nature of this being cannot be a non-complex unity. All the manifestations of being are in terms of beings-in-themselves as they are for-itself; that is, each and every being-in-itself has a correlate which is for-itself. This is the tension which renders the multiplicity of particular beings-in-themselves their unitary manifestation *qua* human being. There are many beings-in-themselves which are for-a-particular-self. Ontologically being itself is the ambiguity of beings-in-themselves that are for-itself. Ontologically, the ambi-guity is given as a totality of beings-in-themselves-for-itself in a tension (the tension of beings-in-themselves as they are united by a being-for-itself).

To restate this point in terms of the 1965 position, we see that each object (the chair, the root of the chestnut tree, or a person's *ego*) is a signified. By itself, this collection of signifieds would be a multiplicity, just as a bundle of impressions is for Hume. However, no signified is ever by itself—it is always that which is signified by a signifier or more precisely, a signifying act. The multiplicity is given as in tension, because each signified is bound to a signifier and, since consciousness is always consciousness of something, each signifier is bound to many signifieds. There are many objects which a signifier can signify (in the sense of human signification, not linguistic signification). A signifier (a signifying consciousness) can signify a chair, the root of a chestnut tree, his ego, etc. The signified could be signified by many signifiers, but then we would be discussing the ontology of objects, and not that of persons. By describing the nature of the relationship of the multiplicity of signified objects to a signifying consciousness we are discussing what Sartre referred to as the "singular universal" in his paper on Kierkegaard.[7] Human experience as a relation of many signified objects to a signifier is universalized in that all humans manifest this ambiguous status; and the individual is singularized as an actualization of this universal condition. The relation forms a tension where the multiplicity of signifieds cannot be separate from a signifying consciousness. There is always meaning, which is the being of the relation. Hence, a person is always meaningful—full of meanings. There is always ambiguity, for, ontologically, this multiplicity of meanings (actualized and describable in words) is always held in tension because of the irreducibility of the signifier-signified relation.

This ambiguity is precisely that which Sartre describes in the following passage:

> Man is the being who transforms his being into *meaning* (*du sens*) and through whom *meaning* comes into the world. The singular universal is this meaning: through his *self*—the practical raising up (*assomption*) and surpassing of being as it is—man restores the unity of envelopment to the universe, by engraving it as a finite determination and a mortgage on future history in the being which envelops him.[8]

Man is human being which is transformed into meanings by experience and activity. His being is the means by which meanings enter the world, since, by being in-itself and for-itself, a man actualizes being itself. We have already shown that being is the precise status of the signifier-signified relation. The status of this relation is the constitution of human meanings, generally describable experientially as *sens* and linguistically as *signification*. This being is ambiguous because a multiplicity of signifieds are related to a signifier and held together in totality by the signifying process. The signifier has this characteristic since it can signify many objects—apart from itself. There would be no signifying if there were not at least one signified to create meaning.[9] But the moment that the signifying signifier has a signified to constitute a meaning, it also constitutes itself as a signifying process, revealing at least one other meaning. This addition of meaning arises, not out of an act of reflection, but in the very signifying itself. In signifying itself, the process empties itself of any special substantial status as a signifi*er*. This ambiguity from the ontological perspective (which can only manifest the multiplicity of meanings in tension *qua* totality) is what Sartre called the "subject-object paradox" (*US*, p. 23) in the Kierkegaard lecture.

The multiplicity of meanings in tension is not reducible, even at a minimum, to only two meanings. Each consideration of the being of being-in-itself and being-for-itself, which is the meaning of that which is signified by a signifying consciousness, reveals not only an object and itself, but also other people. Other people participate in my totality of meanings, as I participate in theirs. It is not enough to say, as Sartre notes in *Being and Nothingness*, that "being is itself . . . it is neither passivity nor activity. It is an immanence which cannot realize itself, an affirmation which cannot act, because it is stuck to itself" (*EN* p. 32; *BN*, p. 27). This characterizes the unity of being—that which makes our experience a totality and not simply a multiplicity of meanings— or, at this point, an ambiguity rather than simply a duality of meanings. But we must also consider that other people are necess- arily implicated in that ambiguity as well. Part of this presence of others can be considered in terms of the body. The body is a sensible center of reference which is "being-in-the-midst-of-the- world." "In so far as I *am for others*, the Other is revealed to me as the subject for whom I am an object" (*EN*, p. 918; *BN*, p. 460). The look of the Other renders this situation concrete. I am the object of his look. The body is given not only as "lived experi- ence," as the center of reference of my own meanings, but also as the locus of those meanings which imply other people. My body is in situation and limits my being in relation to the body of another. In terms of my body I am an object for others. Since my being is also my being *qua* signifier-signified, the other not only *is* for me, as a being-in-itself that is for-itself for me, but also a meaning signified by me.

Now we have at least three meanings (with the first serving as the paradigm case): (1) subject signifier/object signified (or the relation between signifying consciousness and an object such as a chair), (2) subject signifier/subject signified (or the relation between signifying consciousness and the transcendent ego), and (3) subject signifier/object signifier-signified (the relation between signifying consciousness and another person, whose experience is itself a signifier-signified relation). Therefore, not only am I ambiguous, but the other is also ambiguous, unless I should treat him as a signified without an inherent signifier—which, in terms of real being, would be impossible since all signifieds must have a signifier or signifying process to give them meaning. In such a case, the other would not *be* just a signified, even though I might consider him in that way. I would then be treating him as unambiguous, as non-human, as a pure object, as a thing. Such a reduction has specific ethical implications, which we cannot elaborate upon here, except to indicate that it is undesirable to treat another person as unambiguous when experienced as ambiguous. Of course, this might happen by mistake, such as, when we walk around a room filled with statues and we bump into one, discovering that it is really a person.

The ambiguity of a person is one's multiplicity of meanings in tension and this includes the existence of other people. As Sartre pointed out in his Kierkegaard lecture:

> the profundity of Kierkegaard, his manner of remaining *other*, in me, without ceasing to be mine, is the Other of today, my real contemporary who is the foundation of today. Inversely, he is, in each one of us, the denunciation of the ambiguity in him and in others: understandable in the name of each ambiguity, he is our link, our existential relation, multiple and ambiguous between contemporary existents as they are, that is, as lived ambivalences. (*US*, pp. 61–2)

For Sartre, the meanings of that ambiguity include not only the being-in-itself (the signified), being-for-itself (the signifier), and the other (a totalizing signifier-signified relation), but also a dialectical historical being, which is equally foundational to the being that each person is. (We shall return to this historical role in connection with Lévi-Strauss's critique.) Not only is the singular individual person universal by his very manifestation of human experience, but also the universal—history, the social conditions of today and of all times—is rendered singular through the specific meanings that each person lives ambiguously.

I SARTRE AND LACAN

Sartre's controversy with Lacan is equally a debate with psychoanalysis in general. The problem for Sartre has always been one of accounting for human subjectivity without appealing either to a reified ego-center or to a hidden realm of experience which is unavailable to personal inspection. Subjectivity, as we have seen in response to de Saussure and the semiological tradition, is elaborated by a signifying consciousness that makes way for an experienced meaningful totality.

The idea of an unconscious simply does not describe human experience. In the interview with Michel Contat for his seventieth birthday, Sartre indicates that he was tempted to be psychoanalyzed, but, he says, "not in order to clarify what I did not understand myself."[10] He had asked Pontalis, a psychoanalyst and friend of twenty years, to undertake his analysis. The reason he offers is curiosity for the mechanisms of the psychoanalytic method rather than self-understanding. Pontalis's refusal on the grounds of long-term acquaintance led Sartre to drop the whole idea. Fundamentally, delving the unconscious is an intriguing conceptualization, but one which, for Sartre, was hardly necessary. In *The Transcendence of the Ego*, he had distinguished two types of consciousness: reflective and unreflected (*irréfléchi*). Reflective consciousness is a knowing consciousness that reveals immediately the object of awareness. Unreflected consciousness, however, is not given in an act of reflection. This is not to say that it is unconscious. What is unreflected at a particular moment is nevertheless available for reflection at any further time. The unreflected can be known by simply reflecting again. It is not a repressed realm of the psychical, nor is it contained within an *id*-cell, unable to break out. If there is to be an analogue in psychoanalytic theory, unreflected consciousness might be compared with what Freud has called the "preconscious," the latent desires and interests both at the level of the *id* and the *ego*. What is similar is the availability of the pre-conscious for conscious awareness by some trigger, accident, or temporal occasion. But even here the preconscious is often concerned with libidinal drives and object-cathexes which delimit significantly the nature of what is preconscious. For Sartre, unreflected consciousness is unreflected because it is given non-thetically in a conscious act of reflection. A content or noematic meaning is given in the reflective act, but so too is the subjectivity and freedom of selfhood that allows for present and possible experience. This subjectivity and projective freedom of possibilities is given non-thetically, non-positionally, but at the same time as reflective consciousness. It could be called "latent" only in the sense that it can be made available to self-knowledge in a future reflective act. The future act, however, will bring with it its own unreflected consciousness.

In *Being and Nothingness*, Sartre's term "pre-reflective cogito" (which replaces the previous notion of unreflected consciousness) further emphasizes the parallel with a Freudian "preconscious." The "pre-reflective *cogito*" is again non-thetic. But it is also "being-for-revealing," consciousness which when consciousness of something is also consciousness of itself, an "immediate, non-cognitive relation of self to itself" (*EN*, pp. 16–23; *BN*, pp. 9–17). Sartre designates this "pre-reflective *cogito*" consciousness (of), for example, counting. The "of" in parenthesis indicates that reflective consciousness of numbers counted does not, as such, reveal the cognitive life which enters into the experience of counting itself. When Sartre calls this cognitive life "nothingness" he does not always illuminate his position, but fundamentally the term is to show, as I have already mentioned in the first section, its transparent, non-substantial character. The Freudian "preconscious" however establishes a tripartite *substantial* self which is the proper domain of psychoanalytic research.

Sartre's recent 1975 interview with Michel Contat reiterates his basic attitude toward the pre-reflective *cogito* as distinct from the unconscious:

> There are things, which cannot be said, which I can say to myself but which don't allow me to say them to others. Like everyone, I have a grey area which refuses to be spoken.
> —*The unconscious?*
> —Not at all. I am talking about what I *know*.
> There is always a little fringe which is not spoken, and which does not want to be spoken, but which wants to be

206

known, known by me. We can't say everything. You know
that. But I think that later, after my death and perhaps after
yours too, people will say more about themselves and that
will make significant change. Furthermore I think that this
change is linked to a true revolution. (*Entretiens*, pp. 143–4)

The pre-reflective *cogito* refuses to be spoken when we speak, but
it is not a realm unavailable to my knowledge. Indeed, one does
not always say what one knows. What is experienced cognitively,
but not brought out in reflective consciousness or in speech is
nevertheless there. In another time, with different conventions,
what cannot be said now may then be revealed to others. But a
revolution is necessary to take us from our current modes of
interaction—and here Sartre is not far from the Freudian superego which, according to *Civilization and its Discontents*, determines whole cultural prohibitions, inhibitions, and manifestations
of guilt. Our current modes of interaction do not allow us to speak
our minds. This position is representative of the later Sartre, who
sees social situations as conditioned by scarcity both in economic
relations and also in interpersonal relations. The pre-reflective
cogito of 1943 is now imbued with thoughts which remain
unspoken because of social inhibitions. Earlier, it would have
been unspoken because unreflected upon, but nevertheless known
and present in experience. Thus Sartre refuses to affirm a comparable notion of the unconscious as unknown and inaccessible to an
experiencing individual.

Nevertheless, in *Being and Nothingness*, Sartre's enterprise
included a form of psychoanalysis—what he called "existential
psychoanalysis." Its nature was clear and has been much
discussed.[11] The irreducible necessity of choice as a free unification
in the form of a fundamental project is its object of study. Its *goal*
is "to decipher the empirical patterns of man. . . . Its *point of
departure* is *experience;* its pillar of support is the fundamental,
pre-ontological comprehension which man has of the human
person" (*EN*, p. 656; *BN*, p. 726), (*EN*, p. 657; *BN*, p. 727). In
attempting to "reconstitute the life of the subject from birth to the
moment of cure" the existential psychoanalyst seeks to uncover an
original choice which characterizes the totality of the subject's
pre-reflective awareness. In following the itineraries of Baude-

207

laire, Genet, Flaubert, and his own early experiences, Sartre has practiced his own psychoanalysis.

As for other types of psychoanalysis, Sartre has remained particularly ambivalent. The controversy that arose between Sartre and two members of the *Temps Modernes* editorial board (Pontalis and Pingaud) over whether to publish a "Psychoanalytic Dialogue" in the April 1969 issue is indicative of this ambivalence. The dialogue is a transcript of a tape-recorded encounter between an analyst and his patient. What is significant is that the patient brought the tape recorder and turned the tables on his analyst. The analyst is placed in a position of responding to questions and assertions by his patient; he panics, and cries out to be liberated from his uncomfortable circumstances. Pontalis and Pingaud were opposed to publication of the text (and, a year later, they eventually resigned from the journal). The text shows the analyst's fallibility as he is drawn down from his throne and forced into verbal combat. As Pontalis suggests in his published reply to Sartre, the text resembles the type of engaged, but sequestered situationism that characterizes both *No Exit* and *The Condemned of Altona*. It makes a play of the psychoanalytic exchange and turns it into a spectacle for readers of the recorded dialogue.[12] A similar assumption leads Pingaud to assert that, by publishing the patient's transcription of the tape, Sartre is "denouncing both the practice of psychoanalysis and the theory on which it is based" ("Psychoanalytic Dialogue," p. 221).

If Sartre is critical of psychoanalysis in general, or at least if he is wont to take it lightly at times, is his relationship to Lacan of a similar nature? The answer must be equivocal. On the one hand, his positions seem to resemble those of the structural psychoanalyst. On the other hand, Sartre takes issue with the complete dominance of language as a description of the self. In this respect, his critique of Lacan matches his theoretical response to de Saussure.

On the positive side, Sartre agrees with Lacan that the subject is "decentered," but he is not convinced that this poses any problems. Hence, Sartre comments in the 1966 issue of *L'Arc* devoted to his writings:

The disappearance, or what Lacan calls the "decentering" of the subject, is linked to the discrediting of history. If there

208

is no longer any praxis, there can no longer be a subject. What do Lacan and those psychoanalysts who agree with him say? Man does not think, he is thought, just as, for certain linguists, he is spoken. The subject does not occupy a central position in this process. The subject is an element among others. Its essential feature is the "layer" or, if you wish, the structure in which it is held and which constitutes it.

The idea comes from Freud who already assigned an ambiguous place to the subject. Boxed in between the *id* and the *superego*, the psychoanalyst's subject is somewhat like De Gaulle between the Soviet Union and the United States. The Ego has no existence in itself; it is a construct and its role remains purely passive. The Ego is not an actor, but a point of encounter, the place where forces are in conflict. The analyst does not ask his patient to allow himself to be acted upon, while at the same time abandoning himself to his free associations.[13]

The passive role which Freud assigns to the patient is reinterpreted by Lacan as the articulation of a signifying chain in language—where, as Sartre indicates, the subject *is spoken* and *is thought*. According to Lacan, the only way for the analyst to treat his patient is for the self to speak. The self, here, includes the *id, ego* and *superego*. The subject brings about signification, not by acting and self-interpretation, but by revealing symptoms of his unconscious, of a signified experience which he does not know about.[14] The "letter," the true meaning of the patient's words, "insists" in "the chain of signifiers" but none of the explicit elements "consists" in the full meaning itself.[15] The language of the subject then becomes a basis for the analyst's own version of the patient's meaning. The subject is "decentered" in the sense that what the subject says is not the locus of his meaning. The subject *qua* conscious ego is only an element within a total structure. Such a structure denies the priority or dominance of any particular element within the whole. Thus when the subject is "decentered," its experience is disseminated throughout the system and must be interpreted in its dispersed form.

On the point of a "decentered subject," Sartre is quite in accord with Lacan. They disagree as to the significance of that decentering for the subject's modes of self-constitution and acting in the world. Sartre expands on the point in the following way:

> You see, the problem is not one of determining whether the subject is "decentered" or not. In a sense, the subject is always decentered. "Man" does not exist. Marx had rejected "man" long before Foucault or Lacan, when he said, "I do not see man, I see only workers, bourgeois, intellectuals."
>
> If we persist in speaking of the subject as a sort of substantial "I," or a central category, which is more or less given and from which reflection would develop, then the subject died a long time ago. I have myself criticized this conception in my first essay on Husserl. But the initial decentering, which forces man to disappear behind structures themselves implies a negativity, and man surges forth from this negation. There is a subject, or subjectivity, if you wish, from the moment when there is an attempt to surpass the given situation by conserving it. The true problem has to do with this surpassing. We must determine how the subject or subjectivity is constituted on a prior basis, by a perpetual process of interiorization and reexteriorization. (*Sartre répond*, pp. 92–93).

Sartre's long-term critique of human nature and the self-surpassing which he applies to Husserl's transcendental source in *The Transcendence of the Ego* are now given as the groundwork for Foucault's and Lacan's claims to "the death of man" and "the decentered subject."[16] We might go so far as to say that Sartre's position contributes to the conceptual conditions of the possibility for the structuralist claim. But Sartre is not simply concerned with the "decentered subject." For him, although the self does not establish a focal place, subjectivity does appear in its self-surpassing negativity. Selfness is denied, made nothing through human action, and reaffirmed out of that negation. With Lacan, the self is denied as ego-based, but reaffirmed in the analyst's interpretation of patient language. This difference recalls the divergence that we studied between Sartre and de Saussure. Sartre tends toward action and self-surpassing, the structuralist toward linguistic expression and a dispersal of meaning throughout a signifying chain.

Three years after his interview in which he cites his positive relationship to Lacan's views, in another interview entitled "The Itinerary of a Thought," Sartre clarifies the fundamental difference between their orientations:

> Comprehension of a dream occurs when a man can express it in a language which is itself dreamt. Lacan says that the unconscious is structured like a language. I would say that the language which expresses it has the structure of a dream. In other words, comprehension of the unconscious in most cases never achieves explicit expression.[17]

Lacan takes language as his model. The unconscious is therefore structured like a language. The Freudian notions of displacement and condensation within dream experience are presented in terms of metonymy and metaphor. Sartre, on the contrary, takes the dream experience as the model. Comprehension (understanding, *Verstehen*) of the dream has its own modes of expression, a certain amount of which cannot be stated, but is experienced "figuratively" by the dreamer. Comprehension occurs, though it is not necessarily given to the intellect. Sartre refers to this "lived experience" as a new development in his thought and a departure from *Being and Nothingness* with its rationalist philosophy of consciousness. "Lived experience" can be comprehended—given in the totality of human experience. It includes the non-thetic and unreflected, though it is never hidden in the depths of an unconscious realm. Lived experience is "a kind of comprehension of oneself which cannot be named and which perpetually escapes one" ("Itinerary," p. 41). As a dialectical process, lived experience characterizes how we are aware and is continually surpassing itself from one totalization to another.

L'Idiot de la famille explores Flaubert's constitution of his world. Contat has suggested that Sartre characterizes Flaubert's self as compatible with Lacan's idea of the "mirror phase" in which a person identifies with his social and familial circumstances. Furthermore, he proposes that Sartre's descriptions are specific to Flaubert, while Lacan deals with a universal condition. Sartre rejects this latter assertion and reaffirms his prior delineation of the position in question:

> I do not present person constitution as specific to Flaubert. Indeed, it applies to all of us. Constitution consists in

211

creating a person with roles, expected behaviors, derived from what I call constituted being. In other words, what I have written on Flaubert should be done for everyone, showing the constitution and personalization of the individual, i.e., this surpassing towards the concrete aspects of abstract conditioning by family structures. Certainly, the unreal element is total in Flaubert. The difference between Flaubert and someone else—for whom imaginary elements evidently cannot appear—is that Flaubert wanted to be *totally* imaginary.

You know how I conceive of the self—I haven't changed. The self is an object which is before us. That is, the self appears to reflection when it unifies reflective consciousness. Therefore, the pole which I call the self is a transcendent self and a quasi-object. Flaubert *wants* his self to be imaginary. (*Entretiens*, p. 100)

Flaubert presents himself to himself as an imaginary object. In that way he is able to retreat to the oneiric world of poetic fictions. Such a self is nevertheless an object of personal constitution. It is lived imaginatively, which for Flaubert was his manner of experiencing his social and familial relations. For Lacan, the "mirror phase" idea, derived from a child trying to establish or control his image in a mirror, leads to an identification of the self with its image. In Sartrian terms, we all see ourselves as if constituted in a mirror, but the specific definition of that objectification as an image—and further as an imaginary object—is peculiar to Flaubert's pre-crisis situation. With Lacan, the object must be absent from the signifying chain in order for the child to discover it and identify with it as an image of himself. With Sartre, on the contrary, signifying consciousness must be present in its absence, and the projected self must be there for my consciousness—not discoverable since always revealed through comprehension, lived experience, totalization, reflective and pre-reflective consciousness.

The unconscious is missing in Sartre's perspective, though he moves very close to it. The articulation of an unconscious realm in the signifying chain places the burden upon language. Language can reveal all, even that which is hidden (as often indicated by punctuation and gaps in speech). For Sartre, only consciousness, being-for-itself, praxis, comprehension, lived experience can actively bring about self-expression and self-knowledge. Language is simply one form of these modes of experiencing the world. With Sartre, signification extends beyond language to human experience in general.

II SARTRE AND LÉVI-STRAUSS

Where the debate with de Saussure and Lacan remains largely implicit, the encounter with Lévi-Strauss is principally explicit. This is also the domain which brings us closer to the Marxist perspective prevalent in Sartre's later writings. The *Critique de la Raison Dialectique* appeared in its full first volume form in 1960. Lévi-Strauss offered his own critique of Sartre's dialectic only a year later in *The Savage Mind*. The detailed relationship between these two positions has been carefully elaborated in several studies, including those by Klaus Hartmann, Lawrence Rosen, Jean Pouillon, and Lionel Abel.[18] I shall not retrace their steps. Rather I should like to focus on some specific comments which Sartre has made, demonstrating that, for him, diachrony has priority over synchrony—a viewpoint which is reversed in Lévi-Strauss. In this way, it will be clear how Sartre affirms the movement of human history in the light of experience over a structured order that subordinates history to its synchronic elaboration.

Although Sartre speaks generally of anthropology in contrast to philosophy in a February 1966 interview, his most direct accounts of his analysis of the diachrony/synchrony relation occur in the *Arc* interview, published in the same year. He makes four basic points: (1) a structural study is different from a dialectical inquiry; (2) structural systems are already constituted and hence history appears as purely passive; (3) history is a rational disorder, not an ordered form (i.e. structure); and (4) structure is practico-inert and must be surpassed through human praxis. Let us examine each of these in terms of Lévi-Strauss's position.

According to Sartre, societies are basically characterized by historical movement and evolution. Societies change. They also change the lives of individuals by establishing (and reestablishing) conditions of seriality, group, and scarcity. The proper study of individuals in historical societies must be dialectical.

A structural study of historical societies rigidifies and ignores the dynamic aspects of their actual situation. "Even the most archaic societies, the most immobile in appearance—those which Lévi-Strauss calls 'cold' societies—have a history. They simply have a longer period of maturation than 'hot' societies. From a structural perspective, that is, a non-dialectical one, it is impossible to account for this evolution" (*Sartre répond*, p. 90). Structural study is formal; it elaborates an invariant set of relations that can be transformed from one version of the structure to another, irrespective of chronology. The avunculate in one tribal society can bear within it a transformation of the avunculate in another. Similarly the Oedipus myth at one moment with its binary relations of underrating and overrating blood relations, denying and affirming the autochthonous origins of man, can be repeated at another moment. Synchronically, however, neither moment has any priority over the other. The structure remains invariant and reversible.

History however—be it the history of kinship relations in a particular tribe, the development of a myth, economic evolution in a capitalist society, or continual change in conceptual schemes—is variant and irreversible. The diachronic approach reveals only differences from one era, period, or moment to another. The diachronic approach is essentially what Sartre calls "dialectical reason." There is one significant difference: when examining a historical figure or period, Sartre introduces the "progressive-regressive" method, as outlined in *Search for a Method*. By studying the system of cross-references and relations that are directed, through human praxis, toward an objective, and by retracing the original conditions which make the objective possible within a social field, the progressive-regressive method is itself reversible like the structuralist's synchrony. Since the progressive-regressive method is based in dialectical reason, one might say that dialectical reason allows for reversibility. However, that reversibility is grounded in the method and not in the actual movement of totalization, which remains irreversible and unidirectional. The reversibility which concerns Lévi-Strauss, however, can presumably be formed in the social structures themselves. And if Lévi-Strauss is right, these structures are present in the societies themselves. Thus the reversibility, for him, is not only the method, but also in the phenomenon itself. This is, in fact, why in his attack upon Sartre's *Critique*, specifically in the last chapter of *The Savage Mind* entitled "History and Dialectic,"[19] Lévi-Strauss does not see a difference between analytical and dialectical reason. For the structural anthropologist, an investigation of the elements within a social field includes both types of reason. Dialectical reason (which Lévi-Strauss interprets as diachronic) can be understood most fully with the help of analytical reason (i.e., synchronic study). The "discovery of the dialectic," according to Lévi-Strauss, places a requirement upon analytical reason to return to dialectical reason. Without the return, analytical reason (synchronic study) can be pure system spinning, but without analytic reason, Lévi-Strauss argues, "dialectical reason can account neither for itself nor for analytical reason" (*Savage Mind*, p. 25). In fact, he claims that structural study is progressive-regressive in a double way. It not only analyzes the data of experience in the present and tries to grasp its historical antecedents (which Lévi-Strauss thinks is all Sartre's method does), but it also repeats the first movement by establishing the field of endeavor for analytical reason and returning to its applicability in the movements of history as understood by dialectical reason.

Sartre, however, does not agree with this one-upmanship on his own method. And this is his second point: structural systems are already constituted and history appears as purely passive. In studying systems, the investigator presumes that some structure is already there, available for analysis. Thus the structuralist takes particular interest in myths that have been articulated and serve as pure objects of study. The investigator ignores the role of myth as "integrating absurd or unpleasant elements which menace the life of a society" (*Sartre répond*, p. 90). The structural anthropologist is simply not interested in myth as formed by human activity. He is concerned only with the product. The production of knowledge in myths, in kinship relations, in social prohibitions is focused on that which is produced, while the producer and his activity lie outside the proper domain of structural study.

When extended to history as well, the dynamic processes of change are rendered passive. History is left open to examination, but the examiner cannot observe the surpassing that occurs before his very eyes, because he is committed to a synchronic interpretation. "History appears as a purely passive phenomenon, whether

215

the structure carries the original germs of its death with it, or whether an external event destroys it" (*Sartre répond*, p. 90). Whichever case, history is subject to conditions apart from the people who make it. History simply responds, in this view, to conditions either internal or external to it, but without the very human praxis that gives it life. Lévi-Strauss's response to such an account is that Sartre himself has made history into a myth. Sartre's picture is one of people making history and history manifesting itself in people's lives (*Savage Mind*, p. 254). But if true, then Lévi-Strauss has placed the burden back on Sartre. Sartre's proposals for historical action have been turned into a synchronic system awaiting structuralist analysis. Commitment is turned into myth. But then any philosophical position could be set up according to an objectifiable system. What distinguishes the structuralist view from positivist orientations is that the structure or system is a mediating function, not a substance. Myth is not a social fact for Lévi-Strauss; it is a structured form of knowledge. Yet history according to Sartre is nothing of the kind, for history lacks order.

The view of history as rational disorder is my third point. Sartre denies that history is an ordered form of structure. Hence it cannot be a myth available for synchronic investigation, for myths are ordered accounts of human experience. This does not mean that structures do not exist, nor that their mechanism cannot be examined. It only means that any established historical structure is already in the process of reorganization and hence never stable. Thus Sartre claims that "structure is a moment of the practico-inert" (*Sartre répond*, p. 90)—which is my fourth point. The practico-inert, with its parallel but socialized analogy to being-in-itself, lacks the life of human praxis (the active freedom of being-for-itself). Individuals acting in groups and classes create history. Structures are emptied of this active component. Their order is abstracted for creative disorder. As Sartre notes in a 1966 piece published by Contat and Rybalka entitled "Determination and Freedom:"

For *structuralism, history is an internal product of the system.* There are as many *histories* as there are *structured societies;* each society produces its own temporality. Progress is the *development of* order. This historical pluralism seeks to subordinate history *qua* movement to a structural order.[20]

Once again, we find that synchrony is the standard of measurement, while history is that which is measured. Sartre, however, is convinced that the contrary is needed: diachrony must be the point of reference and return. History must be more significant than the structures that constitute it. History is not reducible to the "development of order." Disorder characterizes its ways, since history is elaborated through praxis. Only the practico-inert can be treated as an objectifiable, ordered structure.

Practico-inert structures must be surpassed through human praxis, for man is not lost in the movement of history, as historicists claim. On the contrary, he is "the product of a structure which he surpasses" (*Sartre répond*, pp. 90–1). Since he is engaged in history, he cannot separate his action from its movement. His reception of inert structures becomes his means of going beyond them, of revealing them within his conscious life, and of giving them meaning by his very action.

CONCLUSION

To account for Sartre's positions and reinterpretations of all those whose work has been labelled structuralist is clearly not possible here. Yet a careful examination of his conceptual relationship to Foucault, Barthes, Althusser, Robbe-Grillet, and Piaget—to name only a few—is certainly in order.[21] I have sketched out some aspects of the linguistic, psychoanalytic, and anthropological versions. Turning the signifier/signified (word/concept) relation into a signifying-consciousness object-signified relation paves the road for the articulation of signification within human experience. Since signification or meaning can be elaborated into an ambiguous, but live totality, there is no need for a psychoanalytic unconscious. The Sartrian unreflected consciousness or prereflective *cogito* can, along with reflective consciousness, constitute human lived experience. Such experience cannot be structured according to a language and a signifying chain, as Lacan proposes. Nor can such experience, which gains its life through praxis within a social situation, be reformulated into a myth or structure. Diachrony must prevail and synchrony must follow. Lévi-Strauss's pretensions to the contrary will simply deny the self-surpassing possibilities which Sartre believes are fundamental to human experience whether on an individual or on a contextualized plane. Structural knowledge is produced by human activity—including structuralist activity.[22]

12

SARTRE/PIAGET: BIO-GRAPHICAL SITUATIONS, COGNITIVE STRUCTURES AND HUMAN DEVELOPMENT

In Sartre's biographical accounts of Baudelaire, Genet, and Flaubert, his fictional studies of Lucien Fleurier, Antoine Roquentin, and Franz von Gerlach, and his autobiographical reflections in *The Words* and in subsequent interviews, stress is placed upon developmental description. Although significantly different in theory and methodology from Sartre's conception of the child as an ongoing self-consciousness, Piaget's genetic epistemology nevertheless offers a conception of human growth and development. Where Sartre portrays self-transcendence, Piaget recounts a model of intelligence. Where Sartre delves into the dimensions of consciousness and human praxis in terms of a fundamental project, Piaget establishes a theory of structure for his four stages of development. Sartre formulates a situational context, while Piaget emphasizes assimilation of and accommodation to the environment. Methodologically, Sartre opts for description in coordination with existential psychoanalysis on the one hand and the progressive-regressive approach on the other. By contrast, Piaget observes the performance of specific tasks in relation to certain cognitive structures. In moving through this confrontational analysis, I will show the groundwork for a theory of human development which accounts for both the contextualist and the structuralist perspectives.

(1) *Self-transcendence/development of intelligence*. Sartre established his conception of self-transcendence in one of his earliest publications: *The Transcendence of the Ego*. In this work, Sartre directs his attention to a criticism of Edmund Husserl's notion of

the transcendental ego. Sartre argues that consciousness, which Husserl accurately described as intentional (directed toward objects in the world), is inaccurately characterized as possessing a transcendental source of knowledge. From birth, the individual experiences the world directly and existentially. Consciousness envelops objects of knowledge. Only by the nihilating function of consciousness do such objects acquire an identity different from the person who knows them. As Sartre points out in *Being and Nothingness*, whatever consciousness takes as its object is a being-in-itself. This object could include not only the silverware in Jean Genet's foster-parents' house, the portrait of the Marquis de Rollebon for Antoine Roquentin, or the moustacheless face of Lucien Fleurier in the mirror at the end of *The Childhood of a Leader*, but also Baudelaire's self which he presents to himself in reflection. Any object is in-itself for consciousness, but consciousness cannot have within it a transcendental ego which is *for* consciousness. Consciousness must remain entirely for-itself and not for any consciousness other than itself, hence never in-itself. Such consciousness which is for-itself maintains its condition of unreflectedness or pre-reflectivity just as long as consciousness does not attempt to engage it in its own intentional acts. Once Lucien Fleurier reflects upon himself as a pederast or as a future factory boss, once Baudelaire makes himself appear as though he is another person, or once Hugo in *Dirty Hands* names himself Julien Sorel and Raskolnikov, the reflecting self is not identical with the self reflected upon. The reflected self is ontologically in-itself and no longer characterized by the full freedom of a consciousness which is for-itself and without content (without a transcendental ego). Whatever ego the person can designate as his or her own is a transcendent ego, an object in-the-world like any other.

For Sartre, the development of consciousness involves continual change. The self is constantly transcending itself with a corresponding movement toward a new identity. Consider, for example, Lucien Fleurier. Lucien enters the world as the son of parents who love him, who send him to school, and who expect him to grow up to take over his father's factory. It seems as though his world is determined for him. But, according to Sartre, no life is pre-determined. Every consciousness must nihilate every object it confronts in order to constantly build a new self. Nihilation is not annihilation. Nihilation involves positing an object as an object, as an in-itself. In this respect, the self transcends any particular objectivity in its development toward new objectivities, leaving behind a past full of transcendent objects. Lucien must overcome the perception of himself as a little girl (established by his mother), as a big beanpole (established by graffitti on the bathroom wall at school), as someone with an Oedipus complex (established by his friend Berliac), as a pederast (established by Achille Bergère when he takes Lucien to bed with him), and as an antisemitic proto-fascist (established by his classmates). The protean features of Sartrian development involve a continual process of the self surpassing itself toward a new identity, leaving transcendent egos in its wake.

In Sartre's theory, we find no evidence of pre-established capacities for development. Yet in practically every case Sartre has studied, including his own, he highlights the concept of play-acting. Lucien Fleurier plays the role of a little girl, then that of an orphan. Hugo plays at being an assassin. Sartre even describes himself as a child playing at the role of a hero in a movie. Soon thereafter he notes: "I was beginning to find myself. I was almost nothing, at most an activity without content, but that was all that was needed. I was escaping from play-acting. I was not yet working, but I had stopped playing. The liar was finding his truth in the elaboration of his lies. I was born of writing. Before that, there was only a play of mirrors."[1] Given Sartre's theory, one can escape play-acting, turn it into an object of reflection, a moment to be surpassed in one's future development. And although the individual may return to play-acting in adulthood (as in the case of Hugo), it pervades childhood experience until the child is able to move on to a point where choice of identity is serious.

Even though Sartre is quite imprecise about the particular age at which his biographical figures move on from play-acting, it corresponds roughly to what Piaget describes as a loss of "egocentrism." Egocentrism is the phenomenon whereby the child perceives objects in the world from his or her own perspective. Thus the child will point out a picture of an animal in a book, showing only the back of the book to her friend. Just as the child in the egocentric perspective sees things only from her point of view, so the child who is play-acting has not yet recognized that self-identity can be anything but a role enacted for oneself and for others.

For Piaget, intelligence characterizes the general manner in which the child relates to the world throughout development (during egocentrism and thereafter). Sartre claims that the individual is always conscious of something whenever he is conscious (reflectively or pre-reflectively), while Piaget indicates that the individual always employs some form of intelligence when learning to cope with reality. Thus Piaget writes:

> Intelligence for the child is the solution of a new problem, the coordination of the means to reach a certain goal which is not accessible in an immediate manner; whereas thought is interiorized intelligence no longer based on direct action but on a symbolism, the symbolic evocation by speech, by mental pictures, and other means, which makes it possible to represent what the sensorimotor intelligence is going to grasp directly.[2]

Since thought is more specific and dependent upon symbolism rather than upon direct action, it corresponds most appropriately to what Sartre calls "reflective consciousness." Intelligence, like pre-reflective consciousness (or non-thetic self-consciousness), is the general category according to which the individual relates to the world. In Sartre, all reflective consciousness of something is at the same time pre-reflective consciousness of itself, and in Piaget all thought presupposes intelligence.

Intelligence for Piaget is couched in a notion of genesis. Piaget conceives of the child as developing. This is the type of development which Piaget calls "organic or individual" as opposed to the geneological or collective type. Ontogenesis (or organic-individual development) which parallels Sartre's view of the existing self, is patterned after the evolution of species, but maintains an interdependence of its differentiating and integrating functions—unlike phylogenesis which keeps differentiation and integration of environmental features relatively distinct. In *Biology and Knowledge*, Piaget characterizes both types as "diachronic." Diachrony, however, is intimately bound up with synchrony: the particular structural formations which result from integration and differentiation.

(2)*Fundamental project/structure of knowledge*. According to

Sartre, the individual enters upon a fundamental project which he or she carries throughout life (diachronically) as an original choice.

> To be, for Flaubert, as for every subject of "biography," means to be unified in the world. The irreducible unification which we ought to find, which is Flaubert, and which we require biographers to reveal to us—this is the unification of an *original project*, a unification which should reveal itself to us as a *non-substantial absolute*.[3]

The whole life is unified by this project through which Flaubert, in this case, expresses himself in a variety of circumstances. My fundamental project is "nothing other than the choice of myself as a totality in these circumstances."[4] The process of self-transcendence is a continual condition of making choices, nihilating what *is* in favor of what can be and in opposition to what has been. Thus at any particular moment a new choice can be made, but individual choices all participate in the unification which forms individual experience. Unlike original sin, for which an individual is responsible due to the transgression of Adam and Eve, original choice is "original" because of the initial orientation which a particular individual has selected. Such choices are "fundamental" because they are established in childhood, but always available for revision in terms of new choices. I am never bound by my choices nor am I unable to make new choices.

Consider the case of Baudelaire. Sartre writes:

> Baudelaire chose the sort of person he would be—that irrevocable choice by which each of us decides in a particular situation what he will be and what he is. When he found himself abandoned and rejected, Baudelaire chose solitude deliberately as an act of self-assertion, so that his solitude should not be something inflicted on him by other people. The abrupt revelation of his individual existence made him *feel* that he was *another person*: but at the same time and in a mood of humiliation, rancor and pride, he asserted this otherness of his own accord. From this moment, he set to work with an obstinate, painful fury to *make* himself another person, to make himself into someone different from his mother, with whom he had been identical and who had

223

rejected him; someone different from his coarse, carefree companions. He felt and was determined to feel that he was unique; and he pushed this sense of uniqueness to the point of extreme solitary enjoyment and of terror.[5]

Baudelaire's fundamental project is his choice of himself as someone different from everyone else, as someone who can live his own solitude uniquely. He subsequently reiterates this original choice in whatever he does or writes. In this same respect, Lucien Fleurier chose to become a leader, Jean Genet chose to become a thief which crime had made of him, the young Jean-Paul Sartre chose to become the writer which his grandfather did not want him to be and Flaubert chose to become an artist over against the poet which constrained him. In each of these cases, the biographer notices a moment of self-recognition. This is the moment at which the individual decides to be someone distinct and unique. The generalized version of this moment of self-recognition is highlighted in Antoine Roquentin's celebrated epiphany. As Roquentin records in his journal, one day while sitting in the park, he suddenly became aware of his own existence. He saw beneath the veneer of essences, such as the park bench, the root of the chestnut tree, and the grass. Underlying all of these things was his own existence which was conscious of them. Existence was there in them and at the same time not determinate as any one particular essence. Roquentin's recognition of his own existence was an unsettling consciousness. Sartre describes it as nausea or elsewhere as anguish. In *The Childhood of a Leader*, he writes that the perplexity of whether one exists is "like wanting to sneeze."[6] The moment of recognition can be characterized by these various physiological reactions—reactions which cause momentary discomfort. These moments, however, are difficult to maintain. Indeed, one would not want to prolong them—yet they do bring an awareness which reveals the basic condition of the developing person's experience of self and world.

In Sartre's later philosophy, especially that of the *Critique of Dialectical Reason*, the notion of praxis is substituted for being-for-itself. In this case, the growth of the individual cannot be isolated from social conditions—even when a person stands in a series: someone waiting in line for the bus, Genet in a bookstore asking to see a book which is in the back room so that he can steal one in the front room, Franz von Gerlach carrying out orders in Hitler's army, etc., these relations of isolation, reciprocity, and massification still result in alterity. Conditions of otherness permeate each individual's relations with the others despite the collective which unites them in a practico-inert totality. Particular praxis is possible as each person responds to the inert totalities that surround him or her. However, only synthetic praxis allows individuals to operate along with others in a totalizing process whereby the group acts in relation to History at large.

Piaget is not concerned with the larger movements of History in his genetic epistemology. Yet the development of knowledge does presume a notion of praxis and an ability to deal with particularized situations. Piaget reports:

> Praxis or action is not some sort of movement but rather a system of coordinated movements functioning for a result or an intention. To take but one example, the displacement of an arm which interferes in the act of putting on or of removing a hat is not praxis; a praxis consists of an action in its totality and not of a partial movement within this action. Praxis is an *acquired* as opposed to a reflex coordination; this acquisition can derive not only from the child's experience or education in the large sense (instruction, example, etc.), but also eventually from the internal operations of equilibrium which express a regulation or a stabilization acquired from coordination.[7]

Praxis, then, cannot be accounted for in the Skinnerian behavioral model. Praxis is acquired and results not only from experience or education, but also from the very structures of intelligence. Sartre would certainly agree up to the point that conscious action or praxis results from experience. Education could be the general rubric for the type of epiphany he is wont to detect. The individual passes through an educative process as he becomes aware of his own existence, or as he becomes aware of the practico-inert conditions of his social life. However, the structures of consciousness are limited to a possible filling with anguish and nausea, or alternatively with emotions and imaginative life, but consciousness (and similarly, praxis) remains empty of any particular acquired content. Consciousness is purely projective—toward a new self-definition and further self-transcendence—or it is oriented toward a past which the self has been (which the individual must accept if he is not to be in bad faith, but which cannot limit future choices). Praxis is more complicated in that our choices are limited by scarcity and need. However, within the context of such conditions, we cannot be bound by the practico-inert totalities which surround us. Thus the structures of consciousness are qualified only by the nothingness that is its essence and the projective historicalizing movement which accompanies the reiteration of an original choice.

Piaget, on the contrary, devotes considerable time to an elaboration of the structures of knowledge. In his *Introduction to Structuralism*, Piaget outlines three features present in any concept of structure: (1) wholeness, (2) transformation, and (3) self-regulation.[8] Epistemological structures form a synchronic whole at specific stages of human development. Each stage achieves an equilibrium by which all elements within the whole interrelate such that tasks are accomplished according to a framework appropriate to the child at a given level of development. At a particular moment—but certainly not the sudden moment of recognition which Sartre recounts—the individual begins to undergo a transformation in the given conceptual scheme and tasks are reinterpreted according to a new structural whole. The transformation is the condition under which a particular structure is turned into another structure at a subsequent stage of development. The mechanism by which one structure is transformed into another whole is called "auto-regulation." A particular structure transforms itself into another structure at a subsequent stage. Just as Sartre's individual is able to reiterate or deviate from his fundamental project, Piaget's individual has structures which regulate themselves as they are transformed into new structural wholes.

Piaget is quite specific as to the number of stages and the general age levels at which new structures are formed. He enumerates four successive levels and stages of development:

First, we have a stage, before about age eighteen months, which precedes speech and which we will call that of the sensorimotor intelligence. Secondly, we have a stage which begins with speech and lasts for about seven or eight years. We will call this the period of representation, but it is preoperatory. . . . Then, between about seven and twelve, we will distinguish a third period which we will call that of concrete operations. And finally, after twelve years, there is the stage of propositional or formal operations.[9]

These four stages, recited in practically every one of Piaget's theoretical books, constitute the fundamental framework of his genetic epistemology. Each stage forms a whole or a totality. The movement of one stage into another occurs as a transformation of the totality into a new whole. The change in totality takes place by factors internal to the totality itself. This continuous construction is the elaboration of an ontogenesis whereby "genesis emanates from a structure and culminates in another structure."[10] Furthermore, "every structure has a genesis."[11] This means that diachrony is dependent upon synchrony for its movement and that synchrony carries the possibility of diachronic movement within it. Diachrony or genesis is not a general background of movement against which synchronic structures are painted. Rather they are each mutually bound up with each other. Genesis emanates from a structure which carries the genesis to start with. For a child to move from a stage at which he can see and touch a rattle to a stage at which he can represent the name "rattle" for the object involves both the movement from one totality to another, one structure of knowledge to another, and the presence of the possibility of that movement within the first structure.

While knowledge for Sartre involves reflective consciousness and presupposes a notion of intentionality with its positing or thetic function (also called nihilation), knowledge for Piaget involves the assimilation of reality into systems of transformation. In Sartrian terms, understanding or comprehension is a generalized consciousness (of) something. With Piaget, understanding follows from the transformation of reality into certain conceptual schemes. A scheme is whatever is repeatable and generalizable in an action. While knowing for Sartre is a sub-category of consciousness and understanding, knowing for Piaget incorporates understanding which is itself dependent upon the structures of knowledge. In this connection, Piaget elaborates:

Knowing an object does not mean copying it—it means acting upon it. It means constructing systems of transformations that can be carried out on or with this object. Knowing reality means constructing systems of transformations that correspond, more or less adequately, to reality. They are more or less isomorphic to transformations of reality. The transformational structures of reality; they are simply possible isomorphic models among which experience can enable us to choose. Knowledge, then, is a system of transformations that becomes progressively adequate.[12]

While Piaget claims that knowledge means providing a model which is more or less adequate to reality, he also asserts that knowledge has structures which are distinct from reality. For Sartre, the very task of knowledge is to experience reality in the most immediate fashion—such that our knowledge of reality takes the form of reality as an object of nihilation, as an object of choice, as a transcendent object.

(3) *Situation/environment*. Sartre's philosophy is built upon a concept of situation. The ongoing collections of Sartre's articles, plays, monographs, etc. are still entitled *Situations*. Ten volumes of these collections have been published already. All consciousness and hence all knowledge occurs in a situation. Repeating the phenomenological dictum "all consciousness is consciousness of something" makes the point even clearer. If nihilating consciousness must posit something as in-the-world, consciousness itself (which is for-itself and without content) must also be in-the-world. Sartre describes the particular manner in which the individual is in-the-world as "facticity." Facticity is the character of the individual's place in a situation as identifiably of the world. The situation of the body makes this condition particularly evident. In *No Exit*, Sartre attempts to show that even though his three characters are no longer alive, they find themselves in a closed context from which they cannot escape. They are *in situation* whether bodily or not. In the case of *No Exit*, their bodies are especially significant. Inez is interested in the body of Estelle, Estelle in that of Garcin, and Garcin in his own. Because they are in a hell with self-imposed limits, the situation is particularly noticeable.

Genet's situation is precisely the opposite. He is born an orphan—he never knew his true parents. As Sartre recounts in *Saint Genet*, when Genet at the age of seven was placed in the home of foster parents, he possessed nothing. Everything was given to him: his clothes, his room, his food, and even his name.

Whenever he took something, such as silverware for eating (or to sell), he was taking something which did not belong to him. Genet was unreflectively conscious of his situation. One day, he was caught reaching his hand into the silverware drawer. When his foster parents called out "Thief!", he acquired an identity. His situation was sufficiently open-textured that this new identity forced itself upon him—it was the only one available. In choosing to accept what his own crime had made of him, Genet went on to become a thief, a pederast—in short, a pariah. In this way, he chose his situation. Even writing became a means of entering the homes of fashionable bourgeois readers in order to make himself alien from them—to bring his socially unacceptable life into their world through autobiographical novels. Although his actual situation was often limited by prison walls, he would be able to extend it through his poems, his novels, and ultimately his plays.

Piaget's view is that the developing individual, like any organism, is constantly adapting to his environment. Adaptation takes the forms of accommodation and assimilation. The child makes his or her cognitive processes conform to the environment and selects aspects of the environment to fit his or her own cognitive processes. Sartre does not allow for assimilation because assimilation would presume a cognitive content or at least a scheme, while Piaget stresses the interdependence of the two notions. In *Biology and Knowledge* he writes:

> We shall apply the term "accommodation" to any modification produced on assimilation schemata by the influence of environment to which they are attached. But just as there is no assimilation without accommodation (whether previous or current), so in the same way there is no accommodation without assimilation; this is as much as to say that environment does not merely cause a series of prints or copies to be made which register themselves on the subject, but it also sets in motion active adjustments; which is why every time we speak of accommodation the phrase "accommodation of assimilation schemata" is to be understood. For example, in an infant five or six months old, the seizing of things by both hands is an assimilation schema, but the stretching out or bringing nearer of the

hands according to whether the object is near or far is an accommodation of that schema.[13]

Accommodation and assimilation demonstrate the individual's direct relationship with his environment. However, it should be remembered that these biological functions, which have applicability to the cognitive domain, are also part of a developing process.

Coordinate with accommodation and assimilation is the pair: differentiation and integration. This latter pair is involved in the establishment of equilibration throughout the various stages of development. Piaget describes three types of equilibration. (1) An equilibrium can occur between the assimilation of schemes in action and the accommodation of these schemes to objects. (2) Equilibration results from the interactions between subsystems of a particular structure. And (3) equilibration arises as relations between differentiation and integration unite subsystems to the totality which includes them.[14] Consider, for example, the case of a train passing by telephone poles as an exterior referential and passengers walking about in the train as the interior referential. Integrating both the exterior and the interior motion is a matter of assimilation. Accepting that two different types of motion are operative requires accommodation. The exterior referential constitutes one subsystem; the interior referential constitutes another. In the second type of equilibrium, these two subsystems can be regarded as equilibrated. The differentiation between the two types of motion and the integration of the two into a single totality or whole is exemplary of the third case of equilibration. The extent to which an individual is able to conceptualize these various relationships and cognitively hold them in equilibrium, depends upon the stage of development. At each stage, an equilibrium is maintained. However, the particular equilibrium depends upon the ability of the child to understand the set of relationships present in the environment.

In Sartre's theory, equilibrium is also a framework according to which the individual perceives his situation. However, disequilibrium is not simply a mechanism for reorganization to a subsequent stage of intellectual development. As long as equilibrium is present, the person is contented and at ease with his place in the world. Only when someone reflects upon his situation and confronts his existence is that equilibrium upset. Such moments are precisely those when we are most conscious of what it is to be in the world. Hence instances of disequilibrium bring the greatest awareness and understanding. In the *Critique of Dialectical Reason*, equilibration continually takes place in one's comprehension of social conditions. However, usually this equilibrium is based on an economic condition of need and scarcity. There may be something like a consciousness of equilibrium within the factory in the relations between the number of workers, the amount of work, and the quantity produced. However, because imbalances invariably arise within society, some workers regard themselves as expendable (in the case of a surplus of workers) or some consumers regard themselves as expendable (in the case of a scarcity of products). As an aspect of cognitive structures, Piaget finds the notion of equilibrium not only desirable but universal. Sartre views it as a type of self-deception or social acceptance which does more camouflaging than highlighting of fundamental conceptual features of the human condition.

(4) *Conflict of methodologies.* Like Piaget, Sartre is principally concerned with the status and role of the individual—even in the *Critique*, both the conditions of alterity and the praxis which responds to them are based on a model of the individual. However, Sartre's perspective also stresses the uniqueness of the individual since a particular fundamental project is elaborated within a specified situation. Piaget, on the other hand, is concerned with the universality and cross-cultural features of cognitive structures. For Sartre, the individual develops his original choice in the process of self-transcendence. Although all individuals, in principle, undergo this basic experience, there are no repeatable structures which can be transferred from one individual in one context to another individual in another context. Hence it is no surprise that Sartre's methods are called "existential psychoanalysis" and "progressive-regressive study" with their stress upon singular contextualized conditions, while Piaget offers a "genetic epistemology" with its claims to universal stages of human development.

As I have shown elsewhere, existential psychoanalysis is not a psychoanalysis in the sense that it relies upon a notion of the unconscious.[15] On the other hand, like Freudian psychoanalysis, Sartre's method does take the individual case and return to the childhood experiences which subsequently result in a certain manner of relating to others and to the world. Unlike the Freudian model, Sartre's account is not based on infantile sexuality, but rather on the determination of a childhood project: Lucien Fleurier's decision to become a boss, Baudelaire's resolution to make himself unique in the act of reflecting upon himself, Genet's acceptance of the role of thief, Flaubert's commitment to become an artist, and Sartre's own orientation toward the role of a writer. In each case, the project differs. Hence the task of an existential psychoanalysis is to attend to the biographical situation of the individual in which the choice is made and carried out.

Sartre's reformulation of his methodology in terms of the progressive-regressive approach relies upon two features of personal development: (1) that the individual is oriented toward some end as based on a choice, and (2) that the individual exists within a context of social, political, cultural, and other concerns of his own time. The progressive-regressive method attempts to examine both of these aspects. It follows the general lines of development through time (i.e., diachronically) and it returns to the practico-inert (i.e., synchronic) conditions out of which the original choice was made. Sartre first evolved the progressive-regressive method in *Search for a Method*, but oddly enough, though it serves as a sort of introduction to the *Critique* (and is published with it in the French version), Sartre states at the beginning of *L'Idiot de la famille* that this three volume study of Flaubert is a continuation of *Search for a Method*. As he noted in the 1957 work, the method is both historical and structural. It accounts for both development and the situational structures of a particular moment. With reference to Flaubert in *L'Idiot*, Sartre notes: the regressive analysis can lead the biographer up to the point at which a phenomenological description of a child's sensibility would begin, while the progressive synthesis itself retraces the genesis of this sensibility.[16] Sartre appeals to an encounter with different structures, each leading to directive schemes, but the description of these structural features all lead to historical considerations.

Piaget's account, it will be remembered, indicates that genesis emanates from structure, but also that every structure has a genesis. Hence where structural features are necessarily present in the development of knowledge for Piaget, for Sartre the structural aspects are indicated in the study of an individual and do not constitute the conditions of knowledge itself. For Sartre, the progressive synthesis prevails. With Piaget, the formation of equilibrated cognitive structures predominates. In this respect, Piaget is able to distinguish between the reversible and irreversible operations of a genetic epistemological study. The particular development of knowledge as evolved by an individual is irreversible. No child can return to a previous stage of cognition irrespective of the subsequent experience he has undergone. In this same respect, the irreversible historical movement or development of consciousness is prevalent in Sartre's method. For Piaget, however, it is equally possible to compare the different stages with their corresponding schemes. Hence the action schemes of the formal-mathematical (fourth) stage can be compared with those of the preoperatory and representational (second) stage. This reversibility demonstrates the notion of structure which is basic to all four stages, but which is transformed from one into another in the course of irreversible cognitive growth.

In Sartre's existential psychoanalysis, the closest analogue of this reversibility is the possibility of specifying the recurrence of a particular choice, e.g., Lucien Fleurier's decision to be a leader. By noting the repetition of this choice, Sartre might have identified a reiterated element. However, in each case, the situation and the phenomenon would be quite different. In the progressive-regressive method, the identification of a regressive analysis is the specification of a structural context which could be compared with previous and subsequent contexts. Yet once again, the context itself and the variety of such situations would tend to make such a systematic association impracticable. Piagetian schemes, on the contrary, are repeatable and generalizable across individuals, across countries, and across cultures.

(5) *Pentimento: a multi-contextual experiential structuralism*. In the face of these conflicting methods, where, on the one hand, continual development and uniqueness is valued, and on the other, generalization and structural reversibility is prized, can we develop a theory of biographical understanding which will also permit the examination of cognitive structures? In conclusion, I propose to offer a multi-contextual experiential structuralism which will respect both the situation out of which an individual develops and the structures of knowledge which are repeatable in a variety of situations.

Lillian Hellman explores the significance of the term "pentimento," which she borrows from painting for the title of her book. Pentimento arises when the painter repents and paints over the picture with another. As time passes, the previous version begins to show through and a new synthesis of the old and the new occurs:

> Old paint on canvas, as it ages, sometimes becomes
> transparent. When that happens it is possible, in some
> pictures, to see the original lines: a tree will show through a
> woman's dress, a child makes way for a dog, a large boat is
> no longer on an open sea. This is called pentimento because
> the painter "repented," changed his mind. Perhaps it would
> be as well to say that the old conception, replaced by a later
> choice, is a way of seeing and then seeing again.[17]

The particular representation or account which a painter offers is unique and individual—even if it is a copy. What I wish to suggest here is that each stage is like a new painting. Although a previous stage or equilibrium may be scorned and rejected (which Sartre would call "bad faith"), nevertheless, it is formative of the individual's growing self. Yet the style of each painting is characteristic of one painter, or more specifically, the style identifies itself in its various versions—all of which are available on one canvas. A progressive synthesis takes place. The individual can change direction, add new paintings onto his previous work, but at each moment a new equilibrium, a new totalization takes place. However that new totalization *qua* totality has aspects in common with totalities in the development of other individuals. Comparisons and contrasts with the moments of recognition, the cognitive skills and capacities, and the conceptual limitations of other individuals can be offered. Even a typology of these differing moments, skills and capacities, limitations and possibilities might serve as a catalogue of human developmental situations.

Each situation would bear the conditions according to which identities and differences might be drawn across individual experiences. In this respect, developmental situations interpret themselves as participating in a framework and a typology in which they do not themselves participate directly. Situations are not only autoregulative from one structural whole to the next, but they are also self-sorting from one context to another. By the very

234

articulation of one life, a multiplicity of alternative experiential wholes are identified and indicated. The methodologist must therefore not only study the development of particular biographical conditions, responses to particular questions, and solutions to particular problems, but these conditions, responses, and solutions should be explored for the inter-biographical features in which they already participate.

Such a study would be cross-cultural in the sense that similar structural features might arise across different cultures and different historical periods. Yet the repetition of paradigms of the self or of social ideals cannot be de-contextualized. Each repetition must be founded and elaborated in a particular biographical circumstance with its multifarious individual characteristics. These characteristics are built into the development and experience of a particular life. That there may be features of a stage in an individual's life which are held in common with those of another person's biography only identifies a commonality which does not itself deny the syntagmatic elaboration of individual experience. Thus a phase of Lucien Fleurier's life may have features in common with that of Sartre himself (if not by affirmation, then by negation). For example, Sartre grew up without a father. As he notes in *The Words*, "I had no Superego." Hence, it is precisely the continual presence of a Superego—one which identifies Lucien's career—which Sartre highlights in his character's experience. This identity by negation demonstrates a structural feature which does not permeate all of Lucien's and Sartre's own development. The coincidence of structures however does allow for the indication of a typological relation. Such a relation is not as universal as Piaget would propose for the four stages of cognitive development, but it is also not as individual as Sartre's existential psychoanalysis presumes. The point is that the text of an individual's life is not without both context and intertext. A multi-contextual experiential structuralism brings out all three of these aspects: biography, situation, and structural identities and differences.

13

SARTRE/BARTHES: WRITING DIFFERENCES

Q. "You hardly see anything more than a 'mini-praxis' in literature today." Contat & Rybalka
A. "Yes. But anyway, there is no more literature."

J.-P. Sartre (1971)

The discourse on the Text should itself be nothing other than text, research, textual activity, since the Text is that *social* space which leaves no language safe, outside, nor any subject of the enunciation in the position of judge, master, analyst, confessor, decoder. The theory of the Text can coincide only with a practice of writing.

R. Barthes (1971)

The debate about the meaning and practice of literature has occupied a considerable amount of attention since 1945—particularly in France. Jean-Paul Sartre and Roland Barthes are not the only proponents in this debate. However, there is a certain overdetermination and specificity to their formulations, which, when juxtaposed, identify the principal lines of the debate.

The preliminary opposition between Sartre and Barthes is located in the difference between two essays: one entitled *What is Literature?* (1947), the other called *Writing Degree Zero* (1953, with significant portions appearing in *Combat* between 1947 and 1950). The varying meanings given to the function of Writing in these two works serve as the specific locus of opposition between what it is to write (*écrire*) and writing (*écriture*). Similarly, a decade later, the difference in these two positions lies in the opposition between work and text. These oppositional frame-

236

works elaborate a context for the theoretical or critical practice which they conjointly establish in the name of Writing.

LITERATURE/WRITING

From the English translations of *What is Literature?* and *Writing Degree Zero*, it would seem that Sartre and Barthes ask the same question: "What is writing?"[1] However, the difference located in "writing" is the place of divergence between the two. Sartre asks: *"Qu'est-ce qu'écrire?"* Barthes asks: *"Qu'est-ce que l'écriture?"* Hence, the opposition: *écrire* (to write)/*écriture* (writing). With the question "What is writing?" either "to write" or "writing" could be read into the term "Writing." The "Writing" which appears in English is both *écrire* and *écriture*, but it is not resolvable by turning one into the other. What then is this hinge between *écrire* and *écriture?*

Sartre's attention is devoted to the *act of writing*. What is it *to write (écrire)?* Writing, in this active sense, is what a writer (*écrivain*) engages in. Sartre distinguishes two types of writer: *le prosateur* (prose-writer) and *le poète* (poet). Only the prose-writer creates literature. The poetry-writer, whose activity is excluded from the concerns Sartre attributes to literature, produces absolutized words. The poet's words are transcendent objects like books, tables, and trees. They are opaque and reflect back the poet's image as in a mirror. They create a myth in which the poet seeks to live and they serve as the realization of that narcissistic end. The prose-writer, by contrast, creates words as a means toward an end beyond the words. Through the transparency of words, the prose-writer communicates with the reader.

To write (*écrire*) is a verbal activity which is most appropriately called literature when produced by a prose-writer. This does not mean that everyone who writes verse is excluded from the academy of prose-writers. Prose-writers are discriminated by the activity in which they engage, not the form of their product. Sartre is not concerned with what is produced but rather with the way it is produced and the intersubjective effects of that production.

What is it to write? For the poet, to write is to construe the world and things in it as inessential. The poet's words are the essential elements in the foreground of experience. But to write

237

in this way is not to write at all, it is to poetize. To write is to produce words and works whose essentiality serves as a medium for the writer to communicate his essentiality to the reader. The writer is essential to the communicative act in that he produces a work through which the reader can perceive his own essentiality. This essentiality on the part of both writer and reader is a curious one—and certainly unlike the essentiality of the poet's words. Both the writer and reader are essential to the dialectic in which communication arises and in which their freedom is identified. Paradoxically, both the prose-writer and the reader of prose-writing are essentially existing individuals and essentially free. The freedom of the writer is communicated to the reader through the inessentiality of the work. Since the existing writer is to appeal to the freedom of the reader, the created literary work must serve as only a means. Thus only the engaged writer—one who is fully cognizant of his situation—is able to recognize and reveal the freedom of others. The engaged writer "appeals to the reader's freedom to collaborate in the production of his work."[2] Writer and reader participate in a common enterprise. "Thus, whether he is an essayist, a pamphleteer, a satirist, or a novelist, whether he speaks only of individual passions or whether he attacks the social order, the writer, a free man addressing free men, has only one subject—freedom."[3]

Once again, we can reformulate our question: What is it to write? To write is to be free, to demonstrate freedom, and to appeal to the freedom of others—in short, to write is to be engaged. Since, for the Sartre of the 1940s to be conscious of something is to be free, to write is also to be conscious of one's world. Being is acting and writing (to write) is to act.

Roland Barthes's question is formulated differently: What is *écriture*? *Écriture* is not an action in which a particular writer (*écrivain*) engages. Neither is *écriture* the product of *écrire*. Sartre's question is oriented toward the writer who writes. Barthes's inquiry is located at the site of the signifying process. His attention is not placed at the origin or end of the signifying process, but rather upon writing as a historical activity and a social function.

The same *écriture* could be located in distinctively different historical contexts. Barthes notes that Fénélon and Mérimée have the same *écriture* even though a century and a half stands between them, while Mérimée and Lautréamont, Mallarmé and Céline, Gide and Queneau, Claudel and Camus have different *écritures* even though they are each paired chronologically. Although Sartre might speak of similar projects on the part of different writers, and although he would situate a writer within a historical context, he would not want to claim that the writing of a seventeenth century writer is the same as that of a nineteenth century writer. Indeed, to write is to create within and in relation to a particular situation such that writing as act cannot be examined apart from its situation—unless the writing is of the poetizing sort in which case it only reflects the mirror-image of the poet anyway. For the prose-writer, however, an act of communication with the reader means that both are historically located. To write in the seventeenth century is to write in the seventeenth century and not in the nineteenth—writing (*écrire*) in a particular situation means that one is not writing in another. Hence the paradoxical difference between *écrire* and *écriture:* the historical context does not determine writing (*écriture*), but writing (*écrire*) must occur within just such a context.

For the elements of the paradox one could appeal, on the one hand, to the vertical, experiential, active characteristics in Sartre's notion of writing (*écrire*) and, on the other hand, to the horizontal, delimited, signifying, sign systems which predominate in Roland Barthes's formulation of writing (*écriture*). Nevertheless both are "writing." What needs to be elucidated is where, on Barthes's side, this difference occurs.

Écriture is derived from a problematic of language. In Barthes's more recent *Elements of Semiology* (1964), he distinguishes language *qua langage* from language *qua langue*. Following de Saussure, *langue* is associated in a binary opposition with *parole*. *Langue* is a "social institution," a "system of values," and a "collective contract."[4] English, French, and German are all languages in the sense of *langue*. However, theatre, clothing, and cars are each a *langue* also. *Parole* occurs when any one *langue* is selected, articulated, and actualized in a particular act. *Parole* is the speaking subject expressing his thought in terms of the codes and sign systems of a *langue*. *Parole* is the enactment of a *langue* at a particular moment or in a series of moments. *Parole* and *langue* are dialectically interdependent. An uttered sentence in English, a theatrical gesture, and the advertisement of a new model car all demonstrate the interdependence of *langue* and *parole*.

What about the relationship between *langue* and *langage*—both of which can be translated as "language"? Barthes notes in *Elements of Semiology* that "a *langue* is *langage* minus *parole* (speech)."[5] This means that *langage* is *langue* plus *parole*. In other words, a *langage* is the system of codes and their articulation. A *langage* is the discourse or treatment of a particular topic in a particular *langue*. A novel written in French would be a *langage*—that is, a limited discourse in which the *langue* French is enacted within a specific domain. Similarly, in clothing, there is a *langage* of suits—the particular custom of wearing a combination of matching jacket and pants—which is not presented as an ideal type but rather as that which is enacted by individuals.

When Barthes states in the introduction to *Writing Degree Zero* that Literature as a whole, from the time of Flaubert to the present, has become a problematic of language, he is speaking of *langage* not *langue*. As a problematic of *langage*, Literature is *écriture*. This does not imply that all *écriture* is literature. On the contrary, much *écriture* cannot be called literature. But inasmuch as *écriture* raises the question of Literature as a *langage*, the concern about writing is already a concern about Literature. Literature elaborates the signs of *écriture* as its signification. Just as *écriture* delimits a domain of *langage* in order to define itself, Literature depends upon the production of signifying signs in order for it to achieve a status of its own apart from *écriture*.

The question of writing raises the question of Literature. To think the problem of writing is to think the problem of Literature. But writing itself is situated between language (*langue*) and style. Language and style are objects for study. Language is the material with which writing is created, while style is the "vertical and solitary dimension of thought."[6] Style is such that:

> imagery, delivery, vocabulary spring from the body and the
> past of the writer and gradually become the very reflexes of
> his art. Thus under the name of style a self-sufficient language
> (*langage*) is evolved which has its roots only in the depths
> of the author's personal and secret mythology, that subnature
> of expression where the first coition of words and things

takes place, where once and for all the great verbal themes of his existence come to be installed.[7]

Where style is vertical, the individualized and personal contribution to writing, language (*langue*) is horizontal and transindividual. Style is on one side of writing and language (*langue*) is on the other. Or, one might say (in terms of cartesian coordinates) that *langue* is the x-axis and style is the y-axis. Thus writing (*écriture*) is situated at the intersection of language (*langue*) and style. Since writing is the problematic of language (*langage*) and *langage* involves both *langue* and *parole*, it is likely that style is a type of *parole*. Hence, one could construe the *langue/style* opposition as mapped onto the *langue/parole* opposition. The difference is that *langage* incorporates the *langue/parole* opposition, while *écriture* occurs at the juncture between *langue/style*. *Écriture* (writing) is the problematic of language. Hence writing is mapped onto the problematic of the *langue/parole* opposition. And since the question of writing is already the question of Literature, the *langue/parole* opposition also raises the question of Literature.

What does it mean to say that writing, which is situated at the intersection between *langue* and style, is mapped onto the opposition between *langue* and *parole*? It means that writing which is at the zero degree on the x/y axis announces a language and a style on the one hand—hence a literary concern—and language in relation to speech on the other hand—hence a linguistic concern. Thus Literature which is introduced when writing is introduced is situated in a context which itself is founded on a linguistic framework. In other words, Literature is constructed upon writing and writing is constructed upon a linguistic science (specifically, semiology: the science of signs). Literature is an edifice but one which is in question only at the zero degree, only where *langue* and *parole, langue* and style intersect. This is why it would not be possible to live in the edifice of Literature; one could only produce it. It would not be possible to use Literature, for there is nothing to use. Literature cannot be a vehicle. It cannot serve as the transparent means of communicating the writer's freedom to the reader so that the reader will recognize his own freedom.

Writing is the production or process at the zero degree. Its activities may engage Literature but they will not engage the writer or reader. Literature "becomes the Utopia of *langage*" in that out of the multiplicity of *écritures*, a new Literature is instituted.[8] But this suggests that the structure is not static—which is indeed the case. The z-axis which meets the x/y-axis at their intersection delineates the path of History. Writing is situated along a diachronic line whereby Literature can change its shape and where Literature can reorganize itself as the model which is implicitly appealed to in the multiform varieties of writing. Hence if one were to follow writing along the z-axis at degree zero, one would find different *écritures*, but sometimes one would find *écritures* which repeat previous ones, which reiterate and reaffirm those of earlier Historical moments. It is possible to study the same *écriture* in Fénélon and Mérimée, in Dostoevsky and Ralph Ellison, in Goethe and Mann. These *écritures* can be compared as two points along a Historical line and the comparison can take place irrespective of the diachronic line because it occurs at degree zero. Breaks and new beginnings are always possible along this line.

The zero degree of writing is the place where Literature as a *langage* is put into question. Literary *écriture* is only one of a variety of *écritures*. These include political *écritures*, bourgeois *écritures*, mathematical *écritures*, etc. Writing only raises the question of Literature, it does not necessarily announce Literature, though Literature remains its ideal type. Literature in turn depends upon writing. It depends upon *écriture*—not what Sartre appeals to when he asks, "What is writing?" or "What is it to write?" The question of Literature for Barthes is not the question of *écrire* as it is for Sartre. Writing for Barthes establishes a space at the zero degree of *langue*, style, and along the Historical axis. Writing for Sartre is a creative act which brings about a medium for intersubjective communication.[9] But writing cannot be a medium for Barthes unless one can consider it a neutral terrain for the proliferation and development of sign systems.

What, then, *is* writing? On Sartre's side, it is to write, to create, to communicate, to be free. On Barthes's side, it is to reiterate a linguistic framework of language and speech by establishing its own signs in relation to an authori(ta)tive style and a language which announces the problematic of another language—the *langage* of Literature, just as writing is the *langage* of semiology. But what is writing? Writing must be both the activity of writing and the space in which Literature finds its place. Writing must incorporate both *écriture* and *écrire*. Yet writing operates at the juncture or hinge between the two. There at the hinge between the act of writing and the sign systems of writing, Literature can come into being. Sartre offered a utopian model of Literature in which the freedom of all humanity is realized through the prose-writer's activity. However, it took him a number of years to recognize that it was in fact a utopian formulation, that existentialism was the ideology for which Marxism would be its philosophy. We should therefore not ignore Barthes's claim that Literature becomes the Utopia of *langage*, the utopian question which writing introduces.

WORK/TEXT

The claim that Literature becomes the Utopia of *langage* is situated at the end of *Writing Degree Zero*. That Literature is the problematic of *écriture* and that *écriture* is the problematic of language should already be evident. But that Literature might be the Utopia of *langage* announces the respect in which the ideal place of *langage* is Literature. As Barthes puts it: "The proliferation of modes of writing brings a new Literature into being in so far as the latter invents its language (*langage*) only in order to be a project."[10] From the heterotopia of *langage*, Barthes signals a utopia of Literature. But the discourse of projects is a distinctly Sartrian one. For Sartre, a pro-ject is a directedness or anticipation of a situation which is beyond the present one. The project is the expression of human freedom in that it characterizes the movement of consciousness beyond itself. Literature for Sartre is a project in that it expresses human freedom and takes the writer beyond himself in the art of writing. Literature establishes an ongoing interlocution on the part of the writer with the reader. The human project keeps this condition from turning into a static relation. However, when Barthes speaks of Literature as inventing its language in order to be a project, he means that Literature cannot simply be a type of writing, but rather that it must be the ideal of writing, what Literature would be if it did not have to operate within the frames of language (*langue*), style, and History. Sartre admits our situated location and considers Literature as a function of that situationism, while Barthes sees Literature as an ideal of *langage* and accounts for language as conditioned by contextual frameworks.

When Sartre announces in a 1971 interview with Contat and Rybalka that "there is no more literature,"[11] he achieves a near total reversal of his 1947 position. This transformation in Sartre's view of literature could already be identified in the 1957 essay entitled *Search for a Method*—the *de facto* introduction to *Critique of Dialectical Reason* (1960). Citing Flaubert as his example, Sartre writes:

> The problem is to recover the totalizing movement of enrichment which engenders each moment in terms of the prior moment, the impulse which starts from lived obscurities in order to arrive at the final objectification—in short, the *project* by which Flaubert, in order to escape the petite bourgeoisie, will launch himself across the various fields of possibles toward the alienated objectification of himself and will constitute himself inevitably and indissolubly as the author of *Madame Bovary* and as that petit bourgeois which he refused to be. This project has a *meaning*, it is not the simple negativity of flight; by it a man aims at the production of himself in the world as a certain objective totality.[12]

The writer's project, in this instance, is one of going beyond the objectifications that define and alienate him. Writing is, in effect, the instrument by which the writer establishes his meaning and goes beyond the totalized (practico-inert) conditions in which he finds himself. Writing cannot appeal to the freedom of all mankind because the writer himself is not free. The writer writes in order to overcome and totalize (through his own praxis) the totality which is presented to him in his place in History. The existential version of Literature, which Sartre announced in 1947, becomes an ideal model in 1957. Out of his conditions of need and scarcity, the writer seeks to bring about the situation of the engaged but free author who can communicate his freedom to his readers. However, instead of Literature serving as the instrument of writing, it is now the ideal of writing. If the existential conception of Literature could be realized in practice, it would no longer be necessary as a conception, for it would be the writer's actual *praxis*. Since it has not been realized, it remains a form of ideology. Sartre concludes *Search for a Method* with the remark:

> From the day that Marxist thought will have taken on the human dimension (that is, the existential project) as the foundation of anthropological Knowledge, existentialism will no longer have any reason for being. Absorbed, surpassed and conserved by the totalizing moment of philosophy, it will cease to be a particular inquiry and will become the foundation of all inquiry.[13]

Consistent with his earlier position, Sartre notes, in a 1959 interview entitled "The Purposes of Writing," that in contradistinction to ethnologists who describe, writers must take sides.[14] Taking sides means recognizing one's insertion within a particular historical, political, social circumstance. And the function of literature is to "offer man a critical image of himself."[15] Engaging oneself as a writer means providing a picture of our actual situation—not of an idealized form. As Sartre remarks, we live in the midst of images and Literature offers us a critical image of ourselves. In this critical mirroring, Literature must reveal, demonstrate, and represent. But if Sartre is obliged to claim, as he does in the *Critique of Dialectical Reason*, that we exist in situations of seriality and as practico-inert totalities, then Literature would have to portray those conditions—albeit critically. In other words, Literature can demonstrate a *praxis* as a response to the practico-inert. What Literature does is what the writer does. The writer writes. To write "is the highest form of the basic need to communicate."[16] With the transformation which occurred in the decade or so since *What is Literature?* what is communicated when the writer writes is no longer freedom, but rather conditions of need and scarcity against which freedom can be projected.

It is perhaps still not clear yet why Sartre claims in 1971 that there is no more literature. The 1965 essay "A Plea for Intellectuals," for example, moves closer to the edge which Sartre announces for the termination and completion of literature. He writes:

> The literary work must appertain to the whole epoch, in other words to the situation of the author in the social world, and on the basis of this singular insertion, to the entire social

245

whole—in so far as this insertion renders the author, like any other man, a being *concretely* in question in his being, who *lives* his insertion into the world in the form of alienation, reification, frustration, want, solitude, against a *suspected* background of possible plenitude.[17]

The work (*l'oeuvre*) is part of a socio-historical time (regressively assessed). The author of the work, i.e. the writer, elaborates both his singularity in the world and the universality of his totalizing process. Totalization takes the writer's singularity and through the work universalizes his concrete situation. The work is what the writer creates and the work is his means of bringing about the totalization which he projects as a writer. The work is "both a restitution, on the plane of non-knowledge, of the experience of being in a world which crushes us, and a lived affirmation that life is an absolute value and an appeal for freedom addressed to all other men."[18] In continuing to characterize the task of the writer as appealing to freedom, Sartre maintains the ideology, the utopia, and particularly as a contrast to the heterotopian conditions of adversity.

When writers write literary works, they create literature. By 1971, Sartre himself had stopped writing literary works. His last work of this sort was *The Condemned of Altona* (1959). This does not mean that he stopped writing—before his avowed blindness in 1975. *The Words*, the three-volume *Idiot of the Family*, and several volumes of *Situations:* were added to the corpus, but not as literary works. Even though Sartre claims that works develop out of the activity of singular universals in their concrete situation, he would not base his whole claim about the absence of literature on the fact that he himself no longer writes works. Could it be argued that his study of Flaubert indicates more explicitly his view that literature has come to an end? In "Itinerary of a Thought," he states that Flaubert represents the exact opposite of his own conception of literature.[19] But whether he finds Stendhal or Flaubert more representative of his own view of literature does not bring us closer to the position that literature is at an end.

Literature is at an end because the nature of literature is to bring about the freedom of all mankind. This is the task the prose-writer sets for himself when writing and creating works. The writer must communicate with readers and portray their freedom. But if they are not free, how can the writer write in order to show them their freedom? Works are crafted. Works (*oeuvres*) are man-oeuvered into communicative situations. Though we remain in situation, our situation is more appropriately accounted for by the totalizations and personalizations that a political or perhaps theoretical practice might provide. Literature, it seems, can no longer accomplish the task which Sartre set for it in 1947. The manoeuvres of *oeuvres* do not account for the condition of our times. What is needed at the edge of literature is a discursive space which can account for the situations and conditions in which we find ourselves. Located at the edge of literature, at the limit of the space delimited by literature, is the text.

In the 1961 essay entitled "Literature Today," Roland Barthes notes that literature is only one of a variety of signifying systems. Food, clothing, pictures, films, fashion are all signifying systems like literature.[20] As a signifying system, literature is a text like the others. Since texts can comprise texts, the former Utopia of *langage* is now a *locus operandi*. "The discourse on the Text should itself be nothing other than text, research, textual activity, since the Text is that *social* space which leaves no language safe, outside, nor any subject of the enunciation in position as judge, master, analyst, confessor, decoder. The theory of the Text can coincide only with a practice of writing (*écriture*)."[21] The text is a practice of writing. With the opposition between *écrire* and *écriture* forming the activity and operation of writing, on the other side of the literature/text opposition we find an opposition: work/text. This can be inscribed diagrammatologically in the following way:

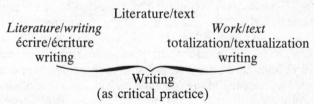

Literature/text

Literature/writing   Work/text
écrire/écriture   totalization/textualization
writing   writing

Writing
(as critical practice)

Sartre has opted for the position that there are still writers and there are still literary works, but that there is no more literature. For Sartre, then, *écrire* means to produce writing and to produce writing means to create literary works (*oeuvres*). Ideally the function of literary works is to appeal to the freedom of all mankind through a communicative act. Since however that function, which is the character of literature, remains utopian, the task of the writer is to totalize the totalities that form the practico-inert situations in which we find ourselves. To write, then, in the second Sartrian formulation, is to totalize. To create works is to perform a totalizing operation. Close to the place where Sartre identifies totalization, we find Barthes announcing textualization. The discourse on the Text is itself textual activity and hence a form of textualization. Textualization is the practice of the text and approximate to Sartrian totalization. In other words, totalization is the experiential process which can be characterized in terms of signifying sign systems, such as literary works, clothing, films, etc. These signifying sign systems are actualized in a textualizing practice of the text.

In order to identify the place of juncture between work and text, we need to understand the framework of the 1960s and 1970s. The Sartrian elaboration of the place of the work *qua* literary work has already been characterized, but what of Barthes's account? Barthes consolidates his position most succinctly in the 1971 *Revue d'esthétique* essay "*De l'Oeuvre au texte.*"[22] However, in order for him to set up the opposition between work and text, he needed to mold his own conception of *oeuvre* (work). The appropriate place for this clarification to occur was in his response to Raymond Picard's accusation against "new criticism." With the proper venting of spleen in Part One, the second half of *Critique et vérité* (1965) sets forth the relationship between *oeuvre* and *langage*. *Langage* touches many domains including philosophy, the human sciences, and literature. In *Writing Degree Zero*, writing is the problematic of *langage* and Literature is placed in question with the realization of writing. Indeed, the question of literary criticism is also raised by writing (*écriture*). The interrogation that literary criticism introduces is also in relation to writing and hence to *langage*. Literary criticism is therefore situated alongside (and within the same domain) as Literature. Yet literary criticism is concerned with works while Literature is appealed to in the appearance of writing. One might say that writing molds and opens up works which, in turn, announce both Literature and literary criticism. As Barthes puts it: "a work is 'eternal,' not because it imposes a unique meaning (*sens*) on different individuals, but because it suggests different meanings to unique individuals who all speak the same symbolic language (*langue*) across multiple times: the work proposes, the individual disposes."[23] The polyvalence of the work is determined in an individual reading. Each reading establishes the work, because the individual reader is situated in a particular situation. Hence, the ambiguity of the work and its pluri-significational qualities are reduced by an individual critical reading. "The situation composes the work, it does not find it."[24] Hence the distinction between a science of literature (or writing) and literary criticism. A science of literature (or writing) is a discourse whose object is not one meaning or another, but rather the plurality of the work's meanings, while literary criticism openly seeks to give a particular meaning to the work.

But what is a work? Granting that the work has a plurality of meanings, we now turn to the 1971 essay in which Barthes distinguishes the work from the text. The work is what a writer or author writes in his or her singularity. It is man-oeuvred. The work is a fragment of a substance and occupies a part of the space held by books, for example, in a library. The works of Shakespeare, Goethe, and Flaubert can all be found on shelves and held by readers. A work closes in on a signified, for example, Plato's *Symposium* is *about love*, for "love" constitutes the signified of the work. A work is created and produced. It functions as a sign. Dante's *Divine Comedy* operates as a sign and represents the civilization of the Sign (including the eschatological features of Christianity). The work is caught in a process of filiation: determined by a world, a race, History, etc., it has a father: its Author. The work is the Author's offspring and its siblings are other works by the same Author. The Author is privileged, paternal, and aletheological. The work is an organic whole and cannot be broken or divided. As an object of consumption, it cannot be sold piecemeal.

The text, by contrast, is a methodological field. The text can be approached, experienced, and understood in reaction to the sign. For example, if "love" is the signified in the *Symposium*, in the respect that it is a text, it practices the infinite deferment of the signified, of the concept of "love." Its field is that of the signifier, whose action is that of deferral. The text can be experienced only in an activity of production, not as a static unity. Indeed, a text may cut across one work or even several works; for example, Diotima's account of love is a text associated with and perhaps even part of the discourse on love in the last book of Castiglione's *Courtier* and Stendhal's *On Love*. Together these three texts constitute fragments of the text of love.[25] The play in the infinite deferral of the signified establishes the field of the signifier as it forms rules of enunciation, rationality, and readability. The limits of its domain open onto its paradoxical features (the features which go behind the limit of *doxa*). The text is structured, but it is also off-centered and without closure. The authorial self is de-centered in the text and in the plural meanings of the text. The demand that there be a distance between writing and reading is abolished, though the author may return to the text—but only as a guest. The text is explicitly intertextual. One particular author has no more authority than any other. As Barthes puts it in *The Pleasure of the Text* (1973):

> Reading a text cited by Stendhal (but not written by him) I find Proust in one minute detail. The Bishop of Lescars refers to the niece of his vicar-general in a series of affected apostrophes (My little niece, my little friend, my lovely brunette, ah, delicious little morsel!) which remind me of the way the two post girls at the Grand Hotel at Balbec, Marie Geneste and Celeste Albaret, address the narrator (Oh, the little black-haired devil, oh, tricky little devil! ah, youth! Ah, lovely skin!) Elsewhere, but in the same way, in Flaubert, it is the blossoming apple trees of Normandy which I read *according to* Proust. I savor the sway of formulas, the reversal of origins, the ease which brings the anterior text out of the subsequent one. I recognize that Proust's work for myself at least, is *the* reference work, the general *mathesis*, the *mandala* of the entire literary cosmogony—as Mme de Sévigné's letters were for the narrator's grandmother, tales of chivalry for Don Quixote, etc., this does not mean that I am in any way a Proust "specialist": Proust is what comes to me, not what I summon up; not an "authority," simply a *circular memory*. Which is what the inter-text is: the impossibility of living outside the infinite text—whether this text be Proust or the daily newspaper or the television screen: the book creates the meaning, the meaning creates life.[26]

The "I" which is in play in the inter-textuality which Barthes describes is a "paper-I," part of the network of the intertextual reading. The readerly self is at work in the textual operations of textuality.

The difference between the pleasure of the work and the pleasure of the text is on the side of the text in the literature/text opposition, but the pleasure of the work certainly approximates that of literature. The pleasure of the work is a pleasure of consumption. I cannot re-write Proust, Flaubert, Balzac *et al.* I can however acquire them and enjoy them. The pleasure of the text comes in the text, it is the *jouissance* which cannot be separated from the textualization of the text, for the reader loses himself in the text and opens himself up to its joy. The *jouissance* happens in the site of the text, which is already atopic, just as writing is situated at the zero degree. It has no particular place, but is, at the same time, everywhere. The critic's pleasure in the text indicates the possibility of a *jouissance* which happens in the text. Barthes's pleasure in the inter-texual "circular memory" which he describes when reading Stendhal only opens up the possibility of *jouissance*. As pleasure, however, it is an experience which is not limited by or bound to a particular work. The space of the work has a pleasure of adoption, while the *jouissance* which is derived from the text is atopic and hence an inter-textual textualization.

Barthes demonstrates in *S/Z* (1970) that there are two types of text: the readerly text and the writerly text. The readerly text is the text as it is written—in its serial, syntagmatic form. The readerly text is the text read through from beginning to end. The readerly text is the text treated as a work. The writerly text, however, is a rewriting, an establishment of the codes at work in the textuality of the text, and an ordering of their predominant elements. The writerly text can become a work—as *S/Z* has become—but as a text, it identifies a process of textualization.

LITERATURE/TEXT

What, we may ask, does textualization accomplish? On the one hand, it may account for the establishment of works. However, the integration of texts into works is like falling from authenticity into inauthenticity for Heidegger. Textualization operates within texts, not within works. Works, as Sartre has shown, achieve communication and the appeal to human freedom. Texts however do not accomplish anything—they have no place and hence cannot be placed within an economy of consumption. They can be the locus of pleasure and even *jouissance*, but only as their self-fulfillment, not as their localization. Textualization is the activity of texts in a readerly or writerly fashion. Textualization is the process whereby the text announces its signifying sign systems, its plurality of meaning. In the case of Sade, Fourier, and Loyola, whom Barthes has studied in one work, the associative (systematic) relation between their textualities is the specifically "logothetic" character of their texts. Hence logothesis becomes an element of their textualization as it is re-written in *Sade/Fourier/Loyola* (1971).[27] Textualization, then, is the process whereby intertexuality is transformed into inter-textualization, where the experience of the plurivalent meaning of texts is not confined by the constraint of univalence. In textualization, the ambiguity of the text is maintained and codified.

Textualization is indeed the practice of the text. The activity of the text is identified as an on-going process and even as a site of *jouissance*. Totalization for Sartre achieves a similar function. Totalization takes the totality of a situation or of a work and opens it up to the possibility of future totalities. The operation on the situation or work is the operation of totalization. In the case of the situation, the writer performs the totalization, in the case of the work, the praxis is that of the reader. There is no more literature because the practice of the writer as a totalizer of a practico-inert totality cannot realize an ideal, but it can achieve a literary work.

How close is the literary work to the text? It is as close as totalization is to textualization. On the one side, the totalization of a work is the reiteration and transformation of the writing of literature. But since it is no longer possible to write literature, what is written is a work which gives a picture of the alienated conditions of our time. At its best, the work can totalize the situation with which the totalizer (writer) is faced. Ideally, it will bring the current situation into conformity with a social domain of human freedom. On the other side, the textualization of the text identifies the meaning and codes of the text. Textualization demonstrates that it is not limited to an established work. Textualization can therefore perform the task that the writing (*écriture*) opens up. Writing here can be found in a variety of works. Hence the codes of the writing are not limited to a particular work. Totalization is accomplished by an individual or a group of individuals in a common situation. Textualization is performed by a single text or a group of texts which have a common textuality. Yet both are forms of writing. Totalization is writing one's situation for potential readings. Textualization is writing as a plurality of meanings whose significations are already textual.

Liberate totalization from its situational context and allow it to draw from a multiplicity of texts, liberate textualization from its textual purity, and there arises the possibility of a critical practice in which the sign systems of a text can be experienced in a totalizing activity of writing and re-writing. To achieve such a critical practice, it would be necessary to identify the interpretive experience of certain significations and codes and to indicate where they are located within a historico-social context. This critical practice operates within an epistemological framework, but is not devoted to the production of works. Rather it elaborates relations within texts, between texts, and around texts. Writing of this sort is a signifying theoretical practice in which individuals or groups participate. In order to achieve such a signifying critical and theoretical practice, it would be necessary to situate both writing and reading at the slash, on the line, in the interface between work and text, between totalization and textualization, between the problematics and pleasures of literature/text. Efforts at crossing-over the line are admirable, but they are also codifying. Binary operations are not easily traversed. Crossing-over can mean crossing-out. For this reason, Sartre and Barthes remain on their respective sides—though in their practice they move as close as possible to the line between them—allowing another self, in this reading, to annul itself by standing on the line at degree zero as a critical practice of Writing.

14

SARTRE/FOUCAULT:
DIALECTIC AND EPISTEMÉ

To interrogate History is to establish its place. The place of History is the context in which alternative theoretical practices operate. History is not a list of events, an inventory of conceptions, or a report of conflicts. History is wherever it is located. The locus of History can be understood topologically, that is, its place depends upon an epistemology which elaborates how it is interpreted by those who live it.

By juxtaposing a theoretical practice such as that offered by Michel Foucault with Jean-Paul Sartre's existential Marxism, the place of History will become evident. On the one hand, Foucault's archaeology of knowledge demonstrates that History as a continuous series of occurrences, discoveries, decisions, and theories is out of place in the contemporary knowledge framework otherwise named Epistemé. On the other hand, Sartre's critique of dialectical reason indicates History's place at the end of a road along which individuals as series and as totalized practico-inert entities overcome their oppressed condtions through praxis. This movement is named: Dialectic. In this chapter, I will show that the place of History is located at the frontier between Dialectic and Epistemé. Sartrian dialectic, as formulated in the 1950s and 1960s, provides the achievement and fulfillment of History such that Foucault in the 1960s and 1970s can offer an account of discontinuous, reversible, and self-regulating knowledge frameworks. In effect, History has no place of its own in dialectical reason and yet once dialectical reason is complete, History appears, but only in time for it to be situated at the threshold of a new positivity, at the edge of a topological delimitation in which the discourse that made it possible has been supplanted by a different discourse. History, then, is located in the context of Dialectic and Epistemé, at the interface between Dialectic and Epistemé.

In *Search for a Method* (1957) which serves as the introductory essay to *Critique of Dialectical Reason* (1960), Sartre distinguishes his own approach from "the Marxist method:"

> The Marxist method is progressive because it is the result—
> in the work of Marx himself—of long analyses. Today
> synthetic progression is dangerous. Lazy Marxists make use
> of it to constitute the real, a priori; political theorists use it
> to prove that what has happened had to happen just as it did.
> They can discover nothing by this method of pure *exposition*.
> The proof is the fact that they know in advance what they
> must find. Our method is heuristic: it teaches us something
> new because it is at once both regressive and progressive. Its
> first concern—as it is for the Marxist too—is to place man
> in his proper framework.[1]

By adding a regressive component to the standard Marxist methodology, the concept of historical inevitability present in dialectical materialism is qualified and reformulated. Civilizational study can no longer simply account for the progressive development of a society, culture, and class scheme toward an already determined *telos*. We learn nothing new from such an account. Economic conditions prepare the ultimate direction which the civilization will take. The progressive-regressive method however provides an element of discovery. We must consider where the society is headed, but we must also return to the period in question in order to understand the set of cross-references characterizing the civilization at that time.

Sartre generally focuses his attention on an individual—a remnant from his earlier existentialism. For example, to study Flaubert regressively, one must consider his early childhood (objective testimonies about his family and subjective statements by Flaubert about his parents, brother, sister, etc.), the type of intellectual petite bourgeoisie living at that time under the Empire, the impeded advance of family capitalism, the return of landed proprietors, contradictions in the government, the misery of a still insufficiently developed proletariat, differences between Flaubert's family and that of Baudelaire, the Goncourt brothers, and others, the real relations between scientists, professionals, and industrialists, etc.[2] This system of cross-references establishes the particular conditions emanating out from Flaubert and elaborating a full picture of a particular civilizational context. The context is developed from the individual and filled out in terms of aesthetic, literary, familial, social, economic, institutional, and political relations. What we discover is the full network of interrelationships characterizing the time of Flaubert. Indeed, in that respect, "Man is placed in his proper framework." The "Man" is Flaubert, the "framework" is the nineteenth century. The concept of "Man in a framework" is, as I shall show, what Foucault takes as a nineteenth century understanding, as opposed to what Sartre would call an understanding of the nineteenth century.

The regressive aspect of Sartre's method brings together a field of possibles and a field of instruments. As fields these domains establish a totalizing context *of* and *for* understanding. Sartre calls this synthetic factor the element of *"compréhension."*

> The movement of comprehension is simultaneously progressive (toward the objective result) and regressive (I go back toward the original condition) . . . . Thus comprehension is nothing other than my real life; it is the totalizing movement which gathers together my neighbor, myself, and the environment in the synthetic unity of an objectification in process.[3]

The movement of comprehension requires that there be a sense of the progressive inevitability of historical change, but also that a return be instituted: the reestablishment of the framework that progresses. Both development and return are given unity by the inquirer who understands these conditions. This element of *Verstehen* as Sartre acquires it from Dilthey and Heidegger highlights what is specifically phenomenological in the later Sartre. *Verstehen*—comprehension—understanding—is the form of intentionality at the foundation of a civilizational hermeneutic. The regressive content is the noematic element which reveals its temporality in the historical development established by the progressive account. To make the point another way, consider the Husserlian notion of *Lebenswelt* (lifeworld) in his later *Crisis of the European Sciences and Transcendental Phenomenology*. Some, such as Ingarden and Schutz, attempt to consider the *Lebenswelt* still within the transcendental sphere as Husserl conceived it. Others, such as Paci, Merleau-Ponty, and Sartre, offer a phenomenological Marxism which existentializes the *Lebenswelt* and show it to be the lived character of a phenomenal field of History. For them, such a field is understood as it is lived, rather than lived as it is understood (which would be the Husserlian version). Foucault's account would announce the inter-section of the two. But on Sartre's side, what he calls "the profundity of the lived" is revealed by the procedures of regression and cross-reference. The lived is shown by progression to be a condition of development and genesis.

Each individual in each historical moment is a project. By understanding the indivdiual as a project, even the progessive account may be integrated into the regressive version. As a trans-formation of Sartre's notion of "fundamental project," which, according to *Being and Nothingness*, is uncovered by existential psychoanalysis as a basic choice underlying a person's action and career, the project in his *Search for a Method* is a surpassing of a generalized situation. "Man defines himself by his project. This material being perpetually goes beyond the condition which is made for him; he reveals and determines his situation by tran-scending it in order to objectify himself—by work, action, or gesture."[4] One's self-objectification is practico-inert, which only *praxis* can overcome. The individual within a civilizational context surpasses his condition in order to objectify himself in it—this means that the project can be integrated into the field of possibles brought out by the regressive account. Though it is directed toward the ultimate outcome of History, the project is part of the civilizational domain of a particular period—even if the individual is not aware of it. The study of Jean Genet in 1952 is transitional in this respect. Sartre's *Saint Genet* shows Genet as an individual with a fundamental project—to become a writer in spite of his orphanhood and his total dependence upon others. By a regressive project, conditions of total need, created by his foster parents, oblige him to steal. He overcomes these conditions of adversity by reintroducing the details of his homosexuality and his various crimes against society into the bourgeois world through his novels

257

and plays—even while he is in prison. Decent folk's horror is his delight; his objective conditions become a delineation of a total social context.

The "Man" of a period is an orientation toward History itself. It is a series of individuals, each with a personality, a set of interests, a class status, a social place, an economic base, and a system of contemporaries. Such a "man" is a signifying being both for himself and for others: "Man constructs signs because, in his very reality, he is signifying; and he is signifying because he is a dialectical surpassing of all that is simply given. What we call freedom is the irreducibility of the cultural order to the natural order."[5]

What Sartre means by the cultural order is the framework in which the individual "signifies," that is, where the individual elaborates his own projective meaning, which aims toward future conditions by realizing the conditions in which he finds himself.

For Foucault, what is problematical about the progressive-regressive method with its theory of comprehension, projection, and signification is that it is archaeologically unsound. An archaeology of knowledge rejects the purely progressive aspect of what Sartre has called "lazy Marxism." Foucault goes even further: the concept of discontinuity undercuts a progressive procedure. Instead of following the traditional conception of a history of, for example, ideas, the arts, cultures, institutions, civilizations, an archaeology of knowledge discovers limits to a particular epistemological formation by showing how each element changes, develops, "progresses." The Renaissance has its own conditions of knowledge-formation, which is quite unlike that of the Classical Age. Where Foucault finds "resemblance" to be the epistemé of the Renaissance, "representation" characterizes the epistemé of the Classical Age. The epistemé is a system of knowledge-production which arises in a number of different contexts within the same period. Each epistemé is comprised of discourses such as general grammar, analysis of wealth, and natural history in the Classical Age. Each discourse is formed by a set of enunciations or statements [*énoncés*], which constitute the claims central to the articulation of a particular discourse—in other words, the conditions for operating a particular system of signs within a general field of science. Science here is the knowledge produced at a designated moment and the formalization of the perception of a situational or civilizational practice.

In stressing the notion of discontinuity, Foucault excludes the progressive procedure altogether. What Sartre has called the regressive aspect, however, is much closer to Foucault's position even though this repetition of a contextual and cross-sectional account occurs on the other side of the slash between Sartre and Foucault. An archaeology of knowledge "questions the already-said at the level of its existence; of the enunciative function that operates within it, of the discursive formation, and the general archive system to which it belongs."[6] Such a method would elaborate knowledge as it exists, for example, in the nineteenth century under the labels of philology, political economy, and biology. These discursive practices are the "already-said at the level of its existence." The period is therefore understood according to its discursive practices and not by examining the familial, social, political, institutional, and literary situation of a single individual such as Flaubert. Hence, when Foucault speaks of "existence," he is talking about the existence of "positivities" or "correlations" between signs, statements, discourses, and disciplinary domains. He is not talking about the existence of the individual introducing signification by surpassing a set of determinate conditions in order to objectify himself. The practice of the archaeologist is discursive practice; practice, for Sartre, is the *praxis* of the individual overcoming the practico-inert in the face of scarcity and need, while at the same time showing dialectically that the individual is bound to his situation. Hence the regressive procedure for Sartre works from the existing practice of the individual, while that of Foucault elaborates a whole civilizational framework of existing discourses as they play a practical role in relation to other discourses.

The opposition between these two methodologies is tantamount to claiming that Foucault has neither the progressive nor the regressive analysis since Foucault's notion of Epistemé calls for a new mode of understanding and particularly one independent of Sartrian Dialectic. Foucault's emphasis upon (1) difference—between epistemological formations, and (2) transformation or threshold—as the conditions of restructuration from one epistemé to another, points to a denial of the progressive view. Continuity is excluded and, with it, progression. Similarly, although more subtly, the regressive position falls out—partially because, for Sartre, the regressive depends upon the progressive, and partially because regression implies a center of emanation from which a whole civilizational understanding can arise. Without the centered individual, projects, signifying beings, and comprehension would be meaningless. In Foucault's own words, the rejection takes the following form.

> There remain two traditional recourses. (1) The historical-transcendental recourse: an attempt to find, beyond all historical manifestation and historical origin, a primary foundation, the opening of an inexhaustible horizon, a play which would move backward in time in relation to every event, and which would maintain throughout history the constantly unwinding play of an unending unity. (2) The empirical or psychological recourse: seeking out the founder, interpreting what he meant, detecting the implicit meanings which were lying silent and dormant in his discourse, following the thread of the destiny of these meanings, describing the traditions and the influences, fixing the moment of awakenings, of lapses, of awareness, of crises, of changes in the mind, the sensitivity or the interest of men. Now it seems to me that the first of these recourses is tautological, the second extrinsic and unessential.[7]

Roughly speaking, the first recourse corresponds to the "progressive procedure" with its foundation maintained as a unity throughout history; and the second recourse corresponds to the "regressive procedure" with its traditions and influences at moments of awakenings for the sensitivities or interests of individuals. Naturally, we cannot be too rigid in our equation, but the correspondence is strikingly suggestive.[8]

Foucault distinguishes two types of history: *total* history and *general* history. Total history, which is the older type, "seeks to reconstitute the overall form of a civilization, the principle—material or spiritual—of a society, the significance common to all the phenomena of a period, the law that accounts for their cohesion—what is called metaphorically the 'face' of a period."[9] In the *Critique of Dialectical Reason*, Sartre elaborates his notion of totalization. The individual engaged in a situation responds to conditions of practico-inert objectivities with *praxis*. In this way, seriality is overcome and the possibility of a totalizing fused group or institution is realized. Only the "pledge," the general totalization of the individual totalizing process, can be brought together into a greater totalization—one which Sartre ultimately calls History. The goal is not the kind of history that Burckhardt, Gibbon, or Toynbee have constructed; however, the methodological claim to the achievement of totalization might well result in the "face" of a period—with History as its aegis and consummation.

According to Foucault, a total history (History for Sartre) develops a network of causality, explores relations of analogy in the domains of historical knowledge (e.g., social structures, economic strata, technological instruments, cultural concerns, and political practice), and elaborates large units, phases, or stages—each of which exhibits its own principle of cohesion. By starting with the individual as center, Sartre cannot help but unify all knowledge in accordance with its reference back to the individual(s) in question. By contrast, a general history (situated at the beginning or *arché* of a new knowledge framework called Epistemé) will discover "series, divisions, limits, differences of level, shifts, chronological specificities, particular forms of rehandling, possible types of relation"[10]—in short discontinuities and breaks will predominate. Although Sartre argues for a set of differentials in working out his system of cross-references, the ultimate goal is a reunification of disparate qualities and elements within a period. One might even say that the "heuristic" of which Sartre speaks is precisely this discovery of links and interconnected relations within a particular civilizational context. However, Foucault's general history, in its comparative evaluation of different epistemés or knowledge frameworks, excludes the ultimate goal of comprehension and the reunification of that which can be totalized (into History).

According to Foucault, the figure of Man, as an empirico-transcendental doublet, arose somewhere at the end of the eighteenth century. Now in its last phases, the concept of Man is on the way to its own disappearance in favor of a new epistemological formation. Foucault adds, with rhetorical flourish, that "Man is a quite recent creature, which the demiurge of knowledge fabricated with its own hands less than two hundred years ago."[11] What he means is that with Kant's Copernican Revolution, Man is presented as a combination of an empirical domain and a transcendental aspect. Empiricities are unified through a schematism of categories by a transcendental unity of apperception. These are the characteristics of the man of the Enlightenment, but also, and more particularly, of Romanticism. An inner, subjective, transcendental realm of experience is combined with an outer, objective, empirical realm of givens. Whether it takes the form offered by Hegel's consciousness/self-consciousness, Marx's economic conditions/ proletarian class-consciousness, or Husserl's natural attitude/ phenomenological attitude, in each case, the empirico-transcendental doublet is reiterated. This figure of Man in the anthropological discourse of the philological-economic-biological complex fills out the particular epistemological space of the modern era and replaces the epistemé of "representation" which preceded it.

In proposing a new epistemological formation succeeding that of anthropologism, Foucault announces the prevalence of the human sciences, and particularly ethnology (e.g., Lévi-Strauss), psychoanalysis (e.g., Lacan), and linguistics (e.g., Jakobson). These human sciences do not, however, reintroduce a concept of Man in his empirico-transcendental doublethood. Rather Man is decentered into a play of elements, structures, systems, and discourses. What Derrida calls an interplay is a decentering of any primordial structure.[12] The subject-object paradox—the expression by which Sartre refers to Kierkegaard[13]—is absent in a system of representations just as the King is absent from the scene in which Velasquez's painter in *Las Méninas* is portrayed. This dispersal of subjectivity, not into objectivity, but into the multiplicity of structures, demonstrates the peculiarly deontological form of the contemporary epistemé.

Can we say, however, that Sartre fits simply within the outmoded epistemological space of anthropologism? Sartre has certainly argued for existentialism as a humanism; he has sought to define man in terms of his project; he has asserted the importance of individuality in understanding the role of totalization. And yet, if we turn to an early text, *The Transcendence of the Ego* (1936),[14] we find that the case for a transcendent ego is the very condition for Foucault's claim to an absent subject. The transcendence of the ego is not simply the move from a pre-reflective to a reflective consciousness. In his critique of Husserl, Sartre wants to maintain a pre-reflective consciousness which is unreflected, while that which is reflected falls prey to the objectifications of consciousness. This does not mean on the other hand that Sartre maintains a conception of the unconscious. Rather the contentless pre-reflective consciousness attains a state of absence—the presence of an absence, like Foucault's "being" of the human sciences. This absent domain, for Sartre, is not filled with repressed and inaccessible drives. On the contrary, it is always available to a knowing act which seeks to understand and reveal it. In stressing the absence of content and its accessibility, Sartre—like Zarathustra pre-figuring the death of God—has announced the death of "Man" as an empirico-transcendental doublet at the same time that he has shown the finitude of the "human nature" concept.

Sartre, however, does not fulfill the enterprise he announces. Just as he establishes the nothingness of the for-itself and the totalizing character of the praxis of an individual or group, he also affirms the place of History as that which embodies the totalizations of individuals and groups in the face of scarcity and need. But in this respect, Sartre is unable to initiate a place for the human sciences as the replacement of the knowledge framework in which human achievements are realized in History. Although Sartre can indeed move close to the edge of the epistemé in which History prevails, he cannot fully traverse the threshold which leads to a new positivity—a production of knowledge in which there is no reference back to a subject, center, individual or act. At the threshold between Dialectic and Epistemé, two types of history are operative. Sartre can at most affirm a total history in which the comprehension of the era is achieved through a regressive analysis, while Foucault, in announcing a new beginning, indicates the viability of a general history in which different types of knowledge production are possible. Yet cutting across all of these different types, a pervasive epistemé is operative. Epistemés establish spaces of knowledge, they do not produce such spaces nor are they the product of them. The Epistemé is the formation of all knowledge at a particular time. The task of an archaeology of knowledge is to make epistemés explicit. Foucault has achieved this sort of task in certain delimited areas such as madness, the clinic, prisons, and sexuality. Yet *The Order of Things* and *Archaeology of Knowledge* are the places in which it becomes evident how Foucault participates along with other concerns in the contemporary human sciences to show that what was Dialectic—the achievement of praxis over the practico-inert—has been transformed into a discursive practice which has its beginnings where History leaves off and archaeology begins.

The problem which faces archaeology is its efficacy with respect to the knowledge framework from which it derives. Its operations and tools are effective with epistemological spaces other than the contemporary one. But how does archaeology work when it demonstrates its own conditions of knowledge, its own positivity? What will an archaeology of the archaeology of knowledge look like? Indeed, how can it account for its own discursive practice on the other side of Dialectic and after History? Must it not always stand facing Dialectic, operating with respect to the very History which separates human praxis as the overcoming of scarcity and need and which begins to examine the discourses that exclude the mad, repress the oppressed, and deny sexual practices? If attention is no longer placed upon relations between individuals and groups but rather upon the language in which individuals and groups affirm what and how they know, what is acceptable and what is unacceptable, what is true and what is false, then how does this sort of archaeological knowledge know itself? Can rhetorical devices suffice? Will the study of the tropes of our own discourse help to situate our own knowledge with respect to History? I would suggest that a topology such as the one I have put into practice here—one which demonstrates the place of History at the slash between Dialectic and Epistemé—can help to provide an interpretation and understanding of the orientations and possibilities which enterprises such as the archaeology of knowledge embody.

15

SARTRE VERSUS STRUCTURALISM

Philosophies do not develop in a vacuum. They originate and spawn within a context. Contextualization is often modified by opposition. Yet opposition is not necessarily agonistic. Philosophical contexts are the spaces in which philosophical texts proliferate and sometimes disappear. The oppositional or diacritical relationship between philosophical texts arises out of the problematics of identity and difference. Those texts which operate according to identities may be authorially or trans-authorially linked. Those texts which operate according to differences may cut across an authorial practice; they may distinguish authorships *in toto;* or they may establish certain authorial groupings as distinct from others. That there are similarities—even identities— in the philosophical practice of a variety of "structuralists" such as de Saussure, Lévi-Strauss, Lacan, Piaget, Barthes and Foucault, does not deny the differences among them. That there are differences in the textual practice of Sartre in relation to that of de Saussure, Lévi-Strauss, Lacan, Piaget, Barthes and Foucault does not deny the place of similarities. Yet within the philosophical context of recent continental thinking, the oppositional or diacritical relation between Sartre and each of the aforementioned "structuralists" is marked by features of difference. Differences also arise between Sartre's early existential phenomenology, his existential Marxism, and his more recent syntheses in the study of Flaubert. I shall review the fundamental opposition and divergences enacted by Sartre on the one hand and the various "structuralists" on the other. This differential analysis will require an

265

assessment of transformations within the authorial practice of each of the structuralists under scrutiny but also within Sartre's diverse writings.

The philosophical context in question began to articulate itself during the mid-1930s with the appearance of phenomenology in France. As Husserlian phenomenology and its Heideggerian existentialization shaped what Sartre called "a theory of consciousness" and "phenomenological ontology" or what Merleau-Ponty dubbed "phenomenology of perception," structuralism—in the form of structural linguistics—established a sub-text in the practice of Russian formalism and in the disciplinary concerns of various linguists, such as Roman Jakobson and André Martinet. From the mid-1930s to the 1950s existential phenomenology established itself as the dominant textualization of French philosophy with Sartre, Merleau-Ponty, and Simone de Beauvoir as its authors. Yet the intrigue of structuralism for Claude Lévi-Strauss while he was teaching at the New School for Social Research in New York City during World War II and in his conversations with Roman Jakobson gave a distinctively different style to his work and especially to his 1949 *Elementary Structures of Kinship*. Hence when Lévi-Strauss returned to France, he imported structuralism in the form of structural anthropology. Though it was still a number of years before it achieved official parity with the varieties of existentialism spearheaded by Sartre, it was definitely part of the philosophical context in the 1950s. The French Nouveau Roman—which brought Robbe-Grillet, Butor, Simon, and others to the fore—was one form in which it achieved some notice, but by the late 1950s and early 1960s when Sartre had turned to existential Marxism, structuralism took on a diacritical status with respect to the varieties of existentialism associated with Sartre. That structuralism also acquired proponents in the forms of psychoanalysis with Lacan, genetic epistemology as Piaget announced it, literary criticism through Barthes, and history of thought in Foucault was a sign of its growing strength.

When the sub-text of structuralism replaced existentialism as an anti-text in the 1960s and early 1970s, it achieved a contextual dominance and an oppositional value. Despite more recent developments in post-structuralism, deconstruction and *la nouvelle philosophie*, this oppositional value opens up a relationality for the articulation of a philosophical enterprise of the 1980s. The juxtaposition of Sartrian existential thinking with the concerns of various structuralists announces a difference in which a number of investigations might arise. Considering the two independent domains together both establishes the places of intersection and introduces a type of positionality which is different from either taken on its own. This new complex arises out of the juxtaposition itself and is characterized specifically by the slash (or stroke) which both separates and brings them together, which qualifies them as different and distinguishes them as articulating common concerns.

The space of the slash indicates at least six problematics, each of which corresponds generally to a binary relationship between the Sartrian position and that of an individual structuralist thinker: (1) the theory of language (Sartre/ Saussure), (2) the theory of social organization and myth (Sartre/Lévi-Strauss), (3) the theory of the self (Sartre/Lacan), (4) the theory of human development (Sartre/Piaget), (5) the theory of literature (Sartre/Barthes), and (6) the theory of history (Sartre/Foucault). Instead of filling out each of these particular problematics in detail, I shall examine three types of relationality which cut across some of these theories and which highlight the character of the differences between Sartrian and structuralist positions. The three thematics can be characterized as follows: (1) existence (or praxis)/structure (or system), (2) situation (or comprehension)/ discontinuity (or epistemé), and (3) project (or personalization)/transformation (or version). Each of these thematics and its formulation in terms of the slash articulates an intersection in which the examination of the relation between Sartre and the structuralists becomes possible. The repetition of these three thematics at the place of the slash delineates the field of the relation itself. I shall elaborate each thematic in turn in order to delimit and establish a theoretical practice for the study of Sartre and the structuralists.

In each case an alternative reading is offered on either side. For not only has Sartre restated his position in different ways and at different times, but also different "structuralists" have offered modified accounts of what goes under the general heading of a structuralist position. This modulation should help to characterize both the scope and limits of the diacritical oppositional relation.

(1) *Existence (or praxis)/structure (or system)*. Sartre has neatly divided up his theortical concerns between what could be called

the cult of existence and the call for praxis. In the first instance the claim is ontological, in the second it is dialectical. In both cases, his task has been to account for how human individuals can consider their relationship to their particular modes of being in the world and what needs to be done within that context. Human existence—that dimension which one often overlooks when concentrating upon what is essential—appears when the very character of one's consciousness is brought under scrutiny. Human existence describes how an individual is conscious of things in his or her world. Instead of determining the essence of being human as an essence, Sartre understands it to be precisely the negation of an essence, the denial of any substantialization of the individual, any determination as exclusively what is in-itself, objectified, static. Human existence is the affirmation of something as a thing while at the same time determining the self as not that thing, as the absence which establishes a presence, and as the non-thetic self-consciousness which accompanies all acts of awareness.

The Sartrian conception of existence is conditioned by its distinction from a conception of essence. The self *is* not any particular essence—though it may *have been* any number of them in the past.

At the limit of human existence is always an essence of some sort. Essences take their place wherever existence has surpassed them. Structures for Sartre would be types of essence. They would be examples of the in-itself and could never take on the status of being-for-itself, of existing consciousness. Even consciousness itself—in contrast to Husserl's view—has no structures. Consciousness is pure directedness toward and beyond things and can never be a thing itself. Consciousness has no structure because it has no content and no form—it is at most a nihilating activity. For various structuralists however structure is not a thing. Structure is the set of relationships between elements constituting a repeatable framework. The structure is not a social fact, nor is it in the mind. Structure is the character of the relationship between mind or subjectivity and world. The structures of language are neither mental nor material; they operate between the mental and the material in that they are formed by signs and signs are made of the relationship between signifiers and signifieds, words or acoustical images and concepts. A complex of signs constitutes a structure which also cannot be either fully material (the signifier as sound) or mental (the signified as concept). Thus each of the signs in "I walked to the park" has a relationship to each other such that the five signs constitute a variously repeatable structure.

For example, a similar structure might read "He crawled from the pub." The set of relationships forming the two statements is the same such that the same structure is reiterated in each case. Similarly the structure of the Orpheus myth involves a poet musician who loses his wife Eurydice and who is told that if he turns around and looks at her before they leave Hades he will lose her forever. He does turn around and does lose her forever— even to the extent that he himself is torn apart by maenads and his head floats ashore on the Island of Lesbos. Each of the units or elements of the myth constitutes a sign. Each sign is related to the others in a complex forming the structure of the Orpheus Myth. The myth itself is the whole narrative as rendered by any number of different versions such as that given by Ovid or Virgil, Bacon or Cocteau. The structure is the unity formed by the set of elements or signs. Similarly, again, when a patient speaks to a psychoanalyst, he or she may report the events of a dream. For Lacan, the structure of the unconscious is patterned after the structures of language. The patient speaks and employs language such that the chain of signifiers constitutes a narrative which is either metaphorical (condensing into a sign a number of different signifieds) or metonymical (displacing signifieds which are not indicated but which veer off into successive signifiers).

These are only a few examples of structures as they operate between self and world, as they distinguish themselves from individual psychological states and from the reified conditions which Sartre proposes for them. Yet structures, if taken as things or essences, if taken *in abstracto*, lose their dynamic and vital features. Structures are thereby turned into material objects. Yet the limits of the structure take it to the boundary where it could be treated as a thing or essence. This boundary is the place of the slash between Sartre and the structuralists. It is the place at which structures which can be proliferated and examined endlessly meet existing beings which themselves when self-conscious open up a field of possible experience which has no limit (except perhaps death).

The alternate form of the existence/structure diacritical relation announces the possibility of substituting praxis for existence and system for structure. Both substitutions need not be effected at once. They are independent of each other. The same holds for each of the three binary oppositions announced in this account. The rationale for substituting praxis for existence is motivated by Sartre's concerns since the late 1950s with the possibilities of dialectical reason, his recognition that individuals queuing for a bus or looking around a supermarket for groceries are in "series." They have a practico-inert relationship to each other. However when individuals respond to their practico-inert condition with praxis—as when they are in a group or responding to some sort of terror which affects them all—then their mutual relationship changes. At this juncture, praxis operates in relation to a situation which is characterized by alienation and alterity.

Sartre has claimed that Lévi-Strauss's account of structure places it in the domain of the practico-inert. Structure is inert, not dynamic, without praxis and hence without any possibility of dealing with what is created in language, myth, or dream. But this is Sartre's view and he pushes structure into his own framework—a framework which disallows the very features which Lévi-Strauss and others provide for their notion of structure. Transforming structure into system indicates the possible multiplication of structures. Structures sometimes form systems of structures. Sometimes systems are part of a general structural account where the system is the dominant principle of organization, as in the case of Roland Barthes's system of fashion. Barthes examines the structures of clothes as they are worn above the waist, below the waist, on the feet, etc. The syntagmatic articulation of an individual's clothing on a particular day or in a particular picture of *Vogue* magazine is understood in terms of the associative possibilities of alternate sweaters, blouses, turtlenecks, etc. for above the waist. In this sense, the clothes one wears at a particular moment are a type of *parole* and the whole language of fashion is a *langue*. High fashion dress is a *langage* which restricts its systematic associative or paradigmatic features to certain types of clothing. Barthes does not treat clothes as a thing. On the contrary, they incorporate a practice on the part of those who wear them. What is distinctive about the account itself is that the stress is not placed upon the practice of wearing clothes (and in this sense Sartre distinguishes himself) but it is also not placed upon the clothes as a practico-inert entity. Rather the systemic or more broadly semiological description accounts for the elements that make the practice possible. These are not Kantian conditions of possibility although they are regulative and parameter-setting if not also categorial. The difference is that in the Kantian schematism the conditions of possibility are set and delimited prior to particular practices. In the semiological or structural view, the parameters are set by the practice. Thus the systemic practice points to but does not coincide with Sartrian praxis—they are separated by a slash.

(2) *Situation (or comprehension)/discontinuity (or epistemé)*. The Sartrian conception of situation extends back to his writings of the early 1940s. To be *en situation* is to be engaged, to be committed to the context in which one finds oneself and to be able to accept that situation in order to go beyond it. We are all in a situation, whether it be the hell of Garcin, Estelle, and Inez in *No Exit* or the little boy Jean Genet caught stealing by his foster-parents or Jean-Paul himself actualizing his decision to become a writer. To be conscious of one's situation is to recognize one's existential condition. Situation can mean a particular context in which one finds oneself or it can mean one's being-in-the-world in general. In either case a full understanding of one's existence involves understanding one's situatedness. Sartre's literature of extreme situations (the prisoner about to be executed in *The Wall*, Marcelle who has just discovered that she is pregnant in *The Age of Reason*, Hugo who is told that he must assassinate the party leader Hoederer in *Dirty Hands*, etc.) demonstrates the extent to which our different situations can force us to recognize our very existence in its varied dimensions.

In order for a situation to be understood, it must be lived. Sartre's notion of the *vécu* brings out the respect in which the living of a situation opens up the domain of the pre-reflective consciousness and through praxis makes it available for the comprehension that will encompass it and make it meaningful. This notion of *compréhension* (a type of *Verstehen*) is recounted particularly clearly in Sartre's *Idiot de la famille* in which comprehension is not simply an individual's interpretation of his or her world. Rather the interpretation is placed in the context of a whole historical complex of relations that characterize the moment in which one lives and the progressive orientation which that situation implies. Thus the consideration of Flaubert delineates not only the future of the nineteeth century novel and the destiny of the bourgeoisie and the orientation of economico-historical conditions of the time, but also the whole framework in which Flaubert lived as the son of a surgeon, as a budding writer, as a youth in early nineteenth century France, etc. The comprehension of that situation is not rendered total, rather the totalizing and signifying activity of understanding is what counts.

Whether one is considering the conception of situation or the comprehension which totalizes the more general historical conditions according to what Sartre calls the progressive-regressive method, continuity is the prevalent characteristic. There may be crises as in the case of Flaubert's psychosomatic experience at Pont l'Évêque but on the whole Sartre's account delineates development without break. For structuralists (and even those who refuse the title such as Michel Foucault) the notion of a break—an epistemological break as Bachelard called it—indicates the fundamental discontinuity of history and the comprehension of it. While situation and comprehension are not simply a flow of experience, they are also not characterized by breaks, thresholds, and reformulations of epistemological frame-works. Yet the thematic of history constitutes the membrane or slash which distinguishes situation from discontinuity. Situations are always changing, while epistemological frameworks (or epis-temés) predominate for a certain period of time and then they are replaced by subsequent frameworks with a similar structure but with totally different features. Their discontinuity identifies their more distinctively synchronic rather than diachronic aspect. Thus Foucault is more concerned with the relationships between general grammar, analysis of wealth and natural history than he is with the relationships between general grammar, philology and contemporary linguistics—all of which could be said to have some historical lineage. His concern with the historical cross-section (instead of the development of ideas and approaches) marks his distinctively synchronic viewpoint. Furthermore the confluence of the situational and the epistemological in the notions of epistemo-logical framework and epistemé suggest that when they meet the Sartrian account at the slash, they correspond to what remains dual in the Sartrian view. Even though Sartre in his more recent phases does incorporate situation through comprehension, it is still by an additional gesture of understanding which, for

272

Foucault—to cite one example—is unnecessary. For Foucault, the history of madness and its treatment, the history of institutional punishment, and the history of the human sciences themselves are all conceptual histories as much as they are accounts of the conditions of the times. These "histories," if they can be so entitled, are accounts of the ways in which human situations are understood, interpreted and implicitly related to correlative institutions.

Even Piaget's view of the four stages of human development interprets human development both epistemologically and according to a stage theory. For Piaget, the four stages of development are (1) the sensori-motor stage, (2) the linguistic stage, (3) the stage of concrete operations, and (4) the stage of formal-mathematical operations. At each successive stage, a total reformulation takes place. For example, from the sensori-motor stage, in which the child moves around a room touching, turning, and crawling ahead according to its senses alone, to the linguistic stage, in which the child is able to speak and employ symbolic expression, the whole character of the child's experience has changed. At the second stage, the child's complete understanding of the world has been revised and re-created. Piaget calls his work "genetic epistemology" in order to demonstrate his concerns for development and its delineation according to stages and for the frameworks of knowledge that are also implicated. Hinged at the intersection of continuity and discontinuity, the positions of Piaget and Sartre (like those of Foucault and Sartre) entertain the place of human development and human history.

(3) *Project (or personalization)/transformation (or version)*. The third binary opposition provides another perspective to the juxtapositional relationship between Sartre and the structuralists. These three oppositions cannot be construed as exclusive and exhaustive. Yet they do constitute antipodian relations which turn on an axis and thereby delineate the position of the slash, the place "between," where the announced theoretical practice operates.

The Sartrian notion of project is the activity or vitality of consciousness when orientated toward some future act or way of acting. Consciousness is directed toward the object of consciousness, toward something. Each individual act of consciousness determines a thing in a particular way, as an essence. Consciousness however distinguishes itself from the essence which it determines. Consciousness remains pure existence, pure for-itself and not for anything else, while the thing becomes pure essence, pure in-itself. The nihilating activity of consciousness necessitates its ongoing character. Whenever consciousness attempts to determine itself in a particular way, it establishes itself as other, it goes beyond the determination. This character of going-beyond is called the project. Projects, however, are not restricted simply to individual acts of consciousness, they can also characterize a whole orientation on the part of an individual toward the future, toward how one will live, toward how one will comport oneself as a life project. Near the end of *Being and Nothingness*, Sartre provides an account of the fundamental project in terms of one's original choice of being. Sartre terms this account a type of "existential psychoanalysis." Baudelaire, for example, made an original choice of being which in Sartre's version involved making himself the wound in which he regularly inserted a knife. This attitude toward himself produced in Baudelaire precisely the way of being-in-the-world which allowed him to create poetry. This original choice became his fundamental project and he sought to live by it. Similarly Sartre himself chose to become a writer. In *Words*, his autobiography, he recounts the passage from reading to writing. His choice of being as a writer includes not only growing up in the absence of a father (who died when Sartre was two years old—"I had no Superego," he writes), but also his negative responses to his grandfather Charles Schweitzer, and his decision to save himself by the very activity of writing—even though he relegates Salvation (in the traditional Christian sense) to the room where stage props are kept.

Sartre's variation on the notion of project in his book on Flaubert, published in the early 1970s, is entitled "personalization." Sartre had already modified his conception of project as a feature of existential psychoanalysis when he developed his "progressive-regressive method" in *Search for a Method* (1957). This stress upon the role of the individual in a context and in relation to the development and continuity of history is reformulated again in *Idiot de la famille* in terms of personalization. The continual process of totalization with its detotalizing and retotalizing movement places the person in a situation which is neither a case of complete submission nor one of simple construction. Personalization is the activity in which the person makes himself as a continual assimilation and surpassing of the lived.

Notice that this continuity, with its projective and personalizing characteristics, has only one version in the living of it. As I have already indicated, there may be crises such as those of Genet, Sartre and Flaubert by which they create themselves, make themselves what they will be—in short, choose themselves in a situation or totalize their practico-inert conditions—but the life must be lived as it is and as it develops. It cannot be otherwise. The best one can accomplish is to become what Sartre calls "the singular universal," a description he offers to characterize Kierkegaard. The singular universal is the generalization to all men of what is oneself. In this same vein, Sartre describes himself in *Words* as "a whole man, composed of all men and as good as all of them and no better than any" ("*Tout un homme, fait de tous les hommes et qui les vaut tous et que vaut n'importe qui*," p. 214). His own move from reading to writing is not a transformation of his original choice but rather a fulfillment of it.

The structuralist position, however, requires that there be alternative accounts, versions or readings. Lévi-Strauss's myths involve a variety of versions of one another. The Oedipus myth traced diachronically from its earliest signs down to Antigone's burial of her brother against the edict of her uncle Creon is rewritten according to four categories (overrating of blood relations, underrating of blood relations, the autochthonous origin of man, and the non-autochthonous origin of man).

The story is given a synchronic character by placing elements of the story in each of these categories as they arise within the flow of the myth. At each level, the story is retold with different characters but with the same structural features. A simple transformation—that which is necessary to get from one structure to another—will allow for the translation of one structure into another. For Lévi-Strauss, the same sort of transformational account can be offered in assessing kinship relations in a variety of different societies throughout the world. In this same way, Foucault appeals to a whole discourse and its epistemological framing in order to demonstrate that the epistemé "resemblance" in the renaissance is replaced by the epistemé "representation" in the classical age, and the "theory of man" in the modern era. Each epistemé has the same structure. The historical discontinuity

275

occurs at the place where one breaks down and another takes over. For Foucault, Don Quixote is the threshold figure between the age of resemblance and that of representation, the Marquis de Sade stands between that of representation and the age of man. But how does the concept of transformation and its sub-study, that of version, meet Sartrian projects and personalizations?

For Sartre, the account is individual and personal; for the structuralist, it characterizes a general epistemology which might be either individual or social. What is significant is that the project takes one out of the present state of affairs and into a future condition. This is where it bears similarities to the structuralist's transformation. Transformations are devices whereby the present structure can be reformulated into another structure. The structuralist operates a transformation through an act of methodology, while the existentialist does so by fulfilling an individual choice of being. They meet at the slash between ontology or social theory and epistemology or some human science such as linguistics, anthropology, or archaeology of knowledge. When the existentialist account becomes a psychology, it matches the type of structural psychology which Piaget and Lacan provide in very different ways. Stage theory in human development and the comparison of signifying chains provide a rubric for the understanding of human experience. What they cannot understand is the individual's project—this element of personalization stands firmly on Sartre's side.

What sort of practice does this type of study imply? I have called it a theoretical practice, one in which the juxtaposition of theoretical approaches announces both a relationality and a difference. Sartrian existential phenomenology (or Marxism) calls for a practice in which existence, situation, and project are its fundamental features. The structuralist purview calls for a practice characterized by structure, discontinuity, and transformation. The interposition of the two, which is not itself a synthesis nor a third position, operates precisely at the juncture of the two—at the place of the difference. Such an enterprise must itself be undertaken in order for there to be any meaning to it. In its practice, the juxtaposition indicates a boundary at the slash where the differing accounts meet. Once the existential position has been elaborated, the possibility of proliferation and repetition becomes almost infinite—existential studies are almost boundless. Similarly, structural analyses in the past three decades have resulted in numerous books, journals, and articles. They could go on without end. There are however limits to existential and structuralist positions. These limits are set at the place of the slash, where they meet and where they identify themselves as different.

PART IV

THE DIFFERENCE BETWEEN (AND BEYOND)

16

THE LIMITS OF
LOGOCENTRISM

In the discourse of the history of metaphysics, Logos occupies a variety of contexts. In order to demonstrate where the thesis of the prevalence of Logos reaches its limits, an articulation of the operations of deconstruction is needed. In this way, logocentrism can be situated along with the other principal centrisms, that is, phonocentrism, ethocentrism, phallocentrism and egocentrism. The examination of logocentrism departs from the instance of Heidegger's "Logos" essay. By juxtaposing Heraclitus' account with that of Heidegger, it becomes evident that Heidegger has transposed the place of Logos. Logos is no longer the universal structure of what is said apart from we who listen to it. With Heidegger, I show that we are situated alongside Logos in the ontological difference. In the process, it becomes clear that Logos *qua* language is both the house and the name of the Being of beings. On this basis, Logos is taken to its limits where language itself occupies the place of the indecidable or hinge at the edge of the discourse of metaphysics.

Unlike Michel Foucault's discourse of epistemic spaces and knowledge frameworks, where every couple of centuries a new episteme supplants the previous one, Jacques Derrida elaborates only two basic "epochs" —that of metaphysics and that which arises at the closure of metaphysics. Metaphysics began, at some point— though Derrida does not date its *arché*. He only remarks that it developed out of the exteriority of writing and the exteriority of the signifier. Along with the *destruction* of this exteriority comes the *construction* of interiority. With the construction of interiority comes the *appurtenance* of metaphysics.

Metaphysics pertains as a whole in the form of a metaphor. Writing in the epoch of metaphysics is "a sign signifying a signifier itself signifying an eternal verity."[1] Writing is taken as that which is literal (itself a sign). As a sign, writing serves as the signified for a signifier, i.e., the letter. The letter is that which forms the word. In the literal sense, writing is the concept associated with the letter. Metaphorically, however, the letter is the signifier for another signified. This metaphorical signified is the "eternal truth," the signified "truth," which goes under the name of *Logos* and is inscribed in the Book of Scripture. This metaphorical scheme was most prominent in the medieval system.

In the medieval appurtenance of metaphysics, the Book of Nature, which is the place of the letter as signifier, is signified by its association with the Divine Word (*Logos*) which speaks as a voice. The Divine Word leaves its sign in the form of the letter. Writing is the exteriorization of the Divine Word. When the *Logos* speaks, the intelligible is made sensible. The transcendental signified leaves its mark in the empirical signifier. When external and empiricized, the letter is elaborated as a multiplicity of signs which are read literally within the Book of Nature. The signified of the letter is the sign itself, and as a signifying system, a literal writing is proliferated. Since, however, the signifier-signified relation is itself a sign, it can also be interpreted allegorically— recalling the metaphorical, scriptural sign.

Rousseau reiterates the medieval system by substituting natural writing for the Divine Word. Natural writing is given its form by an arché-speech, an interior holy voice, which provides the "beginning word." The beginning word, however, is readily corrupted in the form of ordinary writing as it becomes "representative, fallen, secondary, instituted." This writing (as a type of social contact) is the replacement for medieval literality. What was a metaphorical sign in the Book of Scripture is now a natural sign formed by the articulation of the beginning word, and what was literal writing in the Book of Nature is now ordinary (i.e., conventional) writing in social commerce.

Similarly Heideggerian thought "would reinstate rather than destroy the instance of the logos and of the truth of Being as '*primum signatum*': the 'transcendental' signified . . . implied by all linguistic signifiers."[2] Thus entities or beings (*Seiendes*) respond to the call of Being (*Sein*), that is, they correspond to the *primum signatum* of which they are only the *signans*. Their ontic character is always conditioned by an ontological voice. Dasein as a sign leaves its signature in the ontological difference between Being and beings, while the ontic distinction between beings indicates the place occupied by Rousseau's social sign and the medieval Book of Nature.

The history of metaphysics in Derrida's terms is the history of a series of ruptures or breaks. These include the break between the Divine Word and the Book of Nature, between speaking and writing, and between Being and beings. Such oppositions, crystallized as binary oppositions in semiology, form the center of the epoch of metaphysics. One could add other pairs such as intelligible/sensible, mental/physical, interior/exterior, etc. Together they constitute the metaphysical discourse, which begins to achieve its closure with the advent of writing (arché-writing), the *differance* which *deconstructs* the text of metaphysics.

I have now appealed to the earmark of Derridian discourse: "deconstruction." Deconstruction is the praxis which is employed in the movement to the limit, border, or hinge, and by which *differance* is inscribed as arché-writing. Deconstruction is structured. It situated itself at the intersection of the inside and the outside, the word and the concept, ordinary writing and speaking. Deconstruction is neither destruction, a tearing apart, analyzing into atomic units nor construction, a bringing together, synthesizing into a unified totality. Deconstruction involves both destruction and construction. It operates at the juncture which Merleau-Ponty described as the chiasm or intertwining between the visible and the invisible, between philosophy and non-philosophy; it fills out the Heideggerian "in-between" [*Inzwischen*] as indicated by the crossing out of Being (*Sein*) in the *Seinsfrage*. In its own right, it determines the literal meaning of writing as metaphoricity itself. The citing of writing as literally metaphorical places Derrida's texts at the interface between the closure of metaphysics which Nietzsche, Heidegger, and Merleau-Ponty inaugurate and the post-closure which remains pure *differance*.

At the edge of the epoch of metaphysics, deconstruction takes its place. Now thoroughly proliferated, deconstruction—the mark of Derridean discourse—has achieved both the renown and the imprecision of a celebrated event. Although the task here is to demonstrate the space in which a certain type of discourse reaches its limits, it would be unwise to simply put deconstruction to work. This caveat becomes especially important when attempting to situate Heidegger near the border of metaphysical language. Thus a deconstruction of Heideggerian discourse would hide the respect in which Heidegger has taken the history of metaphysics to its final moments and thereby established himself as one of the last outposts on the way to grammatology. We must therefore reconstruct the Heideggerian discourse in order to deconstruct it.

Deconstruction involves the examination of texts taken to their extreme form. Here texts or discourses can neither build models nor tear them down. Theory construction and objections to these have no place. Deconstruction establishes itself at the interface between thesis and anti-thesis, between history and post-history, between truth and lie.[3] It should not be supposed that deconstruction has any *proper* place nor for that matter any *improper* one. One might expect therefore that deconstruction is either Kantian or even Hegelian in character. In the first instance, the function of *critique* is to establish the conditions of the possibility of, for example, metaphysical questions. Kantian critique however delimits what can be known and how it can be known. It would seem that critique avoids assertions and only establishes conditions of knowledge. However, it does not recognize that even critique itself is conditioned by a certain play and limit-setting; it does not consider that it builds these—particularly that of human action created against a backdrop of a transcendental and empirical formation. Furthermore, it does not admit that its very procedure has become the foundation for a whole era of metaphysical thinking. Similarly, the Hegelian *Aufhebung* permits the reestablishment of higher truths constructed on the basis of prior oppositions. It does not go to the tear between one type of discourse and another. Rather it attempts to surpass both. Hence the Hegelian enterprise is a paragon of theoretical knowledge: of destruction and construction.

Kant and Hegel, luminaries of the metaphysical establishment, give credence to the idea that critique and *Aufhebung* can provide tools for the fulfillment of a *telos*. All that is can be known or at least known in a certain way. Deconstruction however can inscribe neither teleology nor archaeology. It can only work with (and play at) the traces, supplements, and edges of discourses which presuppose and incorporate metaphysical features. In short, deconstruction looks for the crack, the hinge, and the tear in the manifold of a metaphysical texture. Deconstruction situates itself there at the place where placement spills over.

Heidegger operates within the metaphysical texture which calls for origins and announces ends. Yet if we could speak of horizons, Heidegger would approach the one beyond which metaphysics no longer functions. What would it be like to stand on the other side? If Heidegger has a vision of that possibility, he is nevertheless firmly entrenched on this side. Though he may offer an account of the end of metaphysics, the end of philosophy, the version itself is provided from within metaphysics. This end is not the same as that which Kant offered when he admonished us to never treat man merely as a means, or which Sartre proposes when he describes our fundamental project. It does however resemble the type of end which Michel Foucault notes when he indicates that man is at an end.[4] Metaphysics will achieve its completion, metaphysics will be fulfilled and will no longer stand on its own. But Heidegger the metaphysician brings this about within a metaphysical discourse. Here is a philosophy which announces the end of philosophy.[5]

Where is the edge between philosophy and non-philosophy?[6] At what place can we say that philosophy turns into non-philosophy? What are the parameters for identifying the difference between them? Is there a location in which the indecidable operates? A topology in which the *topos* is both a *locus* and a topic will help, but only in that we can employ geographers and rhetoricians. Heidegger is neither of these. He can of course look for the clearing [*Lichtung*] or for country paths and he can point out the place of speech, but neither of these activities will help us to discriminate between philosophy and non-philosophy, to interpret the signs at the edge of the metaphysics where metaphysics can no longer identify itself as such. Nevertheless Heidegger does offer an account of difference, particularly the ontological difference, which introduces the question of limits—the limits of that-which-is (beings), the limits of that which is present, and even the limits of truth (at the place where truth comes out of concealedness). While Heidegger falls decidely *on this side* of the history

285

of metaphysics, he also moves quite close to the deconstructive machinery. However, advancing with care, he keeps himself from becoming enmeshed in the interface.

Derridean deconstruction takes to task the five great centrisms which characterize the epoch of metaphysics: (1) phonocentrism, (2) ethnocentrism, (3) phallocentrism, (4) egocentrism, and (5) logocentrism. Phonocentrism is particularly prominent in the medieval appeal to the Divine voice and in Rousseau's substitution of an original speech (an arché-speech) for the Divine Word. Lévi-Strauss places ethnocentrism sufficiently in question for Derrida to examine its closure. The purloined texts of Lacan and Nietzsche indicate where the deconstruction of phallocentrism can occur. Since I enter the fray on the question of egocentrism in the next chapter, I shall not belabor it now.[7] Rather the discourse which is of concern here is that of logocentrism, for logocentrism is precisely the domain in which Heidegger gives form to his own language. It is also where the deconstruction of metaphysics must predominate.

Logocentrism takes Logos as central. But what sort of centrality can it have when it is regarded as that which permeates everything? Can that which is all, or one, be central? Centering announces a circumference, an encompassing domain for which there is a center. Decentering the self (as transcendental ego), for example, conforms to this model. In logocentrism, however, the centrality of Logos is due to its all-pervasiveness, for it is, in that way, the point of reference and return for all that is said, expressed and meant.

It would not be suitable to reiterate (any more than I have already done) the diachronic account of the changes in the conception of Logos within the history of metaphysics from Logos as universal structure to Logos as Divine Word to Logos as natural speech to Logos as language. Rather we shall turn to the place where Logos is most prominently in question and where Heidegger has attempted to demonstrate how he moves it to the edge of the history of metaphysics. Here is where Heidegger allows for the beginning of a de-logocentralization of language in grammatological arché-writing. I refer to a passage from the essay entitled "Logos" in Part Three of Heidegger's *Vorträge und Aufsätze*. This text itself questions another text—Heraclitus' Fragment B 50—which reads: "When you have listened not to me but to the Logos, it is wise within the same Logos to say: One is All" (οὐκ ἐμοῦ αλλέ τοῦ Λογου ακουσαντας ὁμολογειν σοφον ἐστιν Ἕν παντα). The passage from Heidegger goes as follows:

> Ὁ Λόγος, τὸ Λεγειν, is the Laying that gathers. But at the same time λέγειν always means for the Greeks to lay before, to exhibit, to tell, to say. Then would be the Greek name for speaking, saying, and language. Not only this. Ο Λόγος, thought as the Laying that gathers, would be the essence of saying [*die Sage*] as thought by the Greeks. Language would be saying. Language would be the gathering letting-lie-before of what is present in its presencing. In fact, the Greeks *dwelt* in this essential determination of language. But they never *thought* it—Heraclitus included.[8]

Not only is Heraclitus and, in spite of himself, also Heidegger included here but so too is the translator David Farrell Krell. The text speaks a certain reading which incorporates both the self and language of a whole company (a community) of readers, speakers, and writers. For example, and this is the most obvious trace, the translator inserts "*die Sage*" as the correlate of "saying." The task here is not to reiterate the self-decentering, but rather to deconstruct the logocentrism and hence the community of language speakers—what Roland Barthes (in *Sade/Fourier/Loyola*) has called "logothetes." What is logothetic in Heidegger's text is the positing and *re-placing* of Logos.

Logos is transferred from its unifying place in Heraclitus to its role in the Heideggerian differencing which carries the name of the ontological difference. With Heraclitus, Logos is the unifying Reason which gives form and structure to all that *is*. Logos therefore holds the central spot in that it establishes an encompassing totality which brings diversity together under one roof. As one might expect, this unity does not depend upon Heraclitus himself, for Heraclitus (along with the rest of us) is also integrated into the Logos—our rationality participates in a more general *Nous* (an assertion which can also be ascribed to Aristotle at the end of the *De Anima* where he distinguishes two types of mind—a particular and a universal one). The flux in which we find ourselves makes it impossible for us to speak—to enter into the discourse of—Logos. Logos must speak for itself—from its own center.

Heidegger, however, takes as his enterprise the transportation of Logos from its home in the One where only identity and homology can live in the place of difference: the Being of beings. As we learn from Paul de Man,[9] among others, this transportation or transfer is already metaphorical—the epistemology of metaphor prescribes the substitution of one place for another. Hence Heidegger's operation is itself metaphorical, that is, a tropological (rhetorical) language where Logos (language) is in question. Heidegger's transposition of Logos is logothetic—a discourse in which a different language is brought into play. However, by that operation his language is situated between the logocentrism of Heraclitus and its logodecentering.

We have not yet considered the character of Heidegger's reconstruction (transposition) of Logos: he is unequivocal when he writes that "language would be saying" (Ὁ Λογος [language] is τὸ Λεγειν [saying]). Logos speaks and we should listen to Logos. When the Greeks think Logos, they think the essence of saying [*die Sage*], but it is Heidegger who says this. Thus it is not really the Greek placement of Logos, but rather Heidegger's replacement which is in question—particularly when we remember that Heidegger calls Heraclitus a thinker who does not teach doctrines, but who only "gives us to think." In the millenia thereafter we have allowed his saying to enter into forgetfulness, to remain unthought.[10] The task is to *think* the saying which is Logos. *We* can *think* the saying which is language, even though Heraclitus denied that we could have such a role. Heidegger prescribes that we begin thinking and that in so doing we think speaking, saying, language. Throughout Heidegger's texts, he affirms the need to think the ontological difference as the Being of beings.[11] But what about thinking that difference as language?

In section 34 of *Sein und Zeit* (1926), language (*die Sprache*) is an ontic existentielle and different from *Rede* (discourse, discursivity) which is one of the three equiprimordial features of Dasein's Being (along with *Befindlichkeit*—state-of-mind—and *Verstandlichkeit*—understanding). Thus in *Sein und Zeit*, Heidegger could not yet think the ontological difference as language (*die Sprache*), for *die Sprache* was still an ontic form, a being among others. *Logos* on the other hand was equated with *Rede* and therefore with Being rather than with the ontological difference between Being and beings. However, by the time of the essay entitled "Language" (1950–1) in *Unterwegs zur Sprache*, included in *Poetry, Language, Thought*, Heidegger writes: "What is important is learning to live in the speaking of language . . . Man speaks only as he responds to language. Language speaks. Its speaking speaks for us in what has been spoken."[12] Thus language speaks in the ontological difference and no longer as an ontic characteristic or a being among others. Here Heidegger has moved away from his own equating of *Logos* with *Rede*. He has located *Logos* where language speaks and removed it from its privileged ontological state.

Heidegger asserts that Logos (language) is the "Laying that gathers." This is consistent with Heraclitus' account when he claims that, in effect, the Logos both gives unity (gathers) and is that unity (the Laying). Heidegger also indicates that language is the "gathering letting-lie-before of what is present in its presencing." On the surface, this could be considered identical with Heraclitus' version. But when we notice that the presencing of what is present corresponds to the Being of beings in opening up the ontological difference, it becomes evident that the "gathering letting-lie-before" is another formulation of the same difference. Logos is located in that difference. As Heidegger states, "Logos is the name for the Being of beings."[13] Furthermore, "whatever essentially occurs in the λεγιειν of ὁμολογείν and in the λεγειν of the Λόγος has a more primordial origin—and this in the simple middle region between both."[14] In the Being of beings is this middle region which Heidegger calls the ontological difference.

The reciprocal genitive (the Being of beings) opens a clearing (a lighting) in which saying can take place, for to say language (the *legein* of the *Logos*) is to reassert the ontological difference. The λεγειν of the ομολβγειν indicates that the clearing of the difference is saying the same again. In other words, there is a homology between the saying of every ontological difference— but that homology is a *homo-legein* (saying the same Logos in the Being of beings).

We should not be confused by this sort of language, a language which can only speak itself. Unlike the metaphysics of Heraclitus, there is no Logos outside of us to which we can refer, to which we must listen, and which does not depend upon us. With Heidegger, the Logos enters into our own activity—we cannot be separate from it. Thus just as we are located within the Being of beings, just as we are that identity of difference,[15] saying the Logos (and thinking the saying of the Logos) means that we are said as well. Here is the place where Heraclitus and Heidegger diverge: a self about to decenter itself is given a name when we think what deserves to be thought, i.e., the ontological difference, and that name is the Logos (or language) of that which is said. Hence we are involved in the making of language (Logos), it cannot make us and stand apart from us (as Heraclitus would suggest). We dwell within the language which we speak and which says us. Language is the house of Being as it differences (and defers) itself from beings. Although we dwell within that house, it is necessary for us to think it, and by thinking it, we bring out our saying it in the same difference (the homologous place) in which we are. Therefore, there is indeed much that needs to be thought: saying the word (language) is saying that which is said; and saying that which is said is presencing that which is present; presencing that which is present is the Being of beings, and we are located in the Being of beings.

In the essay on "Language," Heidegger writes: "To discuss language, to place it, means to bring to its place of being not so much language as ourselves: our own gathering into the appropriation."[16] Saying that which is said is the expression of language. Language does not happen anywhere. Rather it happens in the appropriation—the *Ereignis*, the event itself. The event, however, is not simply *any* event—it is the happening in which what is *Eigen* occurs—what is *one's* own. Language is one's own and cannot be other. Language is placed or situated in difference. This difference is spoken as we are gathered within it. What is *Eigen* is what is *proper*. *Ereignis* is the happening of the proper in the ontological difference spoken as Logos. Hence Logos happens; it is one's own; it is proper; and it places itself as it gathers us.

Common to both *Eigentlichkeit* and *Uneigentlichkeit* is the *Eigen*. To be *Eigen* is to be the occurrence (*Ereignis*) between the authentic (*Eigentlichkeit*) and the inauthentic (*Uneigentlichkeit*). Here the *homologein* speaks because it is *Eigentlich* (its own). Out of the difference between the authentic and the inauthentic (as articulated in *Sein und Zeit*), there is an identity of a difference—the *Eigen*. We are our own. What is most proper to us is what is neither ontic nor ontological, neither inauthentic nor authentic, but the difference in-between. We are the *authors* of our own language—language speaks us as authors of our own speech. Our authority is the authenticity which is proper to us, which even becomes our proper-ty. Our proper-ty cannot stand apart from what is said, nor from the care which we call our own in the saying of it. Our property is not in the material (*hylé*) of the thing—nor is it in its Being. Property (*Er-eignis*) happens as Logos.

Where is proper-ty placed? It is situated no-where—continually deferring itself as difference. The authority of language therefore is neither a transcendental *Ich Denke* nor an empirical objectivity. The authority of language is taken to the limits of what is one's own. Once it is pure dispersion, dissemination, difference, it will have achieved both the fulfillment and the closure of metaphysics.

At the moment of closure, language no longer *ap*propriates as such, nor does it *ex*propriate. Rather it places itself at the juncture between the appropriation (*Er-eignis*) and the expropriation (*Ent-eignis*). A *crossing* takes place where the difference between the authentic, authorial, ownedness of *Eigentlichkeit* and the inauthentic, readerlike, disownedness of *Uneigentlichkeit* intersects with the difference between the happening, occurrence, appropriation, and property of *Er-eignis* and the dispersal, diffusion, dissemination, and communality of *Ent-eignis*. At that event of crossing is where Logos speaks. Logos speaks as a question—the question of Being, that is, the crossing

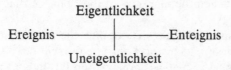

Eigentlichkeit

Ereignis ————————Enteignis

Uneigentlichkeit

out of Being in the *Seinsfrage*. But what is the "crossing out"? It is not the elimination of the Being of beings—rather it is the *marking* of the Being of beings in the difference of ownedness. Language *qua* Logos speaks in that difference. As Heidegger puts it: "Language speaks. Its speaking bids the difference to come which expropriates world and things into the simple onefold of their intimacy."[17]

The speaking of language is where we are logocentrically located. The onefold is the place of the *Eigen* which is repeated *at*

291

the crossing. Although the crossing out is difference and although language is situated there, it is still a metaphysical language which crosses itself out as a self, a language, or Logos which *calls* both for its home (the *heimlich*) and for what is not at home (the *unheimlich*). On the one hand, it is the call of Being; on the other, it is the call for the end of metaphysics. As a call, language speaks as *parole* and writes itself as *langue*, but it also traces its own deconstruction at the point of crossing. This moment of difference is where Heideggerian discourse takes itself to its own limits.

Staying now with the Heideggerian discourse from which Heidegger can extricate neither himself nor us, admitting that it is the same discourse (ὁμολογεῖν) as saying language (the λεγειν of λογος) and accepting that a transposition from Heraclitus to Heidegger has taken place (a transposition which incorporates them both in a metaphorical, metaphysical discourse), we must turn to a troubling opposition. In metaphysics, with Heidegger as its last proponent, Logos is the name or meaning of the ontological difference. But it is also the house in which that difference dwells. This would suggest that Logos is both inside the Being of beings and outside it, both its inner structure and its outer shell. But how can language be both inside and outside? Or would it not be better to say that language (Logos) is the hinge between the inside and the outside, that language itself is at the juncture between the container and the contained? If we could accept the deconstruction, it would mean that language itself is the indecidable, wavering between the inclusion of the Being of that-which-is and its inner necessity.

In this respect, language is not only the rubric under which all of metaphysics (in its history) must be thought but also its identity and meaning. As language spreads itself throughout the discourse of metaphysics, it also serves as that which is said when metaphysical language is offered. But it is just another metaphysical thesis to claim that language as Logos is both what includes and what is included when we think the ontological difference. If however we go to the hinge itself, there we find only traces of a metaphysical discourse which is about to achieve its own closure. Deconstructing Logos will de-logocenter it. Logos will then become only the supplement, that which is left over, the trace of metaphysical discourse. Language will itself be taken to its limits and philos-

292

ophy, in the guise of metaphysics, will be on the way to
grammatology.

In grammatology, writing has priority—as arché-writing, where
neither phonocentrism nor logocentrism prevails. Arché-writing
is the textualization of experience, the traces of the letter and the
voice which vie for the lead position. But neither written language
nor spoken language can succeed, for at their juncture is language
itself, cultivated by metaphysics—a metaphysics which calls for its
own end. Therefore, to what does language belong? It cannot
belong (*gehören*) uniquely to the Being of beings any more than
it can uniquely hear (*hören*) the call of Being. Language has lost
its center when it incorporates itself into a disseminated self whose
meaning is wherever the Logos can be said. But the place in which
the Logos is said remains at best a trace (a *grammé*) of a de-
logologized language—which we still call metaphysics because it
has not quite reached its end, it completion, its fulfillment.

17

SELF-DECENTERING: DERRIDA INCORPORATED

Differance is neither a *word* nor a *concept*.
                                    Jacques Derrida, "Differance"

Heidegger reminds us constantly that the sense of being is neither the word "being" nor the concept of being.
                                    Jacques Derrida, *Of Grammatology*

Differance is neither a thing nor a concept, and the writing that represents it turns out not to be ordinary writing but what Derrida (*OG* 60ff.) calls "arché-writing."
                                    Newton Garver, "Derrida on Rousseau on Writing"

. . . we could perhaps consider this "word" or "concept" *différance* "which is literally [. . .] neither a word nor a concept."
                                    J. L. Houdebine, *Positions*

The motif of *différance*, when indicated by a silent *a*, does not, in fact, work either as a "concept" or simply as a "word."
                                    Jacques Derrida, *Positions*

Self-decentering is the elaboration of identity throughout a play of *differances*. The self is dispersed and disseminated in writing, specifically what Derrida calls "arché-writing." Conventionally such claims are ascribed to a single author: the "self" according to Derrida is such and such, or Derrida's central thesis concerning the "self" is so and so. The "epi-grammes" cited above reiterate a self-decentering of which Derrida is both tenor and vehicle.

The inscription of *"Differance* is neither a *word* nor a *concept"*

294

is not present in the French text of *"La Différance"* as published in *Théorie d'ensemble*[1] nor as it is reproduced in *Marges de la philosophie* (1972).[2] Yet it appears within the first five paragraphs of David Allison's translation of the essay, none of which are in the aforementioned French texts. Who then is the author of *"Differance* is neither a *word* nor a *concept"*? Has the authorial self been de-centered into the position of the translator? Is there an unpublished letter by Derrida to the translator providing the five paragraphs in question? Or is there another published text which begins with these paragraphs and which includes the statement that *"differance* is neither a word nor a concept?"

Further along in the text, we do find *"Je dirais donc d'abord que la différance, qui n'est ni mot ni concept, m'a paru stratégiquement le plus propre à penser, sinon à maîtriser . . . "*[3] A corresponding passage in David Allison's translation reads: "I will say, first of all, that *differance* which is neither a word nor a concept, seemed to me to be strategically the theme most proper to think out, if not to master . . . " We therefore are reassured that most of the translation does render the French text to which it corresponds. But what of the first five paragraphs? Are they a *pre-text* for announcing Derrida and Derrida's text? If the first five paragraphs are a sort of introduction to Derrida's text, it is curious that we find a translator's note which reminds the reader that *"differance"*, or difference with an "a," incorporates two significations: "to differ" and "to defer."[4] This footnote to Derrida's *own* discussion of the verb " 'to differ' [*différer*]" simply crystallizes the point that differ-*ance* as a substantive and a participial involves both non-identity and sameness (but delayed sameness). Are Allison's five paragraphs a pre-text for Derrida's essay in the same way that the "Editor's Note" in Sartre's *Nausea* is a pre-text for Roquentin's diary? If so, should we conclude that Allison is a pre-text for Derrida, that is, Derrida's self de-centered, deferred, and spatialized into another place?

The preliminary note to the translation indicates that the essay "Differance" was "reprinted in *Théorie d'ensemble*, a collection of essays by Derrida and others, published by Editions du Seuil in 1968" and "it is reproduced here by permission of Editions du Seuil." The reader therefore turns to the July-September issue of the *Bulletin de la Société Française de Philosophie* in which the text was first printed. In that version, one finds Jean Wahl's

introduction to Derrida's lecture and the Derrida text again
without the first five paragraphs. However, further searching
provides an answer to the enigma which so effectively demonstrates the process of self-decentering in the textual differance.
The *Bulletin* generally publishes an abstract of the full lecture
preceding the transcription of the presentation and subsequent
discussion. This abstract appears as part of the complete text in
the translation but is absent in the more generally accessible
versions of *"Différance"* in *Théorie d'ensemble* and in *Marges de
la philosophie*. Without the difference between the translation and
these more commonly available "reprintings," there would be no
textual difference and hence no trace of a de-centered self.

In *Of Grammatology* (1967), published a year before the *"Differance"* essay was delivered before the *Société Française de Philosophie*, Derrida had himself written: "Heidegger reminds us
constantly that the sense of being is neither the word 'being' nor
the concept of being."[5] (This is my second epi-gramme.) Here
Gayatri Spivak does not engage in pre-texts. She is more faithful—
but to whom? Certainly not to Heidegger (or at least not to
Heidegger's translators)! The French text reads: *"Sans doute le
sens de l'être n'est-il pas le mot 'être' ni le concept d'être, Heidegger
le rappelle sans cesse."*[6] The French word *"être"* corresponds
conveniently to the German word *"Sein"*; and *"étant"* corresponds
to *"Seiende."* Unfortunately English usage has not worked out as
neatly. A variety of conventions have been operative. Spivak opts
for the distinction being/entity, which is hardly the most common.
In fact, if the reader reads Derrida along with collateral texts such
as *The Question of Being*, one finds the distinction Being/being.[7]
Reading Heidegger's text and Derrida's text in English will show
"being" as *Sein* in Spivak and "being" as *Seiende* in the Wilde-
Kluback translation of Heidegger's *Zur Seinfrage*. Indeed, the full
sense of Being (*Sinn des Sein*) would be lost if one thought that
Spivak's "being" were the same as the "being" which Wilde and
Kluback cite. The sense of Being is situated in the ontological
difference (the difference between Spivak's being and entity,
between Being and being, between Being and beings). Hence the
sense or meaning of Being (*Sein*) cannot be a word (an entity)
nor a concept (Being as idea). But Heidegger does not "remind
us constantly" of this—he "recalls it incessantly" (*Heidegger le*

rappelle sans cesse)! The ontological difference is the place of the "call of Being." The self is situated in the ontological difference, as I have indicated elsewhere (an intertext).[8] If the self *is* in the sense or meaning of Being, then the self must also be neither a word nor a concept. This does not of course signify, with any necessity at all, that the self is *differance* (which is also neither a word nor a concept), for that would not make good Aristotelian logical sense. However it is possible that the self which established itself as a pre-text with *"Differance* is neither a word nor a concept" and which was verified in a subsequent French text of *"La Différance"* might be reiterating itself in Heidegger's ontological difference. This would mean that Derrida's self is decentered into Allison's translation, Derrida's *"La Différance,"* Spivak's *Of Grammatology* and the corresponding *De la Grammatologie*, and now also into Heidegger's "ontological difference."

Why should Derrida be prompted to articulate *"differance"* as different from a word or a concept in the first place? Since *differance* implies both distinction and delay, *differance* must be not only different from (non-identical with) a word and a concept, but also spatially and temporally posterior to (although the same as) a word and a concept. In the first instance, *differance* cannot be identified with a word or a concept. De Saussure objected to the common usage of the sign as word. He noted that the sign is both a word (or acoustical image) and a concept, for example, of a tree. In order to avoid confusion, he named the word as signifier (*signifiant*) and the concept as signified (*signifié*). The sign then is the relation between a signifier and a signified. Signification is the act or process of relating the signifier to the signified within a system of differences between signs. *Differance* is neither a signifier nor a signified. Could *differance* be a sign? Not exactly. A sign is characterized by the arbitrary conjunction of signifier and signified, while *differance* is neither one nor the other. In his text on Saussure ("Linguistics and Grammatology"), Derrida writes: "It is not to the thesis of the arbitrariness of the sign that I shall appeal directly, but to what Saussure associates with it as an indispensable correlative and which would seem to me rather to lay the foundations for it: the thesis of difference as the source of linguistic value" (*OG*, p. 52). Linguistic value is associated with signification. Both arise out of a system of differences. Value is determined by an economy of the sign in which some signs are

worth more than others. The name or convention of one environment (eco-nomy) is to be preferred over another. Value is founded
upon differences between signs. There is non-identity between
the signifier and the signified. A contiguous or even distant sign
is nevertheless a sign even though it is *deferred* to a later moment
and another place. If *differance* were purely static, it would have
the structure of the sign with its accompanying linguistic value.
Since however differ*ance* is active—perhaps "differencing" is a
more accurate translation—it also engages the signifying process
which characterizes the self. *Differance*, therefore, is the self
engaged in the signifying process.

Unlike signification, *differance* is actualized by negation. It
cannot affirm itself. It can, at most, distance itself by being another
substance or by being in another place and at another time. *Differance* can have no center, no focus, no point. Perhaps this *differance* which indicates the place of the self (Derrida, his translators,
Heidegger) also includes Newton Garver, author of a preface on
the translation by David Allison of Derrida's (?) *Speech and
Phenomena*, formulator of a paper on Derrida on Condillac on
Rousseau at a conference (at SUNY/Stony Brook) where Derrida
him*self* was *present*, and writer of an article in the *Journal of
Philosophy* (November 1977) which was read at a session of the
1977 American Philosophical Association meetings on "The Philosophy of Derrida" where Derrida him*self* was *absent* (he was not
invited). Can the *differance* be too great? What of the statement
by Garver that "*differance* is neither a thing nor a concept" (my
third epigramme)? At Stony Brook, Garver was quite explicit in
his reiteration of "Differance is neither a word nor a concept."
Why then does he write (in his *Journal of Philosophy* article):
"Differance is neither a thing nor a concept"? The question is
raised again when placed in the *con*text of the rest of his sentence:
"Differance is neither a thing nor a concept, and the writing that
represents *it* [my emphasis] turns out not to be ordinary writing
but what Derrida (*OG*, pp. 60ff.) calls 'arché-writing.' " This "*it*"
which is not a thing is different from the "*it*" which is not a word.
Because of the variation in the formula, the question arises as to
whether this difference between a word and a thing plays a role
in the meaning of *differance*. One wonders whether Garver is not
himself switching over to the logical tradition of, for example,
Frege, Husserl, and Russell, which he carefully distinguished (in

his preface to *Speech and Phenomena*) from the rhetorical tradition of Saussure, Austin, and Derrida.[9] Frege differentiates sense and reference, Husserl distinguishes noema and thing, while Saussure qualifies sign functions and Austin emphasizes the ordinary language function with its illocutionary force. In certain respects it makes no difference whether Garver says that *differance* is neither a thing nor a concept or that it is neither a word nor a concept. He could also have said that *differance* is neither a book nor a concept. The similarity to the re-iterated formula raises the question of the non-present difference between a thing and a word. I will have more to say about this non-present difference later in connection with Husserl (my deferment of the difference).

This demonstration of self-decentering could go on . . . Indeed Derrida's interviewer for "Positions" again raises the question of *differance*. Houdebine rewrites the *differance* and extends its status as arché-writing. Houdebine cites the literality of *differance:* ". . . we could perhaps consider this 'word' or 'concept' *différance* 'which is literally [. . .] neither a word nor a concept . . .'" Houdebine's reinscription calls *differance* a word or a concept which is not a word or a concept. He cites *differance* in its role in ordinary writing so as to show how its literality in arché-writing is of another order. Since the formula was raised in an interview, Derrida responds actively:

> The motif of *différance*, when indicated by a silent *a* does not, in fact, work either as a "concept" or simply as a "word."
> I had tried to show that. That does not keep it from producing conceptual effects and verbal or nominal concretions, which are, moreoever, and this is not immediately apparent, both imprinted and disrupted by the angle of this "letter," by the incessant workings of its strange "logic." The "cluster" that you recall is a point of historical and systematic intersection; it is especially the structural impossibility of closing this network, of stopping its fabrication, of tracing a margin around it which would not be a new mark.[10]

Differance pushes ordinary writing to its limits and each time it does so a new mark or trace is left in the process: the marking and tracing itself, the limiting and bordering, the writing and differencing itself.

The whole *company* of Derridians—doubtless they would not want to be so incorporated—decenters the self into a series of traces, marks, remainders, supplements, limits of an arché-writing which both distinguishes and defers itself into each instantiation (event) and variation of *"Differance* is neither a word nor a concept." Each of the discourses which is represented by the five epigrammes at the head of this essay bears the *signature* of Jacques Derrida. This disseminated signature is the marking of Derrida's style, which I re-mark here. The statement *"Differance* is neither a word nor a concept" is an event. Like the Austinian speech act, it performs itself. The *demonstrans* is the actualization of the *demonstrandum. Differance* is shown by the difference it makes. Derrida reinscribes his own identity in the variety of inscriptions just as he communicates "communication" in his essay "Signature Event Context." As he uncovers in "Limited Inc. a b c . . . ,"[11] the French is more revealing: *"Signature Evénement Contexte."* With *Contexte (qu'on texte)*, Derrida instaurates a new verb *texter* ("to text"). The signature event is "texted." The event of signature is made into a text. *Differance* is spaced and temporalized into a word and/or a concept; and *differance* is shown to be distinct from words and concepts. Each event of spacing, temporalizing, and distinguishing is a Derridian signature made into a text, incorporated into the *company*, the *"société anonyme,"* or some other group. Similarly, John R. Searle (whom Derrida calls Sarl as in *société anonyme à responsabilité limité*) is characterized as the self who wrote a reply to Derrida's "Signature Event Context" (a text which Derrida describes as *dry*—a translation of *"sec"* and an acronym for the title). However, because Searle indicates his own indebtedness to D. Searle and H. Dreyfus (who knows Derrida, has talked with Derrida—to which I can attest—and therefore brings some of Derrida's signature to Searle's text), his self is dispersed into a multiplicity of texts.

I

The "epoch" of *differance* takes place at the border of the "epoch" of metaphysics. Unlike Michel Foucault's discourse of epistemic spaces and knowledge frameworks, where every couple of centuries a new epistemé supplants the previous one, Derrida seems to elaborate only two basic "epochs"—that of metaphysics and that which arises at the closure of metaphysics. Metaphysics began, at some point—though Derrida does not date its *arché*. He only remarks that it developed out of the exteriority of writing and the exteriority of the signifier. Along with the *destruction* of this exteriority comes the construction of interiority. With the construction of interiority comes the appurtenance of metaphysics.

Metaphysics pertains as a whole in the form of a metaphor. Writing in the epoch of metaphysics is "a sign signifying a signifier itself signifying an eternal verity" (*OG*, p. 15). Writing is taken as that which is literal (itself a sign). As a sign, writing serves as the signified for a signifier which is the letter. The letter is that which forms the word. In the literal sense, writing is the concept associated with the letter. Metaphorically, however, the letter is the signifier for another signified. This metaphorical signified is the "external truth," the signified "truth," which goes under the name of *Logos*. This metaphorical scheme, which was most prominent in the medieval system, can be inscribed diagrammatologically as follows:

Metaphorical sign (Book of Scripture)	Sd = eternal truth, Divine word, *Logos* or Writing	
	Sr = the letter	Sd = the sign or writing $\left(\dfrac{\text{Sd}}{\text{Sr}}\right)$

Literal sign (Book of Nature)

Medieval scheme

In the appurtenance of metaphysics, the Book of Nature, which is the place of the letter as signifier, is signified by its association with the Divine Word (*Logos*) which speaks as a voice. The Divine Word leaves its sign in the form of the letter. Writing is the exteriorization of the Divine Word. When the *Logos* speaks, the intelligible is made sensible. The transcendental signified leaves its mark in the empirical signifier.

Rousseau reiterates the medieval system by substituting natural writing for the Divine Word. Natural writing is given its form by an arché-speech, an interior holy voice, which provides the "beginning word." The beginning word, however, is readily corrupted in the form of ordinary writing as it becomes "representative, fallen, secondary, instituted." This writing is the substitute for medieval literality.

Natural sign	Sd = arché-speech or natural writing	
	Sr = beginning word	Sd = ordinary writing

Social sign

Rousseau's scheme

Similarly Heideggerian thought "would reinstate rather than destroy the instance of the logos and of the truth of Being as '*primum signatum*': the 'transcendental' signified . . . implied by all linguistic signifiers" (*OG*, p. 20).[12] Thus entities or beings (*Seiendes*) respond to the call of Being (*Sein*), that is, they respond to the *primum signatum* of which they are only the *signans*. Their ontic character is always conditioned by an ontological voice.

Ontological difference (*Dasein* as Sign: the meaning or call of Being)	Sd = Being (*Sein*)	
	Sr_1 = being or entity (*Seiende*)	$Sr_{2...n}$ = being or entity

Ontic distinction
(between beings)

Heidegger's scheme

The history of metaphysics in Derrida's terms is the history of a series of ruptures or breaks. These include the break between the Divine Word and the Book of Nature, between speaking and writing, and between Being and beings. These oppositions, crystalized as binary oppositions in semiology, form the center of the epoch of metaphysics. One could add other pairs such as intelligible/sensible, mental/physical, interior/exterior, etc. Together they constitute the metaphysical discourse, which begins to achieve its closure with the advent of writing (arché-writing), the *differance* that *deconstructs* the text of metaphysics.

302

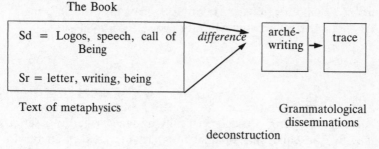

Derrida's scheme

I have now appealed to the earmark of Derridian discourse: "deconstruction." Deconstruction is the praxis which is employed in the movement to the limit, border, or hinge, and by which *differance* is inscribed as arché-writing. Deconstruction is structured. It situates itself at the intersection of the inside and the outside, the word and the concept, ordinary writing and speaking. Deconstruction is neither *destruction*, a tearing apart, analyzing into atomic units, nor *construction*, a bringing together, synthesizing into a unified totality. Deconstruction involves both destruction and construction. It operates at the juncture which Merleau-Ponty described as the chiasm or intertwining between the visible and the invisible, between philosophy and non-philosophy;[13] it fills out the Heideggerian "in-between" as indicated by the crossing out of Being (S̶e̶i̶n̶). In its own right, it determines the literal meaning of writing as metaphoricity itself. The citing of writing as literally metaphorical places Derrida's texts at the interface between the closure of metaphysics which Nietzsche, Heidegger, and Merleau-Ponty inaugurate and the post-closure which remains pure *differance*.

Deconstruction unrewinds the five great centrisms which characterize the epoch of metaphysics: (1) phonocentrism, (2) logocentrism, (3) ethnocentrism, (4) phallocentrism, and (5) egocentrism. I have cited the role of the first two in the history of metaphysics by reference to Rousseau and the medieval system, whose closure is transcribed, but not accomplished, by Heidegger and Merleau-Ponty respectively. "Structure, Sign and Play in the Discourse of the Human Sciences"[14] indicates the function of Lévi-Strauss in establishing the closure of ethnocentrism. "The Purveyor of

Truth"[15] works on Lacan's position at the terminus of phallocentrism. I shall turn to Sartre in order to show his place in bringing the metaphysical predominance of egocentrism to closure.

II

Egocentrism operates at the heart of pure phenomenology. Although the term is used specifically by Jean Piaget to describe the stage in child development in which the child is unable to take on the perspective of another person, egocentrism is also characteristic of the transcendental-constituting self paradigm.[16] In Western Philosophy, the predominant representative of the transcendental-constituting self paradigm is Edmund Husserl. For Husserl, all intentional acts start from and are conditioned by a transcendental ego. The transcendental ego occupies the central place in subjectivity. The field of consciousness *qua* transcendental subjectivity forms the domain in which things in the world are reinterpreted according to the phenomenological perspective. Thus the empirical self which brings its natural attitudes to that which is to be studied takes on a different function when it becomes a transcendental self. In the place of the initial opposition between an empirical self and an empirical object, the phenomenological attitude reveals a transcendental self and an empirical object.[17] Michel Foucault calls this second opposition, the empirico-transcendental doublet[18] which began sometime at the end of the eighteenth century (probably with Kant). Foucault's archaeology demonstrates that the doublet also goes under the name of "man." Since Husserl is exemplary, caution should be invoked in order to indicate that this "man" has a center and the center is the transcendental self or even more precisely the transcendental ego. In this sense, Husserl's phenomenology is *concentric*.

With Husserl, the self is not only at the center of consciousness but also at the center of man. Since intentional acts of constitution can be re-iterated and repeated continuously and since each act can be traced back to a center (the transcendental ego), man acts *without end*. As long as there is a pure phenomenologist, there will be a transcendental ego, and hence there will be *no end* to man. Man is *not without end* as long as the egocentric doctrine is

304

propounded. In Derrida's article "The Ends of Man,"[19] three types of "end" are considered: (1) end as opposed to means, (2) end as goal or project, and (3) end as termination.

(1) In Kant's second critique and the associated *Foundations of the Metaphysics of Morals*, man is described as "an end in itself" who does not exist "merely as a means." In all of his actions, man "should always be considered *at the same time as end*." Never treat man only as a means, Kant said, for at the center of man is a noumenal self which is associated with man's freedom. Compromise the center of man and man's freedom is compromised. In this sense, Kant inaugurates an ethical egocentrism whereby man should act according to the thesis that man always has a center (end) and that this center must be considered in all rational and moral interaction. Man should never be considered only as a means.

(2) The concept of end as goal is itself multiple. Throughout the Christian tradition man's ends have been described as eschatological. One does not become fully one*self* until salvation is achieved. The life of corporeality and terrestrial desires leads the self astray from its center. The city of God is the place in which the self accomplishes its end, its unity, its identity. The self *qua* soul must prepare itself through faith and with the help of reason for entrance into the Empyrean. Dante's model depicts a truly virtuous self as whirling around the spheres of paradise until it achieves the center.

Self-development is also an end of man: man's *telos*. Derrida writes with respect to Hegel's *Anthropology:* "the development of the soul, as it is traced by anthropology, passes through natural soul (*natürliche Seele*), sensitive soul (*fühlende Seele*), and real and effective soul (*wirkliche Seele*). This development is carried out, completed, and opens on consciousness, precisely that form from which proceeds the *Phenomenology of Mind*, in the first chapter on *Sense-Certainty*. Consciousness, the phenomenological element, is thus the truth of the soul; namely, the object of anthropology. Consciousness is the truth of man; phenomenology is the truth of anthropology" (*EM*, pp. 40/1). As man surpasses himself into consciousness, he moves closer to the fulfillment of himself in the absolute through self-consciousness. Man's end is to achieve absolute knowledge in mind (*Geist*). At the center of the Hegelian phenomenology is man's sense-certainty. Absolute knowledge encompasses all. Though it demonstrates the absolute universal self paradigm, man is at its center and origin.

While the self for Kant is identifiable with "man," for Hegel man is within the movement of the self toward absolute knowledge. Husserl places the self within man and in that respect switches to another paradigm, one more closely associated with Descartes' *cogito*. While Heidegger identifies man and the self, in the tradition of Kant, he nevertheless maintains a difference. Man and the self are situated *qua Dasein* in the difference between Being and beings, in the ontological difference. The Kantian center is retranslated by Heidegger from an end as freedom to an end as authenticity (*Eigentlichkeit*). *Eigentlichkeit* is literally own-li-ness or more simply ownness—that which is most *properly oneself*.[20] But *Eigentlichkeit* is situated in a difference (*das ontologische Differenz*) and therefore does not have a center as such.

Confronted with the spectrum including the Hegelian model of man within the self of absolute knowledge, the Kantian and Husserlian conceptions of the self within man, and the Heideggerian formulation of the identity of man and the self in difference, no wonder Sartre at the closure of metaphysics places the end of man outside man, but at the same time denies that man has a center. For Sartre, the "true self" is nothingness, without content, without center. Consciousness is the nothingness of the "true self." Consciousness is also freedom, yet not a centered Kantian freedom. Sartre even says in *Existentialism is a Humanism* that when I act, I am responsible for all mankind. Self-consciousness cannot become absolute in the Hegelian sense, for it only produces transcendent object-like selves which are no longer the existing self of consciousness. Similarly, consciousness has no transcendental ego within it. Every act of consciousness directed at itself reveals only an object outside itself: a being-in-itself. Nevertheless man does have an *end*! Man's end is his fundamental project, which underlies all of his activity. He also has *ends*, which are the projects he announces for himself. They are beings-in-themselves like the just-having-been which he calls him*self*. However, the projective activity itself characterizes consciousness even though it does not fill out consciousness. Sartre finds no center to man. In this respect, his position is similar to that of Heidegger. "Difference" for Heidegger is "nothingness" for Sartre. Both move close to the edge of the epoch of metaphysics.

(3) *End* can also mean termination. According to Foucault, man is at an end. "As the archaeology of our thought easily shows, man is an invention of recent date. And one perhaps nearing its end" (*OT*, p. 387). With the disappearance of man comes the disappearance of the possibility of a center. At the edge of the epoch of metaphysics, the self is de-centered, disseminated, dispersed into grammatological traces, remainders, supplements, etc. The Derridean de-centering, announced by Foucault, takes place in grammatology.

The *epistemé* in which man predominates is an epoch wherein the centering of the self comes of age. All the discursive forms of life, labor, and language (as articulated in biology, political economy, and philosophy) are the productions of a transcendental signified, a producer whose productions are multiple. Foucault indicates, however, that with the functioning of the contemporary human sciences, especially structural psychoanalysis, structural anthropology, and structural linguistics, the self-decentering begins to take place. According to Foucault, this reorientation into a new post-modern *epistemé* was announced by Nietzsche and Mallarmé, both of whom stand at the threshold of the new *epistemé*. The Derridean enterprise, however, operates at the end(s) of man and puts the self-decentering into practice.

III

In "Fors," Derrida writes (or does he?—note that what follows is my transcription of Barbara Johnson's translation), " 'I' can only *save* an inner safe by putting it inside 'myself,' *beside(s)* myself, outside."[21] This transcription could have been placed at the head of the section I am about to begin and the essay I am about to conclude. The transcription is of course a citation, but it is also an "exergue," the place of an inscription (as on a coin) of Derrida de-centering himself into a crypt. The cryptic space is the *topos* of "Fors,"—*fors* itself, as Barbara Johnson indicates, is both subjective interiority ("the tribunal of conscience") and exteriority ("outside," "except for, barring, save").[22] A safe implies "keeping in;" the preposition "save" implies "keeping out." Hence when the self, cited and quoted as "I", is able to maintain its inner fortress, it does so by placing itself outside itself, excluding itself from any inner domain, or safe. When "I" am *beside* "myself," "I" am both excluded from the domain which is mine and at my wit's end. But then who else is there *beside* myself? The en-crypting (read: encoding) of this crypt (read: hidden, secret place) needs to be de-crypted (read: deciphered), the de-encrypting begins with the question "What is a crypt?" In this case the self is a crypt—but no doubt one on the way to its own decentering.

The crypt occupies the position of the "undecidable." Is it the self which is inside or is it the self which is outside? Like *differance* (which is different from itself), and communication (which needs to be communicated), the crypt requires de-en-crypting, i.e. a decoding of the encoded codes. The question is raised as to which is its *proper* meaning. But then what is the *propriety* of the *proper*? The proper is itself an undecidable. It could be (1) that which is literal as opposed to figurative, or (2) that which is appropriate, or (3) that which is one's own.

(1) The proper is that which is not figurative, not metaphorical. In "White Mythology: Metaphor in the Text of Philosophy," Derrida makes the distinction in terms of Aristotle: "The Aristotelian problem of metaphor does not go back to a very simple and clear (that is, central) distinction between what will be called the proper sense and the figurative sense. Nothing prevents a metaphorical *lexis* from being proper,—that is, appropriate (*prepon*), suitable, decent, proportionate, becoming, properly related to subject and situation, to things as they are."[23] Hence, the undecidable "proper" leads to another undecidable—"metaphor." Metaphor can be proper just as much as the proper can be metaphorical. Metaphor is "classified by philosophy as provisional loss of meaning, a form of economy that does no irreparable damage to what is proper, an inevitable detour, no doubt, but the account is in view, and within the horizon of a circular reappropriation of the proper sense" (*WM*, p. 73). Philosophy, Derrida announces, will accept metaphor as long as it leads back to the proper. Metaphor, as a brief but *acceptable detour*, indicates that metaphor has some *propriety* in philosophical discourse and that it serves as a means of *reappropriating* the *proper* meaning. Certain philosophical discourses scorn the metaphorical: they consider it a breach of clarity, something entirely *improper*. Can they avoid it? Is it not constantly an *obstacle* before them?

(2) In considering the propriety of the metaphorical in philosophical texts, the issue of the proper as appropriateness has already been invoked. What is proper or improper as a distinction stands firmly within the epoch of metaphysics. To inquire into the appropriateness of a thing, word, or concept is to appeal to an opposition, a binary pair, in which a choice of one or the other is required. To accept that which is proper is to exclude that which is improper. In this sense, just as the very question of the distinction between the metaphorical and the literal is within the metaphysical domain, so too the appropriateness or inappropriateness of one or the other within specified contexts is part of the history of metaphysics. Similarly what is properly metaphysical and what is not properly metaphysical also enters into the metaphysical problematic. Only the deconstruction of the *differance* will avoid the Scyllas and Charybdises of metaphysical discourse.

Near the edge of metaphysical discourse (but not quite near enough), Heidegger interprets the problem of time. Heidegger is involved in the "destruction" of classical ontology, as Derrida recounts in "Ousia and Grammé: A Note to a Footnote in *Being and Time*."[24] Destruction is not yet deconstruction. The difference is marked; the deconstruction is deferred to another time. Heidegger's concern with temporality is not an ethical matter, yet Derrida asks, "why characterize temporality as authentic or proper (*eigentlich*) and inauthentic or improper after having suspended all ethical considerations?" (*Ousia*, p. 89). Proper temporality is that form of temporality which is appropriate to the meaning or sense of Being. Improper temporality is inappropriate to the meaning or sense of Being. Falling from primordial, authentic temporality is falling into inauthenticity, into the ordinary conception of time, which remains strictly within metaphysics. Authentic temporality is appropriate to Dasein. Falling into the ordinary conception of time is inappropriate to Dasein.

(3) The appropriateness of authentic temporality signals the third sense of proper. What is proper is one's own. This is the oldest sense associated specifically with *proprius* in Latin, meaning "one's own, particular, or special." What is proper belongs to oneself. Not only is it suitable, fit, or acceptable (i.e. appropriate to) oneself but the proper is specifically "mine." That which is authentic (*eigentlich*), as I have noted, could also be translated as *ownly;* authenticity (*Eigentlichkeit*) as *ownness*. Authentic

temporality is therefore not only appropriate for Dasein, but it is also *Dasein's own*. In other words, authentic temporality *belongs* to the self *as its own*. Hence inauthentic temporality (the ordinary conception of time) is not particular to the self.

Inauthentic temporality does not *belong* to the self. It is not the *proper-ty* of the self. The self can make no claim to it. However, in establishing the difference (distinction), the self is as such unable to de-center itself. As Derrida comments in *Spurs: Nietzsche's Styles* "The question of proper-ty (*propre*) has only to loom up in the field of economy (in its restricted sense), linguistics, rhetoric, psychoanalysis, politics, etc., for the onto-hermeneutic interrogation to reveal its limit."[25] What is one's own, one's property, is inscribed in a variety of domains. What is one's own becomes disseminated into a variety of places (*heterotopoi*). The self—that which is proper to it as well as that which belongs to it—is reiterated as proper-ty in these different places and thereby demonstrates the limit (shows itself as the limit) of the "onto-hermeneutic interrogation" (such as that of Heidegger). It is precisely the onto-hermeneutic interrogation which distinguishes between what is authentic and what is inauthentic, claiming that the self is literally (properly) and most appropriately (properly) situated in that which is authentic (proper).

It would be naive "to conclude that, since the question of proper-ty (*propre*) is no longer derivative of the question of Being, it is thus available to direct examination. Proper-ty (*propre*)—as if one even knew *what it is*—propriation, exchange, give, take, debit, price (*coût*), etc. The discourse that does not expand on this problem, that settles comfortably into its own private domain, this discourse also never departs from the onto-hermeneutic presupposition, but remains in its pre-critical relation to the signified, in the return to the presence of the spoken word, to a natural language, to perception, visibility, in a word, to consciousness, and its phenomenological system" (*Spurs*, p. 113). Settling into the private domain of proper-ty, having accepted that it is not derived from the question of Being, does not free the self from its metaphysical place. The formulation of the proper as located in a multiplicity of domains *in which one belongs* is a movement of decentering, but as long as one is at home there in the safe-ty and comfort of the inside, of the *heimlich*, the deconstructive decentering is not yet operative. On the other hand, what is uncanny (*unheimlich*) can equally well be *one's own*. To be at home in the uncanny invokes the movement of self-decentering, it does not establish its place.

Property can occur in a number of places—in the loci where one's own inscriptions are reiterated. Self-decentering is an event (*Ereignis*), pure differ*ance*. "Once the question of production, doing, machination, the question of the *event* (which is one meaning of *Ereignis*) has been uprooted from ontology, the proper-ty or propriation is named as exactly that which is proper to nothing and no one. Truth, unveiling, illumination are no longer decided in the appropriation of the truth of Being, but are cast into its bottomless abyss as nontruth, veiling and dissimulation. The history of Being becomes a history in which no being, nothing, happens except *Ereignis*' unfathomable process. The proper-ty of the abyss (*das Eigentum des Ab-grundes*) is necessarily the abyss of proper-ty, the violence of an event which befalls without Being" (*Spurs*, p.119). The "unfathomable process" of *Ereignis* is the process of self-decentering. *Ereignis* is the occurrence of that which comes about as one's own (*Eigen*). What is one's own is neither truth nor non-truth, but rather what happens in the difference between the two—often cited as the discourse of truth by Derrida. How is the discourse of truth the event of that which is one's own? *Ereignis*, which is often cited in French as "*avènement*," brings the sense of that which comes to be, but it is the translation in English as *appropriation* which is most relevant (I shall not write "appropriate"). Appropriation is the act of making something one's own. Derrida's appropriation of the discourse of truth is at the same time its expropriation (by which arché-writing *qua* discourse of truth is dispersed). In this unfathomable process of ex-ap-propriation (which is analogous to de-construction), the self (one's own) is decentered in the *differance*.

If the self is de-centered into the *differance* of arché-writing, which is itself dispersed, what does one *own*? Is that which I write *my* writing? Are Derrida's texts *his*? Are they his property? Can he copyright them such that he can make claim to them? By placing quotes around "Copyright © 1977 by John R. Searle" (which I cite here from Derrida: " 'Copyright © 1977 by John R. Searle' ")[26] Derrida ex-appropriates the mark. He does not appropriate it—for that would be plagiarism; nor does he simply multiply it by taking it out of its context and putting quotes around it. Rather he ex-appropriates it as a mark which deconstructs itself, i.e. remains Searle's *property* but also becomes Derrida's *property*, but only in the process of becoming so, not in its realization.

Another case, in which the question of property arises, occurs in "The Purveyor of Truth," where Derrida comments upon Lacan's commentary on Edgar Allan Poe's "The Purloined Letter." A letter is stolen from the Queen by the Minister D . . . The theft of this letter could be quite incriminating to the Queen, so she engages Dupin to recover it. When Dupin discovers its location, crumpled up in a conspicuous place, he replaces it with a similarly crumpled up piece leaving his own mark so that the Minister would know who purloined it from him. However, doubtless the Minister would not realize its loss for some time. This deferral of the discovery would enable the Queen to possess the letter, even though the Minister at the same time thinks he has the letter and the accompanying power over the Queen. Thus Derrida remarks: "The letter apparently has no owner. It is no one's property. It has no proper meaning, no proper content which bears on its trajectory. Structurally, therefore, it is in flight [*volante*] and purloined [*volée*]" (*Purveyor*, p. 42). In the same way that the letter is both in flight and stolen, the self is in an "unfathomable process" and taken up by someone else in arché-writing. The possessed property is not one's own. What is one's own happens in the *differance* of arché-writing and therefore does not remain in my safe or crypt any more than in his. Whatever is in my safe-keeping, or in Derrida's, always has a remainder, a supplement, a surplus—something left over, postponed for another time and also different from itself.

But what of one's proper name—can I not say that my proper name is mine? Once again the self-decentering goes to work. Derrida cites the example from *Tristes Tropiques* in which Lévi-Strauss recounts the situation of the Nambikwara, who are prohibited from using their "proper names." Derrida considers this prohibition derivative from the general position in which the proper name is effaced in arché-writing. In arché-writing, the identification of a proper name with the self is not possible. Writing one's name as *properly* one's own is opposed to speaking one's name as one's own. The "effacement" (erasing the face or identifying feature) constitutes an erasure of the name in the

312

differance between the word which is written and the concept which is spoken. In the *differance*, the proper name has no proper place, for it is distinguished from what is written and postponed to another place and time. When Lévi-Strauss taunts one little Nambikwara girl into divulging another little girl's proper name, he learns that the first little girl has *given away* that which is not to be given. In retaliation, the second little girl gives away the name of the first. By this procedure, Lévi-Strauss acquires the names of all the children in the village. When one little girl gives away the proper name of the other, a transgression of a societal prohibition has occurred. In effect, however, by revealing a Nambikwara proper name, it is no longer a proper name. It is no longer the property of the little girl who kept it. Arché-writing gives away what is proper, but without taking on what is improper, i.e. that which is inscribed in the name which is given out of the prohibition. Therefore, the name that continues is neither proper nor improper. By producing a proper name, it loses its proper status. The name of the self is situated in the play of *differances*, for the proper name obliterates itself in *being named*. The prohibition of the proper name, Derrida writes, "is necessarily derivative with regard to the constitutive erasure of the proper name in what I have called arché-writing, within, that is, the play of difference. It is because the proper names are already no longer proper names, because their production is their obliteration, because the erasure and the imposition of the letter are originary, because they do not supervene upon a proper inscription; it is because the proper name has never been, as the unique appellation reserved for the presence of an unique being, anything but the original myth of a transparent legibility present under the obliteration; it is because the proper name was never possible except through its functioning within a classification and therefore within a system of differences, within a writing retaining the traces of difference, that the interdict was possible, could come into play, and, when the time came, as we shall see, could be transgressed; transgressed, that is to say restored to the obliteration and the non-self-sameness (*non-propriété*) at the origin" (*OG*, p. 109). The dispersal at the origin of the non-self-sameness is the place at which the name leaves a trace of the obliteration in the play of *difference*. Just as the Minister and subsequently Dupin have stolen the Queen's letter (but to whom does the letter belong?),

313

similarly one little girl has stolen the proper name of the other. Is not Lévi-Strauss like Dupin who in turn possesses the letter or name but not as his own property? Like the letter, the name is decentered. Like the name, the self is decentered.

In the case of the Queen's letter, "Who *signs?*" Derrida asks. "Dupin wants to sign, indeed, doubtless, the last word of the last message of the purloined letter. First by being unable to resist leaving his own mark—the seal, at least, with which he must be identified—on the facsimile that he leaves for the Minister" (*Purveyor*, p. 111). "The initial—the same, D, for the Minister and for Dupin—is a facsimile on the outside *but on the inside it is the thing itself*" (*Purveyor*, p. 112). The letter is the trace of both the inside and the outside, but it is also a signature—of the Minister D . . . at first, then of Dupin (both names begin with the letter "D"). Or perhaps it is the signature of the narrator, or even Poe. Surely not, since Lacan's "Seminar on the Purloined Letter"[27] steals it away from Poe. But what happens when Derrida purloins it from Lacan in the "Purveyor of Truth"? (the French is more appropriate: "*Le Facteur de la vérité*" for a "*facteur*" is also a person who brings the mail—or letters). So Derrida brings the letter of truth (read: discourse of truth). "Who signs?" Derrida—with a D.—unless it is stolen again by his translators or someone such as Barbara Johnson who has an essay in the *Yale French Studies* issue on "Literature and Psychoanalysis" which is itself a commentary on Derrida's commentary on Lacan's commentary on Poe's commentary on his narrator's commentary on Dupin's commentary on the Minister's commentary on the Queen's commentary on the original sender of the letter. But who sent the letter? We do not know—the whole company does not know. Hence there are only a series of signatures, each of which postpones its inscription until a subsequent signature comes along in the unfathomable process . . .

What is signature? "Spurs: Nietzsche's Style" raises the question because of the status of the words "I have forgotten my umbrella," which were found, isolated in quotation marks, among Nietzsche's unpublished manuscripts (*Spurs*, p. 123). Presumably these are Nietzsche's words, formulated in his "autograph signature." Was this a casual note to himself? Was it a philosophical point? Was it jotted down for the rhythm of the sentence? Was it written to jog his memory? In any case, it was written in Nietzsche's hand.

He signed it,—or did he? "What after all is handwriting? Is one obliged merely because something is written in one's hand, to assume, or thus to sign it? Does one assume even one's own signature?" (*Spurs*, p. 127). Is one's signature one's own—particularly when placed in quotation marks? Is not a signature in effect a deferred sign?

In the *Positions* interview, Derrida speaks of "conceptual effects." We may ask: what are the effects of a *differance* which displaces and disseminates one's proper name, one's signature, and ultimately one's self? There are surely no *causal effects*, except in the sense that a chain of reactions takes place. One event follows another, one appropriation succeeds another. The relationship between one signature and the next is arbitrary. But there are other effects: *stage effects*, for example. Derrida is continually putting traces and *differances* into play. The discourse of truth is as if on stage. The scene of writing is the place in which acts—speech acts, for example—occur. The stage effects produce verisimilitude—the semblance of truth—which is the most the discourse of truth could produce. Above all, however, there are *personal effects*. Each time that *differance* is inscribed in a text in the form of a trace, mark, remainder, supplement, etc., it becomes part of the effects of a self which incorporates them. The self's personal effects are its baggage, that which belongs to the self, its property. The effects of property, however, as we have recounted, are not as such one's own—they are shared with a host or company of selves all of whom sign the text which is not actually written any more than it is spoken. Each effect is a mark along a decentered structure. The self is written at the origin of every point along such a structure, but it is written as *differance:* neither a word nor a concept. "Beyond Being and beings, this difference, which would differentiate and defer (itself) incessantly, would also trace (itself); such a *differance* would be the first or last trace—if we could still speak here of origin or end (*fin*)" (*Ousia*, p. 93). The End. HJS

18

FOUCAULT AND THE
ANTHROPOLOGICAL SLEEP

What does it mean to *think* the nineteenth century in a nineteenth century fashion? Asking Michel Foucault's question about the nineteenth century in this Heideggerian way will help us to understand Foucault's problematic from a different perspective. How, in other words, can the nineteenth century be thought as it would be thought by a nineteenth century thinker? This question about knowledge production in the nineteenth century could, has, and does lead to specific studies of particular literary, sociological, and scientific products. The very dispersal of knowledge production throughout a de-centered space is to think *about* the nineteenth century. But what is it to *think* the nineteenth century? Surely one must elaborate the meanings and sign systems that articulate themselves at that moment in time. However, what Whitehead calls "inert ideas" cannot account for nineteenth century thinking. To simply cite Baudelarian correspondences, Balzacian monetary misadventures, or Dumasian historical reenactments, to announce naively the postulates of Fourier's utopian vision based on passionate attraction, De Tocqueville's account of American democracy, or Comte's religion of positive knowledge, and to forthrightly characterize the science of Claude Bernard's experimental medicine, Lamarck's de-tailed rats, or Charcot's hypnotic treatments of hysteria is to *speak* the elements of the nineteenth century. Yet nineteenth century thinking—though it passes through these disseminated elements—does not rest with them. To think the nineteenth century is to uncover the signification of these elements. A pure semiotic would reveal the multiplicity of

316

their production. A pure hermeneutic would give them a meaning. A hermeneutic semiology, presented in the form of an archaeology, will subtend their multiplicity and intend their meaning as an epistemological space. For Foucault, such a space both announces the *epistemé*—the knowledge formation—called "man" and establishes the threshold of its disappearance.

In order to understand knowledge production in the nineteenth century, the method of understanding must be distinct from what is understood—unless the method can somehow show itself to be its own object. Although the model of differentiating the subject from the object of investigation could be shown to have its origins in the experimental method of a Francis Bacon or the procedural discriminations of a René Descartes, the opposition, albeit binary, has its grounding in the Kantian delineation of an empirical sensibility and a transcendental deduction. The proliferation of the subject-object dichotomy is extended into and throughout the nineteenth century according to the forms given to it by Hegel, Marx, and Kierkegaard. In Hegel, Absolute Spirit differentiates itself from sense-certainty. In Marx, the Proletariat overcomes bourgeois capitalism. In Kierkegaard, subjectivity qualifies objective experience. Thus the nineteenth century opens a space—a *Lichtung* or clearing as Heidegger would call it—in which it is possible to speak of a subjective understanding and an object to be understood. The self makes itself radically other than everything else. The concept of man arises out of the relation. By virtue of "man," things—living things, working things, and speaking things—acquire an identity. The self is their difference.

If the knower is radically other than the known, then all nineteenth century understanding is double. As René Girard, among others, has shown, the nineteenth century is the space in which doubling comes of age.[1] Dostoevsky's Goliadkin is paradigmatic of this self-repetition in both science and literature. Stendhal's Julien Sorel posits an ideal self, while Max Weber's sociological method selects an ideal type. Just as Darwin studies the origin of species, Flaubert announces: "*Madame Bovary, c'est moi!*" The double is the form of nineteenth century knowledge production. Double means difference, subject and object, knower and known. But the idea of production recalls the possibility of identity, the condition under which subjectivity actively enters into objectivity, objectivity becomes the work of subjectivity, and knowledge

317

forms itself. The recollection of identity—not in the Socratic sense of knowing as recollecting, but in the projective sense of Husserlian presentification and Freudian rememoration—affirms the primordial possibility of knowledge acquiring a signifying unity. However, the model of identity in the production of knowledge is unavailable to the nineteenth century. For the nineteenth century, identity can be at most a wish, a desire, in other words, a will to identity. But the will to identity remains the form of difference and hence the impossibility of the method ever acquiring the status of what is to be understood. The object remains the other of the subject.

The name of otherness is repeated throughout the nineteenth century as "alienation." Hegel says that the slave is alienated by his desire of the master's position. Marx says that the worker is alienated by his/her inability to share in what is created. Zola, Dickens, and Dreiser show that individuals are alienated by their working class conditions. Lamartine, Wordsworth, and Thoreau are alienated by the towns and cities which deprive them of nature. Similarly, Ricardo, Cuvier, and Bopp are alienated respectively by the very domains of labour, life, and language which they seek to understand. This discontinuity between subject and object is fundamental to the model of knowledge in the nineteenth century. Try as one may to bring them together, the coefficient of resistance (namely "the will to know") is too strong. The method cannot show itself to be its own object since the method, in its endeavor to interpret the object, is tied up with the investigator.

The task of a twentieth century archeology of knowledge, as proposed by Foucault, involves digging out the conditions of identity between subject and object. The study of knowledge formations, epistemological spaces, and discursive surfaces will attend directly to the active, productive, and emerging aspects of nineteenth century thinking. In this case, the method seeks to be its own object. The uncovering of knowledge production seeks to be the knowledge produced in the nineteenth century. As Althusser would suggest, theoretical practice is indeed possible. This is perhaps one reason why Foucault's discussion of the nineteenth century (and previous epistemological formations for that matter) rarely look like the historical accounts that are generally offered. An archeology of knowledge *qua* twentieth century science involves both "questioning the already-said at the level of its existence; of the enunciative function that operates within it, of the discursive formation, and the general archive system to which it belongs"[2] *and* "a rewriting: in the preserved form of exteriority, a regulated transformation of what has already been written" (*AK*, p. 140) Questioning the already-said must participate in the already-said. Just as thinking the nineteenth century is not mediated thinking about the nineteenth century, questioning knowledge formations is equally unmediated. Nineteenth century discursive practices are already in question. The description of such practices must be a general rather than a total history, for only what is in question needs to be uncovered. The general elements, sign systems, and archival emergences are the domains of concern. Knowledge production can never claim to be exhaustive.

Questioning the already-said also involves "a rewriting." Repetition in this respect is also production—and even creation. The knowledge formations that are in question are productively and creatively in question. Rewriting the nineteenth century involves offering another version of the nineteenth century. *What was* is transformed into *what is* while presented as a general archive system. Knowledge is therefore both the systems of *énoncés* and the interpretation of them. In the nineteenth century, Foucault finds that the particular archive system is delineated by philology, biology, and economics.[3] Although "situated among other discourses," each constitutes a "specific domain" (*AK*, p. 207). No unifying function gives them a transcendental heading under which they may be seen to operate. Such a transcendental heading would be precisely the return to a nineteenth century way of thinking, which the questioning and rewriting overcome through their very practice of thinking the nineteenth century.

If no transcendental unity of apperception, no integrating function applies to an archeology of knowledge, then how do these specific domains relate to one another? Foucault proposes relations between surfaces, which create a de-referentialized discourse. Discontinuity forms between domains of knowledge production within a particular epistemological space—such as the nineteenth century. Each set of signs, each system of dispersion is distinguished from the others. With no point, ground, or foundation of things, each knowledge formation is left to its own devices. Yet there is " a body of rules that enables them to form as objects of a discourse and thus constitute the conditions of their historical appearance" (*AK*, p. 48). Each body of rules is pertinent to a specific domain. As contemporaneous systems, however, rules of relationship are also operative. Any subject that might attempt to understand these rules and their interrelationships according to a standard of measurement or a transcendental principle will be misguided. For Foucault, any attempt at an archeology of knowledge implies a decentered subject. Lacan has called it an excentricity within the signifying chain of the speaking patient in psychoanalysis.[4] Derrida appeals to the de-centering of the structures proposed by Lévi-Strauss.[5] From the perspective of the contemporary human sciences, no ultimate point of reference is available for final appeal as it was in the nineteenth century. The identity of this difference is the archeology which disperses itself into the nineteenth century and into other ages of knowledge formation.

An archeology of knowledge is a dispersive practice. It spreads itself out into a multiplicity of discontinuous domains. Instead of following a historical, continuous, diachronic account of, for example, "the great chain of being,"[6] or "the voice of the people,"[7] or "the perfectibility of man,"[8] the archeologist must question, think and attend to a segmented, discontinuous, synchronic understanding of thought systems. Instead of tracing a single idea through history, the archeologist of knowledge looks for discontinuous formations. Each formation will have sets of rules and each grouping of sets into systems will establish the epistemological signification which Foucault regularly calls the *episteme*.

Epistemic features are characterized by three groups of criteria: the criteria of formation, the criteria of correlation, and the criteria of transformation or threshold. Foucault comments in his 1968 *Esprit* article that "these criteria allow us to substitute differentiated analyses for the broad themes of general history (whether it concern 'the progress of reason' or 'the spirit of a century'). They allow us to describe, as epistemic of a period, not the sum of its knowledge, nor the general style of its research, but the deviation, the distances, the oppositions, the difference, the relations of its multiple scientific discourses: the epistemic is not a sort of grand underlying theory, it is a space of dispersion, it is an open field of relationships and no doubt indefinitely describable."[9] The *episteme* is not a transcendental signified, nor, as I have indicated, a transcendental signifier. It acquires its unity only through its disunity. The *epistemé* is a productive de-centering of knowledge both at a particular moment and in the interpretation of that moment. As a field of relationships, the *epistemé* is a proliferation of knowledge in a multiplicity of specific domains.

Each epistemic dispersal involves a forming of knowledge. Formation is both forming and formed. Within each formation, correlations can be shown among the plurality of elements. Furthermore, the conditions of transformation, the possibility of its reformation into a different morphological structure, are present within each correlated formation. Just as Lévi-Strauss shows that for each version of a particular myth, the basic structure carries with it that which is necessary to move (conceptually) from one version to another, just as Piaget demonstrates that the child's intelligence is changed from the sensori-motor stage to the pre-operational stage by an auto-regulative reorganization of his/her ability to accomplish certain tasks, and just as Thomas Kuhn proposes that the paradigm for scientific activity at a particular moment of normal science bears within it the conditions of a new paradigm due to the work of what he calls "revolutionary" scientific activity, similarly, "transformation" for Foucault is the operation of mutation, modification, and reformation. The concept of threshold describes that moment within an epistemological space in which the *epistemé* is pushed to its limits and a new equilibrium is compelled to follow.

The *epistemé* of the Renaissance is characterized by "resemblance." Romeo and Juliet are described by Shakespeare as "star-crossed lovers." The microcosm resembles the macrocosmic orbit of the stars and planets. In the Classical Age, "representation" delineates the knowledge formation of the seventeenth and eighteenth centuries in terms of (1) general grammar or speaking, in which words are represented, (2) natural history or classification, in which beings are represented and (3) analysis of wealth, in which needs are represented. Foucault describes *Don Quixote* at the threshold of the new positivity of the Classical Age. Don Quixote finds windmills that *resemble* knights, herds of sheep that *resemble* an army of soldiers, and inns that *resemble* castles. In Book Two, however, his own adventures are codified by chivalry books in which he himself is *represented* and known throughout the land.

Similarly, at the limits of representation, we find De Sade's *Juliette*. There *human desire* is represented, but desire also functions as the relation between subject and object, master and slave, transcendental and empirical, lust and desired body. De Sade, for Foucault, is the epistemological threshold of the nineteenth century. De Sade sits at the frontier of an epistemological break. The conditions for the desire of others is the Kantian transcendental subject which serves as the basis for possible syntheses between representations. The founding of a transcendental philosophy corresponds to the new positivity of language, labor, and life, in which the sciences of philology, biology, and political economy are respectively developed. Philology (with Bopp and Grimm) studies kinships between languages, the notion of the radical, and internal variations. Biology (with Cuvier) studies comparative anatomy and anatomic disarticulations. Economics (with Ricardo and Marx) studies scarcity as a matter of life and death; it studies history as a compensating mechanism or as augmenting needs, wants, and other forms of human desire.

This nineteenth century *epistemé* could be called an anthropological formation. "Man" *qua* empirico-transcendental doublet permeates all nineteenth century thinking. From the classical age to the nineteenth century, Foucault offers a four-fold displacement: truth in the classical age becomes being; nature becomes man; the possibility of understanding becomes the possibility of misunderstanding; and philosophical theories which were opposed to science become a philosophical awareness of experiences which cannot be accounted for and in which man does not recognize himself. On this latter point, man *is*, but he is not *represented* in any way. He can *be* without finding himself thematized. The birth of anthropologism is the death of representationalism.

Since *The Order of Things* deals with the relationship between words and things, we find that in the Renaissance, things resemble things. In the Classical Age, words represent both things and ideas. In the nineteenth century, a subject speaks words about things. The anthropological age distinguishes the transcendental self from the discourse it employs in order to describe the way the world really is or the way it ought to be.

In the contemporary epistemological space, which has hitherto remained unnamed—and perhaps remains, as Beckett would suggest, unnameable—words speak themselves. There is no longer recourse either to ideas or to things. The arrival of this archeological event in the twentieth century brings about the disappearance of Discourse and the return of language. In the Classical Age, language—the subject matter of a general grammar, such as that proposed by the Port Royal logicians—turned into Discourse in the nineteenth century. Why? What else could a transcendental subject do but discourse about the world, establish knowledge about the way things are, and fulfill the progressive scientific mission that it had set for itself. Language *qua langage* returns, in the twentieth century, at the provocation of Nietzsche the philologist, and Mallarmé, who enclosed "all discourse within the fragile density of the word" (*OT*, p. 305). The transcendental ego no longer speaks in the twentieth century. The transcendental realm becomes the word itself. The fundamental relation is not that of subject to word, but of word to word. The "event," as Derrida (recalling Heidegger's *Ereignis*) calls the break with modernity, announces the establishment of the human sciences. As Sartre shows, the subject is thought in its transcendence. The transcendental subject has become a speaking subject. The speaking subject is both an embodied intentionality and a series of deconstructed texts leaving their visibility in the form of traces. For Foucault, in the contemporary (post-modern) *epistemé*, Lévi-Straussian ethnology, Lacanian psychoanalysis, and Jakobsonian linguistics are the human sciences that announce the death of man. In the contemporary *epistemé*, nineteenth century "man" has become the absent subject.

To understand this perplexing claim, we must take a clue from Foucault's semiology of Velasquez's painting *Las Meninas*. Since *Las Meninas* is a work of the Classical Age, it surely involves a system of representations. The painter in the painting represents Velasquez; the image in the mirror represents the King and Queen; the represented painter's painting represents the King and Queen; Velasquez's painting represents the court of Philip IV, and so on. In Derrida's words, classical certainty is present in the centered structure (Derrida, p. 278)—the whole structure is centered upon the King and Queen.

Reinterpreted according to the epistemology of the nineteenth century, with its theory of the subject and its concept of man as the empirico-transcendental doublet, the painting is a discourse about the "man" of the Spanish Court in the seventeenth century.

Velasquez brings together a conception of Philip IV's court in its social, economic, artistic, and numerous other forms. Indeed, "man" fills the vacant space in the painting. Foucault writes: "In the profound upheaval of such an archaeological mutation, man appears in his ambiguous position as an object of knowledge and as a subject that knows: enslaved sovereign, observed spectator, he appears in the place belonging to the king, which was assigned to him in advance by *Las Meninas*, but from which his real presence has for so long been excluded" (*OT*, p. 312).

In contemporary thought, with its interplay of presence and absence signifier and signified, knower and known signification is put into practice. The King occupies an ambiguous place as both subject and object, as the presence of an absent subject. The King is not in the painting. The King's place has been de-centered or, in Derridian language, deconstructed at the center of the contemporary *epistemé*. The system of signs that delineates the elements of the painting eclipses the transcendental signified and empirical signifier of the nineteenth century. The King is everywhere and nowhere.

Because of man's place in the nineteenth century as a finite, existing being, like the God of Nietzsche's madman, he is bound to die. Human finitude does not just mean that you and I will die, it also means that the concept of man will die. The analytic of finitude establishes the condition for an anthropological sleep— a slumber as deep as the dogmatism from which Hume awoke Kant. The *anthropos* of nineteenth century is transformed into the activity of the human sciences. De-centered, disseminated, and dispersed knowledge fills out a system of signs, an epistemo-logical space—a human science. "A 'human science'," Foucault notes, "exists, not wherever man is in question, but wherever there is analysis—within the dimension proper to the unconscious—of norms, rules, and signifying totalities which unveil to consciousness the conditions of its forms and contents. To speak of 'sciences of man' in any other case is simply an abuse of language" (*OT*, pp. 364–5).

The method of the archeologist of knowledge is to be faithful to the decentering. The self of the archeologist does not work out of a standpoint—transcendental or otherwise—rather the archeologist disseminates his knowledge out into the Renaissance, the Classical Age, and—for the present problematic—the Nineteenth

Century. Nineteenth century knowledge production is the understanding of the nineteenth century. A semiology, in which the signs of the era are interrelated, demands the hermeneutic that will find meaning in their signification. Such a hermeneutic must produce the signs as they are interpreted—in that way, the nineteenth century can be thought according to the nineteenth century.

19

FROM UTOPIA/DYSTOPIA TO HETEROTOPIA: AN INTERPRETIVE TOPOLOGY

Conventionally, utopian discourse has established itself in opposition to dystopian discourse. The good place—also no-where—is a place of harmony, consolation, and happiness. Its location is extra-terrestrial. In order to attain utopia, some form of vision, journey, or hope is required on the part of the human self. Correspondingly, the bad place is a place of constraint, despair, and unhappiness. Its location is also extra-terrestrial. The human self arrives in dystopia by means of a nightmare, deportation, or fear.

Assuming this binary opposition to be marked out on a vertical axis with utopia above, dystopia below, and the "here and now" at degree zero, the horizontal axis can be described as heterotopian. Heterotopia is a multiplicity of different places; its plurality is "everywhere" in the "here and now." Heterotopias can also be either hypertopian or hypotopian. A de-generate utopia is hypertopian, while a de-generate dystopia is hypotopian. Hypertopian places are desirable situations. Hypotopias are less undesirable—they point below the horizontal axis toward dystopia just as hypertopias point toward utopia.

An interpretive topology provides a means of reading models in relation to the utopia/dystopia axis and within the hypertopia/hypotopia context. Heterotopias (where we live) can be understood by a philosophical sociology which goes under the name of a hermeneutic semiology. This approach involves both a description of places and interpretations which establish the conditions under which a particular heterotopian location is hypertopian, hypotopian, or topologically neutral. This sort of interpretation requires deconstruction: uncovering habitual models of understanding and examining the junctures between those places which function within oppositional frameworks, of which utopia/dystopia, hypertopia/hypotopia, metaphor/metonymy and place/topic are only a few examples.

THE INTERPRETIVE TOPOLOGY

(I) *Utopia/Dystopia*. Ever since Thomas More wrote his fictional *Utopia*, it has been well known that the lexicology of "utopia" indicates a double meaning: both "nowhere" (*ou topos*) and "good place" (*eu topos*). Although a "good place" might be found in the here and now, the presumption has been that the "good place" is also an "ideal place" worth striving for. The interest in achieving utopia as an ideal place which is also a good place has been legitimated by multifarious readings of Plato's *Republic*. The repetition of *eu topos* (good place) as *eu daimonia* (happiness or good daimon) reconfirms the ideality of the republic Socrates proposes. In the Socratic version, utopia is *somewhere*, but that somewhere is necessarily elswhere than where incarnate consciousness, that is, embodied human beings, could live. Plato's ideal-ology is an ideology in that the ideal good place is an idea (*eidos*)—a universal social truth which we can know by practicing the proper dialectic and with which our souls—our*selves*—can become united in happiness. The structure of Plato's otherworld-liness is transformed by Augustine and Dante, for example, into the City of God and the Empyrean itself. Attainable somewhere, but certainly not here and now, paradise is the fulfillment of the soul's journey toward salvation. Love (Beatrice) sometimes with the help of Reason (Virgil) is the Way.

In modern versions, the teleology takes different shapes. The ideal good place turns out to be an active scientific community in Bacon's New Atlantis, a society based on passionate attraction according to Fourier, pure communism for Engels, and a Castle according to Kafka's account. The recent American television serial entitled *Logan's Run* (based on a novel by William F. Nolan and George Clayton Johnson) calls it "Sanctuary." Utopia will provide consolation, happiness, and harmony—the *telos* of a journey, vision, or hope. But in order to attain it the human self must go outside, beyond, and without the everyday present in which one finds oneself. The difference between here and there is a great distance. Utopia begins, however, where the difference is delineated. For Dante, the *arché* of utopia is a dream; for Plato, it is an intuition; for Bacon, Fourier, and Engels, a "science," for Thoreau, Logan, and the Ray Bradbury *Farenheit 451* "Book-people," an escape; for Skinner, a plan; and for Rousseau, a return to the state of nature. An archeology which digs up the origins of an utopian project goes hand-in-hand with the teleology by which the project hopes to realize itself.

Utopian projects can, however, go awry. In *dystopia*—also nowhere (we hope)—the negation of an ideal good place appears. Dystopia is built upon the Manichaean presupposition that Satan is at war with God, that evil can oppose good, that our visions, journeys, and hopes can turn into nightmares, deportations, and fears. The origins of dystopia are as manifold as the origins of utopia: for Dante, it is sin; for Plato, ignorance; for Rousseau, society; for Orwell, big brother authoritarianism; for Zamiatin, a mechanistic totalitarianism; for Huxley, technology; for Logan, the holocaust; and so on. Dystopias usually achieve order through enforced accord and agreement. The result is despair and unhappiness. The only recourses available beyond simple acceptance are escape, revolution, or destruction. The shape of dystopia varies from an Inferno to a Brave New World. Logan's City of Domes and Bradbury's world of book-burning firemen repeat Zamiatin's United State and Dostoevsky's Crystal Palace. Just as much as our upward vision hopes to actualize utopia, our downward look makes us cringe at the thought that an antiutopia might come about. Binary oppositions, one a positive element, the other negative, constitute the vertical line from the point where the human self stands here and now (*hic et nunc*)—a phrase often recited by the Palanese bird in Huxley's *Island*. Utopia/dystopia takes us outside ourselves in offering a picture of what our lives might be like: good/evil, happiness/unhappiness, dream/nightmare. Utopia and dystopia are fictions, but fictions we live by and project into and out of everyday life.

(II) *Heterotopia*. Along another axis, the horizontal line, the fictions of utopia/dystopia become an epistemological and discursive reality. We can walk through degenerate utopias, as Louis

Marin has shown with reference to Disneyland, and we can encounter degenerate dystopias, as Nazi Germany and American Ghettos bear witness. "A de-generate utopia," writes Marin, "is a fragment of the ideological discourse realized in the form of a myth or a collective fantasy."[1] Unlike many myths and collective fantasies, de-generate utopias are sign systems that we live through and experience in certain well-defined and well-crafted locations (*topoi*). Their special characteristic is that they are generated, i.e., derived from an utopian model. In Disneyland, a neutrality can be cited in relation to utopia and dystopia. The structure of Disneyland with its Adventureland, Frontierland, Fantasyland, Tomorrowland, and Main Street USA delineates what Roland Barthes calls a "limit-text" (as opposed to a "limited text"). The "limit-text" is a *topos* mapped out such that we can walk through it in a predeterminable amount of time. Walking through it, however, is at the same time writing or creating the space itself. Thoreau's home near Walden Pond is paradigmatic as he establishes his place in the context of nature recovered. The space we create as we journey through the Concord Woods or Disneyland is our reading or interpretation of the de-generate utopia. Though we can read the map of C.S. Lewis' extra-terrestrial utopia in *Out of the Silent Planet* or Huxley's paradise in *Island*, we cannot create them as we can create Disneyland (California), Sturbridge Village (Massachusetts), Old Bethpage (New York), or even downtown Munich and the Parisian Beaubourg (Pompidou) Center.

De-generate utopias and de-generate dystopias are heterotopian—they partake of the "here and now." A de-generate utopia is also a special type of hypotopia. Hence along the horizontal axis, we find heterotopias which are hypertopian, hypotopian, or topologically neutral. Heterotopias are the multiple places in which we operate throughout our daily lives. They are not limited to a particular circumscribed space; rather they are everywhere. Formed out of common sense, but articulated as plural and varied, heterotopias are the types of social life as we know and experience them. Since a *topos* is both a place and a topic, heterotopias are also the discourse which we employ in order to account for our living spaces. These discourses are articulated for us by people such as Michel Foucault, Jorge Luis Borges, and Buckminster Fuller who formulate both utopian and heterotopian

329

discourses in our own time. We could also turn to Henri Bergson, James Joyce, and Werner Heisenberg in a period prior to our own as formulators of the discursive spaces of the early twentieth century. The heterotopias of our age are many different places and different ways of saying the same thing, i.e., the conventional wisdom of our era: care for environment, curtailment of inflation, reform of prison systems, transformation in the relations between men and women, decentering of selfhood. These are the *topoi* which are formulated and reformulated in contemporary knowledge production. Disagreements with the conventional *dicta* simply constitute new *topoi*. Heterotopias proliferate everywhere and in a multiplicity of forms. Like rhisomes, following Deleuze's metaphor, heterotopias spread everywhere without linearity, hierarchy, or geneology. Heterotopias form the texture and network of communication by which we establish our territories and move into new ones. As Foucault writes,

> heterotopias are disturbing, probably because they secretly
> undermine language, because they make it impossible to
> name this and that, because they shatter or tangle common
> names, because they destroy "syntax" in advance, and not
> only the syntax with which we construct sentences but also
> that less apparent syntax which causes words and things (next
> to and also opposite one another) to "hold together."[2]

Heterotopias are the physics, biology, psychology, art, and philosophy of a community of language-speakers. As both the discourses of our contexts and the respects in which they constitute the meanings of our lived spaces, heterotopias are continually open to the possibility of reformulation. Heterotopias are disturbing because there is no apparent unity or coherence to all these discourses. As hard as we may try to extract ourselves from our heterotopias, we are doomed to reiterate them. We form and are formed by our *topoi*. Instead of trying to escape our heterotopias, an alternative route is to undertake an archeology of heterotopias—to describe their plural sources and origins in the discontinuous segments of history.

Heterotopias are the places and discourses of the spaces which we occupy, the architecture of our knowledge, and the frames of our interaction. Hypertopias are the types of heterotopia which enrich the text of our city and country places. While heterotopias

330

are paramount, only some places are hypertopic. Hypertopias are the metaphors of our contexts. A building well-designed, a garden nicely planned—a novel carefully crafted, a city thoughtfully organized—these are the hypertopias which we need to read, to interpret, to know, and to re-create. A hypertopia is a place to live. A hypertopia is a deconstruction of the utopia/heterotopia opposition. In hypertopias, the fictional, mythical, and oneiric qualities of utopias are deconstructed, that is, given structure as a text that is already interpreted, already experienced in the heterotopian here and now. They cannot account for what ought to be—except as models of what can be accomplished in alternative contexts. The domains of a hypertopia can be developed and its richness qualified as a lived fiction of human life.

A hypertopia is the delineation of a heterotopian place in which surplus of meaning is repeated everywhere and nowhere. Its topology may show its metaphorical features in certain places but, on the whole, the overdetermination of sense is experiential, decentered, and social. The inscribed traces of a knowledge production constitute the domain in which human interaction articulates an exquisite and artistic creativity without necessarily bearing the mark of any one particular author. The proliferated sign systems, which are architectural, economic, cultural, and technological, form (and perform) a living space without origin or goal, *arché* or *telos*, but with self-understanding and self-expression. The task of a human science of hypertopias is to elaborate and interpret their multiple directions and cultural richness as if all society were metaphorical.

In those places in which hypertopias have not arisen, places which nevertheless constitute domains of human movement, we may find *hypotopias*. Hypotopias are the opposite of hypertopias. Just as hypertopias indicate an excess, supplement and over-determination of aesthetic meaning, hypotopias are underdetermined. Hypotopias demonstrate a lack, an absence of topological fullness. Hypotopias, by their very nature, require reconstruction, restoration, or reformulation. In order to improve hypotopic situations, planning, imagination, and attention are needed. Hypotopias are the metonymical conditions of human habitats. They are strung out all in a row—often "ticky-tacky." One might cite, for example, the houses outlining South San Francisco as one drives toward the city on the Bayshore Freeway, or the apartments piled high and wide along the Belt Parkway heading toward Staten Island in New York, or the *bidonvilles* in France. Contiguity and under-determination mark these hypotopias. Of all the heterotopias we can describe, these are the greatest affront to humanity, just as our hypertopias are its tribute.

Most heterotopias are simply not noticed at all; they fall between hypotopias and hypertopias. Nevertheless they remain the discourses of our daily life. Heterotopias constitute the frame-works in which we find ourselves. They rarely distinguish them-selves as specifically hypertopian or hypotopian and yet, when they are identified, they are typically determined in one respect or the other. The task of an interpretive topology is to understand the respects in which social formation takes on hypertopian or hypotopian character. The deconstruction of heterotopias will demonstrate that the opposition itself is only artificial, that is, that hypertopias require hypotopias for their meaning and the converse. Hence it is the dispersed multiplicity of heterotopias in which a deconstructive operation must take place. Here at the interface between desirable places and undesirable ones is the locus of social formation, meaning, and structure.

It would be inappropriate to expect that all hypertopias are interpreted as such. On the other hand, hypertopias (like hypo-topias) acquire their determination according to their placement—both geographical and discursive. To change the discourse is to alter the respect in which a particular heterotopian situation is understood. The interpretation of a context as hypotopian can be reformulated as hypertopian in another time or in another framework. This does not mean that a particular place is simply open to a variety of different perspectives. Rather it means that the manner of articulating the character of a place is readily reoriented, which is to say that the *topos* itself is reoriented. Change the interpretation of the *topos* and the *topos* itself is altered. Interpretation is situated between hypertopian and hypo-topian discourses at the deconstructive moment.

TOPOI (PLACES/TOPICS)

Interpretation passes between hypertopian and hypotopian contexts. It takes as points of reference the utopian and dystopian paradigms which constitute the text of a particular tradition. In order to reinforce the role of topological interpretation, consider the following *topoi:*

(I) *The Paris Latin Quarter.* The Parisian Latin Quarter is hyper-topian in that it corresponds to an ideal of university life integrated into the city, situated just outside the central core known as the *Ile de la Cité.* It offers immediate access to bookstores, cultural life (including the Odéon, the Comédie Française, etc.), and the great libraries (such as the Bibliothèque de la Sorbonne, the Bibliothèque Sainte Geneviève, and, across the Seine just beyond the Théâtre Français, the Bibliothèque Nationale). The Sorbonne serves as a geographical reference point, but only because the Ecole de Médecine, the Ecole des Beaux Arts, the Ecole des Hautes Etudes, and the Ecole Normale Supérieure, for example, are not far away. Until May 1968, one could say that, interpret-ively, the hypertopian Latin Quarter was situated in relation to an ideal model of the Academy as a center of learning in which access, reunification, and hierarchized intellectual rigor are achieved.

Situate the Latin Quarter as an educational locus at the moment of 1968. On the one hand, interpretation takes as its ideal this sense of unity, organization, and academic achievement which is provided in a carefully circumscribed domain. On the other hand the university context excludes a variety of potential students. The spaces are not sufficiently large for everyone who might be qualified and who could benefit. The centralization is stifling: it does not allow for popular culture, for personal flexibility and freedom. In short, the French academic center takes on a hypo-topian aspect. Its reference point therefore becomes no longer the ideal model, but rather its opposite—a system of repressions, exclusion, and oppressive authority.

Out of the interpretation which arises between the utopian and the dystopian models, a reformulation was called for in 1968. The result was that the locus of university experience in the Latin Quarter became disseminated: the University of Paris was divided into some twelve universities dispersed throughout Paris and its suburbs. The model of desirability became that of openness, anti-hierarchization, and diversification. In this respect, the interpret-ation came as an attempt to repeat the American system taken as a hypertopian model, perhaps even perceived as a degenerate utopia. Its features included a multiplicity of universities, with faculties which can teach essentially the same domains but in their own self-determined fashion, and which operate according to a regulated degree system (BA, MA, PhD). Hence the *"licence"* is taken as the first cycle, the *"maîtrise"* as the second cycle, and a doctorate as the third cycle. At the same time, the new hypertopia retains many aspects of the old model as they are integrated into the new format. The *agrégation* and *doctorat d'état* are retained and competitive national examination is preserved for those who hope to teach in the new system as in the old. Hence the new hypertopia incorporates previous features. The utopian models are combined in a hypertopian context. Its interpretive twin is the dystopian model of a dissolved rigor, a locus of control over quality, a dissolution of the previously respected classical education, but also a disorienting absence of a known locus for sound thinking. In its dispersal throughout a multiplicity of places, the feared projection seems realized in the development of an impractical practicality.

Interpretation therefore reunites both the utopian and the dystopian models through hypertopian and hypotopian spaces. The task of an interpretive topology is to open the understanding of such spaces, but also to enter the deconstruction of the hypertopian/hypotopian opposition, for the text of human spatial experience is situated at the juncture between the two, in the articulation of heterotopian formations. Such would, in this case, be the reading of the text of the Parisian Latin Quarter as it is juxtaposed with the text of an enlarged Parisian university context which reaches out even beyond the Boulevard Périphérique.

(II) *Sartre's No Exit.* Topological interpretation situates itself at the moment of the textuality of a place, that is, the respect in which a particular space can be read as a text. For example, the Parisian university framework, which we have just considered, is both a place and a discourse about a place. Furthermore, both the place and the discourse about the place serve as a text along with others (hence a "con-text") which can be read interpretively. However, a topos can be formed and interpreted equally well through the textuality of a literary place. In Jean-Paul Sartre's play *No Exit*, the text opens up a locus. Even the title stresses its spatial character. *Huis Clos* is not only a place from which, or through which, one cannot leave, but it is also a circumscribed area which remains closed to those who are in it. *No Exit* is a place where three characters find themselves unable to leave, where they can observe what people say about them after they have died, where they are forced to relate to each other directly either by affirmation or by negation, and where their personal differences are brought into the unity of a particular situation.

That Inez is a lesbian, Estelle an extroverted heterosexual, and Garcin a self-directed introvert creates an uncomfortable circle which characterizes the textuality of the room where they find themselves. They each have a desire to escape this place until the door opens and they recognize that there is nowhere else to go. Garcin concludes, near the end of the play, that, in view of all the experiences one can have in life and thereafter, it is neither the decor nor the geographical limitations, nor the punishments and rewards of a deity, but rather other people who constitute our "hell." When he states *"l'enfer c'est les autres,"* ultimately he is not speaking of another world but rather of our own. He is speaking of interpersonal relationships as we constitute them and as they constitute us.

No Exit is a text which is readily juxtaposed with Dante's *Divine Comedy*. In Dante's account, one finds the utopian "Paradiso," the dystopian "inferno," and the dysutopian "Purgatorio." "Purgatorio" has features of paradise: a possibility of forgiveness, mobility, and salvation, and those of hell: punishment, suffering, and distance from the divine. However, since it is a projection, like the utopian Paradiso and the dystopian Inferno, it is most appropriately *dysutopian*. Since each of these places is in fact an account of Dante's own world (the sinners, the repentant, and the blessed) the *Divine Comedy* is a portrait of a degenerate dystopia, a degenerate dysutopia, and a degenerate utopia and hence an account of a thirteenth century heterotopia with its hypotopian and hypertopian features. The temporal ruptures between Dante's heterotopias and those of Sartre's epoch are manifold. However the juxtaposition of *No Exit* with the *Divine Comedy* makes it evident that the duality that existed in Dante's formulation between the ideal projection and the heterotopian accounts *generated from it* is no longer present in the Sartrian version. *No Exit* is explicitly a sort of degenerate dysutopia. But since it is not generated from any ideal model (or its opposite),

No Exit would more appropriately take on heterotopian features with hypertopian and hypotopian characteristics. Indeed, *No Exit* is a de-con-structed heterotopia in which the duality of hypertopia/hypotopia no longer operates, especially not in its degenerate forms. Thus *No Exit* is situated precisely at the juncture between the hypertopia which accounts for constructive relations between individuals, where people seek to understand and work together, and the hypotopia which considers people as enmeshed in antagonistic relations taking the forms of masochism, sadism, and indifference. At the interface between a hypertopia and a hypotopia, the deconstructive machinery of an interpretive topology can provide an appropriate discourse on how we relate to each other. The play *No Exit* is already a variant of this kind of discourse.

(III) *Pinturicchio's Spoleto.* In the Duomo of the Italian city of Spoleto, one finds a large Fillippo Lippi fresco of the dying Virgin located in the apse behind the altar. But off to the left near the back of the cathedral is a small chapel which is generally kept locked. There one discovers a Pinturicchio of the Madonna with the Christ Child and two Saints. This fresco is rather simple in composition: the Madonna and child are located in the center with the expressions of a quattrocento Italian. A saint is situated on either side, one dressed in clerical garb (on the right), the other in the habit of a shepherd (on the left). What is remarkable about this painting are not the figures in the foreground but rather the landscape behind. Here we find a curious mixture of mountains which resemble those viewed from Spoleto itself and a city spread out in a valley behind the four central figures. There is also a processional flowing out toward the Madonna and advancing on the right between her and the clerical saint. The city could be Spoleto itself, or a number of other Umbrian towns. Behind the city is a lake or sea, the Mediterranean, or, perhaps, in fact Lake Trasimeno which lies north of Spoleto near Perugia. There are two trees on either side of the Virgin and Child, one a tree such as one might find in the vicinity of Spoleto, the other a palm tree. There are practically speaking no palm trees in that part of Italy. One would have to travel to the Italian Riviera on the western coast near France before one could find palms.

The fresco, then, portrays an ideal *polis:* the community of the holy (Madonna, Child and Saints) with followers advancing for the adoration and admiration. The picture is utopian, yet its depiction makes it de-generate. On the one hand, it is a discourse of a degenerate utopia in that it is only a painting. It is the *topos* of the holy family but not the heterotopia itself. On the other hand, it is an account of the heterotopia in its hypertopian aspect: the people are quattrocento and early cinquecento Italians, the town is Italian, the countryside is Italian, and even the principal figures are "Italian." Yet the palm tree in particular is the call of another world—a context which accompanies that which is portrayed, but one which comes from another world. The palm tree, perhaps even more than the golden halos around the heads of the principal figures, is a metaphor for the utopian discourse which is framed in a heterotopian scene. In this respect we are able to read the fifteenth to sixteenth fresco as it is situated between the utopian model and the discourse of a hypertopian (and more specifically de-generate utopian) space. Such an interpretive topology allows us to read not only the fresco itself but also the localities and the communities of the Italian Renaissance.

Each of the three topological models that I have just examined constitutes a different kind of space: an actual place, a spatially oriented play, and a painted location. Nevertheless each *topos* is an example of how heterotopian discourses are elaborated at particular temporal and spatial locations and also how they are situated deconstructively in relation to utopian pro-jections or dystopian de-jections. The deconstructive moment demonstrates how the interpretation of heterotopias can serve as the context for the understanding of spatial frameworks and for the design of new—presumably hypertopian—places.

337

20

FOR A HERMENEUTIC SEMIOLOGY OF THE SELF

"Understanding the world of signs is the means of understanding oneself."

Paul Ricoeur[1]

To a modern day semiologist, the philosophical perspectives of hermeneutics appear to be alien to the destiny of the human sciences. Similarly, hermeneutics can continue to understand texts without the lessons of semiology. The task of a hermeneutic semiology of the self, however, will be to establish a direct correlation between the self as interpreter and the system of signs produced in the interpretation. If the hermeneutic project is the formation of meaning through interpretation, it will explore the status of the "how" (personal knowledge and philosophical style) in contradistinction to the semiological "what" (identifiable body and language) that can be read by any self.

For the interpretation of the self, one must turn to the possible interpreter. Socrates setting out to fulfill the imperative of the priestess of Delphi ("know thyself"), Don Quixote questing forth imaginatively as the ideal knight errant, Hume at work with the dilemma of personal identity, and Kafka's Land Surveyor searching after an unattainable yet self-fulfilling castle—each is the interpreter of his own self-image. The narcissistic project originates from the beginning—the *arché* of the interpretation is the interpreter, whose objective is self-knowledge. The presumed source, the genesis of interpretation, receives the name of cogito (Descartes), transcendental unity of apperception (Kant), pure

338

ego (James), and transcendental ego (Husserl). This interpreter is both the condition for all acts of understanding and the standpoint of all such acts. Without such an interpreter, self-knowledge would not be possible.

By what compulsion are we forced to the beginning? The Augustinian conception of linear history motivates a need for self-genesis. We avoid the interpreted object until we can grasp the source of knowing, just as the natural scientist refuses the value judgments of an interpreting self until the inquiry into the object-ivities at hand has been initiated and completed. The interpreter will be at the heart, at the center of consciousness—and surely we must first turn to the heart of things. But as Sartre tells us, consciousness is not a realm of thingness. If it were, there would be no doubt as to where to find the center. The problematic of mind-brain identities depends upon the resolution of the question of a center. On the one hand, we are told that the brain is the center. On the other, it is argued that the innermost area of conscious life satisfies the conditions of centrality. A Freudian would even take the quest for sources into the unconscious in order to delve back into the true origins of infantile sexuality. We go to beginnings—as adumbrated in a recent study by Edward Said[2]—in order to uncover the intentional starting point of the interpreter's project.

Why not direct an inquiry alternatively at the middle? The middle of the classical tragedy is where the denouement occurs. The middle is the focus of elucidation. The middle is neither the source—the interpreter—nor the object-pole—that which is to be interpreted. The middle is the system of interpreted signs. Phenomenologically speaking, this system of signs occurs at the level of intentionality and constitution. Caught in the act of interpretation, the interpreter cannot help but reveal himself. He is not uncovering a self under self-reflection. Both Sartre's expulsion of the reflected self from the paradise of consciousness[3] and Merleau-Ponty's critique of reflection as incapable of carrying out the task of interrogation[4] indicate that the self's realization will not lie in an end any more than in a beginning. The self will not be the *terminus* at which all self-knowledge consolidates. The locus of the self obtains neither at the *arché* nor at the *telos*, but rather in the spanning of the two.

The spanning of the middle can be stated semiologically as a system of signs. The sign is the relation between the signifier and the signified. If the signified is the beginning, then the signifier is the end and the sign will be the place in which the self finds a piece of its identity. For de Saussure, the signifier (*signifiant*) is a word and the signified (*signifié*) is a concept.[5] The sign is the arbitrary relation. Because he claimed that linguistics is a part of semiology, he can restrict his inquiry to these terms. However, if one follows Roland Barthes in his assertion that semiology is a part of linguistics,[6] then it will be possible to transfer the signifier-signified relation to the human experiential realm in order to elucidate the nature of the self. In this Barthesian model, the signs to be read are not confined to the level of language. Rather languages (*langues*) appear in the context of fashion, menus, custom, and here, selfhood. This latter—selfhood—is perhaps the most fundamental of all semiological systems. Since a language in the sense of *langue* includes both a mode of discourse (*langage*) and particular articulations, performatives, speech acts (that is, *paroles*), the conception of the self as both formed and forming is not alien to semiological analysis. Thus in forming its place as middle, the self articulates and activates (*parole*) its own formed level of actualization and discourse (*langage*). Together this forming self and formed self constitute what has been called, in connection with Lacan[7] and Beckett,[8] the "language of the self"— language here in the sense of *langue*.

The self must be the interpreter of its own interpreted signs. The signs are united into a system. The system is dependent upon a language (*langue*) in which there is coherence of signs. Without that coherence, it would be unclear *which* self is in question. Although one can speak of a language of the self, when a particular analysis is to be undertaken, a particular self must be interpreted. The language of the self establishes a framework in which the inquiry can take place. Thus the language of the self is distinguished from the language of fashion and of fictional worlds. But the particular manner in which this self is distinguishable from that one is dependent upon an interpretational system. The system of signs is established through the on-going activity of interpretive experience, an experience based neither in the interpreter nor in the interpreted.

Interpreting as a language (*langue*) is the producing of an interpretation, i.e. the self as a system of signs. The production takes place through signification. In semiology, signification is that which accounts for the particular coherence of a particular instantiation (*parole*) of a type of discourse (*langage*). Signs inter-relate only because they form signification. Since signification is also associated with value, the special importance of certain signs within a system is achieved through the comparative value of particular signs and their significations. A sign does not hold signification on its own. It must be placed in the context of other signs for there to be meaning, just as a penny has no meaning or signification without other pennies, nickels, dimes, quarters, and dollars. Aspects of a particular self have signification or meaning only in connection with the whole. This point can be restated in phenomenological terms, since, as Ricoeur claims, meaning is "the most comprehensive category of phenomenology."[9] For Husserl, an aspect of the noema of the self has no meaning without its relationship to the whole thetic component as given in a noetic act. The analogy proposed is between the noematic field with its horizons and the system of signs. The difference is that for Husserl the noematic realm is transcendental, while the semiological view disallows the special status of signs. This is not to say that signs are transcendent, for this would reduce the sign to the level of the signifier. Even when Lacan speaks of the self as operative in the chain of signifiers,[10] he does not mean to abolish signifieds and the resultant signs. Rather he wishes only to establish a cairn for a direction that will identify the self in operation. For Lacan, one must look to the chain of signifiers as a signifying chain in order to discover the self's significations. This is quite different from Sartre's claim that the self, when treated thetically, becomes a transcendent self, a just-having-been or a projected future self. For the Sartre of *Being and Nothingness*,[11] meaning occurs in the context of consciousness—that free realm of insubstantiality—but without the possibility of being known as such in its pure state. In this early Sartre, to name the self is to posit an inapplicable identity. That identity is not to be denied entirely if at one time it was appropriate—for that would be bad faith—but it is also not to be accepted as a full description of the self. With Lacan's chain of signifiers, signification is presumed from the chain, while for Sartre signification is proposed from one's consciousness of something.

In a hermeneutic semiology of the self, meaning cannot be

relegated on the one hand to pure consciousness nor on the other hand to a simple chain of signifiers. Pure consciousness is only another substitute for a beginning and a pure chain of signifiers replaces goal-like objectivities. The system of signs must arise out of the self's interpretive activity. It must be realized through the grasp of consciousness (*prise de conscience*),[12] not through consciousness itself—through the meaning of sign systems, not through their external manifestations. Interpretive experience is an ongoing activity that creates meaning, leaves signs and tends toward the production of new signs. If I *am* my system of signs, the interpretive mode will have turned into a concatenation of objectivized identifications. The non-objective character of these identities cannot be overstressed. The signs of the self are produced through the interpretation and maintained through the ongoing activity of interpretive experience. Self-knowledge therefore will depend upon a careful understanding of signs in relation to one another. These signs, however, are not separable from the understanding that reveals them. This ambiguity is the perplexity of western philosophy and has motivated not only the subject/object dichotomy, but also the separating of soul and mind from body, being-for-itself from being-in-itself, and knowledge from what is to be known. A hermeneutic semiology of the self will show that the separation is artifice.

The self is both absent because of its signs and present through the interpretation of its sign. Signs form a locus for one to say: here is a mark of myself—but to assume that one's self is present in those signs is to ignore the meaningfulness of the interpretation that understands them. Understanding is the full presence of the self in its signs in the same way that for Aristotle the body is the potentiality and the soul its actualization. The potentiality of the self's signs is its realization in understanding. In effect, signs have no meaning without interpretation. To put it in Heideggerian terms, what most merits being thought is the Being of that which is. The differencing of the ontological from the ontic is the semiological space which is also filled with understanding, interpretation, and *Denken*. Signs do not form at the level of the *existentielle*, nor in the realm of *existentialia*. They achieve realization only in *Dasein* itself—for this is the Heideggerian meaning of man's *Sache selbst*. *Dasein* interprets itself and constitutes itself as its own meaning. Heidegger's formulation offers a description of *how* understanding brings about the self in its realization.

In his essay on "Heidegger and the Subject," Ricoeur demonstrates the equivocal character of "subject" as both "I" or "ego" and as *substratum* or ground.[13] The first we have rejected as an instance of origin, source, and beginning. The second, the *substratum*, moves in the direction of a representation of the self's character. In other words, the notion of *substratum* or ground is the basis for the *what* of the self. The system of signs is the ground for what I am. What the self *is* establishes itself through interpretation as a sign that there is Being of that which is (*Seiendes Sein*). The self is absent in this *quod sum* because it requires the presence of the *quomodo sum* in order for it to be complete.

In the coordination of interpretation (the how) and the system of signs (the what), the self is formed. Thought—the Heideggerian *Denken*—is the self at work, operating its own identity in the production of signs. The signs of the self, which thought and understanding produce, are the indication of an absence, an absence which Foucault demonstrates in Velasquez's painting *Las Meninas*.[14] There the signs of the self operate within a system of references which all point to the presence of an absence, the place of the king and queen. In the absence of the subject, these signs are not devoid of identity. They simply lack the fulfillment of their identity in the meaning-producing acts of the hermeneutical project. As Derrida has claimed,[15] they are the "trace," the grammatological index of a complete presence brought about through the self's quest for self-knowledge. For Derrida, if one looks at writing, one finds only the traces of a deconstructed, decentered selfhood that lacks full presence because that presence is already articulated as absent in the trace.[16] The self's decentered character identifies its condemnation to structure—the structure that forms the ground of a system of self-signs. In the play of the structure within the system, the self works out its identity.

The identity of the self is created through its differences. I am different from the other because our basic structure is the same. Differences can be ascertained when repetition of the same structure indicates variations on the same theme. Lévi-Strauss's *pensée sauvage*[17] is savage in that it defies being civilized into a unitary signification. The self forms a sign-system in a particular society, in its own milieu. Here the same structure is revealed as that which appears in another place and/or in another time. What is needed is not a refusal of selfness, not a condemnation to death as the concept of man is for Foucault[18]—but rather a revitalization through the transformation that identify this combination of signs in *the* structure of the self as different from other combinations. That there is a basic *substratum*, a structure that we call "the self," pervades even the semiological formulation. The self that is interpreted by itself through its own activity is the "deep structure" as Chomsky might refer to it.[19] This deep structure is what each act of understanding finds to be undeniable despite its variations in different human contexts. The deep structure of the self remains incomplete as long as it is unknown. By knowing it, I define myself; I provide the final individualizing touch that differentiates it from that of all others. The signification and meaning arising out of its self-positing is unique.

What is posited is not a centered (concentric) individuality. Lacan speaks of the self as ex-centric.[20] A centrifugal force (as opposed to a centripetal force) is paradigmatic here. A system of signs does not require the centrality of one particular sign—in fact, it refuses such an orientation. The system presumes equal distribution throughout—Merleau-Ponty's term was "equilibrium." The equilibrated organism is the form of the body that is lived through by consciousness. Ex-centricity in the sign system is the manifestation not only of balance and harmony, but also of individuality. The self is ex-centric in that it is unlike others—*ab*-normal. Only its structure provides a norm of selfness.

In its dispersed identity, the self is meaningful and that meaning is co-ordinate with the index of meaning. An idea, a gesture, a movement, an expression, an act—each is a sign which also serves as an index of meaning. Meaning depends upon its indices in the context of a whole system. Meaning cannot arise purely through the interpretational act. There must also be the motivators of its occurrence—motivations that are dispersed throughout a semiological framework. In their disparateness they unify in order to bring identity to a particular self-interpretation. The originary producer of meaning—not the origin, but rather the intentional structure of knowing—gathers together as it leaves scattered a full system in which a structured self is made known.

In this act of self-revelation, selfhood seems to be left in the signs themselves. The signs seem to absorb the vitality of the interpretation. They make claims to the possession of the self's identity. They seem to call out: I am this expression of that self, I am its idea, I am its gesture. I can be many of these signs; many names can make claim on who I am; and I am scattered among them. Hence, dispersion, disorder, chaos seem to characterize the self. The self is left helpless. It has offered a manifestation, a sign. But the sign is taken metonymically for the whole and the self is reified, shattered, lost in multiplicity like Beckett's Malone as he has taken the forms of the characters in the dying man's stories.[21] The self, dispersed in multiplicity, can *be* only in its reifications. Its vitality is gone, because its hermeneutic has been forgotten in favor of its signs. The lesson is that the signs are signs *of* an interpretive act just as consciousness for Husserl was consciousness of something. The interpretive act is the presence and actualization of the self's sign system and it yearns to be recovered— through interpretation itself.

NOTES

INTRODUCTION: CONTINENTAL PHILOSOPHY IN AMERICA

1 Oddly, British continental philosophy—still labelling itself primarily "phenomenological"—follows more closely what prevails in some of the American varietals. See especially articles in *The Journal of the British Society for Phenomenology*, but also in *Radical Philosophy*, and *I & C*.

2 For an account of phenomenology in Europe and America, see the now classic survey, Herbert Spiegelberg, *The Phenomenological Movement: An Historical Introduction*, 2 vols (The Hague: Nijhoff, 1981), and also Hugh J. Silverman, "Phenomenology," *Social Research*, vol. 47, no. 4 (Winter 1980), pp. 704–20.

3 For the history of hermeneutics, see Richard E. Palmer, *Hermeneutics: Interpretation Theory in Schleiermacher, Dilthey, Heidegger, and Gadamer* (Evanston: Northwestern University Press, 1969) and for its more recent developments Josef Bleicher, *Contemporary Hermeneutics: Hermeneutics as Method, Philosophy, and Critique* (London and Boston: Routledge & Kegan Paul, 1980). Don Ihde, *Hermeneutic Phenomenology* (Evanston: Northwestern University Press, 1971) offers a review of Paul Ricoeur's thought and David Couzens Hoy, *The Critical Circle: Literature and History in Contemporary Hermeneutics* (Berkeley and Los Angeles: University of California Press, 1978) focuses on the work of Hans-Georg Gadamer and his context. David Couzens Hoy, "Hermeneutics," *Social Research*, vol. 47, no. 4 (Winter 1980), pp. 649–71 provides an account of contemporary discussions on the topic.

4 For the role of Merleau-Ponty in the development of structuralism, see James M. Edie, *Speaking and Meaning: The Phenomenology of Language* (Bloomington: Indiana University Press, 1976), esp. chapter 3 on "Merleau-Ponty's Structuralism," and James M. Edie, "The meaning and development of Merleau-Ponty's concept of struc-

ture," in *Merleau-Ponty: Perception, Structure, Language*, ed. John Sallis (Atlantic Highlands, New Jersey: Humanities Press, 1981), pp. 39–57.

5 Among those philosophers in America who make use of structuralism, see, for instance, Peter Caws, *Structuralism: The Art of the Intelligible* (Humanities Press, forthcoming in the new series "Contemporary Studies in Philosophy and the Human Sciences"), Calvin O. Schrag, *Radical Reflection and the Origin of the Human Sciences* (West Lafayette: Purdue University Press, 1980), Hugh J. Silverman (ed.), *Piaget, Philosophy and the Human Sciences* (Atlantic Highlands, New Jersey: Humanities Press, 1980), and T. K. Seung, *Structuralism and Hermeneutics* (New York: Columbia University Press, 1982).

6 See Martin Jay, *The Dialectical Imagination: A History of the Frankfurt School and the Institute of Social Research, 1923–1950* (for background) and David Held, *Introduction to Critical Theory: Horkheimer to Habermas* (Berkeley and Los Angeles: University of California Press, 1980) for a subsequent overview. Dick Howard, *The Marxian Legacy* (New York: Urizen, 1977), John O'Neill (ed.), *On Critical Theory* (New York: Seabury, 1976), and Fred Dallmayr, *Beyond Dogma and Despair* (Notre Dame: University of Notre Dame Press, 1981) offer contemporary assessments of critical theory.

7 See, for instance, Thomas McCarthy, *The Critical Theory of Jürgen Habermas* (Cambridge, Mass.: MIT Press, 1978) and Raymond Geuss, *The Idea of Critical Theory: Habermas and the Frankfurt School* (Cambridge: Cambridge University Press, 1981).

8 Philosophical studies which draw upon the work of French poststructuralists include the special issue of *Research in Phenomenology*, vol. 8 (1978) on "Reading(s) of Jacques Derrida," David B. Allison (ed.), *The New Nietzsche: Contemporary Styles of Interpretation* (Cambridge, Mass.: MIT Press, 1984), Charles C. Lemert and Garth Gillan, *Michel Foucault: Social Theory and Transgression* (New York: Columbia University Press, 1982), and Alan Sheridan, *Michel Foucault: The Will to Truth* (New York: Tavistock, 1980).

1 THE SELF IN HUSSERL'S *CRISIS*

1 For the specific manner of relatedness to objects in terms of *noemata* and meanings, see Dagfin Føllesdal, "Husserl's notion of noema," *Journal of Philosophy*, vol. 66, no. 20 (16 October 1969), pp. 680–7; also see David Woodruff Smith and Ronald McIntyre, "Intentionality via intentions," *Journal of Philosophy*, vol. 68, no. 18 (18 September 1971), pp. 541–61, and their recent book *Husserl and Intentionality* (Dordrecht: Reidel, 1982).

2 See particularly Maurice Merleau-Ponty, *Consciousness and the Acquisition of Language*, trans. Hugh J. Silverman (Evanston: Northwestern University Press, 1973), pp. 36, 40–5.

3 Jean-Paul Sartre's phenomenological critique of Husserl's "transcen-

dental ego" is elaborated in *The Transcendence of the Ego*, trans. Forrest Williams and Robert Kirkpatrick (New York: Noonday, 1957) and "Consciousness of self and knowledge of self," trans. Mary Ellen and N. Lawrence, in *Readings in Existential Phenomenology*, ed. Nathaniel Lawrence and Daniel O'Connor (Englewood Cliffs, New Jersey: Prentice-Hall, 1967), pp. 113–42. This theme is developed further in chapter 10.

4 See Michel Foucault, *The Order of Things* (New York: Vintage, 1970). See also chapter 9.

5 The phenomenological features of temporal experience are discussed further in my "Imagining, perceiving, remembering," *Humanitas*, vol. 14, no. 2 (May 1978), pp. 197–207. My discussion appeals specifically to the work of Edward S. Casey, *Imagining: A Phenomenological Study* (Bloomington: Indiana University Press, 1976) and subsequent articles, particularly those in the *Review of Metaphysics*, vol. 31, no. 2 (September 1977) and vol. 32, no. 3 (March 1979).

6 See David Michael Levin, *Reason and Evidence in Husserl's Phenomenology* (Evanston: Northwestern University Press, 1970), and the review of it by David Woodruff Smith in *The Journal of Philosophy*, vol. 52, no. 12 (21 June 1973), pp. 356–63.

7 What Merleau-Ponty has called *le corps vécu* corresponds to this notion of *Leib*. The conventional translation for *le corps vécu* however is "the lived body." To conceive of the self as living through the body would add a valuable dimension to the understanding of Husserl's *Leib*.

2 DASEIN AND EXISTENTIAL AMBIGUITY

1 Martin Heidegger, *Sein und Zeit* (Tübingen: Niemeyer, 1926), p. 173. I have made use of the eleventh edition which appeared in 1967. The English translations appearing in my text are based on the version by John Macquarrie and Edward Robinson, *Being and Time* (New York: Harper & Row, 1962), viz. p. 65. Hereafter, indications will be incorporated into the text as, for example, *SZ*, p. 173; *BT*, p. 65.

2 As Walter Biemel remarks, "Husserl thought very highly of Heidegger and saw in him his most important pupil, one who would continue his work . . . Heidegger saw in Husserl a renovator of the philosophy of the twentieth century and over and over again held seminars on the *Logical Investigations*, especially Investigation VI. But he was no disciple" (*Martin Heidegger: An Illustrated Study*, trans. J. L. Mehta (New York: Harcourt Brace Jovanovich, 1976), p. 27). The point is to indicate that thinking Heidegger in relation to the Husserlian enterprise is not at all arbitrary.

3 I will assume that noematic *Sinne* are the central, meaning-laden aspects of *noemata* as they are given in noetic (meaning-giving) acts.

4 Husserl describes a horizon as a "dimly apprehended depth or fringe

of indeterminate reality" in *Ideas* I, sec. 27 and as "predelinated possibilities" in *Cartesian Meditations*, sec. 19.

5 The translations of *Sein* and *Seiende* are manifold. *Sein* is usually given as "Being" or "being." I shall prefer the former. *Seiende* however goes under more names. Ralph Manheim in his translation of *Einführung in die Metaphysik* notes that he was coining the word "essent," "essents," "the essent," "based on the fiction that *essens, essentis*, is the present participle of *sum*" (*An Introduction to Metaphysics* (New York: Anchor, 1959, p. xi). Wilde and Klubach in their translation of *The Question of Being* (New Haven: College and University Press, 1958) employ "being" (as opposed to "Being" which they reserve for *Sein*). A similar usage is suggested by Dreyfus and Todes in "The existential critique of objectivity," *Patterns of the Life-World*, ed. J. M. Edie, G. M. Parker and C. O. Schrag (Evanston: Northwestern University Press, 1970), pp. 346–87. They refer to "a being" for *Seiende* in the singular and 'beings" to satisfy a plural sense. For reasons discussed in the body of the next chapter, I subsequently use "being," "essent" and "that which is" (emphasizing the objective character of *Seiende*). In the present chapter, however, I follow the Macquarrie and Robinson preference for "entity."

6 Following Husserl, quotation marks are used to indicate meanings which are to be reflected upon after the phenomenological reduction.

7 In the work of art, the polyvalent and metaphorical character of the aesthetic object stretches the noematic *Sinn* in such a way that it appears to be multiple. Its multiplicity is an overdetermined unity, which might be called "perceptual ambiguity" but which does not exhibit the same type of co-givenness of noematic *Sinne* that we find in human or existential ambiguity. In the work of art—assuming it is other than one engaged in self-interpretation and self-disclosure—the lived multiplicity arises from a fixed or determinate but polysemous totality. I explore the implications of this thesis in "Artistic creation and human action," *Mosaic: A Journal for the Comparative Study of Literature and Ideas* (Winnipeg: University of Manitoba Press), vol. 8, no. 1 (Fall 1974), pp. 157–64.

8 This conception of the part/whole relation is comparable to that presented by Köhler, Koffka and Merleau-Ponty in the domain of perception.

9 Merleau-Ponty makes this methodological point clearly in the Preface to *Phenomenology of Perception*, trans. Colin Smith (London: Routledge & Kegan Paul, 1962), where he states that phenomenology is "a matter of describing, not of explaining or analyzing" (p. viii).

10 The notion of hermeneutics suggested here is that of the messenger (Hermes) moving back and forth between subject and object. Since, however, the sender and the receiver are one and the same, the message (the interpretation), which arises out of the relation, acquires a polysemous, multi-contextual type of understanding. What is understood is the interpreter, the interpreted, and the meaningful interpretation itself. For the etymology of hermeneutics, see Richard Palmer,

Notes

Hermeneutics: Interpretation Theory in Schleiermacher, Dilthey, Heidegger, and Gadamer (Evanston: Northwestern University Press, 1969).

3 THE IDENTITY OF DIFFERENCE

1 "Man" is understood here in the now outmoded generic sense which includes both men and women. The discussion appeals to this traditional usage.
2 Ralph Manheim, "Translator's Introduction," in Martin Heidegger, *An Introduction to Metaphysics* (New York: Anchor, 1959), p. xi. See also note 5 to Chapter 2 above for further elaboration of this question of translating *Sein* and *Seiende*.
3 See *"Qu'est-ce que la metaphysique?,"* trans. Henri Corbin and R. Munier, in *Questions I* (Paris: Gallimard, 1968).
4 See M. Heidegger, *Vom Wesen des Grundes* in *Wegmarken* (Frankfurt: Klostermann, 1967), pp. 30–1.
5 See M. Merleau-Ponty, *Phenomenology of Perception*, trans. Colin Smith (London: Routledge & Kegan Paul, 1962).
6 *Seminaire tenu par la Professeur Martin Heidegger sur la Differenzschrift de Hegel* (Villeneuve-St Georges: SPIT, 1969), p. 25.
7 Ibid.
8 M. Heidegger, *Nietzsche II* (Pfullingen: Neske, 1961), p. 209. Subsequent references to Heidegger's text are incorporated into the body of the chapter. (The translations are mine.)

4 THINKING AND BEING

1 In "Moira," Heidegger translates Parmenides' fragment τό γὰραντό νοειν εστίν τε καί εἶναι as *"Denn dasselbe ist Denken und Sein."* *Vorträge und Aufsätze*, Teil III (Pfullingen: Neske, 1954), p. 27, [henceforth cited as *VA, III*, with the roman numeral depending upon the volume]. In *Identität und Differenz* (Pfullingen: Neske, 1957) p. 14, it reads: *"Das Selbe ist Vernehmen (Denken) sowohl als auch Sein"* [this work will be abbreviated as *ID*]. Except where an English version reference is cited, translations appearing in this text are mine.
2 *"Hier wird Verschiedenes Denken und Sein, als das selbe gedacht."* *ID*, p. 14.
3 *"Denken und Sein gehoren in das Selbe und aus diesem Selben zusammen."* *ID*, p. 14.
4 *"Inswischen haben wir aber die Selbigkeit von Denken und Sein schon als die Zusammen-gehörigkeit beider festgelegt."* *ID*, p. 15.
5 See note 5 to chapter 2 and note 2 to chapter 3.
6 The ontological difference (*die ontologische Differenz*) is what characterizes the Being (*Sein*) of that which is (*Seiende*). This is a "lived"

350

difference, as opposed to one made for analytical purposes, e.g. "*der Unterschied von Sein und Seiendem*." The distinction between *Differenz* and *Unterschied* is discussed at greater length in chapter 3.

7 "*das Vorliegenlassen*," *VA, III*, "Moira," p. 41.

8 M. Heidegger, *Was Heisst Denken?* (Tübingen: Niemeyer, 1954) p. 147 [henceforth abbreviated as *WHD*]. *What is called Thinking?*, trans. F. Wieck and J. Glenn Gray (New York: Harper & Row, 1968), p. 241.

9 *VA, II*, "*Was heisst Denken?*" p. 13.

10 See Maurice Merleau-Ponty's posthumous work, established by Claude Lefort as *Le Visible et l'invisible* (Paris: Gallimard, 1964) and translated by Alphonso Lingis as *The Visible and the Invisible* (Evanston: Northwestern University Press, 1968).

11 M. Heidegger, *Über den Humanismus* (Paris: Aubier, 1964), bilingual edition with a translation into French by R. Munier, p. 62. This was originally a letter to Jean Beaufret in 1946. [Henceforth cited as *UH*.]

12 M. Heidegger, *Zeit und Sein*, in *L'Endurance de la pensée* (Paris: Plon, 1968), p. 14. This was a lecture given in 1962 at the University of Freiberg, and first published as a *Festschrift* for Jean Beaufret. It was republished in *Zur Sache des Denkens* (Tübingen: Niemeyer, 1969) [*Zeit und Sein* will henceforth be cited as *ZS*, and *Zur Sache des Denkens* as *ZSD*.] An English translation by Joan Stambaugh has been published by Harper & Row as *Time and Being*.

13 M. Heidegger, *Einführung in die Metaphysik* (Tübingen: Niemeyer, 1953), p. 148. English translation by Ralph Manheim published as *An Introduction to Metaphysics* by Anchor Doubleday and reissued by Yale University Press, 1959.

14 M. Heidegger, "Letter to Richardson," in William J. Richardson, *Heidegger Through Phenomenology to Thought* (The Hague: Nijhoff, 1963).

15 M. Heidegger, *Kant und das Problem der Metaphysik* (Frankfurt: Klostermann, 1929), p. 205. Translation by James S. Churchill as *Kant and the Problem of Metaphysics* (Bloomington: Indiana University Press, 1962), pp. 234–5 [henceforth *KPM*].

16 M. Heidegger, *Aus der Erfahrung des Denkens* (Pfullingen: Neske, 1947), p. 9.

17 *VA, II*, "Was heisst Denken?," p. 10.

18 M. Heidegger, *Satz vom Grund* (Pfullingen: Neske, 1957), pp. 210–11.

19 *VA, III*, "Logos," p. 24.

20 M. Heidegger, *Was ist Metaphysik?* (Frankfurt: Klostermann, 1969), p. 18. Original text appeared in 1929, with an "Afterword" added in 1943, and an "Introduction" in the 1949 edition.

5 MERLEAU-PONTY'S HUMAN AMBIGUITY

1 Ferdinand Alquié, "Une Philosophie de l'ambiguité," *Fontaine*, vol. 11, no. 59 (April, 1947), pp. 17–70. Subsequent references to this

Notes

article are incorporated into the body of the essay. The translations for this and subsequent commentaries with only French text references are mine.

2 Alphonse de Waelhens, "Une Philosophie de l'ambiguité," in Maurice Merleau-Ponty, *La Structure du comportement* (1942), 2nd edn. (Paris: Presses Universitaires de France, 1949), pp. v, xv. Hereafter abbreviated *SC*.

3 John Wild, "Foreword," in *The Structure of Behavior*, trans. Alden D. Fisher (Boston: Beacon Press, 1963), p. xv. Hereafter cited as *SB*.

4 Marc Richir, "La Défenestration," in *L'Arc* (issue on Merleau-Ponty), no. 46 (1971), pp. 31–42.

5 Henri Lefebvre, "M. Merleau-Ponty et la philosophie de l'ambiguité," *La Pensée*, no. 73 (May-June 1957), p. 37. Hereafter cited in the text of the chapter.

6 Maurice Merleau-Ponty, *Phénoménologie de la perception* (Paris: Gallimard, 1945), p. 383. Hereafter abbreviated as *PdP*. English translation by Colin Smith, *Phenomenology of Perception* (London: Routledge & Kegan Paul, 1962), p. 332. Hereafter cited as *PoP*.

7 Xavier Tilliette, *Merleau-Ponty ou la mesure de l'homme* (Paris: Seghers, 1970), pp. 41–2.

8 The theme of philosophy becoming experience also permeates Merleau-Ponty's "Philosophy and non-philosophy since Hegel" (1961). This theme is elaborated further in chapters 7 and 8.

9 There are also no poles in the Sartrian relation between being-in-itself and being-for-itself since the for-itself in Sartre's view is always a negating activity and not an entity. Nevertheless Sartre does distinguish the two types of being just as Heidegger distinguishes between Being and that which is. See chapter 10 for a more detailed account of Sartre's position.

10 Maurice Merleau-Ponty, "Un inédit de Maurice Merleau-Ponty," in *Revue de Métaphysique et de morale*, 67th, no. 4 (October-December 1962), p. 409. "An unpublished text," trans. Arleen B. Dallery, in *The Primacy of Perception and other essays*, ed. James M. Edie (Evanston: Northwestern University Press, 1964), p. 11.

11 Merleau-Ponty's particular debt to de Saussure's structural linguistics is presented at some length in his *Consciousness and the Acquisition of Language*, trans. Hugh J. Silverman (Evanston: Northwestern University Press, 1973) and in *The Prose of the World*, trans. John O'Neill (Evanston: Northwestern University Press, 1973).

12 Maurice Merleau-Ponty, *Le Visible et l'invisible* (Paris: Gallimard, 1964), p. 181. English translation by Alphonso Lingis (Evanston: Northwestern University Press, 1968), pp. 137–8.

6 MERLEAU-PONTY ON LANGUAGE AND COMMUNICATION

1 As I indicated in the Preface to *Consciousness and the Acquisition of Language*, trans. Hugh J. Silverman (Evanston: Northwestern University Press, 1973), notes from Merleau-Ponty's courses at the Université de Lyon, where he taught from 1945–8, have been made available to me by F. Jacquet. Jacquet was a student in Merleau-Ponty's Lyon courses.

2 See G. T. Fechner, *Elements of Psychophysics* (1860), trans. H. Alder (New York: Holt, Rinehart & Winston, 1966). This work was subjected to philosophical scrutiny by Henri Bergson in *Time and Free Will: An Essay on the Immediate Data of Consciousness* (1889), trans. F.L. Pogson (New York: Harper Torchbooks, 1960). Bergson demonstrates that Fechner's notion of minimum differences between sensations and Delboeuf's revision in terms of mean gradations both overlook the important role of intensity. "Intensity," Bergson writes, "is situated at the juncture between two streams, one of which brings us the idea of extensive magnitude from without, while the other brings us from within, in fact from the very depths of consciousness, the image of an inner multiplicity" (p. 72). Bergson goes on to examine the concrete multiplicity of inner states of consciousness as they unfold themselves in pure duration and as they are distinct from quantitative enumeration *per se*. It is also worthy to note that Bergson, along with Malbranche and Maine de Biran, was the topic of a course which Merleau-Ponty taught at the Ecole Normale Supérieure in Paris concurrently with "Language and Communication" in Lyon. This other 1947–8 course has been published by Jean Deprun as *L'Union de l'âme et du corps chez Malbranche, Biran et Bergson* (Paris: Vrin, 1968). Curiously, Merleau-Ponty does not cite the French equivalent of *Time and Free Will* (i.e. *Essai sur les données immédiates de la conscience*). Rather he focuses on the 1896 *Matière et mémoire*. He then only mentions the 1903 *Introduction to Metaphysics*, the 1907 *Creative Evolution*, the 1911 *L'Intuition philosophique*, and the 1934 *La Pensée et le mouvant*.

3 Wolfgang Koehler, *The Mentality of Apes*, trans. Ella Winter (New York: Harcourt, Brace & World, 1925).

4 See Merleau-Ponty, *Consciousness and the Acquisition of Language*, p. 9. [Henceforth cited as *CAL*.]

5 W. von Wartburg, *Problèmes et méthodes de la linguistique* (Paris: Presses Universitaires de France, 1947).

6 See in particular, W. von Wartburg, *Evolution et structure de la langue française* (Bern: A. Franche Verlag, 1946).

7 Ferdinand de Saussure, *Course in General Linguistics*, ed. Charles Bally and Albert Sechehaye in collaboration with Albert Riedlinger, trans. Wade Baskin (New York: McGraw-Hill, 1959).

8 See especially André Meillet, *Linguistique historique et linguistique générale*, 2 vols (Paris: repr. 1948–52).

9 See, for example, Noam Chomsky, *Language and Mind* (New York: Harcourt, Brace & World, 1968), p. 25 ff.

10 See Emile Durkheim, *The Elementary Forms of Religious Life*, trans. Joseph Ward Swain (Glencoe, Ill.: Free Press, 1947), and *The Rules of Sociological Method*, trans. Sarah A. Solovoy and John H. Mueller, ed. George E. G. Catlin (New York: Free Press, 1938).

11 See the collection of essays in Marcel Mauss, *Sociologie et anthropologie* (Paris: Presses Universitaires de France, 1950).

12 Jacques-Bénigne Bossuet, *Discours sur l'histoire universelle* (Paris: Garnier Frères, 1873).

13 See, in particular, Merleau-Ponty, *Phenomenology of Perception* (1945), trans. Colin Smith (London: Routledge & Kegan Paul, 1962), chapter 4 of the Introduction, entitled "The phenomenal field."

14 Many of the points raised here were discussed in an earlier version published as "The metaphysical in man" which first appeared in the *Revue de Métaphysique et de Morale*, July-October 1947. This remark should also serve as a correction to footnote 15 of my "Translator's Preface" to *CAL*. The same chronological reversal also occurs in the Métraux bibliography (footnote 10) to X. Tilliette, *Merleau-Ponty ou la mesure de l'homme* (Paris: Seghers, 1970), p. 175. Since "The metaphysical in man" which was republished in *Sense and Non-Sense*, was written and probably published before the 1947–48 course even began, Merleau-Ponty clearly developed and embellished upon the more summary formulations provided in the article. This accounts for the significant differences between "The metaphysical in man" and *CAL*. Indeed, one might consider "Language and Communication" as the missing link between the two.

15 Ivan Petrovich Pavlov, *Lectures on Conditioned Reflexes* (New York: International Publishers, 1928).

16 Adhemar Gelb and Kurt Goldstein, *Über Farbennamenamnesie*, in *Psychologische Forschung*, 1925.

17 See the chapter entitled "The pathology of language," *CAL*, pp. 63–77, and especially the section on "Goldstein's analysis of language," pp. 70–5.

18 See, for example, Kurt Lewin, *Field Theory in Social Science*, ed. Dorwin Cartwright (New York: Harper & Row, 1951).

19 See, for example, Alain, *Eléments de philosophie* (Paris: Gallimard, 1941).

20 Jean-Paul Sartre, *The Psychology of Imagination* (1940). trans. Bernard Frechtman (New York: Washington Square Press, 1948).

21 For a further clarification of the distinction between (linguistic) signification and (experiential) meaning, see chapter 5.

22 See Maurice Merleau-Ponty, "Philosophy and non-philosophy since Hegel," trans. Hugh J. Silverman, *Telos*, no. 29 (Fall 1976), pp. 43–105, and chapters 7 and 8.

23 See Paul Valéry, *The Collected Work of Paul Valéry*, vol. VIII, trans. M. Cowley and J. R. Lawler (Princeton New Jersey: Princeton, University Press, 1971).

Notes

24 For the remainder of the Lyon course, Merleau-Ponty devotes his attention to the explication of Michotte's *La Perception de la causalité* (*The Perception of Causality*).

25 Maurice Merleau-Ponty, *The Prose of the World*, trans. John O'Neill (Evanson: Northwestern University Press, 1973), p. 7.

26 A further consideration of Saussure's semiology was the topic of another course which Merleau-Ponty offered a year later (1948–9) at the Ecole Normale Supérieure in Paris.

27 For Roland Barthes's early semiology see *Writing Degree Zero* (1953), trans. Annette Lavers and Colin Smith (New York: Hill & Wang, 1967) and *Elements of Semiology* (1964), trans. Annette Lavers and Colin Smith (New York: Hill & Wang, 1967). As examples of the more recent orientation, see *S/Z* (1970), trans. Richard Miller (New York: Hill & Wang, 1974) and *The Pleasure of the Text* (1973), trans. Richard Miller (New York: Hill & Wang, 1975).

28 Discussions of this relationship between Merleau-Ponty's phenomenology and structuralism include Michel Lefeuvre, *Merleau-Ponty au delà de la phénoménologie* (Paris: Klincksieck, 1976); James M. Edie, *Speaking and Meaning: The Phenomenology of Language* (Bloomington: Indiana University Press, 1976); Luce Fontaine de Visscher, *Phenomène ou Structure? Essai sur le langage chez Merleau-Ponty* (Bruxelles: Facultés Universitaires Saint-Louis, 1974); and Richard L. Lanigan, *Speaking and Semiology: Maurice Merleau-Ponty's Phenomenological Theory of Existential Communication* (The Hague: Mouton, 1972). Of those just cited, Edie alone notes the important place of the 1947–8 Lyon lectures although he does not elaborate its contents. See, especially, his chapter on "Merleau-Ponty's structuralism." In chapter 8 I indicate some of the respects in which Merleau-Ponty continues to serve as an unspoken presence in contemporary structuralism and post-structuralism.

7 MERLEAU-PONTY AND HEIDEGGER: INTERPRETING HEGEL

1 Maurice Merleau-Ponty, "Philosophy and non-Philosophy since Hegel," trans. Hugh J. Silverman. The original French, edited by Claude Lefort, appeared in *Textures*, no. 8–9 (1974) and no. 10–11 (1975).

2 Martin Heidegger, "*Hegels Begriff der Erfahrung*" in *Holzwege* (Frankfurt: Klostermann, 1950), pp. 105–92. The French translation by Wolfgang Brokmeier, edited by François Fédier as "Hegel et son concept de l'expérience," in *Chemins qui ne mènent nulle part* (Paris: Gallimard, 1962), pp. 101–72, appeared shortly after Merleau-Ponty's death (Merleau-Ponty was closely associated with Gallimard, who published most of his writings). The English version is published as *Hegel's Concept of Experience* (New York: Harper & Row, 1970).

Although the translator of the portions by Heidegger is anonymous, the Hegel passages are translated by Kenly Royce Dove. This text is henceforth cited as *HCE*.

3 In the German original of *Hegel's Concept of Experience*, the full text of Hegel's "Introduction" is given prior to Heidegger's sixteen-part paragraph by paragraph commentary. In the English version, we find not only the complete text at the beginning, but also the reproduction of each paragraph prior ot Heidegger's discussion of it. Thus, in the original, one could study Hegel's text in its entirety and a reexamination of each passage would necessitate a return to the beginning. In the English version, one can readily compare Hegel's assertions with Heidegger's comments.

4 Maurice Merleau-Ponty, *Themes from the Lectures*, trans. John O'Neill (Evanston: Northwestern University Press, 1970), p. 111. Subsequent references to this text are cited in the body of the essay as *TL*.

5 This point is developed further in chapter 8.

6 For Hegel, the claim to the end of philosophy is the assertion that philosophy must become science. In the "Preface" to the *Phenomenology of Mind*, he puts it in the following way: "To demonstrate that the time has come for the elevation of philosophy to a science—this would be the only true justification of the attempts which have this aim. For this would show the necessity of such an aim even while accomplishing it." Translation by W. Kaufmann in *Hegel: Texts and Commentary* (New York: Anchor, 1965), p. 12. Hegel restates his point near the end of the Preface: "Scientific knowledge . . . demands precisely that we surrender to the life of the object or—and this is the same—that we confront and express its inner necessity" (p. 82). In assessing this claim, Heidegger indicates that the result of Hegel's philosophy was to become the dominant position in the nineteenth century: "The completion of metaphysics begins with Hegel's metaphysics of absolute knowledge as the Spirit of will . . . In spite of the superficial talk about the breakdown of Hegelian philosophy, one thing remains true: Only this philosophy determined reality in the nineteenth century, although not in the external form of a doctrine followed, but rather as metaphysics, as the dominance of beingness as the sense of certainty. The counter movements to this metaphysics belong *to* it." Heidegger, *The End of Philosophy*, trans. Joan Stambaugh (New York: Harper & Row, 1973), p. 89. Nietzsche reiterates this completion of philosophy: "With Nietzsche's metaphysics, philosophy is completed. That means: It has gone through the sphere of prefigured possibilities. . . . But with the end of philosophy, thinking is not also at its end, but in transition to another beginning." Ibid., p. 96.

7 This notion of difference—specifically the ontological difference—has been developed in the previous chapter.

8 Maurice Merleau-Ponty, *The Structure of Behavior*, trans. Alden J. Fisher (Boston: Beacon Press, 1963), pp. 162–84.

9 See the discussion of these two attitudes in chapter 1.
10 See M. Heidegger, *The Question of Being*, trans. Jean T. Wilde and William Kluback (New Haven: College and University Publishers, 1958) and specifically Being as ~~Sein~~.

8 RE-READING MERLEAU-PONTY

1 See note 1 and the general discussion in chapter 7.
2 The role of language is elaborated at length in the next chapter.
3 Two series of lectures were offered during 1960–1, for only in the years 1957–9 did Merleau-Ponty consolidate his two courses into one. Thus for 1960–1, there exists another set of inquiries announced as *Cartesian Ontology and Modern Ontology* and not included in *Philosophy and Non-Philosophy since Hegel*. In this other course Merleau-Ponty explored the visible with Cézanne, the invisible in things through Leonardo's perspectival projection, and the oscillating center in the chiasm of visual perception and kinesthetic apperception. Alexandre Métraux summarizes these materials in "Vision and Being in the last lectures of Maurice Merleau-Ponty," in *Life-World and Consciousness*, ed. Lester E. Embree (Evanston: Northwestern University Press, 1972), pp. 332–6. The course parallels specific elements in *Eye and Mind*, trans. Carleton Dallery, in *The Primacy of Perception and other Essays*, ed. James M. Edie (Evanston: Northwestern University Press, 1964). It develops certain aesthetic theories that remained nascent since *Sense and Non-Sense* (1948), trans. Hubert L. Dreyfus and Patricia A. Dreyfus (Evanston: Northwestern University Press, 1964), including particularly the transformation of Cézanne's Gestaltism into the painter's thinking in space as visibility.
4 Maurice Merleau-Ponty, *In Praise of Philosophy*, trans. John Wild and James M. Edie (Evanston: Northwestern University Press, 1963). Subsequent references are cited in the text as *Praise*.
5 Maurice Merleau-Ponty, "An unpublished text," trans. Arleen B. Dallery, in *The Primacy of Perception*, ed. James M. Edie (Evanston: Northwestern University Press, 1964), p. 9.
6 Maurice Merleau-Ponty, *Phenomenology of Perception*, trans. Colin Smith (London: Routledge & Kegan Paul, 1962), p. xix. Henceforth cited as *PoP*.
7 See Maurice Merleau-Ponty, "Philosophy and non-philosophy since Hegel," trans. Hugh J. Silverman, *Telos*, no. 29 (Fall 1976), p. 81, translator's note no. 81.
8 Maurice Merleau-Ponty, *The Prose of the World*, trans. John O'Neill (Evanston: Northwestern University Press, 1973), p. 84. Henceforth cited as *PW* in the text.
9 For an alternative account of utopian thinking which demonstrates the possibility of understanding ideal (future) worlds in relation to the lived present, see chapter 18. There is a sense in which this

account does fulfill the conditions Merleau-Ponty proposes in that any utopian model appears as a projection of the "now."

10 Note Lefort's doubts that the work was fully abandoned and that were there time it could have been revived out of the tissue of *The Visible and the Invisible* (*PW*, p. xx).

11 Maurice Merleau-Ponty, *The Visible and the Invisible*, trans. Alphonso Lingis (Evanston: Northwestern University Press, 1960), pp, 165–275. Henceforth cited in the text as *VI*.

12 See Martin Heidegger, *The End of Philosophy*, trans. Joan Stambaugh (New York: Harper & Row, 1973). This is selected from vol. II of *Nietzsche* (Pfullingen: Neske, 1961).

13 The inherent critique of Heidegger's notion of the *Zwischen* will be discussed later in this chapter.

14 Maurice Merleau-Ponty, *The Structure of Behavior*, trans. Alden L. Fisher (Boston: Beacon Press, 1963). p. 162.

15 Maurice Merleau-Ponty, *Humanism and Terror*, trans. John O'Neill (Evanston: Northwestern University Press, 1969), p. 96. Henceforth cited as *HT*.

16 Maurice Merleau-Ponty, *The Adventures of the Dialectic*, trans. Joseph Bien (Evanston: Northwestern University Press, 1973).

17 Maurice Merleau-Ponty, *Themes from the Lectures*, trans. John O'Neill (Evanston: Northwestern University Press, 1970), pp. 51–61. Henceforth cited as *TL*.

18 See my article "Cézanne's mirror stage," *Journal of Aesthetics and Art Criticism*, vol. 40, no. 4 (Summer, 1982), pp. 369–79.

19 Maurice Merleau-Ponty, *Eye and Mind*, trans. Carleton Dallery, in *The Primacy of Perception*, p. 178. Henceforth cited at *EM*.

20 These notes were published posthumously in *Méditations*, no. 4, 1961–2, pp. 5–9. They are reprinted in *Entretiens: Claude Simon*, ed. Marcel Séguier (1972), pp. 41–6. Dates of these notes extend between October 1960 and March 1961. Therefore they cover the same period as "Philosophy and non-philosophy since Hegel." The text is henceforth cited as *Entretiens*. The translation is mine.

21 For a discussion of the meaning of these events and related issues in Merleau-Ponty's political theory, see Dick Howard, "Ambiguous radicalism: Merleau-Ponty's interrogation of political thought," in G. Gillan, *Horizons of the Flesh* (Carbondale: Southern Illinois University Press, 1973), pp. 143–59. See also his *The Marxian Legacy* (London: Macmillan, 1977).

22 Louis Althusser in his "Introduction" to *For Marx*, trans. Ben Brewster (New York: Vintage, 1969) dubs this break the *coupure épistémologique*, following Gaston Bachelard's description of changes in knowledge as understood through the philosophy of science. In that the epistemological break in Marx announces a shift from an earlier position, the transition that it signals is the move to science and a "scientific socialism."

23 Contrast the position held by Merleau-Ponty as discussed in chapter 5 in relation to that of Husserl elaborated in chapter 1.

24 J.-P. Sartre, "The singular universal," trans. John Mathews, in *Between Existentialism and Marxism* (New York: Pantheon, 1974).
25 See chapter 1 for a further elaboration of Husserl's position.
26 See chapter 3 for an account of selfness as between subjectivity and objectivity (establishing difference) and as inclusive of both (establishing identity).
27 See J.-P. Sartre, *Transcendence of the Ego*, trans. Forrest Williams and Robert Kirkpatrick (New York: Noonday, 1957).
28 See chapter 10 for a further elaboration of this point.
29 This view is developed at length in chapter 5.
30 Ferdinand de Saussure, *Course in General Linguistics*, trans. Wade Baskin (New York: McGraw-Hill, 1959).
31 Claude Lévi-Strauss, *Elementary Structures of Kinship*, trans. James Harle Bell, John Richard von Sturmer and Rodney Needham (Boston: Beacon Press, 1969). Although first published in 1949, a revised edition appeared in France in 1967. A more detailed account of these two thinkers is provided in chapter 11.
32 J.-P. Sartre, "Merleau-Ponty," in *Situations*, trans. Benita Eister (Greenwich, Conn: Fawcett, 1965), p. 211. Henceforth cited as S:M-P.
33 Alain Robbe-Grillet, *The Voyeur*, trans. Richard Howard (New York: Grove, 1958).
34 See Roland Barthes, *Writing Degree Zero*, trans. Annette Lavers and Colin Smith (New York: Hill & Wang, 1967).
35 For examples, see Barthes, *S/Z*, trans. Richard Miller (New York: Hill & Wang, 1974); *On Racine*, trans. Richard Howard (New York: Hill & Wang, 1964); *The Fashion System*, trans. Matthew Ward and R. Howard (New York: Hill & Wang, 1983); *Roland Barthes*, trans. R. Howard (New York: Hill & Wang, 1981).
36 See Jacques Lacan, "The insistence of the letter in the unconscious," in *The Structuralists*, ed. Richard and Fernande De George (New York: Anchor, 1972), pp. 287–323.
37 Louis Althusser, *For Marx*, p. 167.
38 See Michel Foucault, *The Order of Things*, trans. anonymous (New York: Vintage, 1970), and *The Archeology of Knowledge*, trans. A. M. Sheridan Smith (New York: Pantheon, 1972).
39 In 1967, Jacques Derrida published three books: *Speech and Phenomena*, trans. David B. Allison (Evanston: Northwestern University Press, 1973); *L'Ecriture et la différence* (Paris: Seuil, 1967); and *De la Grammatologie* (Paris: Minuit, 1967).
40 See particularly "Différance" in *Speech and Phenomena*, pp. 129–60. This essay was originally published in 1968 as vol 62 of the *Bulletin de la Société Française de Philosophie* after having been read before that society. The significance of its oral exposition is internal to the understanding of the distinction between "différance" and "différence."
41 See Jacques Derrida, "Structure, sign and play in the discourse of the

human sciences," *Writing and Difference*, trans. Alan Bass (Chicago: University of Chicago Press, 1978).
42 See Jacques Derrida, *Dissemination*, trans. Barabara Johnson (Chicago: University of Chicago Press, 1981). The *semé* as unit of meaning is dispersed throughout writing.
43 Jean-François Lyotard, *La Phénoménologie* (Paris: Presses Universitaires de France, 1954).
44 See J.-F. Lyotard, *Discours, figure* (Paris: Klincksieck, 1971).
45 See J.-F. Lyotard, *Dérive à partir de Marx et Freud* (Paris: 10–18, 1973) and *Économie libidinale* (Paris: Minuit, 1974).
46 Reference is made here to Lyotard's "majesterial" lecture for the "Schizo-Culture" *Semio-text(e)* conference held at Columbia University (Fall 1975). The experimentalization of translation methods used in the course of the lecture illustrated not only the proliferation of "desire," but also the repetition of the discourse of the other—in this case, Lyotard's.
47 See Gilles Deleuze, *Empirisme et subjectivité* (Paris: Presses Universitaires de France, 1953); *Spinoza et le problème de l'expression* (Paris: Minuit, 1969); *Kant's Critical Philosophy*, trans. Hugh Tomlinson and Barbara Habberjam (Minneapolis: University of Minnesota Press, 1984).
48 See G. Deleuze, *Présentation de Sacher-Masoch* (Paris: Presses Universitaires de France, 1967); *Logique du sens* (Paris: Minuit, 1969).

9 MERLEAU-PONTY AND THE INTERROGATION OF LANGUAGE

1 James M. Edie has listed Merleau-Ponty's writings on language in his "Forward" to *Consciousness and the Acquisition of Language*, trans. Hugh J. Silverman (Evanston: Northwestern University Press, 1973), pp. xi–xxxii. Since Edie's listing is incomplete due to subsequent publications, I offer a full accounting according to the four framework formulations discussed in this chapter.

(1) The Language of the Body
(1945) "The body as speech and expression," in *Phenomenology of Perception*, trans. Colin Smith (London: Routledge & Kegan Paul and Atlantic Highlands: Humanities Press, 1962), pp. 174–99.
(2) The Philosophy and Psychology of Communication
(1947) "The metaphysical in man," in *Sense and Non-Sense*, trans. Hubert L. Dreyfus and Patricia A. Dreyfus (Evanston: Northwestern University Press, 1964). pp. 83–98.
(1947–8) "Language and communication," Lecture course at the Université de Lyon (summarized and discussed in chapter 6).
(1949–50) *Consciousness and the Acquisition of Language* (cited

above).
(1950–1) "Phenomenology and the sciences of man," trans. John Wild, in *The Primacy of Perception and other essays*, ed. James M. Edie (Evanston: Northwestern University Press, 1964), pp. 43–95.
(1951) "On the phenomenology of language," in *Signs*, trans. Richard C. McCleary (Evanston: Northwestern University Press, 1964), pp. 84–97.
(1951–2) "The experience of others," trans. Fred Evans and Hugh J. Silverman, in *Review of Existential Psychology and Psychiatry* (1985), pp. 43–60.
(3) Indirect Language
(1952) "Indirect language and the voices of silence," in *Signs*, pp. 39–83.
(1950–2) *The Prose of the World*, ed. Claude Lefort, trans. John O'Neill (Evanston: Northwestern University Press, 1973).
(1953) "The sensible world and the world of expression," in *Themes from the Lectures*, trans. John O'Neill (Evanston: Northwestern University Press, 1970), pp. 3–11.
(1953) "Studies in the literary use of language," in *Themes from the Lectures*, pp. 12–18.
(1954) "The problem of speech," in *Themes from the Lectures*, pp. 19–26.
(4) The Language of Visibility
(1959–61) *The Visible and the Invisible*, trans. Alphonso Lingis (Evanston: Northwestern University Press, 1968).
(1960) "Eye and mind," trans. Carleton Dallery, in *The Primacy of Perception*, pp. 159–90.
(1961) "Philosophy and non-philosophy since Hegel," trans. Hugh J. Silverman, *Telos*, no. 29 (Fall 1976), pp. 43–105.

2 See chapter 5.
3 See chapter 8.
4 *Phenomenology of Perception*, p. 197. In the original Gallimard edition (Paris, 1964), p. 229.
5 Ibid., p. 193. (Fr., p. 226.)
6 Ibid., p. 184. (Fr., p. 214.)
7 Ibid., p. 185 (translation altered). (Fr., p. 215.)
8 See my "Preface" to *Consciousness and the Acquisition of Language*, p. xxxvii.
9 See chapter 6.
10 Ibid., p. 174.
11 "The metaphysical in man," in *Sense and Non-sense*, p. 86.
12 Ibid., p. 88 (my emphasis).
13 *Consciousness and the Acquisition of Language*, p. 58 (henceforth cited as *CAL*).
14 *CAL*, p. 98.
15 *CAL*, p. 99.

16 "Phenomenology and the sciences of man," in *Primacy of Perception*, p. 81.
17 Ibid., P. 83.
18 "The experience of others" (1950–51) (cited above).
19 "Indirect language and the voices of silence," in *Signs*, p. 41.
20 Ibid., p. 64.
21 Ibid., p. 67.
22 Ibid., p. 79.
23 Ibid., p. 81.
24 *The Prose of the World*, p. 48.
25 Ibid., p. 50.
26 Ibid., p. 5.
27 "The literary use of language," in *Themes from the Lectures*, p. 18.
28 *The Visible and the Invisible*, p. 270. (Fr. p. 324.)
29 Ibid., p. 154. (Fr., p. 202.)
30 "Eye and mind," in *Primacy of Perception*, p. 162.
31 Ibid., p. 169.
32 Ibid., p. 189.
33 See "Philosophy and non-philosophy since Hegel."
34 See chapter 8.
35 *Phenomenology of Perception*, p. 179. (Fr., p. 209.)
36 *CAL*, p. 31.
37 *CAL*, p. 42–3.
38 "Indirect language and the voices of silence," in *Signs*, p. 53.
39 *The Visible and the Invisible*, p. 155. (Fr., p. 203.)

10 SARTRE'S WORDS ON THE SELF

1 Michel Foucault in *The Order of Things* (New York: Vintage, 1970), originally published as *Les Mots et les choses* (Paris: Gallimard, 1966), speaks of the epistemé as the conceptual scheme or pattern of knowledge characteristic of different periods within Western thought. Sometimes the term paradigm, as employed by Thomas S. Kuhn in *The Structure of Scientific Revolutions* (Chicago: University of Chicago Press, 1962), is substituted for epistemé. The correlation is suggested by Jean Piaget in his *Que sais-je?* volume on *Structuralism*, trans. C. Maschler (New York: Harper & Row, 1970), p. 132. Kuhn speaks of a paradigm as that model of scientific thought under which ordinary scientists work and out of which the extraordinary scientist must break. Although both Foucault and Kuhn are speaking of epistemological time slices within history, Piaget himself directs his genetic epistemology at stages in child development. That Piaget's work deals with the individual, with personal levels of thought, approximates more closely in this particular respect what I am proposing concerning Sartre's development. Kierkegaard's notion of "stages in life's way" is perhaps also worthy of mention. What I am suggesting by my use of the terms epistemé and paradigm is that in Sartre's work there are

different stages of thought in which the relationship between language and self forms different (but comparable) structures.

2 Jean-Paul Sartre, *The Transcendence of the Ego*, trans. F. Williams and R. Kirkpatrick (New York: Noonday, 1957).

3 For a more fully developed discussion of Husserl's notion of the self, see chapter 1.

4 The phenomenological field is referred to as the "transcendental field" by Sartre and is to be distinguished from what Merleau-Ponty calls the "phenomenal field" in *Phenomenology of Perception*, trans. C. Smith (London: Routledge & Kegan Paul, 1962). Merleau-Ponty's conception also includes bodily experience in addition to the Husserlian and Sartrian non-reified consciousness.

5 The expression "catching the ego red-handed" was suggested by Professor Algis Mickunas in "The concept of transparency in Husserl," given during the Husserl Circle meetings, 4–5 April, 1975, at the State University of New York at Stony Brook.

6 All thetic acts are noetic; but, as Sartre shows, not all noetic acts are thetic.

7 Merleau-Ponty writes: "Consider the example in Stendhal's *The Charterhouse of Parma* when the Count fears the first word of love that will confirm the young couple's feelings, which as yet have not been verbally expressed." See Merleau-Ponty, *Consciousness and the Acquisition of Language*, trans. Hugh J. Silverman (Evanston: Northwestern University Press, 1973), pp. 4–5.

8 Jean-Paul Sartre, *Being and Nothingness*, trans. Hazel E. Barnes (New York: Philosophical Library, 1956), p. 103; hereafter incorporated into the main text as BN. Original French edition: *L'Etre et le néant* (Paris: Gallimard, 1943), p. 148; hereafter cited with an "Fr.," abbreviation, as in the case of each original French edition.

9 Jean-Paul Sartre, *What is Literature?*, trans. B. Frechtman (New York: Harper & Row, Colophon Edition, 1965), p. 45; hereafter incorporated as WL. Original French: "*Qu'est-ce que la littérature?*," in *Situations, II* (Paris: Gallimard, 1948), p. 101.

10 Jean-Paul Sartre, *Dirty Hands*, trans. Lionel Abel, in *No Exit and Three Other Plays* (New York: Knopf, Vintage Books, 1949), p. 142. Original French: *Les Mains sales* (Paris: Gallimard, 1948), p. 33.

11 See Maurice Merleau-Ponty, *Humanism and Terror*, trans. John O'Neill (Boston: Beacon Press, 1969).

12 Jean-Paul Sartre, Forward to Jean Genet, *The Thief's Journal*, trans. B. Frechtman (New York: Grove Press, 1964), p. 7. Note that the "foreword" is a word before other words: the other words in this case are those of Genet's autobiography.

13 Jean-Paul Sartre, *Saint Genet*, trans. B. Frechtman (New York: Braziller, 1963), p. 85; hereafter incorporated as SG. Original French: *Saint Genet: comédien et martyr* (Paris: Gallimard, 1952), p. 86.

14 Jean-Paul Sartre, *Search for a Method*, trans. H. Barnes (New York: Knopf, Vintage Books, 1963), p. 9; hereafter incorporated as SM.

Original French: *Questions de méthode* in *Critique de la raison dialectique* (Paris: Gallimard, 1960), p. 18.

15 Roland Barthes, *Elements of Semiology*, trans. A. Lavers and C. Smith (Boston: Beacon Press, 1967), pp. 9–11.

16 Jean-Paul Sartre, "Kierkegaard: the singular universal," in *Between Existentialism and Marxism*, trans. John Mathews (New York: Pantheon, 1974), pp. 141–69. Original French: "L'Universel singulier," in *Situations, IX* (Paris: Gallimard, 1972), pp. 152–90.

17 For the distinction between self and man, see chapter 3. Also see chapter 11 for a study of Sartre's formulation of the Saussurian signifier/signified relation.

18 Jean-Paul Sartre, *The Condemned of Altona*, trans. Sylvia Leeson and George Leeson (New York: Knopf, Vintage Books, 1961), p. 60; hereafter incorporated as CA. Original French: *Les Séquestres d'Altona* (Paris: Gallimard, 1960), p. 128.

19 Jean-Paul Sartre, *The Words*, trans. B. Frechtman (Greenwich, Conn.: Fawcett Premier, 1964), p. 160; hereafter incorporated as W. Original French: *Les Mots* (Paris: Gallimard, 1964), p. 213.

20 See Jean-Paul Sartre, *Life/Situations: Essays Written and Spoken*, trans. Paul Auster and Lydia Davis (New York: Pantheon, 1977); and especially "Self-portrait at seventy," pp. 4–92. Original French: *Situations, X* (Paris: Gallimard, 1975). See also *On a raison de se revolter*, discussions with Phillipe Gavi and Pierre Victor (Paris: Gallimard, 1974), and *Sartre: By Himself*, trans. Richard Seaver, a film directed by Alexandre Astruc and Michel Contat (New York: Urizen Books, 1978). Original French: *Sartre* (Paris, Gallimard, 1977).

11 SARTRE AND THE STRUCTURALISTS

1 The interview by P. Verstraeten first appeared in the *Review d'Esthétique*, 1965. It is reprinted in Jean-Paul Sartre, *Situations IX*, (Paris: Gallimard, 1972), pp. 47–8. This and any subsequent note in which no English reference is given signifies that the translation is mine.

2 Note how this Sartrian view of the signification/meaning distinction differs from that offered by Merleau-Ponty. See particularly chapter 5. For Sartre signification and meaning are effectively synonymous. Sartre's minimal stress on the body and hence *sens* (meaning) renders *signification* the more dominant (epistemological) formulation— particularly when understood as an *inversion* of the Saussurian conception.

3 Jean-Paul Sartre, *The Transcendence of the Ego*, trans. Forrest Williams and Robert Kirkpatrick (New York: Noonday, 1957). A French version of this article is entitled *La Transcendence de l'ego: esquisse d'une déscription phénoménologique* (Paris: Vrin, 1966).

4 Jean-Paul Sartre, *Being and Nothingness*, trans. Hazel Barnes (New York: Washington Square, 1966). Originally *L'Etre et le néant* (Paris:

Notes

Gallimard, 1943). Henceforth cited as *EN* for the original and *BN* for the translation.

5 *Néant* has the same etymological implication as "nothing:" a negated thing, a non-entity.

6 Jean-Paul Sartre, *La Nausée* (Paris: Gallimard, 1938), pp. 185–6.

7 Jean-Paul Sartre, "L'Universal singulier," *Kierkegaard vivant* (Paris: Gallimard, 1966), pp. 20–63. Two English translations have been published: (1) "The singular universal," *Kierkegaard: A Collection of Critical Essays*, ed. Josiah Thompson (New York: Doubleday Anchor, 1972), pp. 230–65; and (2) "Kierkegaard: the singular universal," *Between Existentialism and Marxism*, trans. J. Mathews (New York: Pantheon, 1974), pp. 141–69. Henceforth cited from the original French as *US*. Note that the essay was presented at a UNESCO conference in 1964, three years after Merleau-Ponty's death. Although he did not attend, Heidegger also contributed an essay for the conference.

8 Sartre, "L'Universal singulier," p. 50. The passage quoted is modified from the translation in *Between Existentialism and Marxism*, p. 160. Sartre uses the term *sens* instead of *signification*. Both are translated here as "meaning." *Sens* is perhaps closer to what can be called "human meaning" as opposed to "linguistic meaning."

9 This prior condition is not evident in Sartre's earlier presentation of being. It is conceivable that being-in-itself exists without being-for-itself to know it. Signification and meaning require the co-givenness of signified and signifying processes for its very possibility.

10 Jean-Paul Sartre, "Entretiens sur moi-même," *Situations*, X (Paris: Gallimard, 1976), p. 146. Henceforth cited as "Entretiens."

11 See, for example, A. Stern, *Sartre: His Philosophy and Existential Psychoanalysis* (New York: Delta, 1967).

12 First published in *Les Temps Modernes* (April 1969), the transcript is included in *Between Existentialism and Marxism* as "Psychoanalytic Dialogue," pp. 199–223. Henceforth cited as "Psychoanalytic Dialogue."

13 J.-P. Sartre, "J.-P. Sartre répond," *L'arc*, no. 30 (1966), pp. 91–2. The whole issue is devoted to essays on Sartre's work. Henceforth cited as *Sartre répond*.

14 See, for example, Jacques Lacan, "Le Sinthome," *Ornicar?* (1976), pp. 3–20. This comprises Lacan's 18 November and 9 December 1975 lectures. We note also how, in the psychoanalytic situation, the "bar" between the signifier and the signified inhibits a direct meaning relation. Hence, the signifying chain presents, at most, symptoms of a signifying activity.

15 See J. Lacan, "The insistence of the letter in the unconscious," *The Structuralists from Marx to Lévi-Strauss*, ed. Richard and Fernande De George (New York: Anchor, 1972), pp. 287–323.

16 It is actually Derrida who works out the notion of a decentered subject in "Structure, sign, and play," *The Structuralist Controversy*, ed. Richard Macksey and Eugenio Donato (Baltimore: Johns Hopkins

University Press, 1972), pp. 247–72. The essay was given at the Johns Hopkins conference the same year as Sartre's 1966 interview. See chapter 16 for more detail.

17 Sartre, "The itinerary of a thought," *Between Existentialism and Marxism*, p. 41. The interview first appeared in the *New Left Review*, no. 58 (1969). Henceforth cited as "Itinerary."

18 See Klaus Hartmann, "Lévi-Strauss and Sartre," *Journal of the British Society for Phenomenology*, vol. 2, no. 3 (1971), pp. 37–45; Lawrence Rosen, "Language, history, and the logic of inquiry in the works of Lévi-Strauss and Sartre," *The Unconscious in Culture*, ed. Ino Rossi (New York: Dutton, 1974), pp. 389–423; Jean Pouillon, "Sartre et Lévi-Strauss," *L'Arc*, no. 26 (1965), pp. 55–60; and Lionel Abel, "Sartre vs. Lévi-Strauss," *The Anthropologist as Hero*, ed. E. N. and J. Hayes (Cambridge, Mass.: MIT Press, 1970), pp. 235–64.

19 Claude Lévi-Strauss, *The Savage Mind* (Chicago: University of Chicago Press, 1966), pp. 245–69. Henceforth cited as *Savage Mind*.

20 Sartre, "*Détermination et liberté*," *Les Ecrits de Sartre*, ed. Michel Contat and Michel Rybalka (Paris: Gallimard, 1970), p. 743.

21 See chapter 14.

22 "Structuralist activity" is the term employed by Roland Barthes in *Partisan Review*, no. 34 (Winter, 1967), pp. 80–8 to indicate that structuralism is indeed a form of *praxis*—which we might associate here, in conclusion, with the Sartrian *praxis* of dialectical reason.

12 SARTRE/PIAGET: BIOGRAPHICAL SITUATIONS, COGNITIVE STRUCTURES AND HUMAN DEVELOPMENT

1 Jean-Paul Sartre, *The Words*, trans. Bernard Frechtman (Greenwich, Conn.: Fawcett, 1964), p. 95.

2 Jean Piaget, "Time and intellectual development," *The Child and Reality:Problems of Genetic Psychology*, trans. Arnold Rosin (New York: Viking, 1973), p. 11.

3 Jean-Paul Sartre, *Being and Nothingness*, trans. Hazel Barnes (New York: Washington Square Press, 1966), p. 717.

4 Sartre, *Being and Nothingness*, p. 721.

5 Jean-Paul Sartre, *Baudelaire*, trans. Martin Turnell (New York: New Directions, 1950), p. 18.

6 Jean-Paul Sartre, "Childhood of a leader," *The Wall*, trans. Lloyd Alexander (New York: New Directions, 1948), p. 100.

7 Jean Piaget, "Child praxis," *The Child and Reality*, p. 63.

8 Jean Piaget, *Structuralism*, trans. Chaninah Maschler (New York: Harper & Row, 1970), pp. 3–16.

9 Jean Piaget, "Time and intellectual development," *The Child and Reality*, p. 11.

10 Jean Piaget, "Genesis and structure in the psychology of intelligence,"

Six Psychological Studies, trans. Anita Tenzer, ed. David Elkind (New York: Vintage, 1968), p. 147.

11 Piaget, "Genesis and Structure," *Six Psychological Studies*, p. 147.
12 Jean Piaget, *Genetic Epistemology*, trans. Eleanor Duckworth (New York: Norton, 1970), p. 15.
13 Jean Piaget, *Biology and Knowledge: An Essay on the Relations between Organic Regulations and Cognitive Processes*, trans. Beatrix Walsh (Chicago: University of Chicago Press, 1971), pp. 8–9.
14 Jean Piaget, *The Development of Thought: Equilibration of Cognitive Structures*, trans. Arnold Rosin (New York: Viking, 1977), pp. 9–10.
15 See chapter 11.
16 Jean-Paul Sartre, *L'Idiot de la famille: Gustave Flaubert de 1821 à 1857*, vol. 1 (Paris: Gallimard, 1971), p. 51.
17 Lillian Hellman, *Pentimento: A Book of Portraits* (New York: Signet, 1973), p. 1.

13 SARTRE/BARTHES: WRITING DIFFERENCES

1 See Jean-Paul Sartre, *What is Literature?*, trans. Bernard Frechtman (New York: Harper & Row, 1965), pp. 1–31, and Roland Barthes, *Writing Degree Zero*, trans. Annette Lavers and Colin Smith (New York: Hill & Wang, 1967), pp. 9–18. In translation, both of these chapters are entitled "What is Writing?" Susan Sontag even remarks in her preface to Barthes's book that "both Sartre's first chapter and the first section of *Writing Degree Zero* have the same title: ('What is Writing?')" (p. xv). She does not notice (establish and interpret) the difference.
2 Sartre, *What is Literature?*, p. 40.
3 Sartre, *What is Literature?*, p. 58.
4 See Barthes, *Elements of Semiology*, trans. Annette Lavers and Colin Smith (Boston: Beacon Press, 1967), p. 14.
5 Barthes, *Elements of Semiology*, p. 14.
6 Barthes, *Writing Degree Zero*, p. 11. French edition (Paris: Editions du Seuil, 1953), p. 12.
7 Barthes, *Writing Degree Zero*, p. 10.
8 Barthes, *Writing Degree Zero*, p. 88.
9 See Jean-Paul Sartre, *Search for a Method*, trans. Hazel Barnes (New York: Vintage, 1963).
10 Barthes, *Writing Degree Zero*, p. 88.
11 Jean-Paul Sartre, "On *The Idiot of the Family*," *Life/Situations*, trans. Paul Auster and Lydia Davis (New York: Pantheon, 1977), p. 131.
12 Sartre, *Search for a Method*, p. 147.
13 Sartre, *Search for a Method*, p. 181.
14 Jean-Paul Sartre, "The purposes of writing," *Between Existentialism and Marxism*, trans. John Mathews (New York: Pantheon, 1974). p. 26.
15 Sartre, "The purposes of writing," p. 25.

16 Sartre, "The purposes of writing," p. 31.
17 Jean-Paul Sartre, "A plea for intellectuals," *Between Existentialism and Marxism*, p. 283.
18 Sartre, "A plea for intellectuals," p. 285.
19 Jean-Paul Sartre, "The itinerary of a thought," *Between Existentialism and Marxism*, p. 285.
20 Roland Barthes, "*Littérature, Aujourd'hui,*" *Essais critiques* (Paris: Editions du Seuil, 1964), p. 155.
21 Roland Barthes, "From work to text," *Image/Music/Text*, trans. Stephen Heath (New York: Hill & Wang, 1977), p. 164.
22 Barthes, "From work to text," p. 164.
23 Roland Barthes, *Critique et vérité* (Paris: Editions du Seuil, 1966), p. 53.
24 Barthes, *Critique et vérité*, p. 55.
25 This is the direction which Barthes initiates in *The Lover's Discourse*, trans. Richard Howard (New York: Hill & Wang, 1978).
26 Roland Barthes, *The Pleasure of the Text*, trans. Richard Miller (New York: Hill & Wang, 1975), pp. 35–6.
27 Roland Barthes, *Sade/Fourier/Loyola*, trans. Richard Miller (New York: Hill & Wang, 1976).

14 SARTRE/FOUCAULT: DIALECTIC AND EPISTEME

1 Jean-Paul Sartre, *Search for a Method*, trans. Hazel Barnes (New York: Vintage, 1963), pp. 133–4.
2 The example of Flaubert is developed initially in *Search for a Method*, pp. 140–50, and at much greater length in Sartre's three-volume *L'Idiot de la famille* (Paris: Gallimard, 1971–2).
3 Ibid., pp. 154–5.
4 Ibid., p. 150.
5 Ibid., p. 152.
6 Michel Foucault, *The Archaeology of Knowledge*, trans. A. M. Sheridan Smith (New York: Pantheon, 1972), p. 131.
7 Michel Foucault, "History, discourse, and discontinuity," *Salmagundi*, no. 20 (Summer–Fall 1972), p. 227.
8 Foucault's essay appeared in 1968 as a justification for his own approach in *The Order of Things* (1966), while Sartre's position had been set forth in 1957 and elaborated in his *Critique of Dialectical Reason* (1960).
9 Foucault, *The Archaeology of Knowledge*, p. 9.
10 Ibid., p. 10.
11 Foucault, *The Order of Things*, trans. anon. (New York: Vintage, 1970), p. 308.
12 Jacques Derrida, "Structure, sign, and play in the discourse of the human sciences," *The Structuralist Controversy*, ed. Richard Macksey and Eugenio Donato (Baltimore: Johns Hopkins University Press, 1972), pp. 247–72.

Notes

13 Jean-Paul Sartre, "The singular universal," *Between Existentialism and Marxism*, trans. John Mathews (New York: Pantheon, 1974), pp. 141–69.
14 Jean-Paul Sartre, *Transcendence of the Ego*, trans. Forrest Williams and Robert Kirkpatrick (New York: Noonday, 1957).

16 THE LIMITS OF LOGOCENTRISM

1 Jacques Derrida, *Of Grammatology*, trans. G. Spivak (Baltimore: Johns Hopkins University Press, 1976), p. 15.
2 Ibid., p. 20. To avoid confusion, I have changed Spivak's "being" to "Being" as the translation of *être* corresponding to Heidegger's *Sein*.
3 Philippe Lacoue-Labarthe has developed the particular relation between truth and lie in "The fable (literature and philosophy)," trans. Hugh J. Silverman, *Research in Phenomenology*, vol. 14 (1985), pp. 43–60.
4 For Derrida's discussion of these three types of end, see "The ends of man" in *Margins of Philosophy*, trans. Alan Bass (Chicago:University of Chicago Press, 1982), pp. 111–36.
5 See, for example, "What is meant by the talk about the end of philosophy? We understand the end of something all too easily in the negative sense as a mere stopping, as the lack of continuation, perhaps even as decline and impotence. In contrast, what we say about the end of philosophy means the completion of metaphysics." This passage occurs in Martin Heidegger, "The end of philosophy and the task of thinking," *On Time and Being*, trans. Joan Stambaugh (New York: Harper & Row, 1972), p. 56. See also *The End of Philosophy*, trans. J. Stambaugh (New York: Harper & Row, 1973).
6 Heidegger is not the only participant in the delineation of the relationship between philosophy and non-philosophy. See, for example, Maurice Merleau-Ponty, "Philosophy and non-philosophy since Hegel," trans. Hugh J. Silverman, *Telos*, no. 29 (Fall 1976), pp. 42–129. See also chapters 7 and 8.
7 See chapter 17.
8 M. Heidegger, "Logos," *Early Greek Thinking*, trans. David Farrell Krell and Frank A. Capuzzi (New York: Harper & Row, 1975), p. 77. *Vorträge und Aufsätze*, Teil III (Pfullingen: Neske, 1954), p. 24.
9 See Paul de Man, "The epistemology of metaphor," *Critical Inquiry*, vol. 5, no. 1 (Autumn 1978), pp. 13–30.
10 Heidegger, "Logos," p. 72.
11 See chapter 4.
12 M. Heidegger, "Language," *Poetry, Language, Thought*, trans. Albert Hofstadter (New York: Harper & Row, 1971), p. 210.
13 Heidegger, "Logos," p. 77.
14 Ibid., p. 75.
15 A further elaboration of this aspect can be found in chapter 3.

369

16 Heidegger, "Language," p. 190.
17 Ibid., p. 210.

17 SELF-DECENTERING: DERRIDA INCORPORATED

1 Jacques Derrida, "La Différance," *Tel Quel: Theorie d'ensemble* (Paris: Editions du Seuil, 1968), pp. 41–66.
2 *"La Différance,"* in Jacques Derrida, *Marges de la philosophie* (Paris: Minuit, 1972), pp. 1–29. The English translation by David B. Allison is published in *Speech and Phenomena* (Evanston: Northwestern University Press, 1973), pp. 129–60.
3 Derrida, *Marges de la philosophie*, p. 7.
4 Allison, *Speech and Phenomena*, p. 129n.
5 Jacques Derrida, *Of Grammatology*, trans. Gayatri Chakravorty Spivak (Baltimore: Johns Hopkins University Press, 1976), p. 21.
6 Derrida, *De la Grammatologie* (Paris: Minuit, 1967), p. 34. Henceforth cited as *DG*.
7 The spectrum of existing translations of the difference between *Sein* and *Seiende* include Being/being, being/essent, being/entity, etc. For further details see note 5 to chapter 2.
8 In chapter 3, I have shown that for Heidegger, the self holds the place of Dasein in the ontological difference. Since Dasein is characterized as existential ambiguity in chapter 2, it can be assumed that the existential or human ambiguity (of the ontological difference) is the place in which the Heideggerian self occurs.
9 Newton Garver, "Preface," *Speech and Phenomena*, pp. ix-xxix.
10 Interview with Jacques Derrida, conducted by J. L. Houdebine and Guy Scarpetta, entitled "Positions," and included in the small book with the same title, trans. Alan Bass (Chicago: University of Chicago Press, 1981), pp. 39–40. The translation offered here is taken from the earlier version given in *Diacritics*, vol. 1, no. 4 (Winter 1972) p. 35. The interview was originally published in *Promesse*, nos. 30–1 (Fall-Winter 1971), pp. 7–63 and in 1972 as a book by Editions de Minuit.
11 Jacques Derrida, "Limited Inc. a b c . . . ," *Glyph II*, ed. Samuel Weber and Henry Sussman (Baltimore: Johns Hopkins University Press, 1977), pp.162–254. This essay constitutes Derrida's response to the reply by John Searle to Derrida's "Signature event context," both of which were published in *Glyph I*.
12 To avoid confusion, I change Spivak's "being" to "Being."
13 See chapter 8 for an account of Merleau-Ponty's position at the fringe of structuralism and post-structuralism.
14 Jacques Derrida, "Structure, sign, and play in the discourse of the human sciences," *The Structuralist Controversy*, ed. Richard Macksey and Eugenio Donato (Baltimore: Johns Hopkins University Press, 1972), pp. 247–72. Also in *Writing and Difference*, trans. Alan Bass (Chicago: University of Chicago Press, 1978), pp. 278–93.

Notes

15 Jacques Derrida, "The purveyor of truth," *Yale French Studies*, no. 52 (1975), pp. 31–113. The issue is entitled "Graphesis: perspectives in literature and philosophy," ed. Marie-Rose Logan. Henceforth cited as *Purveyor*.

16 For an outline of this transcendental-constituting self concept as a pro-ontological type (along with the absolute-universal and the organic-natural self concepts) in opposition to the de-ontological type, see my article (co-authored with David Dilworth), "A cross-cultural approach to the de-ontological self paradigm," *The Monist*, vol. 61, no. 1 (January 1978), pp. 82–95.

17 A more fully elaborated delineation of the position of the Husserlian self can be found in chapter 1.

18 See Michel Foucault, *The Order of Things: An Archeology of the Human Sciences* (New York: Vintage, 1973). Henceforth cited as *OT*.

19 Jacques Derrida, "The ends of man," trans. E. Morot-Sir, W. C. Piersol, H. L. Dreyfus and B. Reid, *Philosophy and Phenomenological Research*, vol. 30, no. 1 (September 1969), pp. 31–57. Henceforth cited as *EM*.

20 See, for example, Albert Hofstadter, "Enownment," *Boundary 2*, vol. 4, (Winter 1976), pp. 357–77, and his translator's introduction to Martin Heidegger, *Poetry, Language, Thought* (New York: Harper & Row, 1971), esp. pp. xvii-xxii. In both of these instances Hofstadter emphasizes *das Ereignis* as the bringing about that which is "own" or "en-own-ment." In this sense, what is *eigentlich* is own-ly. I develop the link between *Eigentlichkeit* and *das Ereignis* later in this chapter.

21 Jacques Derrida, "Fors," trans. Barbara Johnson, *The Georgia Review*, vol. 11, no. 1 (Spring 1977), p. 68.

22 See the note by Barbara Johnson to her translation of "Fors," p. 64n.

23 Jacques Derrida, "White mythology: metaphor in the text of philosophy," trans. F. C. T. Moore, *New Literary History*, vol. 6, no. 1 (Autumn 1974), p. 47. Henceforth cited as *WM*.

24 Jacques Derrida, "Ousia and grammé: a note to a footnote in *Being and Time*," trans. Edward S. Casey, *Phenomenology in Perspective*, ed. F. Joseph Smith (The Hague: Nijhoff, 1970), p. 54. Henceforth cited as *Ousia*.

25 Jacques Derrida, *Spurs: Nietzsche's Styles*, trans. Barbara Harlow along with the original French *Éperons: Les Styles de Nietzsche* and translations into German and Italian, introduced by Stefano Agosti (Venice: Corbo e Fiori, 1976), p. 88. Reprinted in a bilingual edition by University of Chicago Press (1978), p. 43. Henceforth cited in the University of Chicago Press edition as *Spurs*.

26 Derrida, "Limited, Inc. a b c . . . ," pp. 163–4. Derrida actually repeats the formula several times, adding more quotation marks on each occasion.

27 Jacques Lacan, "Seminar on the 'Purloined Letter,' " trans. Jeffrey Mehlman, *Yale French Studies*, no. 48 (1972), pp. 38–72. This number, edited by Mehlman, is entitled *French Freud: Structural Studies in Psychoanalysis*.

371

18 FOUCAULT AND THE ANTHROPOLOGICAL SLEEP

1 See René Girard, *Deceit, Desire, and the Novel*, trans. Yvonne Freccero (Baltimore: Johns Hopkins University Press, 1965).
2 Michel Foucault, *The Archeology of Knowledge*, trans. A. M. Sheridan Smith (New York: Pantheon, 1972), p. 131. Henceforth cited as *AK*.
3 Michel Foucault, *The Order of Things: An Archeology of the Human Sciences*, trans. anon. (New York: Vintage, 1970). See pp. 250–302. Hereafter cited as *OT*.
4 See Jacques Lacan, "The insistence of the letter in the unconscious," *The Structuralists from Marx to Lévi-Strauss*, ed. Richard and Fernande DeGeorge (New York: Anchor, 1972), pp. 310–11 and 318–23.
5 See Jacques Derrida, "Structure, sign, and play in the discourse of the human sciences," *The Structuralist Controversy*, ed. Richard Macksey and Eugenio Donato (Baltimore: Johns Hopkins University Press, 1972), pp. 242–72. Henceforth cited as *Derrida*. See also chapter 16.
6 See Arthur O. Lovejoy, *The Great Chain of Being* (New York: Harper & Row, 1936).
7 See George Boas, *Vox Populi: Essays in the History of an Idea* (Baltimore: Johns Hopkins University Press, 1969).
8 See John Passmore, *The Perfectibility of Man* (New York: Scribner's, 1969).
9 Foucault, "History, discourse, and discontinuity," *Salmagundi*, no. 20 (Summer-Fall 1972), p. 228.

19 FROM UTOPIA/DYSTOPIA TO HETEROTOPIA: AN INTERPRETIVE TOPOLOGY

1 Louis Marin, "Disneyland: a degenerate utopia," *Glyph I* (Baltimore: Johns Hopkins University Press, 1977), p. 65. See also Marin's *Utopics: Spatial Play*, trans. Robert Vollrath (Atlantic Highlands, New Jersey: Humanities Press, 1984). This is vol. 1 in the Humanities-Macmillan "Contemporary Studies in Philosophy and the Human Sciences" series.
2 Michel Foucault, *The Order of Things* (New York: Vintage, 1970), p. xviii.

20 FOR A HERMENEUTIC SEMIOLOGY OF THE SELF

1 Paul Ricoeur, "The question of the subject," trans. Kathleen McLaughlin, in *The Conflict of Interpretations*, ed. Don Ihde (Evanston: Northwestern University Press, 1974), p. 264.

2 Edward W. Said, *Beginnings* (New York: Basic Books, 1975).

3 See Jean-Paul Sartre, *The Transcendence of the Ego*, trans. Forrest Williams and Robert Kirkpatrick (New York: Noonday, 1957).

4 See Maurice Merleau-Ponty, *The Visible and the Invisible*, trans. Alphonso Lingis (Evanston: Northwestern University Press, 1968).

5 Ferdinand de Saussure, *Course in General Linguistics*, trans. Wade Baskin (New York: McGraw-Hill, 1959).

6 Roland Barthes, *Elements of Semiology*, trans. Annette Lavers and Colin Smith (Boston: Beacon Press, 1967), p. 11.

7 Anthony Wilden, *The Language of the Self* (Baltimore: Johns Hopkins University Press, 1968).

8 See Frederick J. Hoffman, *Samuel Beckett: The Language of Self* (New York: Dutton, 1964).

9 Ricoeur, "The question of the subject," p. 246.

10 Jacques Lacan, "The insistence of the letter in the unconscious," in *The Structuralists: From Marx to Lévi-Strauss*, ed. Richard and Fernande De George (New York: Doubleday Anchor, 1972), p. 297.

11 Jean-Paul Sartre, *Being and Nothingness*, trans. Hazel Barnes (New York: Washington Square Press, 1953).

12 See Merleau-Ponty's use of this expression in the context of the child's language acquisition in *Consciousness and the Acquisition of Language*, trans. Hugh J. Silverman (Evanston: Northwestern University Press, 1973), pp. 16–18, 47–8 and 50. I have translated "prise de conscience" alternatively as "sudden consciousness" and "coming to consciousness." See also Jean Piaget, *The Grasp of Consciousness: Action and Concept in the Young Child* (Cambridge, Mass.: Harvard University Press, 1976).

13 Paul Ricoeur, "Heidegger and the subject," in *The Conflict of Interpretation*, p. 228.

14 Michel Foucault, *The Order of Things* (New York: Vintage, 1970), chapters 1 and 9.

15 See Jacques Derrida, *Speech and Phenomena*, trans. David B. Allison (Evanston: Northwestern University Press, 1973), and *De la Grammatologie* (Paris: Minuit, 1967).

16 See Jacques Derrida, "Structure, sign, and play in the discourse of the human sciences," in *The Structuralist Controversy*, ed. Richard Macksey and Eugenio Donato (Baltimore: Johns Hopkins University Press).

17 See Claude Lévi-Strauss, *The Savage Mind* (Chicago: University of Chicago Press, 1966).

18 In the preface to *The Order of Things*, Foucault writes: "man is only a recent invention, a figure not yet two centuries old, a new wrinkle in our knowledge, and he will disappear again as soon as that knowledge has discovered a new form" (p. xxiii).

19 See, for example, Noam Chomsky, *Language and Mind*, enlarged edition (New York: Harcourt, Brace, Jovanovich, 1972).

20 Lacan, "The insistence of the letter in the unconscious," p. 311.

21 Samuel Beckett, "Malone dies," in *Three Novels*, trans. Samuel

Beckett (New York: Grove, 1956). See also my "Beckett, philosophy, and the self," in *The Philosophical Reflection of Man in Literature, Analecta Husserliana* (Dordrecht: Reidel, 1982), pp. 153–60.

BIBLIOGRAPHY

ABEL, Lionel, "Sartre vs. Lévi-Strauss," in *The Anthropologist as Hero*, ed. E. N. and J. Hayes (Cambridge, Mass.: MIT Press, 1970).

ALAIN, *Eléments de philosophie* (Paris: Gallimard, 1941).

ALQUIE, Ferdinand, "*Une Philosophie de l'ambiguïté*," in *Fontaine*, vol. 11, no. 59 (April 1947).

BARTHES, Roland, *Essais critiques* (Paris: Editions du Seuil, 1964).

BARTHES, Roland, *On Racine*, trans. Richard Howard (New York: Hill & Wang, 1964).

BARTHES, Roland, *Critique et verité* (Paris: Editions du Seuil, 1966).

BARTHES, Roland, *Elements of Semiology*, trans. Annette Lavers and Colin Smith (Boston: Beacon Press, 1967).

BARTHES, Roland, *Writing Degree Zero*, trans. Annette Lavers and Colin Smith (New York: Hill & Wang, 1967).

BARTHES, Roland, *S/Z*, trans. Richard Miller (New York: Hill & Wang, 1974).

BARTHES, Roland, *The Pleasure of the Text*, trans. Richard Miller (New York: Hill & Wang, 1975).

BARTHES, Roland, *Sade/Fourier/Loyola*, trans. Richard Miller (New York: Hill & Wang, 1976).

BARTHES, Roland, *Image/Music/Text*, trans. Stephen Heath (New York: Hill & Wang, 1977).

BARTHES, Roland, *The Lover's Discourse*, trans. Richard Howard (New York: Hill & Wang, 1978).

BARTHES, Roland, *Roland Barthes*, trans. Richard Howard (New York: Hill & Wang, 1981).

BARTHES, Roland, *The Fashion System*, trans. Matthew Ward and Richard Howard (New York: Hill & Wang, 1983).

BECKETT, Samuel, *Three Novels*, trans. Samuel Beckett (New York: Grove, 1956).

BERGSON, Henri, *Time and Free Will: An Essay on the Immediate Data of Consciousness* (1889), trans. F. L. Pogson (New York: Harper Torchbooks, 1960).

BIEMEL, Walter, *Martin Heidegger: An Illustrated Study*, trans. J. L. Mehta (New York: Harcourt Brace Jovanovich, 1976, p. 27).

BLEICHER, Josef, *Contemporary Hermeneutics: Hermeneutics as Method, Philosophy, and Critique* (London and Boston: Routledge & Kegan Paul, 1980).

BOAS, George, *Vox Populi: Essays in the History of an Idea* (Baltimore: Johns Hopkins University Press, 1969).

CASEY, Edward S., *Imagining: A Phenomenological Study* (Bloomington: Indiana University Press, 1976).

CHOMSKY, Noam, *Language and Mind*, enlarged edition (New York: Harcourt Brace Jovanovich, 1972).

DE GEORGE, Richard and Fernande (eds), *The Structuralists* (New York: Anchor, 1972).

DELEUZE, Gilles, *Empirisme et subjectivité* (Paris: Presses Universitaires de France, 1953).

DELEUZE, Gilles, *Présentation de Sacher-Masoch* (Paris: Presses Universitaires de France, 1967).

DELEUZE, Gilles, *Logique du sens* (Paris: Minuit, 1969).

DELEUZE, Gilles, *Spinoza et le problème de l'expression* (Paris: Minuit, 1969).

DELEUZE, Gilles, *Kant's Critical Philosophy*, trans. Hugh Tomlinson and Barbara Habberjam (Minneapolis: University of Minnesota Press, 1984).

DERRIDA, Jacques, *Speech and Phenomena*, trans. David B. Allison (Evanston: Northwestern University Press, 1973).

DERRIDA, Jacques, "The purveyor of truth," in *Yale French Studies*, no, 52 (1975).

DERRIDA, Jacques, *Of Grammatology*, trans, G. Spivak (Baltimore: Johns Hopkins University Press, 1976).

DERRIDA, Jacques, *Spurs: Nietzsche's Styles*, trans. Barbara Harlow, along with the original French *Eperons: Les Styles de Nietzsche* and translations into German and Italian (Venice: Corbo e Fiori, 1976).

DERRIDA, Jacques, "Fors," trans. Barbara Johnson, in *The Georgia Review*, vol. 11, no. 1 (Spring 1977).

DERRIDA, Jacques, *Writing and Difference*, trans. Alan Bass (Chicago: University of Chicago Press, 1978).

DERRIDA, Jacques, *Dissemination*, trans. Barbara Johnson (Chicago: University of Chicago Press, 1981).

DERRIDA, Jacques, *Positions*, trans. Alan Bass (Chicago: University of Chicago Press, 1981).

DERRIDA, Jacques, *Margins of Philosophy*, trans. Alan Bass (Chicago: University of Chicago Press, 1982).

DE SAUSSURE, Ferdinand, *Course in General Linguistics*, trans. Wade Baskin (New York: McGraw-Hill, 1959).

DE WAELHENS, Alphonse, "Une Philosophie de l'ambiquïté," in

Maurice Merleau-Ponty, *La Structure du comportement* (1942), 2nd edn (Paris: Presses Universitaires de France, 1949).

DILWORTH, David and Silverman, Hugh J., "A cross-cultural approach to the de-ontological self paradigm," in *The Monist*, vol. 61, no. 1 (January 1978), pp. 82–95.

DREYFUS, H. and Todes, P. "The existential critique of objectivity," in *Patterns of the Life-World*, ed. J. M. Edie, G. M. Parker, and C. O. Schrag (Evanston: Northwestern University Press, 1970).

EDIE, James M., *Speaking and Meaning: The Phenomenology of Language* (Bloomington: Indiana University Press, 1976).

FØLLESDAL, Dagfin, "Husserl's notion of noema," *Journal of Philosophy*, vol. 66, no. 20 (16 October 1979).

FOUCAULT, Michel, *The Order of Things* (New York: Vintage, 1970).

FOUCAULT, Michel, "History, discourse, and discontinuity," *Salmgundi*, no. 20 (Summer-Fall 1972).

FOUCAULT, Michel, *The Archeology of Knowledge*, trans. A. M. Sheridan Smith (New York: Pantheon, 1972).

FOUCAULT, Michel, *The Birth of the Clinic*, trans. A. M. Sheridan Smith (New York: Vintage, 1975).

FOUCAULT, Michel, *Discipline and Punish*, trans. Alan Sheridan (New York: Random House, 1977).

FOUCAULT, Michel, *History of Sexuality*, vol. 1, trans. Robert Hurley (New York: Vintage, 1980).

FOUCAULT, Michel, *Power/Knowledge*, trans. Colin Gordon, Leo Marshall, John Mepham and Kate Soper (New York: Pantheon, 1981).

GENET, Jean, *The Thief's Journal*, trans. B. Frechtman (New York: Grove Press, 1964).

GILLAN, G. (ed.), *Horizons of the Flesh* (Carbondale:Southern Illinois University Press, 1973).

GIRARD, René, *Deceit, Desire, and the Novel*, trans. Yvonne Freccero (Baltimore: Johns Hopkins University Press, 1965).

HARTMANN, Klaus, "Lévi-Strauss and Sartre," *Journal of the British Society for Phenomenology*, vol. 2, no. 3 (1971).

HEIDEGGER, Martin, *Aus der Erfahrung des Denkens* (Pfullingen: Neske, 1947).

HEIDEGGER, Martin, *Vorträge und Aufsatze*, 3 vols (Pfullingen: Neske, 1954).

HEIDEGGER, Martin, *Der Satz vom Grund* (Pfullingen: Neske, 1957).

HEIDEGGER, Martin, *The Question of Being*, trans. Jean T. Wilde and William Kluback (New Haven: College and University Publishers, 1958).

HEIDEGGER, Martin, *An Introduction to Metaphysics*, trans. Ralph Manheim (New York: Anchor, 1959).

HEIDEGGER, Martin, *Being and Time*, trans. John Macquarrie and Edward Robinson (New York: Harper & Row, 1962).

HEIDEGGER, Martin, *Kant and the Problem of Metaphysics*, trans. James S. Churchill (Bloomington: Indiana University Press, 1962).

HEIDEGGER, Martin, "Letter to Richardson," in William J. Richardson, *Heidegger: Through Phenomenology to Thought* (The Hague: Nijhoff, 1963).

HEIDEGGER, Martin, *Über den Humanismus*, bilingual edition with a translation into French by R. Munier (Paris: Aubier, 1964).

HEIDEGGER, Martin, *Vom Wesen des Grundes*, in *Wegmarken* (Frankfurt: Klostermann, 1967).

HEIDEGGER, Martin, *Qu'est-ce que la métaphysique?*, trans. Henri Corbin and R. Munier, in *Questions I* (Paris: Gallimard, 1968).

HEIDEGGER, Martin, *What is called Thinking?*, trans. F. Wieck and J. Glenn Gray (New York: Harper & Row, 1968).

HEIDEGGER, Martin, *Zeit und Sein*, in *L'Endurance de la pensée* (Paris: Plon, 1968).

HEIDEGGER, Martin, *Identity and Difference*, trans. Joan Stambaugh (New York: Harper & Row, 1969).

HEIDEGGER, Martin, transcript of *Séminaire tenu par le Professeur Martin Heidegger sur la Differenzschrift de Hegel* (Villeneuve-St. Georges: SPIT, 1969).

HEIDEGGER, Martin, *Hegel's Concept of Experience*, trans. anonymous (New York: Harper & Row, 1970).

HEIDEGGER, Martin, *Poetry, Language, Thought*, trans. Albert Hofstadter (New York: Harper & Row, 1971).

HEIDEGGER, Martin, *On Time and Being*, trans. Joan Stambaugh (New York: Harper & Row, 1972).

HEIDEGGER, Martin, *The End of Philosophy*, trans. Joan Stambaugh (New York: Harper & Row, 1973).

HEIDEGGER, Martin, *Early Greek Thinking*, trans. David Farrell Krell and Frank A. Capuzzi (New York: Harper & Row, 1975).

HEIDEGGER, Martin, *Nietzsche*, 4 vols, trans. David Farrell Krell (New York: Harper & Row, 1981–7).

HELLMAN, Lillian, *Pentimento: A Book of Portraits* (New York: Signet, 1973).

HOFFMAN, Frederick J., *Samuel Beckett: The Language of Self* (New York: Dutton, 1964).

HOFSTADTER, Albert, "Enownment," in *Boundary 2*, vol. 4 (Winter 1976).

HOWARD, Dick, *The Manyian Legacy* (New York: Unizon, 1977).

HOY, David Couzens, *The Critical Circle: Literature and History in Contemporary Hermeneutics* (Berkeley and Los Angeles: University of California Press, 1978).

HUSSERL, Edmund, *The Crisis of European Sciences* (1954), trans. David Carr (Evanston: Northwestern University Press, 1970).

HUSSERL, Edmund, *Cartesian Meditations*, trans. Dorian Cairns (The Hague: Nijhoff, 1960).

HUSSERL, Edmund, *Ideas Pertaining to a Pure Phenomenology and to a Phenomenological Philosophy*, trans. F. Kersten (The Hague: Nijhoff, 1983).

IHDE, Don, *Hermeneutic Phenomenology* (Evanston: Northwestern University Press, 1971).

KAUFMANN, Walter, *Hegel: Texts and Commentary*, with translations by Kaufmann (New York: Anchor, 1965).

KUHN, Thomas S., *The Structure of Scientific Revolutions* (Chicago: University of Chicago Press, 1962).

LACAN, Jacques, "Seminar on The Purloined Letter," trans. Jeffrey Mehlman, *Yale French Studies*, no. 48 (1972).

LACAN, Jacques, *"Le Sinthome,"* in *Ornican?* (1976).

LACOUE-LABARTHE, Philippe, "The Fable (Literature and Philosophy)," trans. Hugh J. Silverman, *Research in Phenomenology*, vol. 15 (1985), pp. 43–60.

LEFEBVRE, Henri, *"M. Merleau-Ponty et la philosophie de l'ambiguïté,"* in *La Pensée*, no. 73 (May-June 1957).

LEVIN, David Michael, *Reason and Evidence in Husserl's Phenomenology* (Evanston: Northwestern University Press, 1970).

LÉVI-STRAUSS, Claude, *The Savage Mind* (Chicago: University of Chicago Press, 1966).

LÉVI-STRAUSS, Claude, *Elementary Structures of Kinship*, trans. James Haile Bell, John Richard von Sturman and Rodney Needham (Boston: Beacon Press, 1969).

LOVEJOY, Arthur O., *The Great Chain of Being* (New York: Harper & Row, 1936).

LYOTARD, Jean-François, *La Phénoménologie* (Paris: Presses Universitaires de France, 1954).

LYOTARD, Jean-François, *Discours, figure* (Paris: Klinchsieck, 1971).

LYOTARD, Jean-François, *Dérive à parter de Marx et Freud* (Paris: 10–18, 1973).

LYOTARD, Jean-François, *Economie libidinale* (Paris: Minuit, 1974).

MACKSEY, Richard and Donato, Eugenio (eds), *The Structuralist Controversy* (Baltimore: Johns Hopkins University Press, 1972).

MARIN, Louis, *Utopics: Spatial Play*, trans. Robert Vollrath (Atlantic Highlands, New Jersey: Humanities Press, 1984).

MERLEAU-PONTY, Maurice, *Phenomenology of Perception*, trans. Colin Smith (London: Routledge & Kegan Paul, 1962).

MERLEAU-PONTY, Maurice, *The Structure of Behavior*, trans. Alden D. Fisher (Boston: Beacon Press, 1963).

MERLEAU-PONTY, Maurice, "An unpublished text," trans. Arleen B. Dallery, in *The Primacy of Perception and Other Essays*, ed. James M. Edie (Evanston: Northwestern University Press, 1964).

MERLEAU-PONTY, Maurice, *Sense and Non-sense* (1948), trans. Hubert L. Dreyfus and Patricia A. Dreyfus (Evanston: Northwestern University Press, 1964).

MERLEAU-PONTY, Maurice, *Signs*, trans. Richard C. McCleary (Evanston: Northwestern University Press, 1964).

MERLEAU-PONTY, Maurice, *L'Union de l'âme et du corps chez Malbranche, Brian et Bergson* (Paris, Vrin, 1968).

MERLEAU-PONTY, Maurice, *The Visible and the Invisible*, trans. Alphonso Lingus (Evanston: Northwestern University Press, 1968).

MERLEAU-PONTY, Maurice, *Humanism and Terror*, trans. John O'Neill (Evanston: Northwestern University Press, 1969).

MERLEAU-PONTY, Maurice, *Themes from The Lectures*, trans. John O'Neill (Evanston: Northwestern University Press, 1970).

MERLEAU-PONTY, Maurice, *Consciousness and the Acquisition of Language*, trans. Hugh J. Silverman (Evanston: Northwestern University Press, 1973).

MERLEAU-PONTY, Maurice, *The Adventures of the Dialectic*, trans. Joseph Bien (Evanston: Northwestern University Press, 1973).

MERLEAU-PONTY, Maurice, *The Prose of the World*, trans. John O'Neill (Evanston: Northwestern University Press, 1973).

MERLEAU-PONTY, Maurice. "Philosophy and non-philosophy since Hegel," trans. Hugh J. Silverman, *Telos*, no. 29 (Fall 1976).

MERLEAU-PONTY, Maurice, "The experience of others," trans. Fred Evans and Hugh J. Silverman, in *Review of Existential Psychology and Psychiatry* (1985).

METRAUX, Alexandre, "Vision and Being in the last lectures of Merleau-Ponty," in *Life-World and Consciousness*, ed. Lester E. Embree (Evanston: Northwestern University Press, 1972).

PALMER, Richard E., *Hermeneutics: Interpretation Theory in Schleiermacher, Dilthey, Heidegger, and Gadamer* (Evanston: Northwestern University Press, 1969).

PASSMORE, John, *The Perfectibility of Man* (New York: Scribner's 1969).

PIAGET, Jean, *Six Psychological Studies*, trans. Anita Tenzer, ed. David Elkind (New York: Vintage, 1968).

PIAGET, Jean, *Genetic Epistemology*, trans. Eleanor Duckworth (New York: Norton, 1970).

PIAGET, Jean, *Structuralism*, trans. Chaninah Maschler (New York: Harper & Row, 1971).

PIAGET, Jean, *Biology and Knowledge: An Essay on the Relations between Organic Regulations and Cognitive Processes*, trans. Beatrix Walsh (Chicago: University of Chicago Press, 1971).

PIAGET, Jean, *The Child and Reality: Problems of Genetic Psychology*, trans. Arnold Rosin (New York: Viking, 1973).

PIAGET, Jean, *The Grasp of Consciousness: Action and Concept in the Young Child* (Cambridge, Mass.: Harvard University Press, 1976).

PIAGET, Jean, *The Development of Thought: Equilibration of Cognitive Structures*, trans. Arnold Rosin (New York: Viking, 1977).

RICHIR, Marc, "La Défenestration" in *L'Arc*, no. 46 (1971).

RICOEUR, Paul, "The question of the subject," trans. Kathleen McLaughlin, in *The Conflict of Interpretations*, ed. Don Ihde (Evanston: Northwestern University Press, 1974).

ROBBE-GRILLET, Alain, *The Voyeur*, trans. Richard Howard (New York: Grove, 1958).

ROSEN, Lawrence, "Language, history, and the logic of inquiry in the works of Lévi-Strauss and Sartre," in *The Unconscious in Culture*, ed. Ino Rossi (New York: Dutton, 1974).

Bibliography

SAID, Edward W., *Beginnings* (New York: Basic Books, 1975).

SALLIS, John, *Merleau-Ponty: Perception, Structure, Language* (Atlantic Highlands, N.J.: Humanities Press, 1981).

SARTRE, Jean-Paul, *La Nausée* (Paris: Gallimard, 1938).

SARTRE, Jean-Paul, *The Psychology of Imagination* (1940), trans. B. Frechtman (New York: Washington Square Press, 1948).

SARTRE, Jean-Paul, *The Wall*, trans. Lloyd Alexander (New York: New Directions, 1948).

SARTRE, Jean-Paul, *No Exit and Three Other Plays* (New York: Knopf, Vintage Books, 1949).

SARTRE, Jean-Paul, *Baudelaire*, trans. Martin Turnell (New York: New Directions, 1950).

SARTRE, Jean-Paul, *Transcendence of the Ego*, trans. Forrest Williams and Robert Kirkpatrick (New York: Noonday, 1957).

SARTRE, Jean-Paul, *The Condemned of Altona*, trans. Sylvia Leeson and George Leeson (New York: Knopf, Vintage Books, 1961).

SARTRE, Jean-Paul, *Saint Genet*, trans. B. Frechtman (New York: New American Library).

SARTRE, Jean-Paul, *Search for a Method*, trans. Hazel Barnes (New York: Knopf, Vintage Books, 1963).

SARTRE, Jean-Paul, *The Words*, trans. Bernard Frechtman (Greenwich, Conn.: Fawcett, 1964).

SARTRE, Jean-Paul, *Situations*, trans. Benita Eister (Greenwich, Conn.: Fawcett, 1965).

SARTRE, Jean-Paul, *What is Literature?*, trans. Bernard Frechtman (New York: Harper & Row, 1965).

SARTRE, Jean-Paul, *Being and Nothingness*, trans. Hazel Barnes (New York: Washington Square Press, 1966).

SARTRE, Jean-Paul, "J.-P. Sartre répond," in *L'Arc*, no. 30 (1966).

SARTRE, Jean-Paul, "*Détermination et liberté*," in *Les Ecrits de Sartre*, ed. Michel Contat and Michel Rybalka (Paris: Gallimard, 1970).

SARTRE, Jean-Paul, *L'Idiot de la famille: Gustave Flaubert de 1821 à 1857*, vol. I (Paris: Gallimard, 1971).

SARTRE, Jean-Paul, "Replies to structuralism: an interview with J.-P. Sartre," trans. Robert D'Amico, *Telos*, no. 9 (Fall 1971).

SARTRE, Jean-Paul, *Situations IX* (Paris: Gallimard, 1972).

SARTRE, Jean-Paul, *Between Existentialism and Marxism*, trans. John Mathews (New York: Pantheon, 1974).

SARTRE, Jean-Paul, *Situations X* (Paris: Gallimard, 1976).

SARTRE, Jean-Paul, *Life/Situations*, trans. Paul Auster and Lydia Davis (New York: Pantheon, 1977).

SARTRE, Jean-Paul, *Sartre by Himself*, trans. Richard Seaver (New York: Urizen Books, 1978).

SCHRAG, Calum O., *Radical Reflection and the Onigm of the Human Sciences* (W. Lafayotte: Purdue University Press, 1980).

SILVERMAN, Hugh J., "Artistic creation and human action," in *Mosaic: A Journal for the Comparative Study of Literature and Ideas*

(Winnipeg: University of Manitoba Press, 1974), vol. 8, no. 1, pp. 157–64.

SILVERMAN, Hugh J., "Imagining, Perceiving, Remembering," *Humanitas*, vol. 14, no. 2 (May 1978), pp. 197–207.

SILVERMAN, Hugh J. and Elliston, Frederick A. (eds), *Jean-Paul Sartre: Contemporary Approaches to his Philosophy* (Pittsburgh: Duquesne University Press, 1980).

SILVERMAN, Hugh J. (ed.), *Piaget, Philosophy and the Human Sciences* (Atlantic Highlands, New Jersey: Humanities Press, 1980).

SILVERMAN, Hugh J., "Phenomenology," *Social Research*, vol. 47, no. 4 (Winter 1980), pp. 704–20.

SILVERMAN, Hugh J., "Beckett, Philosophy and the Self," in *The Philosophical Reflection of Man in Literature*, ed. A.-T. Tymieniecka (Dordrecht: Reidel, 1982), pp. 153–60.

SILVERMAN, Hugh J., "Cézanne's mirror stage," *Journal of Aesthetics and Art Criticism* (Summer 1982).

SMITH, David Woodruff and McIntyre, Ronald, "Intentionality via Intentions," *Journal of Philosophy*, vol. 68, no. 18 (18 September 1971).

SMITH, David Woodruff and McIntyre, Ronald, *Husserl and Intentionality* (Dordrecht: Reidel, 1982).

SPIEGELBERG, Herbert, *The Phenomenological Movement: A Historical Introduction*, 2 vols (The Hague: Nijhoff, 1981).

STERN, A., *Sartre: His Philosophy and Existential Psychoanalysis* (New York: Delta, 1967).

TILLIETTE, Xavier, *Merleau-Ponty ou la mesure de l'homme* (Paris: Seghers, 1970).

WEBER, Samuel and Sussman, Henry (eds), *Glyph I* and *II* (Baltimore: Johns Hopkins University Press, 1977).

WILDEN, Anthony, *The Language of the Self* (Baltimore: Johns Hopkins University Press, 1968).

INDEX

Abel, Lionel, 213
action. *See* Praxis
Adorno, Theodor, 3, 5
Alain, Emile, 101
Allison, David, 295, 296, 298
Alquié, Ferdinand, 63–5
Althusser, Louis, 4, 124, 146, 147, 217, 318
anthropology, 124, 145, 146, 213, 307
Aquinas, Thomas, 44
archaeology of knowledge, *ix*, 4, 149, 254, 258, 264, 276, 304, 307, 317–20, 324, 328, 330; task of an, 263
Aristotle, 6, 44, 130, 287, 342
Augustine, 45, 327
Austin, J. L., 6, 299

Bacon, Francis, 269, 317, 327, 328
Balzac, Honore de, *xi*, 251
Barthes, Roland, *ix, x, xi*, 4, 7, 8, 106, 146, 163, 189–90, 217, 236–53, 265, 266, 267, 270, 287, 329
Baudelaire, Charles, 186, 207, 219, 220, 223–4, 256, 274
Beaufret, J., 110
Beauvoir, Simone de, 194, 266
Beckett, Samuel, 322, 340, 345
being: and language, 288–93; and

thinking, 52–62; in Heidegger, 31, 32, 33, 40, 47–51, 52–62, 108–22, 132, 134, 143, 281, 288–93, 296–7, 302, 303, 309, 311, 315, 342, 343, 349n5; in Merleau-Ponty, 133, 147, 168; in Sartre, 199, 200, 238
Benjamin, Walter, 4
Benveniste, Emile, *xi*
Bergson, Henri, 20, 47, 81, 111, 123, 150,, 330, 353n2
Bernard, Claude, 316
Body: in Husserl, 21–5, 26, 27, 28; in Merleau-Ponty, 64, 65, 66, 69, 76, 79–80, 81, 84, 88, 89, 154–6; in Sartre, 203
Boethius, Anacius, 45
Bonaventure, 114
Bopp, 318, 322
Borges, Jorge Luis, 329
Bossuet, Jacques-Benigne, 98
Bradbury, Ray, 328
Brentano, Franz, 14, 88
Buber, Martin, 3
Burckhardt, Jacob, 261
Butor, Michel 266

Camus, Albert, 239
Carr, David, 22
Carroll, Lewis, 151

383

Index

Castiglione, Baldassare, 250
Céline, Louis-Ferdinand, 239
Cézanne, Paul, 132, 162, 163, 167
Charcot, J. M., 316
chiasm, 84, 119, 128, 136, 166, 167, 170, 283, 303
Chomsky, Noam, 97, 103, 344
Claudel, Paul, 239
Cocteau, Jean, 186, 269
code, 240, 252, 253, 308
communication, 95–107, 156–61, 184, 188, 237–8, 242, 244, 246, 247, 308
Comte, Auguste, 316
Condillac, Etienne de, 298
consciousness, 2, 7, 44, 45, 46, 100, 146, 189, 305, 342; in Husserl, 2, 18, 19, 345; in Merleau-Ponty, 64, 68–9, 75, 81, 87, 101, 103, 115–20, 122, 135–8, 144, 151, 154; in Sartre, 65, 101, 136, 173–9, 183–4, 200–4, 205–7, 211, 212, 217, 219–20, 222, 225–7, 243, 262–3, 268, 266, 271, 273–4, 306, 339, 341; internal time-, 18, 20–1, 41; see also ego; self; subjectivity
Contat, Michel, 194, 205, 206, 211, 216, 236, 244
Corbin, Henri, 132, 174
Cousin, Victor, 67
Cuvier, 318, 322

Dante Alighieri, 186, 249, 327, 328, 335
Darwin, Charles, 45, 317
dasein (being-there), 29–43, 44, 54, 55, 56, 132, 142, 174, 282, 288, 306, 309–10, 342
decentering, 143–51, 262, 310–11, 324; self-, 9, 149, 208–10, 250, 286, 287, 294–315, 343
deconstruction, ix, 4, 8, 171, 266, 281, 283–6, 292, 302–3, 309, 311, 327, 331, 332, 334; task of, 284

Deleuze, Gilles, xi, 4, 124, 150–1, 330
Derrida, Jacques, ix, x, xi, xii, 4, 5, 7, 8, 124, 149, 262, 281, 282, 286, 294–315, 320, 323, 343
Descartes, Rene, 6, 13–5, 22, 51, 65, 86, 306, 317, 338
Descombes, Vincent, xi
description, 74–5, 78, 79, 137
dialectic: and Aufhebung (sublation), 8, 88, 143, 284; in Merleau-Ponty, 72–3, 127, 128, 129, 137–9; in Sartre, 151, 204, 211, 213–15, 254–64, 268
Dickens, Charles, 318
differance, 149, 283, 294–300, 302, 303, 308, 309, 311, 313, 315
difference, xi, xii, 7, 8, 128, 149, 150, 166, 171, 276, 317, 343; between unterschied and differenz, 46–7; linguistic, 162, 164, 165, 167; ontological, 47, 48, 49, 50, 51, 53, 54, 55, 56, 57, 58, 59, 61, 62, 110, 111, 115–16, 117, 118, 119, 122, 143, 164, 166, 167, 171, 281, 282, 285, 287, 288, 289, 292, 296–7, 302, 306
Dilthey, Wilhelm, 3, 256
discontinuity, 258, 267, 271–3, 319
dissemination, 149, 150, 209
Dostoyevsky, Fyodor, 242, 317, 328
Dreiser, Theodore, 318
Dreyfus, H., 300
dualism, 64, 65, 68, 79, 85, 106
Dufrenne, Mikel, x, 151
Durkheim, Emile, 98

ego, 44, 46, 49, 148, 343; in Husserl, 14–28, 143, 173, 220, 304, 339; empirical or psychic (soul), 14–9, 23, 25, 173, 304; transcendence of the (Sartre), 19, 144, 172–9,

184, 198–200, 204, 220, 262,
306, 323; transcendental or
pure, 14–19, 20, 21, 23, 24,
25, 26, 27, 143, 173, 220, 286,
304, 306, 339; *see also* self;
subjectivity; consciousness
egocentrism, 221, 281, 286, 304
Ellison, Ralph, 242
Engels, Friedrich, 327, 328
Epictetus, 45
epistemé, 19, 148, 150, 172, 176,
181, 189, 190, 192, 194,
254–64, 267, 271–3, 275, 300,
307, 317–21, 322, 324, 362n1;
definition of, 258–9
epoché: *see* reduction,
phenomenological
equilibrium, 230–1, 234, 344
event of appropriation (*Ereignis*),
56, 116, 119, 290, 311, 323
existence, 2; circuit of, 84–7, 121,
128; in Foucault, 258; in
Heidegger, 35, 54, 132; in
Merleau-Ponty, 64, 68, 76, 77,
81, 84–7, 110, 121, 128; in
Sartre, 200–1, 224, 258,
267–71
existential or human ambiguity,
342; definition of, 34; and
linguistic ambiguity, 70, 72; in
Heidegger, 29–43, 50, 54, 55,
56, 57, 59, 60, 62; in Merleau-
Ponty, 63–91, 124, 126, 128,
137, 138, 140, 142, 144, 153,
168, 169; in Sartre, 201–4,
217
existentialism, 4, 189, 197, 243,
245, 255, 262, 266
experience, 2, 3, 29, 108, 119–21,
122, 135, 262, 293, 340; in
Merleau-Ponty, 76, 81, 89,
124–34, 136, 137, 144, 147,
149; in Sartre, 202, 203, 205,
207, 211, 217–18; *see also*
perception

Fechner, G., 95–6
Fenelon, Francois, 238, 242

Feuerbach, Ludwig, 130, 139, 184
Flaubert, Gustave, 185, 208,
211–12, 219, 222, 224, 232,
244, 246, 249, 250, 255–56,
258, 271–2
Foucault, Michel, *ix, x, xi, xii*, 4,
5, 7, 8, 19, 124, 146, 148–9,
172, 210, 217, 254–64, 265,
266, 267, 272–3, 276, 281,
285, 300, 304, 307, 316–25,
329, 330, 343, 344
Fourier, Francois, 252, 316, 327,
328
freedom, 38, 79, 126, 179, 180,
184, 206, 207, 238, 243–7,
252, 306
Frege, Gottlieb, 298, 299
Freud, Sigmund, 136, 151, 165,
205, 207, 209
Fuller, Buckminster, 329

Gadamer, Hans-Georg, *x*, 3, 5
Garver, Newton, 294, 298, 299
Gavi, Pierre, 194
Gelb, Adhemar, 101, 158
Genet, Jean, 172, 182–9, 190, 191,
193, 208, 219, 224, 228–9,
257
Gibbon, Edward, 261
Gide, André, 239
Girard, René, 317
Godard, Jean, *xi*
Goethe, Johann Wolfgang von,
242, 249
Goldmann, Lucien, *xi*
Goldstein, Kurt, 101, 158, 170
grammatology, *ix*, 149, 284, 307
Grimm, 322
Guillaume, Gustave, 97, 170

Habermas, Jurgen, 4, 5
Hartmann, Klaus, 213
Hegel, G. W. F., *xii*, 1, 4, 48, 108,
109, 110, 116, 120, 121, 122,
123, 124, 125, 126, 130, 131,
134, 137–43, 144, 150, 184,
190, 261, 284, 305–6, 317
Heidegger, Martin, *ix, xii*, 2, 3, 5,

6, 7, 8, 29–62, 108–22, 123,
126, 127, 129, 130, 131, 132,
134, 135, 143, 164, 166, 174,
180, 197, 256, 281–93, 294,
296, 298, 302, 303, 306,
309–10, 317, 323, 343
Heisenberg, Werner, 330
Heraclitus, 45, 59, 286–90, 292
hermeneutics, *x*, 3, 5, 39, 111, 149,
151, 256, 317, 324, 338, 345,
349n10
heterotopia, 243, 246, 326,
328–32, 336, 337
history, 4, 8; and language
(Barthes), 242, 243; in
Foucault, 146, 148, 260–1,
263, 267, 272–3, 320; in
Merleau-Ponty, 82, 98, 103,
124, 125, 126, 128, 139–40,
142–3, 148; in Sartre, 204,
208,, 213–17, 254, 255, 257,
261, 263, 264, 274; total and
general, 260–1, 263, 320
Hobbes, Thomas, 45
Hölderlin, Friedrich, 53, 57, 164
Horkheimer, Max, 4
Houdebine, J., 294, 299
Hugo, Victor, 186
human development, 8, 219–22,
226–8, 234–5, 273, 304
humanism, 132, 262
Hume, David, 19–20, 45, 201, 324
Husserl, Edmund, *ix*, *xii*, 1, 2, 5,
7, 13–28, 32, 33, 41, 42, 51,
73, 76, 88, 102, 104, 111, 115,
117, 123, 126, 131, 132, 143,
156, 157, 160, 161, 162, 163,
173, 199, 200, 210, 219–20,
257, 262, 298, 299, 304, 306,
339, 341, 345
Huxley, Aldous, 328
hypertopia-hypotopia, 326, 331–2,
333–4, 336, 337
Hyppolite, Jean, 124, 143

indecidability, 8, 281, 285, 292,
308
Ingarden, Roman, 257

intentional arc, 85–8, 90, 114, 121,
128, 132
intentionality, 7, 14, 69–70, 88,
102, 136, 137, 150, 157, 158,
173, 227, 256
interpretation, 5, 7, 36–40, 78, 96,
143, 149, 151, 332, 333, 334,
338–45
interrogation, 109, 117, 130,
131–2, 152–71
intersubjectivity, 7, 27–8, 73, 104,
157, 158, 163, 170

Jakobson, Roman, *x*, 96, 170, 262,
266
Jaspers, Karl, 197
James, William, 51, 339
Johnson, Barbara, 307, 314
Johnson, George Clayton, 327
jouissance (pleasure), 106, 251,
252
Joyce, James, 330

Kafka, Franz, 151, 327, 338
Kant, Immanuel, 1, 6, 27, 151,
284, 285, 304, 305–6, 324,
338
Kierkegaard, Soren, 3, 123, 130,
131, 190, 202, 204, 262, 275,
317
Klee, Paul, 162
Kluback, William, 296
Koehler, Wolfgang, 96, 158
Koffka, Kurt, 158
Krell, David Farrell, 287
Kristeva, Julia, *xi*, 4
Kuhn, Thomas, 6, 321

Lacan, Jacques, *ix*, *x*, *xi*, *xii*, 3, 7,
123, 146, 147, 165, 197,
205–13, 217, 262, 265, 266,
269, 276, 286, 304, 312, 314,
320, 340, 341, 344
Lacoue-Labarthe, Phillipe, *xi*
langage (discourse), 146, 149,
240–1, 243, 244, 247, 248,
270, 323, 340, 341; definition
of, 145

language, *xi*, *xii*, 3, 7, 8, 65, 209, 217, 236, 264, 267, 269, 307; and *Logos*, 281–93, 301; and thought, 100–3, 106; in Heidegger, 57, 61, 180, 287–93; in Merleau-Ponty, 95, 124, 126, 133, 147, 152–71; in Sartre, 172–94, 208, 212–13

langue – parole (language-speech), 97, 104, 106, 239–41, 243, 249, 270, 292, 340, 341; definition of, 145

Lautréamont, Comte de, 239

Lefebvre, Henri, 67–8

Lefort, Claude, 25

Lévi-Strauss, Claude, *ix*, *x*, *xi*, *xii*, 3, 123, 145, 197, 204,213–18, 262, 265, 266, 267, 270, 275, 286, 303, 312–13, 320, 321, 343

Lévinas, Emmanuel, 151

Lewin, Kurt, 101

linguistic value, 104, 159, 297–8, 341

literary criticism, 146, 248–9

literature, 8, 133, 165, 168, 179, 236, 237–47, 267

Loyola, Ignatius, 252

Lucretius, 44

Lukacs, Georg, 4

Lyotard, Jean-François, *xi*, 4, 124, 149–50

Mallarmé, Stephane, 186, 239, 307, 323

Malraux, André, 164, 168

man, 350n1; and self, 44–6, 51; in Derrida, 305–7; in Foucault, 210, 261–3, 304, 317, 322, 324, 344; in Heidegger, 47–51, 53–62; in Merleau-Ponty, 89, 134, 143; in Sartre, 13, 190–1, 210, 256–8

Mann, Thomas, 242

Mannheim, Ralph, 47

Marcel, Gabriel, 3, 197

Marcuse, Herbert, 4

Marin, Louis, 328–9

Martinet, André, 266

Marx, Karl, 1, 4, 108, 123, 124, 125, 130, 131, 134, 136–43, 144, 150, 151, 210, 262, 317, 322

Marxism, 129, 243, 245, 255, 258; existential, 254, 265, 266, 276; phenomenological, 257

Mauss, Marcel, 98, 123

meaning, 2, 5, 248–9, 252, 260, 317, 325, 341, 344; in Husserl, 17, 18; in Heidegger, 29–43, 57, 59, 60, 62; in Merleau-Ponty, 71, 72, 73, 82, 83, 84, 85, 88, 89, 102, 126, 133, 147, 149, 154, 156, 162, 163, 167; in Sartre, 174, 175, 178, 179, 180, 181, 185, 199–204, 210, 244; *see also* noema-noesis; signification

Meillet, A., 97

Meinong, A., 175

Merleau-Ponty, Maurice, *ix*, *x*, *xi*, *xii*, 2, 4, 5, 7, 8, 19, 22, 47, 54, 63–171, 178, 257, 266, 283, 303, 339, 344

Merimée, Prosper, 238, 242

metaphor, 3, 65, 66, 78, 147, 165, 171, 282, 283, 301, 303, 308, 337

metaphysics, 55, 99, 100, 130, 131, 132, 149, 281–6, 293, 306, 307, 309; history of, 282–83, 285–6, 292, 300–4

Montaigne, Michel de, 45

More, Thomas, 327

Mounier, Emmanuel, 3

myth, 214–16, 217, 267, 269–70, 275, 321, 329

Nancy, Jean-Luc, *xi*

Nature, 111, 117, 119, 122, 128, 130, 131, 134, 136, 142, 143, 146

Nietzsche, Friedrich, *xii*, 1, 31, 49, 50, 116, 120, 130, 131, 135,

144, 150, 175, 283, 286, 303, 307, 314, 323, 324
noema-noesis, 2, 15, 17, 19, 23, 24, 32, 33, 34, 35, 36, 39, 40, 41, 42, 102, 173, 176, 198, 206, 341, 348n3
Nolan, William, 327

Ortega y Gasset, José, 3
Ovid, 269

Paci, 257
painting, 132–3, 149, 150, 162–5, 167, 168, 170, 234
Parmenides, 52
Pascal, Blaise, 45
Pavlov, Ivan, 100, 101
perception, 7, 16, 23; in Merleau-Ponty, 65, 66, 73, 74, 76, 77–9, 81, 266; *see also* experience
Petrarch, 186
philosophy, 74–6, 115, 117, 293, 308; and non-philosophy, 102, 109, 110, 112, 116, 119, 121, 122, 123–51, 168, 285; the end of, 120, 127, 131, 132, 285, 356n6, 369n5
Piaget, Jean, 7, 103, 159, 217, 219–35, 265, 266, 267, 273, 276, 304, 321
Picard, Raymond, 248
Pico della Mirandola, 45
Pingaud, 208
Plato, 6, 31, 44, 249, 327, 328
Podgorny, Michel, 48
Poe, Edgar Allen, 312
poetry and prose (Sartre), 185–9, 237–8
Pontalis, J. B., 205, 208
positivism, 97, 128
Pouillon, Jean, 213
practico-inert, 191, 192, 193, 213, 216, 217, 244, 245, 248, 252, 254, 257, 258, 260, 264, 270
praxis, 91, 145; in Merleau-Ponty, 112, 119, 121, 130, 134, 135, 138–43, 144, 147, 151; in

Sartre, 180–1, 189, 191, 192, 193, 194, 202, 209, 213–17, 219, 224–6, 236, 245, 252, 254, 257, 258, 260, 263, 264, 267–71
presence, 53–4, 55, 56, 68, 75, 76, 110–11, 112, 114, 118, 120, 121, 126, 143, 149, 151, 162, 177, 324, 342, 345
project: in Merleau-Ponty, 73, 87; in Sartre, 136, 191, 219, 222–8, 243, 244, 257, 267, 273–6, 285
progressive-regressive method, 192, 193, 214–5, 219, 231–3, 255–60, 272, 274
proper, 290, 306, 308–15
Protagoras, 45
Proust, Marcel, 150, 151, 162, 250, 251
psychoanalysis, 23, 124, 146, 147, 156, 158, 198, 205, 208, 323; existential, 207–8, 219, 231–3, 235, 262, 274, 307

Queneau, Raymond, 239
Quine, W. V. O., 19

reduction, phenomenological, 14, 15, 16, 18, 26, 27, 32, 35, 125, 173
Renoir, Auguste, 163
Ricardo, David, 318, 322
Richir, Marc, 66
Ricoeur, Paul, *x*, 3, 5, 8, 151, 338, 341, 342
Rimbaud, Arthur, 184
Robbe-Grillet, Alain, 146, 217, 266
Rosen, Lawrence, 213
Russell, Bertrand, 2, 135, 175, 298
Rousseau, Jean-Jacques, 45, 282–3, 286, 298, 301, 303, 328
Rybalka, Michel, 216, 236, 244
Ryle, Gilbert, 13

Sacher-Masoch, Leopold von, 151

Sade, Marquis de, 252, 276, 322
Said, Edward, 339
Sartre, Jean-Paul, *ix*, *x*, 2, 5, 7, 8,
   19, 65, 66, 82, 84, 87, 101,
   123, 130, 132, 134, 135, 136,
   142, 143, 144, 146, 147, 148,
   151, 157, 163, 164, 172–277,
   285, 295, 304, 306, 323,
   334–6, 339, 341
Saussure, Ferdinand de, *ix*, *xi*, *xii*,
   3, 82, 96, 97, 103, 104, 106,
   145, 154, 156, 157, 159, 160,
   161, 162, 165, 167, 169, 189,
   197, 198, 199, 205, 208, 210,
   213, 265, 267, 297, 299, 340
Scheler, Max, 45
Schleiermacher, Friedrich, 3
Schutz, Alfred, 257
scientism, 95–100, 105, 156
Searle, John, 300, 311–12; and D.
   Searle, 300
self, *xii*, 4, 5, 7, 8, 147, 294–315,
   338–45; and man, 44–6, 51,
   317; in Heidegger, 29–51; in
   Husserl, 13–28, 143; in
   Merleau-Ponty, 63–91, 127,
   144, 148; in Sartre, 144,
   172–94, 206, 210, 212, 220,
   267, 268; *see also* ego;
   consciousness; subjectivity
self-language-world complex, *xii*,
   7, 8
semiology, *x*, 3, 106, 149, 241,
   242, 302, 323, 325, 338;
   hermeneutic, *xii*, 7, 8, 9, 317,
   325, 326, 338–45
sense (*Sinn*); *see* Meaning
Shakespeare, William, 249
sign, 7, 57, 71, 100, 102, 104, 105,
   106, 159, 161, 240, 249, 259,
   268–9, 282, 297, 301, 319,
   325, 340, 342, 341, 345;
   Saussure's definition of, 145
signification, 5, 83, 146, 149, 159,
   161, 170, 171, 209, 240,
   297–8, 316, 324, 341, 345; in
   Merleau-Ponty, 71–4, 83,
   85–6, 88, 98, 100, 102, 144,

162, 163, 167; in Sartre,
191–3, 198–9, 202, 213, 217,
259, 341; Saussure's
definition of, 145, *see also*
meaning
signifier-signified (word-concept),
7, 71, 104, 136, 145, 149, 159,
165, 197, 217, 249, 250,
268–9, 281, 282, 297, 324,
340; in Sartre, 190–3,
198–204, 217, 258
signature, 300, 314–15
Simon, Claude, 133, 266
singular universal, 142, 191, 202,
204, 275
situation, 191, 203, 210, 219,
228–31, 234–5, 239, 243,
245, 249, 252, 259, 267, 270,
271–3, 274
Skinner, B. F., 44, 328
slash, 253, 259, 267, 271, 272,
276–7
Spinoza, Benedict de, 65, 150
Spivak, Gayatri, 296, 297
Stendhal, 162, 246, 250, 251, 317
Strawson, P. F., 45
structure, 2, 5, 15, 36, 41, 71, 72,
83, 85, 89, 145, 148, 154, 158,
179, 211, 213, 216, 217,
222–8, 262, 267–71, 268–9,
275, 344; and genesis, 227;
linguistic, 97, 161, 171, 191,
268; social, 189, 214; *see also*
practico-inert; system
style, 5, 121, 153, 170–1, 240–1,
243, 300
subjectivity, 4, 5, 145, 146, 151,
262, 317; in Husserl, 16, 17,
24, 26, 28, 158, 160, 173, 304;
in Merleau-Ponty, 63, 64, 78,
99; in Sartre, 175, 185, 205,
206, 210, 268; transcendental
or pure, 2, 16, 17, 24, 26, 28,
76, 144, 158, 160, 323; *see
also* self; ego; consciousness
synchrony-diachrony, 4, 83, 96,
97, 148, 157, 158, 197,

213–17, 222, 227, 242, 272, 274

system, 5, 8, 83, 148, 216, 262, 267–71, 319; of differences, 159, 160, 161, 163, 167, 170, 297; of signs, 145, 146, 149, 165, 239, 247, 248, 282, 324, 339–45; *see also* structure

temporality, 2, 20, 29, 30, 40–3, 69, 80–1, 89–91, 309–10
text, 3, 9, 71, 106, 146, 150, 236, 237–53, 284, 300, 302, 329, 334; and intertextuality, 250–2
textualization, 248, 251–3, 293
Thoreau, Henry David, 318, 328
Tilliette, Xavier, 68–70
Tintoreto, Il, 164
Tocqueville, Alexis de, 316
Totalization, 244, 246, 248, 252–3, 260–1, 263, 272, 274
Toynbee, Arnold, 261
trace, 149, 293, 299, 300, 307, 313, 314, 315, 323, 343
transformation, 226–8, 259, 273–6, 320–1
truth, 114, 118–19, 121, 122, 127, 129, 285, 311, 315

unconscious, 8, 147, 150, 197, 205–7, 209, 211, 212, 217, 263, 269, 339
understanding, 29, 32, 33, 36–40, 70, 74–5, 81, 135, 211, 213, 227, 256–7, 267, 271–3, 288, 342; and explanation, 74–5
Utopia, 242, 243, 247; and dystopia, 326–37

Valéry, Paul, 103, 162, 167, 186
Van Gogh, Vincent, 162, 164
Vendreys, 170
Verstrseten, Pierre, 198
Victor, Pierre, 194
Villon, Francois, 186
Virgil, 269, 327
visibility, 66–7, 84, 112, 113, 119, 121, 122, 128, 132–3, 137, 149; language of, 166–8

Waelhens, Alphonse de, 65
Wahl, Jean, 295
Wartburg, W. von, 96
Weber, Max, 317
Wild, John, 66
Wilde, Jean, 296
Wittgenstein, Ludwig, 6
Wordsworth, William, 114, 163, 318
work, 150, 236, 243–51; definition of, 246, 249
world, *xii*, 7, 8, 323, 338, 340; in Heidegger, 29, 35–6, 37, 43; in Husserl, 14, 15, 18, 22, 25–7, 28, 126, 132, 257; in Merleau-Ponty, 64, 65, 66, 70, 73, 74, 80, 82, 84, 86, 120, 121, 122, 125, 130, 151, 171; in Sartre, 202, 213, 268
writing, 146, 149, 162–4, 180, 229, 236–53, 281–3, 299, 301, 312, 315; arche-, 283, 286, 293, 294, 298, 299, 300, 302, 303, 311, 312, 313

Zola, Emile, 318